C000298718

A Wine Atlas of the Langhe

The Great Barolo and Barbaresco Vineyards

sponsored by

Slow Food Editore

Editor
Carlo Petrini

With the collaboration of
Vittorio Manganelli

Authors
Felice Campanello, Gianni Fabrizio, Armando Gambera, Vittorio Manganelli, Marcello Marengo, Marco Mascarello, Francesco Mastrocola, Alessandro Monchiero, Carlo Petrini, Gigi Piumatti, Piero Sardo, Andrea Vannelli

Editorial staff
Bianca Dotta Minerdo, Mavi Negro, Grazia Novellini

Maps
Davide Gandino, Francesco Perona

Cover design
Dante Albieri

Graphic design
Stefano Pallaro

Layout
Maurizio Burdese, Davide Gandino,
Francesco Perona, Cristina Capussotti

Photographs
Tino Gerbaldo, Bra

English translation
Giles Watson

Photo-offset lithography
Ponti, Boves

Printed by
L'Artistica, Savigliano

Previously published in Italian as
Atlante delle Grandi Vigne di Langa, Zona del Barolo: 1990

Previously published in Italian as
Atlante delle vigne di Langa.
I Grandi Cru del Barolo e del Barbaresco: September 2000

Acknowledgements
Piedmont Regional Authority
Cuneo Chamber of Commerce
Vignaioli Piemontesi
Consorzio Tutela Barolo e Barbaresco, Alba, Langhe e Roero
The municipal authorities of the towns mentioned
The producers and growers

Cover photograph
The Gavarini vineyard at Monforte d'Alba

Copyright © 2000, 2002
Slow Food Editore
All rights reserved

Slow Food Editore srl
Via della Mendicità Istruita, 45
12042 Bra (Cn)
tel. + 39 0172 419611 fax + 39 0172 411218

E-mail: info@slowfood.it
Website: www.slowfood.it

ISBN 88-8499-041-6

Contents

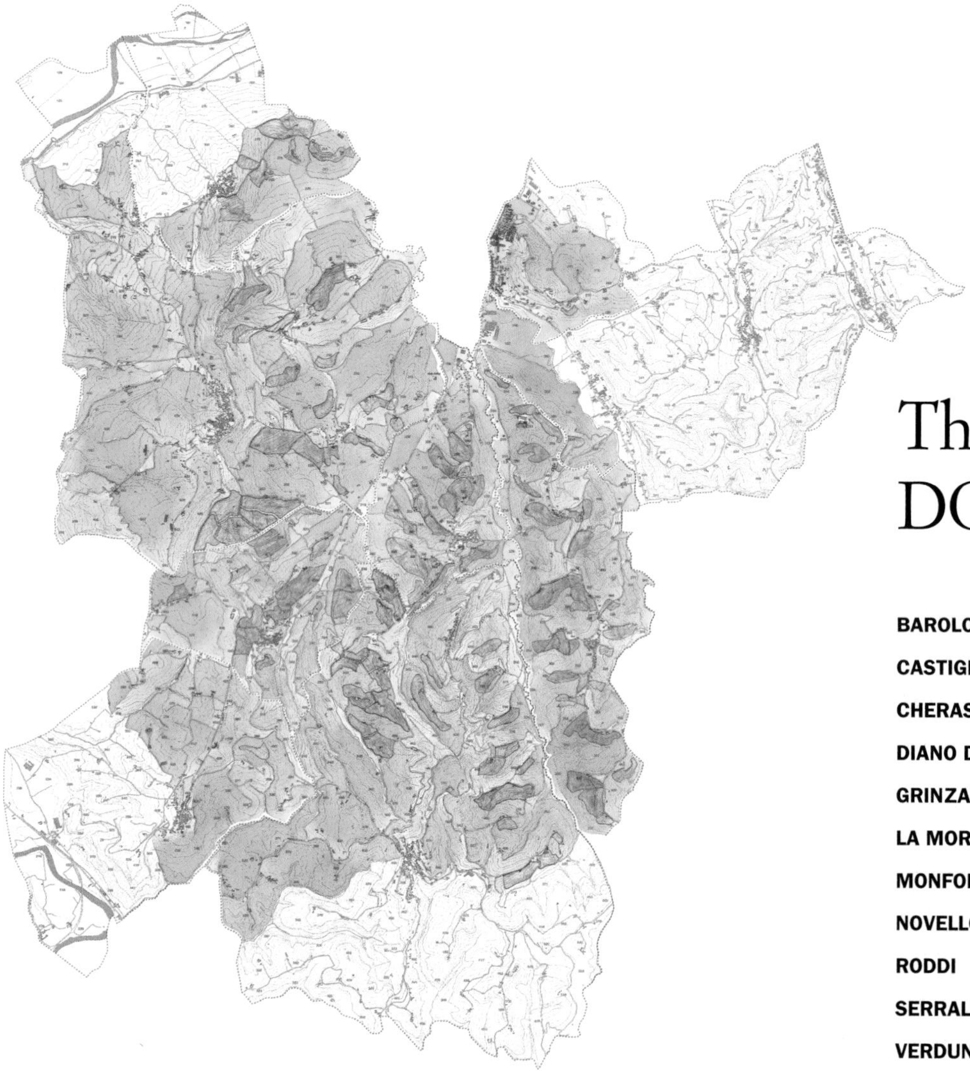

The Barolo DOCG zone

BAROLO

CASTIGLIONE FALLETTO

CHERASCO

DIANO D'ALBA

GRINZANE CAVOUR

LA MORRA

MONFORTE D'ALBA

NOVELLO

RODDI

SERRALUNGA D'ALBA

VERDUNO

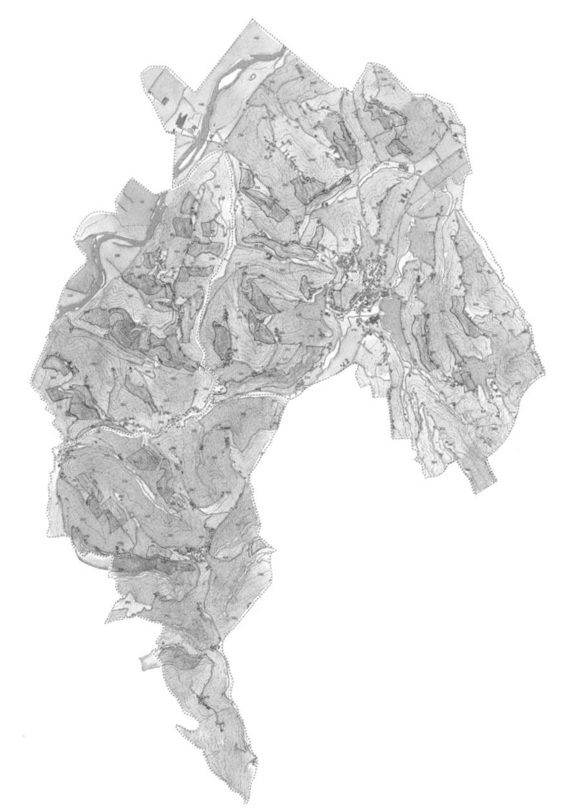

The Barbaresco DOCG zone

BARBARESCO

NEIVE

SAN ROCCO SENO D'ELVIO

TREISO

Barolo and Barbaresco

It was the need to define and describe the finest vineyards in the Langhe that prompted us to publish, in 1990, *Zona del Barolo* (The Barolo DOCG Zone), the first instalment of a larger work with the overall title *Atlante delle Grandi Vigne di Langa* (Atlas of the Great Langhe Vineyards). Over the past ten years, the task of determining the extent of the vineyards has continued, partly through the application of national or local regulations. The worrying absence of regulation is now well on the way to being rectified, although many contradictions remain.

Nevertheless, it would not be in the spirit of this *Atlas* to report in detail every step in the legislation that has led to the current situation. Our aim is to explore in depth the qualities of the great Langhe vineyards, conveying to the reader the importance of the work done by wineries and growers, explaining why the Langhe has been able to emerge as one of the world's major wine areas, and offering eye-witness reports from people who have observed, and made, the history of the past hundred years.

This effort is in response to requests from many interested parties, especially producers, who have been pressing for clarity in the regulation and classification of their estates. Public bodies, too, are interested, as they have been unable to impose order in an area too often approached in a superficial manner. Finally, consumers – those abroad perhaps even more insistently than Italian winelovers – have been demanding to know exactly where these increasingly admired and sought-after wines are grown.

Documents from the past

We decided to begin our task by concentrating on the nebbiolo vineyards in the Barolo and Barbaresco DOCG zones, the ones that, by long-established tradition, are located in the most favourable positions. We then began to study the texts – there are actually very few of them – that have in the past examined the best locations in the Langhe. It is our firm belief that a great vineyard is one that has been held in high esteem by several generations, the more so in a region where the history of viticulture is measured in millennia.

The most complete and scientific work on the subject, and the one we found most useful, was Lorenzo Fantini's late nineteenth-century treatise, *Monografia sulla Viticoltura ed Enologia nella Provincia di Cuneo* (Monograph on Viticulture and Oenology in the Province of Cuneo). It does not include a classification of the vineyards, although it does give quality assessments of the different growing areas.

More limited in scope, but still very interesting, is Ferdinando Vignolo Lutati's essay *Sulla Delimitazione delle Zone a Vini Tipici* (On the Delimitation of Typical Wine Zones), which draws a detailed agricultural map of the municipality of Castiglione Falletto towards the end of the 1920s, highlighting the plots planted to nebbiolo. We would have to wait 50 years to acquire a tool, Renato Ratti's *Carta del Barolo*, or Map of Barolo, whose objective was the complete and systematic classification of Barolo by highlighting the great vineyards. The *Carta* is a courageous, groundbreaking work, for Ratti indicates precisely the first-class growths, the historic wine subzones and, within them, the positions of outstanding quality. Ratti's research was carried out "by following local traditions", gathering first-hand statements and recollections vineyard by vineyard, and *cascina* by *cascina*.

This was our starting point for the Barolo DOCG zone del Barolo. Ratti's results were as significant as his method. We are therefore very happy to be able to republish, with the permission of the Ratti family, the complete *Carta del Barolo*.

Working method

In September 1989, our research into the Barolo DOCG zone entered the operational stage. We brought together the oldest growers, municipality by municipality, and in some cases, hamlet by hamlet. A few were also interviewed individually. In this way, we built up a library of over 500 hours of recordings.
From the meetings and interviews, we gleaned information about the quality of the vineyards but also acquired an extraordinary portrait of family and community life in a rich, unique and very human series of documents. It is an unwritten history, scarred with the indelible mark of poverty, and on occasion despair, conditions that obtained in the rural world until the late 1950s.
The value of this information on the great vineyards was immediately confirmed by the producers, who acknowledged the validity of the opinions expressed by our elderly collaborators, some more than 80 years old. A few interviewees had even taken part in the vast grafting operations required after the arrival of phylloxera in the early decades of the twentieth century.
This initial stage was concluded by site visits to the vineyards and soil analyses, as well as the historically significant collection of the biographies of the great Barolo personalities. Completed in early 1990, that work provided the basic structure for this *Atlas*.
We adopted the same approach – and here, we were pioneers – for the section regarding the Barbaresco DOCG zone. We consulted past researches, we interviewed growers, gathered data in the municipalities, drafted new maps and made lengthy visits to the vineyards.
We added descriptions of the individual vineyards to the maps that point out their location. We have noted the aspect, the nature of the soil, where necessary, the boundaries, altitude and surface area of each. In the more interesting cases, we have added other details gleaned from first-hand reports or relating to special production features.

Classification of vineyards

It was not our intention to draw up a "top twenty"-style classification but we did want to point out the most vineyards that are historically and qualitatively most important. It will be possible, and useful, to make a full classification when the delimitation of subzones currently under way is complete. Above all, such a classification will require meaningful comparative tastings from the various vineyards.
For the time being, we believe we will have achieved our aim if we can indicate to consumers and professionals the exact location of the vineyards, where the best positions are and which cellars vinify their grapes. It was during this research that we came across what may well be the most elegant definition of a *cru*, or great vineyard. It was coined by Paolo Cordero di Montezemolo and it goes like this, "... a great wine, which many compare to a work of art, is actually a work of nature. It is the work of the sun, of the site climate, of the soil type and so on. To use a somewhat paradoxical expression, a great wine is a work of the land".
The vineyard profiles and the related municipal maps, the biographies and the lists of wineries with plots in the selected vineyards have been supplemented by a generous number of eye-witness reports. These constitute a crucial part of this book, not just because they were the main sources of our research but because they describe the world in which Barolo and Barbaresco's leading figures lived. We thought it important that these eye-witness contributions should be reported as accurately as possible. They help us to trace the development of winemaking techniques while offering an overview of history without which even the most up-to-date research techniques would be of little use.

Our collaborators

This book has made full use of the work carried out in recent years by the municipal authorities, particularly in the Barolo area.

We have also taken the opportunity to make the adjustments to the territorial boundaries, indicated in our original work a decade ago, that recent vintages have shown to be necessary.

From 1995, our researches were extended to include the Barbaresco DOCG zone. At first, work proceeded cautiously as we awaited indications from the appropriate public bodies. Later, we began to operate with greater autonomy and decisiveness, in the knowledge that the information collected during our interviews and talks with producers was more than sufficient to describe winemaking in Barbaresco.

Our approach remained the same. We studied maps and charts, visited vineyards, met local administrators and, above all, spoke to the growers and producers.

In autumn 1999 and spring 2000, we collated the material we had collected. You will find here the results of ten years' work, an effort we believe is useful and significant but by no means definitive.

Many of the older interviewees are no longer with us. We offer our thanks to them for enabling us to write this modest page in the history of the great wines of the Langhe.

BAROLO
Gavi

Nebbiolo, Barolo and Barbaresco

The history of nebbiolo

The nebbiolo grape is native to Piedmont, at least in the sense that it has been cultivated here for hundreds of years. When it actually arrived, and whether or not it is the result of the modification of other varieties, are matters for conjecture since it is likely that all varieties of grapes originally came from Georgia or Mesopotamia. The view that nebbiolo derives from pinot noir appears equally unfounded. Both varieties are, of course, among the most richly nuanced grapes in the world, as far as their olfactory profiles are concerned. However, it would be rash to assert that they are related. Genetic evidence is inconclusive.

It is clear that highly prized grapes were grown in this area before the arrival of Christianity but we cannot be certain that nebbiolo was cultivated here more than 2,000 years ago.

The origin of the name, once written *nebiolo*, appears to be the Latin word *nebia*, or mist, and may have been acquired because the harvest takes place when the first mists are rising from the river Tanaro to the tops of the hills. It is also possible – and, according to some commentators, probable – that the name refers to the whitish, waxy bloom that covers the berries.

The year in which the nebbiolo story officially began is **1431**. It was then that Odoninum de Bancho, the public notary of Serralunga, added a new chapter to the town's book of statutes, the **Statuti di La Morra**, which date from 1402 and are perhaps even older. The addition mentions the variety *nebiolium* and its twin *pignolium*.

On 1 December 1431, the term "nebbiolo" was used in the Langhe for the first time to refer to a grape well-established here and from which a much-prized wine was already being obtained. In the statutes of La Morra, there was a five lire fine for those who cut one of these vines, *arbore alleva-ta vel ad filagnos, in bussono et domestica*, in other words, whether the plant was bush-trained or high-trained. Another chapter prescribed cutting off the right hand of repeat offenders and hanging for the most serious cases.

In fact, the name nebbiolo was used for the first time even earlier just outside the Langhe, at Canale in Roero. As early as **1303**, we find a reference to *una carrata de bono puro vino nebiolio* (a barrel of good, pure nebiolio wine).

We can deduce the fame that this farmland, especially suitable for viticulture, enjoyed at the time from an examination of contemporary maps and charts. From the sixteenth century on, unnamed but highly competent surveyors mapped out the plots under vine, indicating with carefully drawn lines the rows of vines and noting the names of the locations. In many cases, the topographical terms have survived to the present day from the beginning of the second millennium, when the Langhe hills were gradually deforested and the land opened up.

The birth of Barolo and Barbaresco

The first step towards the formulation of regulatory safeguards was taken in 1926, with the passing of the law on typical wines. In the Langhe, and in the Barolo area in particular, the question of how to combat adulteration had been on the agenda for at least half a century.

Less than a decade after the death of Marchesa Giulia Falletti in 1864, councillor Ghisolfi had spoken at a meeting of the Barolo municipal council. The date was 27 October **1873**. "It is widely known, and by many acknowledged as deleterious to the general interest, that wines are sold as Barolo on a vast scale, even though they lack those qualities that are now held in high regard by all... I address the council here convened to take appropriate measures, drafting as quickly as possible a list of the names, surnames and domiciles of all purchasers of Barolo grapes this autumn".

Thirty years later, in **1903**, the provincial authority of Cuneo drew up the first *Carta Vinicola*, or Wine Map, indicating the areas of origin of the wines. For the time, the project was revolutionary and, like Ghisolfi's proposal, it was never implemented.

In 1904, Teobaldo Calissano, a member of parliament from Alba, president of the Piedmont Wine Union and minister for the post office and telegraphy in Giolitti's government, called, unsuccessfully, for a law on the designation of wines.

On 16 November **1908**, a meeting was held at Barolo of growers and experts under the chairmanship of Professor Cavazza from Barbaresco to demand measures for safeguarding Nebbiolo wine and the detailed delimitation of the Barolo zone. It was decided to set up an organisation, called Pro Barolo, to support the requests. In **1909**, the Alba agricultural committee defined clearer, but still not detailed, boundaries for the zone of origin, which may be summed up as follows: the municipal territories of Barolo, La Morra, Serralunga, Castiglione, Perno, Grinzane, part of Verduno, part of Monforte and a very small part of Novello. Readers will note that Diano, Roddi and Cherasco were not included. This delimitation retraced the 1896 definition of the ministry of agriculture, used again in the *Carta Vinicola* of the provincial agricultural office of Cuneo in 1903.

On 2 September 1909, the national congress at Alba accepted these boundaries, to the disappointment of the municipality of Barolo, which would have preferred the designation of origin to be restricted to nebbiolo grown at Barolo itself. In 1920, the Lega dei Comuni Viticoli Piemontesi, or League of Piedmontese Wine Municipalities, was set up at Asti with the aims of obtaining recognition and protection for typical wines, encouraging the formation of grower co-operatives and protecting those that already existed. But for the *cantine sociali* (co-operative wineries), it was too late. With no state aid, they all went bankrupt during the 1920s. The co-operative movement that had developed in the Langhe from the late nineteenth century until the crash of 1929, saw the creation of many co-operative cellars. *Cantine sociali* appeared at Barbaresco, Castiglione Falletto, Monforte, Barolo, La Morra and finally Alba, where the co-operative winery was founded on 2 October 1904 and would finally be acquired by Alfredo Prunotto.

At last, on 18 March **1926**, a law was passed that provided, albeit timidly, some protection for typical wines. The following year, the first moves were made to set up the **Consorzio per la Difesa dei Vini Barolo e Barbaresco** (Consortium for the Defence of Barolo and Barbaresco Wines), which would be officially constituted in **1934**. The world of wine at the time was torn by controversy and protests from growers and producers at Castiglione Falletto and Barolo, who felt cheated, were particularly emphatic. The proposed compromise, which would have identified two Barolos, a Classico and a base version, under the umbrella of a single consortium, came to nothing. It has to be said that it would have created confusion and, with hindsight, was unfair.

Ferdinando Vignolo Lutati, a chemist, expert in commerce and botanist, was following the debate. At the same time, he was also preparing his 1930 *Carta Geologica della Zona del Barolo* (Geological Map of the Barolo Zone) and an agricultural and viticultural map of the municipal territory of his home town, Castiglione Falletto.

Little of importance took place during the 1930s

and 1940s. The vineyards were slowly replanted after the ravages of phylloxera had almost entirely wiped them out. Our older informants remember the period as a time of frustration and hard work, with growers rationalising and replanting their rows and grafting the nebbiolo onto phylloxera-resistant American rootstock.
The Fascist regime, with its autarky-based economic policies and ill-starred "battle for wheat", offered no margin for the development of wine, despite the heavily advertised grape fair in 1933 at La Morra and the Alba fairs.
The war years administered the *coup de grâce*. Post-war recovery was arduous and, in viticulture, set itself objectives that today we can clearly see were misguided for the emphasis was on quantity, not quality. Carbon-copy wines were made with indiscriminately blended fruit from unidentified plots, undermining all the hard work carried out in vineyard and cellar.
During the 1950s, there was a massive shift of population in Italy from the countryside to the cities. The myth of a job at Fiat in Turin, or with Ferrero at Alba, took root so firmly that it has only recently begun to fade. Although the governments of the day supported the phenomenon, there were wineries, growers and producers who resisted, convinced that migration was not the answer.
Finally, after years of waiting and discussions, Barolo and Barbaresco were accorded **Denominazione di Origine Controllata** (DOC, or "registered designation of origin") status in a presidential decree dated 23 April **1966**. Other, more recent, important legislative developments date respectively from 1 July and 3 October **1980**, when Barolo and Barbaresco gained **Denominazione di Origine Controllata e Garantita** (DOCG, or "registered and guaranteed designation of origin").

Other nebbiolo designations of origin

The nebbiolo grape has a number of different names, depending on where it is grown. Known as *spanna* around Novara and Vercelli, it is called *picotèner* or *picotendro* in Valle d'Aosta and the Canavese area, and *chiavennasca* in Valtellina.
Varying proportions of nebbiolo, defined by the relevant production regulations, are present in Barolo and Barbaresco DOCG, as well as the Langhe Nebbiolo, Nebbiolo d'Alba, Roero and Langhe Rosso DOCs.
Outside the Langhe, nebbiolo is used with other varieties in many other DOC zones. In Valle d'Aosta, it is used for the Valle d'Aosta Donnas DOC, in Piedmont, in the recent Albugnano, Canavese, Colline Novaresi and Coste della Sesia DOC zones, as well as the longer-established Carema, Gattinara (a DOCG), Boca, Bramaterra, Ghemme (also a DOCG), Fara, Lessona and Sizzano. In Lombardy, nebbiolo is used in Valtellina, Sforzato and Valtellina Superiore (a DOCG), with the sub-designations Sassella, Grumello, Inferno and Valgella.

THE VINE

Nebbiolo has become the uncontested king of Langhe grapes thanks to its superior genetic characteristics of aromatic complexity, tannic power and exceptional ageing potential. The variety is grown in the best positions, the south-facing hillslopes of the 15 municipalities we will be examining, at altitudes between 200 and 450 metres above sea level.
A very vigorous vine, nebbiolo needs to be long pruned – today, it is almost invariably long Guyot pruned, with 10-12 buds – to give rein to its exuberant vegetation. It needs to be thinned and the buds nipped constantly, otherwise the canopy, the part of the plant that grows above ground, will become an impenetrable forest. The vine also needs space, partly because the first two or three buds are infertile. This means that it is not possible to adopt a planting pattern that exploits the row space to the full. The minimum distance between plants in the same row has to be at least one metre but the space between the rows can be reduced. We can still see evidence of nebbiolo's

vigour, especially at La Morra, where there are long-established plots trained according to the *tiràsce*, or *tirasse*, system, with fruit-bearing shoots growing from long, thick canes. Of course, genetic selection and the recovery of clones damaged by virus disease have drastically reduced the problems of excessive vigour and the poor fertility of the first buds. Clones used today permit shorter pruning.

Historically, **four nebbiolo clones** belong to the Alba area. The first is **Michet**, so called because the bunch has the shape of a *michetta*, or "bread roll". Michet is thought to be a virus-contaminated form of the lampia clone but it is still mass selected for its quality profile, including low yield per vine and the high concentration of phenolics in the must. **Lampia** has a larger, longer bunch and a reliable, balanced oenological profile. Today, **Rosé** has been almost entirely abandoned because of its poor oenological qualities. It combines high sugar and malic acid content with low phenolics, especially anthocyans, a feature that jeopardises the intensity of its colour. **Bolla**, named after its Santa Maria di La Morra selector, is no longer permitted because of its over-abundant yield.

The nebbiolo leaf is medium sized, with three to five distinct lobes. Depending on the clone and variety, the bunch is large or medium sized with a pyramidal, or nearly cylindrical, shape.

The **berries** are medium sized and round, tending slightly to oval. The pulp is sweet and juicy while the skin is thin but tough and rich in tannins. Dark purple in colour, it turns greyish in autumn with bloom, the whitish, wax-like substance that covers the berries. Its **early flowering** – in the first ten days of April – and **markedly late ripening** – in the first to the third ten days of October – make nebbiolo a particularly challenging variety and expose it to many weather-related risks.

The harvest is often preceded in July and August by bunch-thinning. The grapes are gathered by hand and selected both during the harvest itself and, if necessary, at the cellar.

Clones and rootstocks

Clonal selection of nebbiolo focuses mainly on the most widely planted clone, Lampia, but Michet and Rosé clones are also available.

The following clones, each with its own special characteristics, are currently the most popular:

CN 36, selected by the Centro per il Miglioramento della Vite, or Vine Improvement Centre, of the CNR (National Research Council) in Turin: Lampia selected at La Morra for wines with medium-term ageing potential. Today, this clone is relatively little planted.

CN 111 (selected by the Centro per il Miglioramento della Vite, or Vine Improvement Centre, of the CNR (National Research Council) in Turin. A fairly high-yielding Rosé clone selected at La Morra. Very vigorous and richly scented, it is suitable for making wines with short or medium-term ageing potential.

CN 142 (selected by the Centro per il Miglioramento della Vite, or Vine Improvement Centre, of the CNR (National Research Council) in Turin. Lampia selected at Neive. Low-yielding, very tannic and well-structured, it is suitable for wines with long-term ageing potential.

CN 230, selected by the Centro per il Miglioramento della Vite, or Vine Improvement Centre, of the CNR (National Research Centre) in Turin. Lampia selected at Neive. It tends to be high-yielding but if appropriately thinned, can achieve excellent balance.

R 1, selected by Vivai Cooperativi Rauscedo. A fairly high-yielding Lampia clone selected in the municipality of Barolo. Suitable for making wines with medium-term ageing potential.

R 3, selected by Vivai Cooperativi Rauscedo. A low-yielding Michet clone selected at Barolo and suitable for wines with long-term ageing potential.

When choosing **rootstock**, it is essential to opt for types that are very resistant to active lime, which comprises nearly ten per cent of the soil in the Barolo and Barbaresco areas. One of the most widely used rootstocks is Kober 5BB, which is easy to root and very productive. Others used include the not very vigorous 420A, more suitable for infertile soils, SO4, a vigorous rootstock resistant to active lime, the very easy to root 157/11 and the slow developing 161/49, which is capable of producing truly great wines.

THE SOIL

The area under study in this book is bounded to the south by the first spurs of the Ligurian Maritime Alps, to the west by the river Tanaro, to the east by the river Bormida di Spigno and to the north by the Tanaro and the hills around Asti. The Langhe, as the area is known, derives its name from the Latin work meaning *tongue*, which gives some idea of its very special morphology. The Langhe is in fact a long strip of narrow and fairly steep hills that extends from Liguria, mainly facing north east, to the Tanaro valley. The formation of the oldest of these hills, the ones to the south, is fairly recent. If we consider the Langhe it in terms of the earth's geochronology, which extends over 4,600,000,000 years, we need go no further back than the middle-upper Eocene, about 30,000,000 years ago. The birth of these hills is closely bound up with the massive geological events that witnessed the creation of the Alps. In that period, the southern supercontinent, **Gondwana**, which included the present-day Africa, south America and Oceania, collided with the northern block, **Laurasia**, formed by Asia, north America and Europe. The thrust generated such massive squeezing and wrinkling effects that it formed the great mountain ranges we know today, the Alps, the Himalayas and Morocco's Atlas range. Similarly, the geological action created a series of inland seas. Piedmont was at that time almost entirely under water and lay in a vast gulf, delimited to the north, east and south by the pre-Tertiary rocks of the Alps, known as the Tertiary Piedmontese Basin. This was a vast sea trough extending from the Ligurian Alps down to western Piedmont and continuing up towards Biella, at the foot of the Pennine Alps. It was in this marine environment that the subsequent sedimentation of mainly terrigenous rocks – conglomerates, sandstones and clays – built up during the Miocene, 15,000,000 to 7,000,000 years ago. The process formed the soil of the Langhe areas we are examining, Barolo and Barbaresco. The land, comprising layers of rock sloping towards what is now the Cuneo plain at an inclination of about 15 degrees, was thrown up later on, during the Pliocene, under the relentless thrust of the African plate. At first, the entire area was a vast marshland. During the Quaternary period, about 1,500,000 years ago, this territory rose further with respect to the sunken plain of Alessandria when changes in the pattern of rainfall caused intense erosion. Deep inroads were made into the soft sedimentary soil to the north east, producing the Langhe hills that we see today.

The north west-dipping monocline is set perpendicular to the valleys. Today, it forms the south east-facing hillsides, the steeper, more stable slopes, called *a reggipoggio*, while the north west-facing slopes that follow the monocline are gentler but also less stable. When there is heavy rain, infiltrating water encourages the upper layers to slide naturally, making an unstable, or *a franapoggio* slope. In general, the Langhe hills present asymmetrical slopes.

The terrains in the Barolo and Barbaresco zones were formed during the Serravallian, or Helvetian, and Tortonian epochs. They comprise sedimentary clay and calcareous marl alternating with grey-blue sandstone (the Sant'Agata marl known locally as *tov* and made up of 30 per cent sand, 55 per cent clay and 15 limestone); more or less loosely packed layers of sand and yellow-brown or yellowish sandstone (Diano sandstone); and layers of sand or reddish-grey sandstone alternating with grey marl, known as the *Formazione di Lequio*. The Sant'Agata marls found at La Morra and Barolo give elegant, richly aromatic wines that evolve slightly sooner whereas the Diano sandstones, at Castiglione Falletto and part of Monforte d'Alba, and the *Formazione di Lequio*, in part of Monforte d'Alba and Serralunga d'Alba, produce a more robust, alcoholic wine with greater ageing potential. Sant'Agata marls from the Tortonian epoch prevail in the Barbaresco DOCG zone.

The high limestone content makes the soil in the Langhe very alkaline, with a pH value of nearly eight. In contrast, the soil in neighbouring Roero, for example, is prevalently sandy and less calcareous, and so more acid.

THE CLIMATE

In the context of a generally temperate, continental climate, records show that the Barbaresco zone enjoys a slightly higher average temperature than the townships in the Barolo area. In consequence, the grapes ripen, and are harvested, about a week earlier than those in the neighbouring zone.

The wettest month in the Langhe is May, when average rainfall is about 100 millimetres. April follows, with about 80 millimetres and then September, with almost 70 millimetres. Obviously, rain can be crucially important during flowering, when it can cause substantial reductions in yield, and during the harvest, when prolonged rain can lead to the formation of mould or rot, and to various other quality problems. This was the case, for example, during the 1994 vintage. Excessive rain, particularly just before the harvest, can cause a drop in acidity without a corresponding increase in sugars. However, nebbiolo is an outstandingly hardy variety and the few days of rain that are generally recorded in late September and early October have little effect on the berries, which are able to ripen normally.

In general, fairly rainy springs are followed by hot and often drought-afflicted summers, when the nebbiolo's vigour is put to the test and the flavour and aroma components in berries gain in concentration. The growing area enjoys excellent sunlight, which ensures the optimal development of chlorophyll-based photosynthesis.

Another particularly important weather phenomenon is hail, which can have a sever impact on both the quantity and quality of the fruit. In especially unfortunate years, hail can cause overall grape losses of 20-30 per cent of the harvest. In some areas, the entire crop may be ruined, as happened during the 1986 and 1995 vintages. Luckily, hail never affects the whole of the nebbiolo-growing area, generally hitting only a few hillslopes in any one year.

VINIFICATION

Naturally enough, cellar techniques vary considerably from one producer to another. We will describe the most widely used approaches, to which there may be occasional exceptions.

Destemming and crushing take place simultaneously, using a machine called a crusher-destemmer. The old practice of keeping back part of the stems during fermentation has now been abandoned, although one or two producers continued to do so until about a decade ago.

Not all the cellars use selected yeasts to start fermentation as nebbiolo has little difficulty in beginning alcoholic fermentation, provided the must temperature is not too low. The usual range is from 13 to 17°C. There is one major difference between the producers who carry out alcoholic fermentation in open wooden vats, containing anything from 30 to 80 hectolitres, and those who use the now very widespread vertical stainless steel tanks. In both cases, great care is taken to prevent the grape refuse, which floats naturally to the surface during fermentation, from drying out, which would lead to problems of volatility and would hinder the extraction of the substances contained in the skins. The must is therefore pumped over the "cap" of refuse that forms on the surface. The cap is also broken up, either manually or mechanically. The period of maceration, when the must is left on the skins and grapeseeds, and primary fermentation, when the sugars are transformed into alcohol and other less important substances,

HL75
HL75

can vary from ten to 30 days, depending on the decisions of the cellar manager.

Over the last ten years, horizontal rotary fermenters have begun to appear in Langhe wineries and these tools enable the fermentation process to be reduced to a very few days. Also known as "rotofermenters", "tanks" and even "cement mixers" for their vague resemblance to such machines, rotary fermenters have been, and continue to be, the subject of much controversy. Some producers maintain that a few hours' skin contact is insufficient to extract tannins while others claim that the process yields rounder, more approachable wines, free of the rough edges that prolonged contact with skins and seeds often entails.

Finally, we should also note that lined cement vats have been almost entirely abandoned in favour of temperature-controlled stainless steel tanks, which are undoubtedly better suited to modern hygiene and temperature regulation requirements. Before instruments for keeping fermentation temperature constant became available (the temperature is generally considered too high if it rises above 35°C), it was not infrequent for excessive volatile acidity to form in, even in good vintages. Occasionally, a young wine might present vinegary aromas. The reason for this defect is that when the temperature rises too high, acetobacter transform the sugars not into alcohol but into acetic aldehyde, and then acetic acid.

The use of vertical or horizontal stainless steel containers enables the producer to programme precisely the temperature cycle of the vinous mass throughout fermentation, monitoring progress according to the requirements desired. Specifically, cellarmen who adopt very brief maceration times, of two or three days, need a fairly high temperature from the beginning of the fermentation process. In contrast, when maceration lasts for 15-18 days, temperatures may be kept lower. It should be remembered that until a few years ago – indeed, the practice has not entirely died out – the outside of the fermentation vessel was sometimes soaked with cold water. In some cases, plastic bags of ice were thrown into the must.

At various stages of cultivation and vinification, above all during racking, **sulphur dioxide** (SO_2) is used for its disinfectant and preservative properties. When ready for drinking, wine contains about 60-90 milligrams per litre total sulphur dioxide whereas free sulphur dioxide varies from 12 to 20 milligrams.

After alcoholic fermentation, we come to another crucial decision, regarding **malolactic fermentation**, or the transformation of strong malic acid into the weaker lactic acid. Should this take place immediately after fermentation or should it begin in the following spring? In the first case, the wine will be heated, either in temperature-controlled containers or by raising the ambient temperature of the cellar to about 20°C. Instead, the winemaker may prefer to wait for the ambient temperature to rise slowly and naturally, which often takes until the summer following the vintage. Both techniques are still widely used. In general, producers who use large barrels for ageing still tend to "forget" the problem of malolactic fermentation since they maintain that the vinous mass will undergo this process naturally when the conditions are congenial. It should not be forgotten that in some years, anomalous weather conditions have prevented malolactic fermentation with the result that the wine bottled was excessively acidic and stalky.

It may come as something of a shock to visitors to see how differently cellars in the Langhe are organised. There are two extremes: 1) producers who adopt only large barrels, containing anything from 2,000 to 10,000 litres, for ageing Barolo and Barbaresco; their few stainless steel vats are used exclusively for maceration and alcoholic fermentation; and 2) wineries where large barrels have been completely abandoned in favour of small ones and stainless steel; these cellars generally use barrels of different sizes, ranging from 225 to 600 litres, and some have been experimenting with even smaller containers.

Two major variables are the type of wood and the period for which the barrels are used. Until a few years ago, barrels were almost all made from Slavonian oak, with a tiny proportion of chestnut. Now, French oak has become increasingly popular, not just in the classic 225-litre *barrique bordelaise* but also in larger containers. Slavonian oak barrels are generally used for several decades whereas the French oak containers are substituted more frequently, about once every ten years on average. Barriques are used for an average of one to four years, depending on the producer's policy.

Most cellars devote special attention to tartrate precipitation, even though it is a natural process that occurs when the temperature is particularly low. The crystals of potassium tartrate that form in the wine have to be deposited on the bottom of the container and eliminated by racking the wine before bottling. This prevents excessive residue forming on the bottom of the bottle. Nevertheless, the presence of sediment of this kind in the glass should cause the consumer no concern. Tartrates are harmless and have absolutely no influence on the taste of the wine.

Maturing in wood

The traditional practice of ageing in wood is a necessary step in the creation of a great red *vin de garde*, or wine for the cellar.

Once, many different woods were used but by far the most common variety today is **oak** (*Quercus sessilis*, *Q. peduncolata* and *Q. alba*) from various sources. Most comes from the forests of central France, from Slavonia, in the former Yugoslav republic, from the countries of eastern Europe and from the USA.

During its stay in wood, the wine undergoes a series of complex processes, which are still the subject of intense study.

Much importance has been attributed to the exchanges of gases that take place through the wood, which are in direct relation to the age and size of the container, and to the effects of the penetration of oxygen into the wine.

This controlled oxidation acts mainly on the phenolic compounds in the wine, favouring two kinds of reaction that are fundamental for maturing: 1) the condensation of tannins and anthocyans; and 2) the polymerisation of the tannins. The first encourages the long-term **stabilisation** of colour-inducing components, which are thus protected from break-down. The combination of the tannins leads to the formation of polymers with a higher molecular weight. The wine then loses some of its astringency, gaining softness and roundness.

Equally important are the substances from the wood that dissolve in the wine, of which phenolics and their derivatives are some of the most important. Oak contains two main types of phenolics, lignins and tannins.

Lignins are non-water soluble, phenolic polymers and their break-down generates the precursors of many aroma-producing substances that can be distinguished on the noses of wines, particularly if they have been aged in small, toasted barrels.

The tannins, which comprise up to ten per cent of the dry matter in the wood, are largely ellagitannins, or water-soluble tannins that release ellagic acid. The behaviour and evolution of **ellagic tannins** in wine are very complex and directly influence the condensation of pigments and the maturing of the phenolics in general. They therefore have a substantial impact on the overall maturing of the wine itself.

Both Barolo and Barbaresco have phenolics characterised by substantial, albeit rather rugged, tannins and delicate anthocyans. They therefore require careful maturing in wood to acquire long-term cellaring potential.

Only the slow uptake of oxygen provided by wood ageing stabilises the wine's colour and enables the condensed tannins to evolve and acquire greater softness. Obviously, the choice of wood container is critical and particular care must be taken when considering barrel size and construction technique.

Traditional large oak casks have a low contact

BAROLO
96 g° 13.5

surface area to volume ratio and relatively thick staves, which means the exchange of gases is fairly slow and limited, racking excepted. In consequence, the wines will require a lot of time to reach full maturity and acquire a warm, evolved hue. For the same reasons, and because of the construction technique and the fact that these containers are used for many years, the release into the wine of substances from the wood is very limited.

In contrast, small oak barrels permit a more intense, regular **exchange of gases**. This leads to a swifter and more complete polymerisation of the tannins and anthocyans, so the wine has a younger-looking, more stable hue, and the tannins achieve an equilibrium on the palate more quickly. The more favourable surface area to volume ratio, and a barrel-making technique that involves **heat-bending** and then **toasting** the staves, help the substances extracted form the wood to dissolve in the wine. The less used the barrel, the more complete is the process of extraction.

That is why different choices of wood lead to different styles of wine.

BOTTLES, CORKS AND LABELS

The bottles currently released are either of the **Bordeaux** or **Burgundy** types, with all the variations that history and the producers' imagination have made on the theme. Nevertheless, all must comply with DOCG regulations that ban excesses of extravagance, imposing an "an *Albeisa* bottle shape or one that corresponds to ancient usage and tradition". Many producers have opted for the bottle shape known as ***Albeisa***, meaning "from Alba", which derives from a bottle used in the nineteenth century and ultimately comes from the Burgundy type. Production regulations also permit the bottling and release of Barolo and Barbaresco in half bottles (0.375 litres). However, few wineries put half bottles on the market, perhaps for fear that the wine might, over time, evolve differently from that released in the standard containers, the bottle (0.75 litres) and the magnum (1.5 litres). Little use is made of double magnums (3 litres), which are also permitted.

While the regulations permitted the practice, quarter *brenta* (or 12.5 litres) containers were fairly widely used. Producers would keep their finest selections in this format in order to slow the ageing process.

Since Barolo and Barbaresco are destined for long-term cellaring, the **cork stoppers** must be first quality, with compact, elastic, regular fibres and a light ochre colour. The diameter of the cork is about 24-25 millimetres and the length is on average between 45 and 55 millimetres, although some producers use 60 millimetre-long stoppers. The increasing scarcity of defect-free corks and the rise in price of bottled wine have led to a further increase in the problem of wine that is "corked". Here, as in other wine zones, producers are experimenting with alternative stoppers made from silicon. We have tasted wines sealed with these stoppers and, unfortunately, the results are not encouraging. It should be borne in mind that DOCG regulations do not, for the time being, permit stoppers made with any materials other than cork.

The first printed Barolo **labels** date from the early nineteenth century, the corresponding Barbaresco labels first appearing 50 years later. They were very plain and uncomplicated, with no indication of the vintage or the producer's name. Sometimes, producers used only metal collars with the topographic designation of the wine inscribed by hand, for example *Cannubi 1776* or *Nebiolo Barbaresco 1871*. From the early twentieth century, a number of labels began to carry the name of the winery and the place of production or the vineyard of origin. Black lettering on a white background was succeeded by gold on black or black on gold. With the passage of time, crests, coats of arms and other decorations have been added to make the bottles more attractive. We should also mention the custom of reproducing trophies, such as gold or silver medals awarded at fairs or exhibitions in

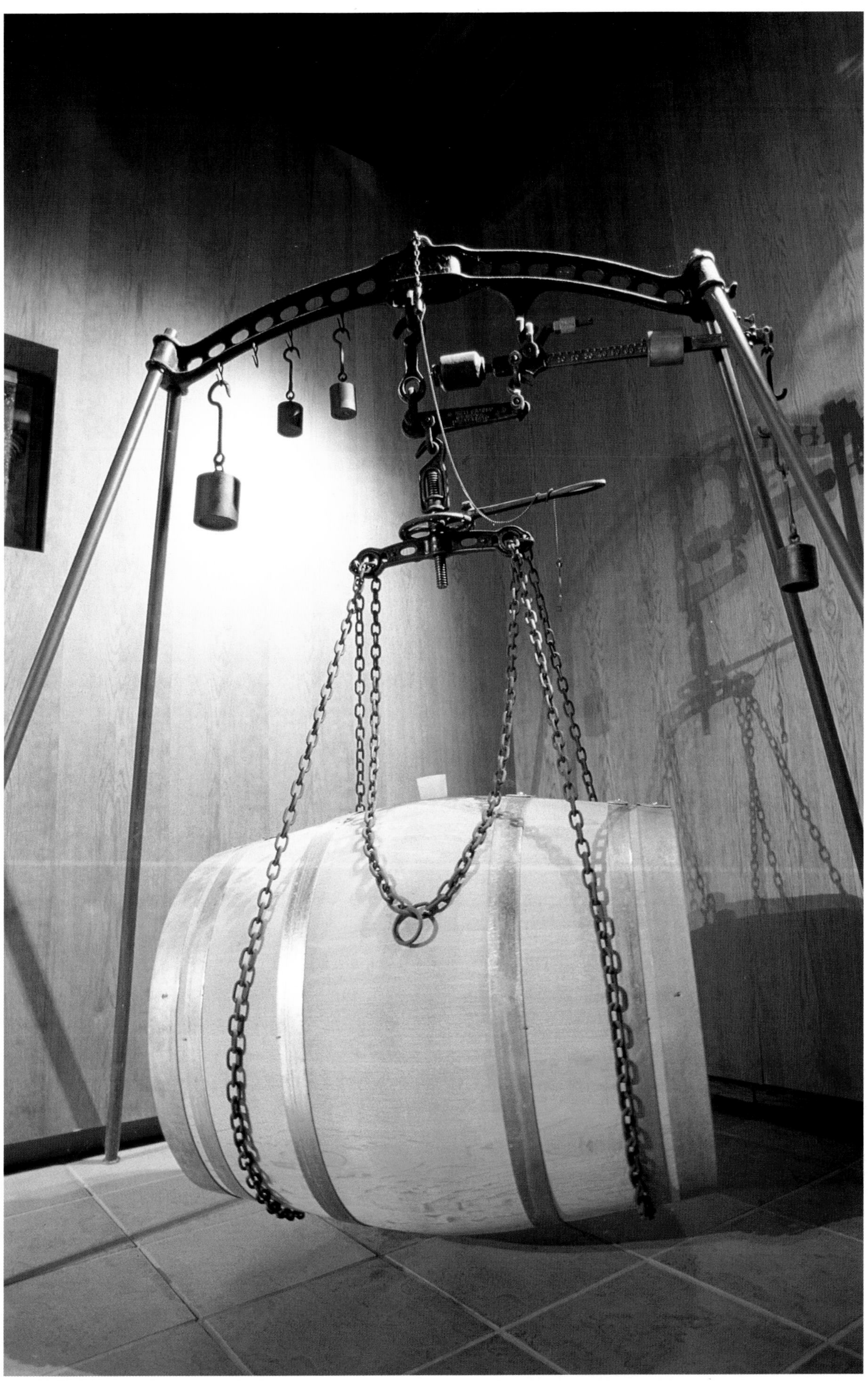

London, Paris and Vienna, or mentioning that the wine was supplied to royal households or pioneering expeditions to the north pole. Labels also carry recommendations on storage, uncorking, serving temperatures or food and wine pairings, some going so far as to provide information on cellar management, fruit selection, soft-crushing and barrique ageing. Currently, Barolo and Barbaresco labels are very diverse. On the one hand are the historic labels that have not changed for many years and on the other are those from recently founded wineries that use geometry and colour, or the inspiration of local and non-Langhe graphic artists, to create distinctive labels that will attract the eye of older and younger wine drinkers.

THE MARKET AND DEMAND

As there are no official data on the markets of consumption for Barolo and Barbaresco, it is not easy to calculate precise figures for exports or to break them down by country. We feel it is reasonably safe to affirm that exports currently account for about 80 per cent of production and that there have been no significant variations in recent years. Demand is well-established in traditional European markets, like Germany, Switzerland and Great Britain, and in north America. Significant progress has also been made in the Asian markets of Japan, Korea and Singapore, where many purchases are made for the purpose of speculation.

Only two decades ago, the situation was very different. Demand for Barolo and Barbaresco was so slack that stocks were piling up in the cellars. The wines were sometimes even given away to customers who regularly purchased Dolcetto or Barbera, and prices were extremely low for wines of this type. The grapes, too, commanded very poor prices and many growers ripped out nebbiolo, even in good positions, to plant dolcetto or moscato. Then increasing interest by the wine press and excellent vintages, like '85, '89 and the legendary '90, contributed to a boom in demand for these two wines. This produced a sharp rise in the wholesale price of grapes, which doubled in 1995 and again in 1998, the year when it reached its peak at about five times more than the level of ten years previously.

In recent years, foreign markets have boosted demand but the Italian market has also, historically, held Barolo and Barbaresco in high esteem. All too frequently, the bottles were left to gather dust in the cellar but things have been slowly improving with the education of a new generation of wine drinkers. Younger people seem more interested in enjoying serious wines than their parents, who are used to less challenging bottles. If we consider that at least 80 per cent of the remaining 20 per cent, accounted for by domestic sales, is bought or consumed in restaurants by foreign tourists, Italian consumers probably buy only four per cent of the total. This represents 400,000 bottles a year out of an average production of 10,000,000 units.

TASTING BAROLO AND BARBARESCO

Appearance

Briefly, we can say that immediately after alcoholic fermentation, nebbiolo is a not very intense ruby in colour, with highlights that tend more towards bright, or even dark, red rather than orange. Later, the wine, which will have become either Barolo or Barbaresco in the meantime, loses a little intensity as the anthocyans, the main colour-producing phenolics, are precipitated. The wine shades into garnet red, and then orangey red, before finally becoming brick red after many years in the bottle. It should be noted that the garnet shade is stable for several years, and sometimes for decades.

One good indicator of the ageing process is the **rim**, the dilute and occasionally colourless part of the wine at the edges when the glass is inclined. The broader and less intensely coloured the rim, the longer the wine has been ageing in the bottle.

Langhe producers have often shown they suffer from an inferiority complex with respect to makers of more intensely hued wines, such as Dolcetto, Barbera and Cabernet Sauvignon, although there are no valid reasons for this. Pinot Noir from Burgundy generally has a less intense colour than Barolo or Barbaresco but that has certainly proved no obstacle to its success all over the world.

Nose

The olfactory profile of Barolo and Barbaresco is probably their most exciting aspect. As with all great wines, the most striking features are the intense impact on the nose and the complexity of the aromatic profile, which evolves with aeration in the glass but above all with the passing of the years as the wine ages in the bottle. Of all the locally grown varieties, nebbiolo is the one that most clearly leaves its mark in the memories of winelovers as emblematic of the flavour and aromas of the Langhe. While it is almost impossible to tell a Barbaresco Asili from a Rabajà, and it is difficult to distinguish a Barolo Cannubi from a Barbaresco Montestefano, experienced palates will find it much easier to identify the nebbiolo variety in a great Barolo or Barbaresco.

We have collected, from notes written by many different tasters, mentions of dozens of distinct aromas that depend on the individual taster's perceptions, the ageing techniques used and the vineyard of origin of the grapes that went into the wine. The most frequently mentioned aromas include red and black berry fruit, especially plums, red and blackcurrants, raspberries, bilberries, strawberries, brambles, morello cherries, plain, bitter and liqueur cherries, and various kinds of jam. Then come various kinds of flowers, especially roses and violets, fresh or dried, herbs, hay, tobacco, tar, Peruvian bark, liquorice, chocolate, pine and wood resin, incense, mint, basil, camphor, eucalyptus, peach, rain-soaked earth, mushrooms, truffle, a range of spices including cinnamon, cloves and pepper, cocoa powder, leather, cakes and milk, including cheese and milk shake. Other aromas reported, usually as indicators of a lack of finesse, various vegetables, rhubarb, minestrone, chicory and artichoke. The aromas that indicate excessive evolution range from coffee to the maderized, or *marsalato*, notes typical of over-oxidised wines. Wines aged in small oak barrels acquire a range of notes from the wood, from vanilla and torrefaction to smokiness, cigar box and spices. It is interesting to note that some aromas, especially the grassy, fresh, balsamic notes, may derive equally from the vineyard where the grapes were grown, such as Ginestra at Monforte, or from barrique ageing.

One of the defects sometimes encountered is an aroma of reduction, the unpleasant, dirty, inelegant sensation that recalls a closed or mouldy room. It is caused by a lack of oxygen in the wine. We do not believe that it is necessary to uncork a bottle of Barolo or Barbaresco hours before serving but the aromas undergo perceptible changes, generally for the better, if allowed to breathe for a few minutes. We therefore suggest gradual aeration during the course of tasting.

Palate

Barolo and Barbaresco have remarkable intensity and persistence on the palate, marked tannins, good acidity and substantial alcohol, which lends the wine warmth and softness. In the early years after the harvest, the wine's balance is generally jeopardised by the tannins, whose astringency and bite tend to have the upper hand over the alcohol-derived softness. But tannins are one of the crucial factors in the wine's success. All great reds have a robust tannin content but few are able to convey the **velvet** softness, or the succulent, palate-enfolding mouthfeel of a Barolo or Barbaresco from a good vintage. It will be useful to remember here that extraction of tannins is in direct proportion to the duration of maceration on the skins, fermentation temperature and alcohol. Longer maceration, higher fermentation temperatures and greater alcohol content also encourage the release of the harsher, more astringent elements in the tannins. That is to say, they bring out the

components that are more difficult to extract but which also appear to ensure greater longevity.
It is also possible to find Barolo and Barbaresco in which the alcohol is preponderant, causing a warm, burning sensation on the palate because the wine lacks sufficient structure.
In quantitative terms, **tannins** can reach or exceed a level of three grams per litre, producing a weight in the mouth that few other varieties can duplicate, while total acidity is on average between five and 5.5 grams per litre, or slightly above the values for the cabernet family and just below those for sangiovese. Alcohol content is very high, at between 13.5 and 14.5 per cent, whereas dry extract ranges from 26 to more than 30 grams per litre. The latter value is comparable to that of other great wines but it is only significant if taken in conjunction with the other figures.
The principal feature of the palate in Barolo and Barbaresco is undoubtedly persistence, in the sense of the length of time these wines stay clearly perceptible on nose and palate. This is often measurable in many tens of seconds.

Ageing potential

When we talk about ageing – or maturing, or cellaring – potential, we are referring to the wine's capacity to improve in the bottle, or at least to develop without deterioration or impairment. In this sense, it is generally true that, with some not infrequent exceptions, Barolo and Barbaresco are at their best after ten to 30 years, provided the vintage is good, the winemaker competent and the bottle cellar suitable. When these three conditions are satisfied, the wines can easily age for up to **40 years** and sometimes longer. They will show no signs of decline and, indeed, will be capable of expressing the inherent characteristics of the nebbiolo grape to a sublime degree. Obviously, perfect wine can also be found in a newly released bottle but the nebbiolo nose will only emerge after a certain number of years in the cellar. The tannins, too, require several years to mellow out and shake off their aggressive edges through polymerisation. Indeed, we have tasted both Barolo and Barbaresco that was still in excellent condition 40 years after the vintage. The uptake of oxygen, however, enhances perception of the sweeter aromas and leads to a sometimes excessive masking of the tannins, and a change in the wine's personality.
Outstandingly good vintages can produce wines that rise above these limitations. For example, it is still possible to taste bottles from the 1958 and 1961 vintages that are astoundingly harmonious and satisfying. Nevertheless, these are wines that have in all probability come to the end of their evolution and will not improve any further. The 1971 vintage is another that looks set to offer us some delicious surprises over the next few decades. Clearly, wines are likely to have greater ageing potential when, as is common practice already with some producers, the corks are replaced every 15-20 years in bottles destined for a prolonged sojourn in the cellar.

Serving temperature, decanting and glasses

The recommended serving temperature for these wines is from 18 to 20°C but we have to admit that we have enjoyed excellent Barolos and Barbarescos, particularly from older vintages, at temperatures a few degrees higher. Equally, these are reds that can be enjoyed at slightly cooler temperatures, particularly when they have only been in the bottle for a few years. It should be remembered that the higher the temperature, the greater the perception of the alcohol in the wine, to the detriment of its tannin content. Drinking Barolo and Barbaresco at a relatively low temperature tends to bring out the astringent elements in the gustatory profile.
Pouring the wine into a carafe before serving is recommended for older bottles as this will prevent any of the sediment that will probably have formed from getting into the glass. For very mature wines, however, it will be advisable to use a narrow-necked **decanter**, which prevents any

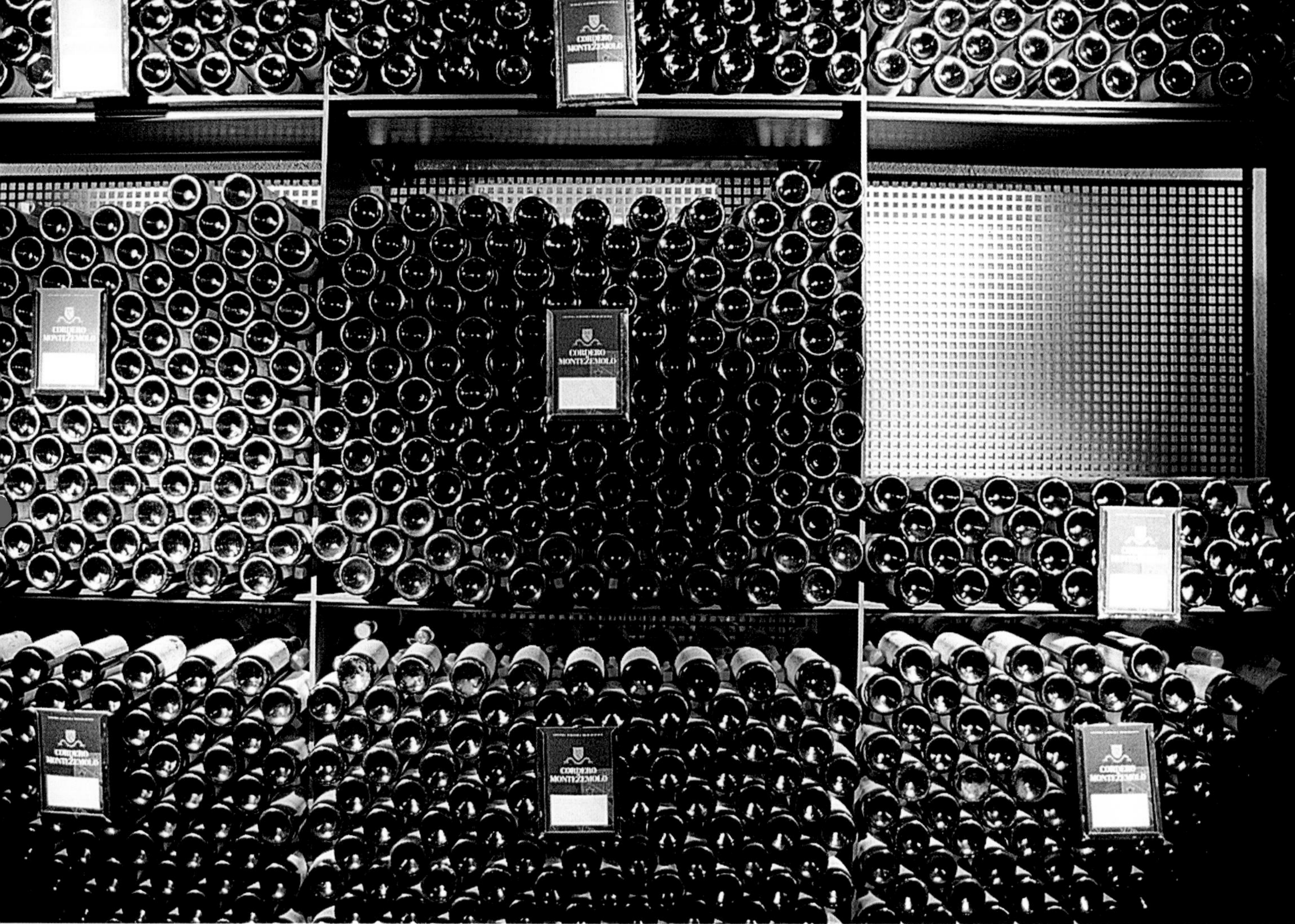

appreciable aeration, as sudden contact with the atmosphere after 30 years in the bottle may cause excessive oxidation and ruin the wine. Aeration is of fundamental importance if we are to appreciate the olfactory qualities of Barolo and Barbaresco so decanting into a carafe is recommended even for recent vintages. The **glass** generally suggested for these wines is the tulip, which has a fairly broad bowl that narrows at the top, opening out again at the rim. In practice, it is sufficient if the glass used permits adequate aeration when rotated gently.

Barolo

THE BIRTH OF BAROLO

Castiglione Falletto
Facing page, Barolo vineyards

Although the first reports of nebbiolo grapes date back to the early centuries of the second millennium, we have to wait for the eighteenth century to find the term *Barol* (without the final "o") in correspondence between the Savoy ambassador in London and some English wine merchants. At the time, Britain was at war with France and no longer imported French wines. Genoa was demanding heavy taxes on wine shipped through her port while Nizza Marittima, the only Savoy outlet to the sea, was too distant and poorly served by roads. Sadly, the chance to export Barolo across the Channel was missed.
The real birth of Barolo took place during the Risorgimento, in the cellars of the castle belonging

to the Marchesi Falletti. King Carlo Alberto and Cavour were its official patrons. They both appreciated the wine and produced it on their estates, thus contributing to its fame, but it was a woman who acted as Barolo's godmother. **Giulietta Vitturnia Colbert di Maulévrier**, the wife of Tancredi Falletti, wanted her Nebbiolo to be called after its town of origin, Barolo.

Barolo was held in very high regard and the story goes that the Marchesa sent a long convoy of ox-drawn carts to the court of the king, Carlo Alberto. On each cart, there was a long, flat, six-hectolitre barrel of Barolo. Legend has it that there was one cart for each of the Marchesa's *cascine*, which were as numerous as the days in the year. Other imaginative commentators counted 325 barrels, were broken up and sold off to meet the huge running costs of the Opera Pia.

The Marchesa was also a friend of **Camillo Benso di Cavour**, whom she used to refer to affectionately as *le petit terrible Camille*. The young Camillo Benso had arrived at Grinzane in 1832 with a royal nomination as mayor in his pocket. At Grinzane, the Cavours had 542 Piedmontese *giornate* (more than 200 hectares), some of which they owned and some they rented. The family also owned the castle. As the estate's land agent, Cavour replanted the vineyards and reorganised the cellars. He planted 14 *giornate* to pinot nero, for he loved the wines of Burgundy. He also had the oenologist **Oudart** summoned from France to create some excellent "modern" wines in the Burgundy style.

Serralunga

representing the 365 days of the year less 40 for Lent, as the Marchesa was very religious. The Falletti estate at Barolo was so vast, extending from Vergne to Alba and passing across the slopes of La Morra, Castiglione Falletto and Serralunga, that almost any such hypothesis was at least credible.

When her husband died in 1838, Giulietta was 53 and she inherited a huge fortune. Alone and childless, she used her substantial income to finance a wide range of charities, including orphanages, boarding schools for young girls and hospitals, as well as the college at Barolo. Today, these constitute the Opera Pia Barolo charitable foundation. In the twentieth century, the estates

It was to her *terribile* friend Cavour, a liberal and a womaniser, that the pious Marchesa Falletti turned to obtain the assistance of Oudart in her own vineyards and cellars. That was how Barolo was born, from the marriage of new winemaking techniques to the nebbiolo variety.

The Marchesa's Barolo had by now charmed the palate of **Carlo Alberto**. As a result, the king decided to take up viticulture and winemaking in the grand style. He purchased, from the administrators of the charity hospital in Turin, the castle of Verduno and all its *cascine*, then the castles of Roddi and Santa Vittoria, which were acquired from the Marchesi della Chiesa. Starting in the 1830s, Carlo Alberto began to reorganise agricultural activity on

estates that extended over 1,800 *giornate* or 685 hectares, some in the municipal territory of Bra, with a total of 14 *cascine*.
From 1818 to 1843, Carlo Alberto built the Agenzia at Pollenzo. This agricultural complex, which was the state of the art at the time, is currently being converted. The castle was reconstructed, the church raised, the cabled-stayed iron bridge over the Tanaro was built and the park with its perimeter walls was renovated. The cellars were dug in the tufaceous rock underneath Santa Vittoria. The complex was named Il Moscatello and, under the direction of a general and wine expert, Paolo Francesco Staglieno, it began to produce mainly *Sciampagna* (pronounced "sham-pan-ya").
Carlo Alberto died in 1849. By 1865, his estates had been rented to the Bosco e Compagnia firm. In 1867, Il Moscatello was sold to Francesco Cinzano. Pollenzo, however, remained the property of the Savoys and Vittorio Emanuele II visited often, partly because Rosa Vercellana, the *Bela Rosin* who was later to be his morganatic wife, lived at Fontanafredda. Vittorio Emanuele's son, Emanuele, Conte di Mirafiore, and then his grandson Gastone, made Fontanafredda into a major wine producer. In 1878, they built the new cellars.
In the meantime, the art of winemaking emerged from the cellars of the nobility to enter, equally triumphantly, those of the wealthier private citizens, lawyers and pharmacists.
Proof of this was the award at the 1873 exhibition of two medals to Matteo Fissore from Bra, for an 1869 Barolo and a Barolo Secco from the 1871 vintage. At Turin in 1881, Giovan Battista Burlotto from Verduno won a gold medal. It was to be the first of 32 such awards. At La Morra, the pharmacist and mayor, Andrea Tarditi, and his son, Giuseppe, produced a much-decorated Barolo vermouth, as well as Langhe wines. In Alba, Luigi Calissano's wines were being exported to France by 1879 and at the turn of the century, they began to be exported to South America and the United States. In Barolo, Giacomo Borgogno and the prize-winning Barale e Rinaldi cellar were releasing successful wines while the Opera Pia continued its activities. At Serralunga, Dottor Giuseppe Cappellano was equally successful with his wines and his Barolo Chinato, as was *Tota* Virginia Ferrero. In Santa Maria at La Morra, Cavalier Luigi Parà, with advice from the director of the new oenological school at Alba, Professor Domizio Cavazza, was setting up an experimental vineyard with the planting system that would be named after him.
A large group of Barolo makers enlivened the scene at the turn of the last century. Many others would follow in their footsteps, despite the ravages of phylloxera in the vineyards and the economic crisis of 1929. Many of the above are profiled in the sections entitled *The Greats of Barolo and of Barbaresco*, where we have attempted to reconstruct the biographies of the people who created today's Barolo.

Grinzane Cavour

Regulations for the production of Barolo

The Barolo Registered and Guaranteed Designation of Origin was instituted by Presidential Decree on 1 July 1980. In brief, it stipulates that:

1. Barolo should be obtained only from nebbiolo grapes of the michet, lampia and rosé clones.
2. Grapes may only come from the entire area of the municipal territories of Barolo, Castiglione Falletto, Serralunga d'Alba, and part of the municipal territories of Monforte d'Alba, Novello, La Morra, Verduno, Grinzane Cavour, Diano d'Alba, Cherasco and Roddi.
3. In this zone, only appropriately located and aspected hillslope vineyards, with prevalently clay and limestone soil, will be considered suitable.
4. The maximum yield of grapes permitted is 80 quintals per hectare while the wine-to-fruit ratio cannot exceed 65 per cent at the end of the compulsory period of ageing.
5. Vinification and ageing must be carried out in the grape production area, with some permissible exceptions for wineries that have previously made Barolo in the provinces of Cuneo, Asti and Alessandria.
6. The minimum natural alcoholic strength of the wine must be 12.5 per cent and the bottled wine should have an alcohol content of at least 13 per cent. The minimum for dry extract is 23 grams per litre and total acidity may not be less than five grams per litre.
7. The minimum ageing period is three years (five for Barolo Riserva) from the 1 January after the harvest.
8. Back blending with younger or older Barolo is permitted, up to a maximum of 15 per cent.

Municipalities	**Registered wineries**	**Total area under vine (ha)**	**Max. yield permitted (q/ha)**	**Max. yield permitted (hl)**	**% of area in DOCG zone**
Barolo	90	163.6465	12,993.15	9,095.21	13.10
Castiglione Falletto	55	126.9446	10,118.61	7,083.03	10.16
Cherasco	1	1.8500	148.00	103.60	0.15
Diano d'Alba	8	22.5905	1,773.88	1,241.72	1.81
Grinzane Cavour	31	23.6143	1,889.14	1,322.40	1.89
La Morra	227	383.6390	30,411.69	21,288.18	30.70
Monforte d'Alba	122	208.3518	16,383.51	11,468.46	16.67
Novello	44	52.3005	4,159.08	2,911.36	4.19
Roddi	17	11.6460	931.68	652.18	0.93
Serralunga d'Alba	98	200.9548	15,969.60	11,178.72	16.08
Verduno	57	54.0911	4,327.29	3,029.10	4.33
TOTAL	750	1,249.6291	99,105.63	69,373.94	100.00

Production of municipalities included in the Barolo DOCG zone (data from 1998)

There were 750 estates registered as growers of nebbiolo for Barolo in 1998, accounting for a total area under vine of 1,250 hectares (an average of 1.67 hectares per estate). In that vintage, the total yield was 99,105 quintals of grapes and 69,374 hectolitres of wine. The production forecast for Barolo in 1998 was 7,612,933 bottles, in comparison with 6,665,467 in 1994, 5,027,867 in 1995, 6,192,267 in 1996 and 7,361,600 in 1997.

Year	Registered area under vine in hectares	Actual production in bottles	Hectolitres per hectare
1967	644.79	4,353,600	50.64
1968	644.79	4,052,933	47.14
1969	688.96	4,341,600	47.26
1970	780.09	5,280,000	50.76
1971	868.17	5,595,200	48.34
1972	981.34	0	–
1973	1,016.29	6,642,800	49.02
1974	1,061.21	6,962,800	49.21
1975	1,076.48	5,035.333	35.08
1976	1,065.44	3,799.467	26.75
1977	1,092.75	3,969,867	27.25
1978	1,112.62	4,223,467	28.47
1979	1,113.29	7,092,400	47.78
1980	1,111.70	7,238,933	48.84
1981	1,195.74	6,233,867	39.10
1982	1,183.43	7,479,467	47.40
1983	1,307.02	7,476,533	42.90
1984	1,247.70	4,310,400	25.91
1985	1,256.04	7,260,533	43.35
1986	1,208.03	3,710,933	23.04
1987	1,181.17	6,317,600	40.11
1988	1,178.69	6,710,533	42.70
1989	1,166.15	5,050,400	32.48
1990	1,163.54	6,110,667	39.39
1991	1,175.63	6,836,933	43.62
1992	1,169.37	6,544,533	41.97
1993	1,178.63	6,408,000	40.78
1994	1,189.62	6,665,467	42.02
1995	1,184.93	5,027,867	31.82
1996	1,238.73	6,192,267	37.49
1997	1,253.60	7,361,600	44.04
1998	1,249.63	7,612,933	45.69

Total area of Barolo DOCG zone

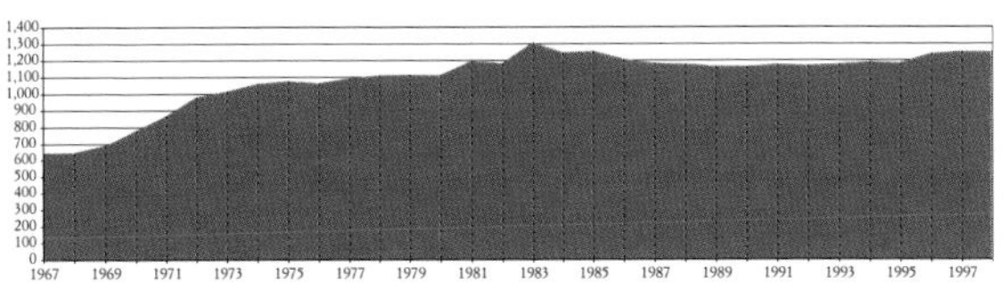

Barolo production (number of bottles)

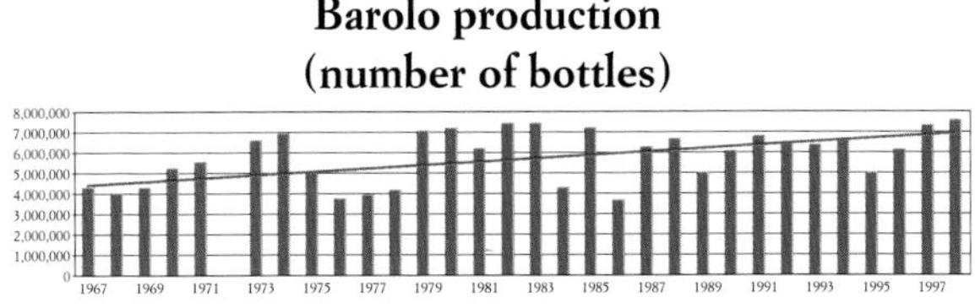

Yields of Barolo DOCG zone

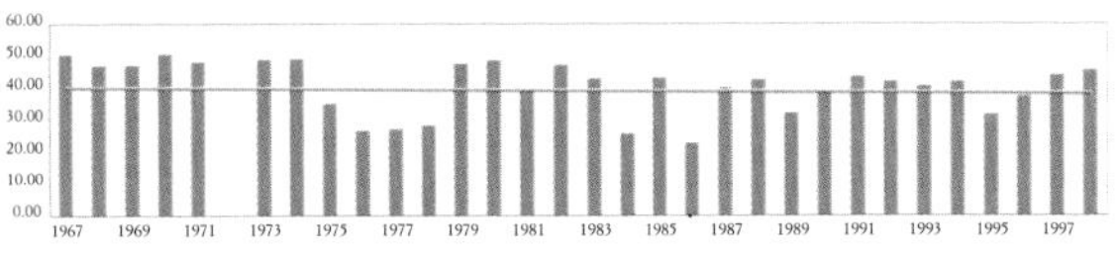

Breakdown of Barolo DOCG zone by municipality

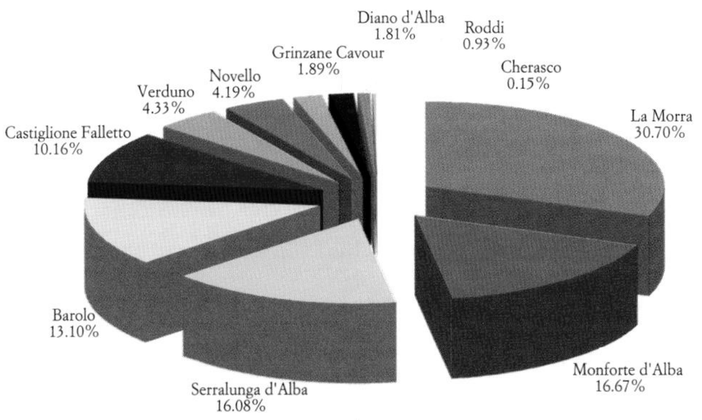

Barolo

In the centre of a sweeping, vine-clad natural amphitheatre sits the town of Barolo, home and eponym of the greatest of Italy's wines. The Barolo adventure started here, on the slopes of this valley, known as Cannubi, and it was from these wineries that Barolo set out to conquer the world's markets. The name itself has Celtic origins: *bas reul* means "low place" and the territory, if not the site of the present-day town, was inhabited in prehistoric times. Stone weapons and utensils from the Neolithic era have been found in the Conca della Fava below.

Unlike neighbouring towns, Barolo does not have a hilltop or ridge as its focal point but lies instead on a sort of plateau, or spur, under the hills themselves, sheltered by the surrounding high ground. The town and its castle come into view suddenly on the outcrop that almost closes off the road for those who come up from Alba on the old highway. Visitors arriving from above, from Novello and La Morra, first pass the small country chapel of San Pietro delle Viole and immediately afterwards, the looming mass of the castle of Volta, at Vergne. The ruined but still rugged castle has recently been acquired by private buyers, who intend to restore it. There is a persistent local legend that Volta is the meeting place for witches and the tormented souls of the participants at an orgy so debauched that the castle floor opened in shame, swallowing them up. Only one man survived, a Falletti who had merely watched the riotous *bal dij patanu* (dance of the naked).

The castle of Barolo, however, is in good condition. No embarrassing memories haunt its past nor are there any importunate ghosts in its present. It was built in the tenth century, when the incursions of the Saracens forced Berengarius I of Provence to grant his vassals and the religious communities in the area

the right to build towers and other defences. In 1250, it was acquired by the powerful Falletti family, able bankers and traders from Alba. Subsequently, the Falettis became *conti*, or counts, with Girolamo III in the seventeenth century, and then *marchesi*, or marquises, in the eighteenth century under Girolamo IV. The line became extinct with Carlo Tancredi, who was twice mayor of Turin, and his wife, the celebrated, cultured Juliette (Giulia) Colbert di Maulévrier, a generous benefactress and the leading light in a generation of Barolo makers who laid the foundations of the town's future fortune. Her contemporaries had names like Borgogno, Rinaldi, Mascarello and Pira.

Since a public subscription in 1971, the castle has belonged to the municipal authority and today it is a mandatory port of call for tourists visiting Barolo. The castle's current appearance is the result of transformations imposed by the changing times and uses to which it has been put. From a defensive shelter, it became a noble country residence and was finally converted into a strict religious school. Each change left its mark on the castle's austere architecture. Today, the cellars – where Marchesa Giulia first christened the king of wines – house the regional authority-run Enoteca Regionale del Barolo.

In the square in front of the castle, there is an interesting parish church dedicated to Saint Donatus, which was formerly the Falletti family chapel. Extended so as to be suitable for public worship, it is still a very compact building and looks as if it is about to be crushed under the massive weight of the castle walls. Under the presbytery is the funeral chamber of the former feudal landlords, with tombs dating from the end of the sixteenth century until the family became extinct.

The great vineyards

The castle is the historic powerhouse that drives Barolo. The wine was created here and the Enoteca Regionale acts as a showcase for all the municipalities in the DOCG zone.
Cannubi, the Barolo vineyard *par excellence*, overshadows the other subzones in the municipality. This preeminence is, however, happily acknowledged by the entire Langa del Barolo and is a source of pride for Cannubi's "neighbours". It should also be borne in mind that some of the best locations – Brunate and Cerequio – lie mainly in the municipality of La Morra. Nor should we forget that traditionally, many producers in the municipality of Barolo – Borgogno and Bartolo Mascarello, to name but two – made their reputations with blended wines containing grapes from various locations, not vineyard selections.
The long central strip of Cannubi is flanked by two vine-growing hills of considerable interest. On the slopes facing the municipality of Monforte are the vineyards of Castellero, Zuncai and Monrobiolo while there are three superb crus on the border with La Morra: Brunate, Cerequio and Sarmassa.

DOC and DOCG	Total area under vine in hectares	% of area in municipality	% of area in zone
Barolo	**163.6455**	**62.13**	**13.10**
Dolcetto d'Alba	55.7750	21.18	2.98
Barbera d'Alba	35.2471	13.38	2.04
Langhe Chardonnay	4.7867	1.82	1.87
Other DOC zones	3.9300	1.49	
TOTAL	263.3843	100.00	
Other DOC zones			
Langhe Rosso	0.7800	0.30	1.11
Langhe Nebbiolo	0.6300	0.24	2.52
Langhe Freisa	1.9900	0.76	3.32
Langhe Bianco	0.5300	0.20	1.99

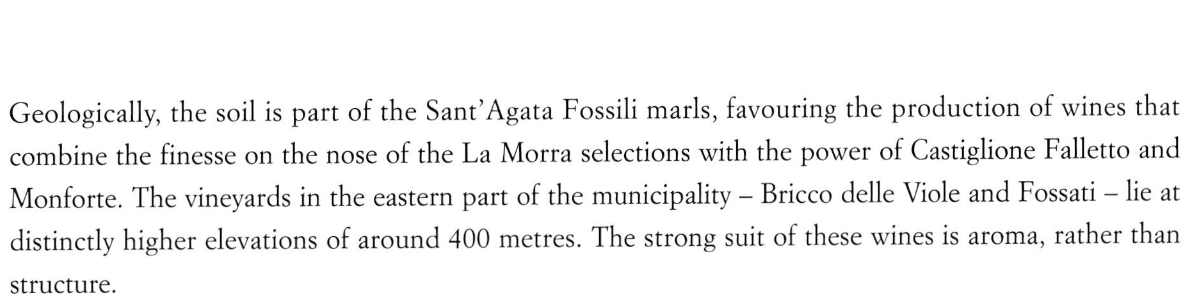

Geologically, the soil is part of the Sant'Agata Fossili marls, favouring the production of wines that combine the finesse on the nose of the La Morra selections with the power of Castiglione Falletto and Monforte. The vineyards in the eastern part of the municipality – Bricco delle Viole and Fossati – lie at distinctly higher elevations of around 400 metres. The strong suit of these wines is aroma, rather than structure.

Many of the names here will already be very familiar to winelovers. In pointing out their precise geographical location, this Atlas hopes to bring their special characteristics into sharper focus and thus encourage informed, intelligently inquisitive wine tourism.

Production

There are 90 wineries in the municipality, with 164 hectares and a potential production of 9,095 hectolitres of wine a year, or 13 per cent of the entire Barolo DOCG zone.

THE GREAT VINEYARDS

BRICCO VIOLE
BRUNATE
CANNUBI
CASTELLERO
CEREQUIO
FOSSATI
LE COSTE
LISTE
MONGHISOLFO OR CANNUBI BOSCHIS
MONROBIOLO OR BUSSIA DI BAROLO
MUSCATEL OR CANNUBI MUSCATEL
PAIAGALLO
PREDA
SAN LORENZO OR CANNUBI SAN LORENZO
SAN SEBASTIANO
SARMASSA
VALLETTA OR CANNUBI VALLETTA
VIA NUOVA
VIGNANE
ZUNCAI

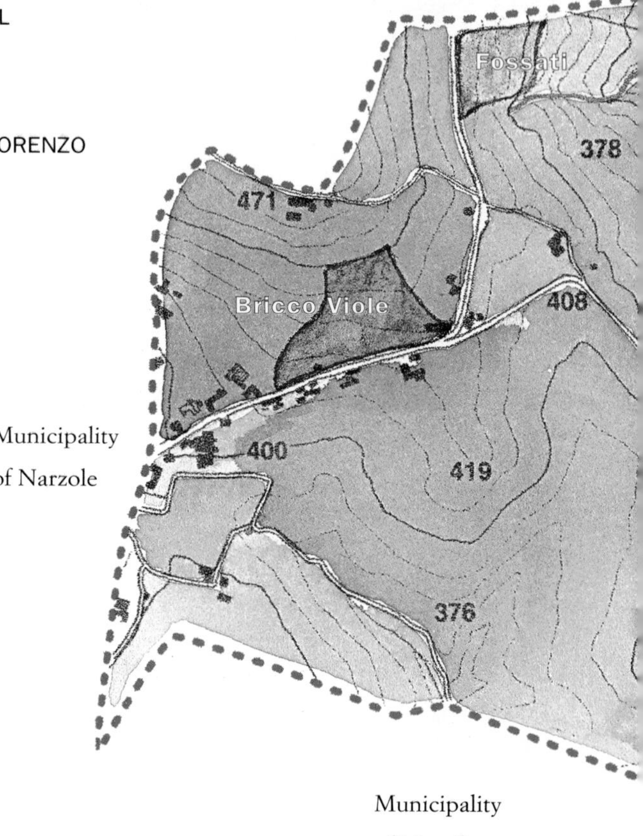

Municipality of Narzole

Municipality of Novello

BAROLO DOCG ZONE

GREAT VINEYARDS

Municipality of La Morra

Municipality of Castiglione Falletto

Municipality of Monforte d'Alba

N

Bricco Viole

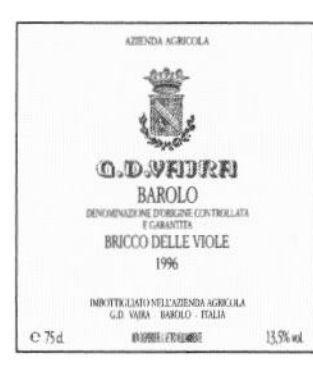

Bricco Viole belongs to the district of Vergne di Barolo and its charming name (literally, 'violet hill') is a reminder of the flowers that bloom here in springtime. And of course, violets are very much part of the aromatic profile of Barolo. This great vineyard can be clearly seen from the road that leads from the centre of Vergne to La Morra. We prefer the plots that are less exposed to the cold winds that blow off the mountains across the tip of the Po flatlands. The vines here are south-facing. Ownership is split among several cellars and a number of very interesting wines indeed have emerged from this vineyard.

MAIN LABELS

*Barolo Bricco delle Viole – G. D. Vajra, Barolo

*Barolo Bricco delle Viole – Giovanni Viberti, Barolo

Brunate,Cerequio, Fossati

These vineyards are shared by the municipalities of Barolo and La Morra. Brunate and Cerequio lie in the part below the ridge and Fossati lies on the brow that skirts the provincial road from Vergne to La Morra. We refer readers to the profiles on these vineyards in the chapter on La Morra but not without first underlining the extraordinarily high quality of Brunate, also called "Brinate", and Cerequio. Both are undoubtedly among the very finest Barolo crus in absolute terms.

MAIN LABELS

*Barolo Crus Vigneti Brunate – Francesco Borgogno, Barolo

*Barolo Brunate – Marchesi di Barolo

*Barolo Vigneto La Brunata – Francesco Rinaldi & Figli, Alba

*Barolo Brunate-Le Coste – Giuseppe Rinaldi, Barolo

Cannubi

The oldest bottle anywhere in the Langhe is conserved at Bra by the Manzone family. It bears the words "CANNUBI 1752". This precious relic shows that the Cannubio (or Canubbio or Cannubi) vineyard was already famous and well-respected even before the appearance of Barolo. Cannubi's prestige has never dimmed. In fact, Cannubi has always served to bring prestige to the wineries that acquired its grapes, or better still, owned small plots there. For many years, the name Cannubi even used to be printed on the labels of wines that did not come from the vineyard itself. In short, it was a name to bank on. It is interesting to note that small producers almost invariably used to blend grapes from Cannubi with fruit from other, less prestigious vineyards. There are many reports of blending the fruit from this superb vineyard. Here are a few: "Pira (a much-respected producer who died in 1980) used to blend Cannubi and Vignane because Cannubi mellows and acquires aromas earlier. Vignane never matures. It's much rawer" (Natale Ronzano, nick-named *Talin*). "Once, the old Donati family used to blend Cannubi with Le Coste because, especially in dry years, the wine from Cannubi would benefit considerably" (Donato Camerano). "In dry years, you have to blend Cannubi with other subzones because it has a low must weight and is missing something. When it's been rainy, it's the finest wine you can make" (Bruno Boschis).

We would be poor reporters if we failed to point out that Cannubi is unrivalled as the leading vineyard for Barolo. The prices of fruit from Cannubi have always been higher than those for other vineyards and the consolidated experience of many vintages bears witness to the wine's quality. "Cannubi never lets you down. You can get the yield wrong but not the quality" (Natale Ronzano).

Although there can be no debate over the quality of Cannubi, there is plenty of argument about where it begins and ends. The prestige of the name Cannubi and the outstanding nature of the vineyard have, over the years, encouraged a very elastic definition of its area. According to older growers, today's Cannubi no longer corresponds to the original vineyard. "For me, the Cannubi hill goes from the Viganò holding to the former Canonica vineyard above the cemetery" (Donato Camerano). This detailed description was shared by all our interviewees and our map reflects the definition. It is, however, equally true that for many years most people have had a wider interpretation of the territory indicated in the phrase "go to Cannubi". In this way, the original Monghisolfo area has over time acquired the name Cannubi Boschis, as may be seen from the priceless *Monografia sulla Viticultura ed Enologia nella Provincia di Cuneo*, or "Monograph on Viticulture and Oenology in the Province of Cuneo", written by Lorenzo Fantini towards the end of the nineteenth century. In more recent years, in 1972 to be precise, Renato Ratti prefixed the term "Cannubi" to the traditional Muscatel subzone. Ratti, too, in his first map of Barolo, lumped together under the single name, Barolo, the entire band of hillside that runs from Muscatel to Monghisolfo, classifying it as an "historic viticultural subzone with a traditional vocation". Obviously, we have here a number of distinct interpretations of "Cannubi" that over the years have come into conflict, with one or other prevailing for a certain period. We acknowledge this situation but will take our cue from a statement on which all the sources agree. We think it is the most crucial and significant element in the entire debate: the unquestioned prestige enjoyed by grapes from all these subzones. The quality of the fruit harvested at Muscatel, Valletta, San Lorenzo, Cannubi and Monghisolfo is almost indistinguishable, even though within each vineyard there are plots whose location is more or less felicitous. "Once, the estates had a cow or ox and so at the bottom of Cannubi, or Valletta, or other similar subzones, there was meadowland or maize. Then they began to put in peach orchards and finally they planted nebbiolo right down to the bottom. In those

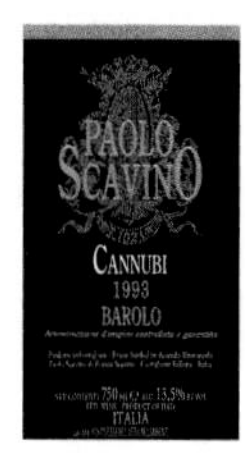

plots, grapes in the last 50 or 60 metres will struggle a little to ripen". This interesting comment comes from Bruno Boschis, known as *Brunone*, or "Big Bruno", and universally acknowledged as a man who is intimately familiar with the Barolo DOCG zone after working here as a grower and grafter for more than 60 years. Bruno's words focus on the gradual changes that the productive geography of this particular part of the Langhe has undergone. Today, the area at the bottom of Cannubi, where the terrain is almost level, is in part planted to barbera.

To return to the problem of the precise location of Cannubi, the existence of two distinct opinions confuses the issue. Some use the name only to indicate the traditional area while others extend the definition to include fruit that matches strict quality criteria, or for specific commercial reasons. Some producers, following Ratti's broader definition, obtain Barolo Cannubi with grapes from Monghisolfo or Muscatel. Others call Monghisolfo itself Cannubi Boschis and still others, as we have already mentioned, use fruit from Cannubi in blends with other grapes to make excellent Barolos.

The numerous reports we have recorded all agree that the Cannubi vineyard lies between the main Alba-Barolo road and the Crosia road, embracing the *cascine* of Ferrere and Viganò. They say in these parts that the best sites are the ones that face the cemetery. A small west-facing area was once planted to dolcetto and barbera.

Although we are duty-bound to define the precise location of Cannubi, we feel obliged to mention that the broader use of the name has been in the past, and continues to be, encouraged by the superlative quality of the grapes and wines involved. The name Cannubi, albeit in a rather haphazard way, has brought prestige to other deserving vineyards, just as in Burgundy, the Romanée vineyard has passed its name to Romanée Conti and Romanée Saint-Vivant. We must acknowledge that this small hill, with an area of about 40 Piedmontese *giornate*, or 15 hectares, has been able to enhance the potential of the surrounding area in a way that has no equal in Italy.

Main labels

*Barolo Cannubi – Fratelli Serio e Battista Borgogno, Barolo
*Barolo Cannubi – Giacomo Brezza & Figli, Barolo
*Barolo Vigneto Cannubi – Commendator G.B. Burlotto, Verduno
*Barolo Cannubi – Michele Chiarlo, Calamandrana
*Barolo Cannubi – Guido Damilano, Barolo
*Barolo nei Cannubi – Poderi Luigi Einaudi, Dogliani
*Barolo Cannubi – Giacomo Fenocchio, Monforte d'Alba
*Barolo Cannubi – Marchesi di Barolo
*Barolo Cannubi – E. Pira & Figli (Chiara Boschis), Barolo
*Barolo Cannubi – Prunotto, Alba
*Barolo Vigneto Cannubbio – Francesco Rinaldi & Figli, Alba
*Barolo Cannubi – Paolo Scavino, Castiglione Falletto
*Barolo Vigneti in Cannubi – Tenuta Carretta, Piobesi d'Alba

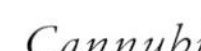

Cannubi

Castellero

The Castellero vineyard lies north east of the town of Barolo, on the last hill in a range that starts at Castiglione Falletto. The vineyard extends over about 15 Piedmontese *giornate*, or less than six hectares, with a uniformly west-facing position. On one side, Castellero is bounded by the ridge of the hill and on the other, a *capezzagna*, or unsurfaced road, marks it off from Vignane, which is part of the same strip of territory. The lower part of the vineyard descends to the flatland, where most of the vines planted are chardonnay and pinot nero.

In the past, Castellero, too, was no stranger to the practice of blending grapes from different vineyards. "I remember when the co-operative winery was here, they tried to mix these grapes with fruit from other subzones with less clayey soils" (Baldo Demagistris).

Main labels

*Barolo Castellero – Barale Fratelli, Barolo

*Barolo Castellero – Giacomo Brezza & Figli, Barolo

Le Coste

"Le Coste starts at the Battista Rinaldi house and come down to the Rivassi road. There have always been excellent nebbiolo vines there" (Bruno Boschis). That statement sums up the location and potential for growing Barolo nebbiolo in this zone. Le Coste enjoys excellent sunshine as it is almost entirely south-facing. Here's a comment on the soil, "At Le Coste, it's different from Paiagallo and is already a little bit more like Cannubi" (Natale Ronzano). Comprising less than ten Piedmontese *giornate*, or four hectares, Le Coste lies at no more than 300 metres above sea level. The vines are dominated by the lovely early twentieth-century residence that now houses the Giuseppe Rinaldi cellar.

As we have already mentioned, the Donati family used to blend Le Coste nebbiolo with fruit from Cannubi in the late nineteenth and early twentieth century. It was such a well-established practice that Fantini, in his work on viticulture and oenology, refers to a "Cannubio-Le Coste" subzone.

*Barolo Le Coste – Giacomo Grimaldi, Barolo

Liste

Liste is the name given to the ten or so east-facing *giornate* – less than four hectares – situated below the minor Pascolo road. All the reports we collected agree that, "It's a good vineyard, particularly below the Borgogno *cascina*", while further up and over towards the woodland, the terrain is fairly cold and damp. "There are a lot of holes up there and the soil isn't stable. There could be some running water underground" (Natale Ronzano). The vineyard is easily visible from the curves of the Alba-Narzole provincial road, as you come down from the castle at Volta.

Main labels

*Barolo Liste – Giacomo Borgogno & Figli, Barolo

Monghisolfo or Cannubi Boschis

It is common knowledge that the name of a territory often derives from that of its former owners and the family to which this area once belonged was probably called Ghisolfi. Subsequently, the estate passed to the Boschis family, which owned the *cascina* Boschis that is now called Rinaldi. That explains the two names for this excellent nebbiolo-growing vineyard, whose almost seven hectares under vine have always produced outstanding grapes. Bounded by the Crosia road, Monghisolfo borders on a less well-aspected vineyard called Vezza, which forms a buffer with neighbouring Cannubi. We find the name "Canubio Boschis" in Lorenzo Fantini's previously cited *Monografia sulla Viticultura ed Enologia nella Provincia di Cuneo*. This invaluable source mentions that at the time, the latter half of the nineteenth century, as many as four locations were named "Canubbio". In 1972, Ratti was to report the name "Cannubi Boschis", classifying it as a subzone with special quality characteristics. The vineyard includes the Rinaldi cellar, known as *'l Palas*, or "the Palazzo", and enjoys a particularly sunny location, facing south east, south and then south east again.

MAIN LABELS

*Barolo Cannubi Boschis – Luciano Sandrone, Barolo

Monrobiolo or Bussia di Barolo

It seems that the name "Monrobiolo" is very old but over the years, it has been used along with Bussia di Barolo, since the area is situated just below Bussia Soprana in the municipality of Monforte and has similar characteristics. In addition, the vineyard is principally comprised of a hill whose peak lies in the municipal territory of Monforte. Here, too, not all of the area known as Monrobiolo is suitable for the cultivation of nebbiolo. Only ten or so *giornate*, less than four hectares, has a south west-facing position where nebbiolo will ripen fully. In another part of the vineyard, the main variety is dolcetto. The soil is dark clay, alternating with more friable whitish marl.

MAIN LABELS

*Barolo Bussia – Sylla Sebaste, Barolo

Muscatel or Cannubi Muscatel

Located at the beginning of the hillslopes which continue to the Monghisolfo vineyard, and which can justly be considered to be the heart of Barolo country, Muscatel has in part suffered because of poorly regulated urbanisation. The vines cover an area of about five hectares in a south east and south-facing position that borders on the Valletta vineyard. The building known as the "Gancia house" stands in the middle. The quality of the fruit grown here is excellent while the soil is slightly less friable, and a little more fertile, than in the neighbouring vineyards. There are several theories about the origin of the name "Muscatel". Some say that before the arrival of phylloxera, there were nebbiolo scions here grafted onto

moscato rootstock. Others maintain that moscato was actually grown in the vineyard. The designation "Cannubi Muscatel" was introduced by Renato Ratti in the early 1970s and in subsequent years was picked up on a number of labels. Much of the subzone is owned by the Marchesi di Barolo winery.

Paiagallo

The Paiagallo vineyard lies between the Novello-Barolo provincial road at the top and the Barolo-Monforte road below. To the north, it borders an area called Drucà, where the cemetery is – *drucà* means "the fallen" in dialect. On the opposite side, Paiagallo is bounded by San Sebastiano and Via Nuova.

Paiagallo, also known as "Peiragallo" or even "Pelagallo", embraces about 20 Piedmontese *giornate*, almost eight hectares, with a range of positions. At *cascina* Mirafiore, the vines face east, then south east, south and east again on the far side of the steep Paiagallo road.

The vineyard lies between 300 and 400 metres above sea level and has a relatively favourable topoclimate, thanks to the shelter afforded by the small escarpment that descends from the provincial road for Novello. From here, you can enjoy a marvellous panoramic view of the lower Langhe.

Main labels

*Barolo La Villa Paiagallo – Fontanafredda, Serralunga

Preda

The vineyard lies opposite Vignane and Zuncai. Its soil is whiter and more tufaceous while the vines can be considered uniformly south east-facing.

Preda includes the *cascina* of the same name, which once belonged to Luigi Pira, the celebrated Barolo maker who died in 1980. Luigi used to regard Barolo from Preda as a little "raw" and inelegant, for use in blends with other subzones. Natale Ronzano, nicknamed *Talin*, used to work here as a tenant farmer. We interviewed him as he is respected in the village as one of the, sadly, ever more restricted circle of older growers who are both experienced and highly competent.

The lower part of Preda is also known as Coste di Rosa, from the name of the road that winds along the valley floor. Production is uneven at Preda but, in some years, achieves remarkable heights.

Main labels

*Barolo Preda Sarmassa – Lodovico Borgogno, Barolo

Le Coste

San Lorenzo or Cannubi San Lorenzo

"Here, the soil is a light and sandy as it is at Cannubi. This vineyard is as good as Cannubi" (Bruno Boschis). San Lorenzo includes about eight Piedmontese *giornate* and bears the name of a church that stood here at the time of the plague described in Alessandro Manzoni's classic, *The Betrothed*. There was a lazar house here and also the old cemetery. "When they were ripping, they would find a bone from an arm or a leg every so often" (Bruno Boschis).

Cannubi San Lorenzo enjoys a fine south east-facing position, looking towards Bussia. It stands on the strip of hillside over Cannubi Valletta. On the far side of the road, the aspect changes and the slope runs down to Sarmassa, facing south west. The more correct name for this vineyard is San Lorenzo. The soil of Cannubi San Lorenzo, like that of Cannubi, Cannubi Muscatel, Cannubi Valletta and Cannubi Boschis, is fairly loose-packed, dry and unfertile. It comprises mainly sand and the whitish siliceous marl known in the local dialect as *tov* while dark, nutrient-rich clay is found only sporadically. The topoclimate and soil type are the key elements that enable growers to obtain from these five stupendous hectares fruit to be transformed into elegant San Lorenzo wines. Typically, they are already drinking well in the first years after bottling but they also age magnificently in the cellar.

Main labels

*Barolo Cannubi San Lorenzo – Camerano e Figli, Barolo

*Barolo Cannubi San Lorenzo-Ravera – Giuseppe Rinaldi, Barolo

San Sebastiano

This vineyard takes its name from the chapel dedicated to Saint Sebastian that was erected near the vines in 1470. The chapel was demolished in the early twentieth century.

Bounded by Via Nuova and Paiagallo, San Sebastiano covers about ten Piedmontese *giornate*, or just under four hectares, half facing east and half south east. The soil here is fairly similar to that of the two neighbouring vineyards. It is relatively fertile and comparable to the terrain at Castellero and Vignane. Vines here tend to bear fruit generously, unlike those at Cannubi, where it is difficult to reach the 80 quintals per hectare maximum permitted by the DOCG regulations. It is therefore up to the growers at San Sebastiano to keep yields low and quality high.

Sarmassa

Sarmassa is an historic vineyard, considered by old growers to possess truly outstanding potential as a location for nebbiolo. "Nebbiolo from here has always been regarded as being every bit as good as Cannubi" (Donato Camerano).

As was confirmed to us by several sources, the former Cantina Sociale di Barolo, which went bankrupt in 1929, used to classify vineyards into three categories. Sarmassa was in the top group. In fact, the area adjudged to be of outstanding growing potential and indicated on the map, includes only part of what is known as Sarmassa. The whole of the area extends to the valley floor and goes on a little way up the opposite slope towards the Crosia road. This is where the *cascina* of Sarmassa stands. Once, its estate extended over 20 or so hectares around the building.

The finest growing plots enjoy particularly sunny positions. Starting from Rio Fossati, there is a south-facing slope and the hillside continues, turning first south east, then south, and south east again. The upper part of Sarmassa borders on the equally historic Cerequio vineyard. The growing territory lies at an altitude of between 250 and just over 300 metres, embracing ten or so hectares and presenting a white marly soil, the celebrated Langhe *tov*. Free of sand and relatively unfertile, it restricts the

Sarmassa

vegetation of the vines and ensures yields are not excessive. Moreover, the site climate is particularly favourable and "Sarmassa is always one for the first places where, at the end of winter, *la fioca a' scianca*", ("the snow melts", according to *Talin*). The area includes the *cascina* Marenda, behind which lies the much prized "vigna d'la Mandorla" plot and the *cascina* Bergeisa.

MAIN LABELS

*Barolo Sarmassa – Silvio Alessandria, La Morra

*Barolo Sarmassa – Bergadano, Barolo

*Barolo Bricco Sarmassa – Giacomo Brezza & Figli, Barolo

*Barolo Sarmassa – Giacomo Brezza & Figli, Barolo

*Barolo Sarmassa – Marchesi di Barolo

*Barolo Vigna Merenda – Giorgio Scarzello e Figli, Barolo

Valletta or Cannubi Valletta

In an area that extends over about ten Piedmontese *giornate*, or less than four hectares, Valletta forms a trough facing south, south east and east which enjoys a particularly favourable mesoclimate. To the west, it borders on San Lorenzo, to the north with Cannubi, to the south with Muscatel and to the east, in the lower-lying

part, with the Alba-Barolo highway. Down near the main road, the grapes do not always ripen perfectly. However, in the middle and upper part of the vineyard, grape quality is absolutely superb. In the heart of Valletta is the house of Burlotto, the celebrated Commendator Burlotto from Verduno who at the turn of the twentieth century successfully exported Barolo and promoted its image all over the world.
What we said about the combination of "Cannubi" with the original, authentic name of the vineyard also holds true at Valletta. You will find Cannubi Valletta, just as you find Cannubi San Lorenzo or Cannubi Muscatel. We have no particular objections to this practice but we would be sorry to see the second part of the name disappear, and with it valuable information for consumers and Barolo's many admirers around the world.

MAIN LABELS

*Barolo Cannubi Valletta – Marchesi di Barolo

Via Nuova

The 15 or so *giornate*, or just under six hectares, that make up Via Nuova border at the top with Paiagallo. To the south, the vineyard is marked off by a steep path that separates it from an area called Terlo, considered an excellent location for dolcetto, as well as nebbiolo. Via Nuova is uniformly east-facing and is remembered by locals above all as the estate of the former Italian president, Luigi Einaudi. Einaudi "sometimes came to inspect his vines but never went into the town in case he was recognised" (Teobaldo Prandi). Here, you can see a training system for nebbiolo that was very popular in the past. The vines are joined together with thick garlands of shoots several years old. Each vine is extended to cover the space of the five or six ones after it. The reasons for this practice are a little complicated to explain. However, the system was employed because the nebbiolo shoot's first two or three buds are not fruitful.

MAIN LABELS

*Barolo Costa Grimaldi – Poderi Luigi Einaudi, Dogliani

Vignane

Vignane can be thought of as a continuation of Castellero and it shares the latter's orientation. Nor are their any significant differences in their soil types. Situated between Castellero and Zuncai, Vignane comprises about ten hectares at an elevation of between 250 and 300 metres. It has always been a location planted to nebbiolo for Barolo. According to our informants, the wines obtained at Vignane are slightly less elegant than those from Cannubi or other comparable vineyards.

"Vignane and Zuncai have higher must weights but they don't have the aromas of Cannubi" (Bruno Boschis); "Vignane is very good but you couldn't compare it to Cannubi" (Natale Ronzano).

Zuncai

This is the last vineyard on this hillslope. It is mainly south west-facing. The upper part borders on the municipal territory of Monforte, the lower section goes down to the Vignane road and to the side, the vineyard extends to the small valley that rises to Bussia Soprana.

Zuncai covers an area of almost ten Piedmontese *giornate*, or less than four hectares. The terrain is similar to the rest of the hillside and the prevalent soil type is clay. This means the soil is fairly compact and cool. Reddish in colour, it is rich in nutrients that encourage vegetation so the vines tend to give fairly generous crops. The various reports we recorded agreed that "of all the vineyards on the hill that starts at Castellero, Zuncai is the best because it has the most favourable position" (Baldo Demagistris).

MAIN LABELS

*Barolo Bricco Zuncai – Franco Molino, La Morra

Cannubi

Our selection

Population 682
Height 301 metres asl

INFORMATION

Town Hall
Piazza Caduti
per la Libertà, 3
Tel. + 39 0173 56277

Castello di Barolo
Piazza Falletti
Tel. + 39 0173 56277

THE WINERIES

Barale Fratelli
Via Roma, 6
Tel. + 39 0173 56127
One of the longest established wineries in the area, Barale Fratelli makes outstandingly cellarable Barolos, as recent tastings of their 1961 vintage have confirmed. The wines in the range relevant for this Atlas are Sergio Barale's Barolo Castellero and Bussia, as well as a standard-label Barbaresco and a Rabajà selection.

Giacomo Borgogno & Figli
Via Gioberti, 1
Tel. + 39 0173 56108 - 0173 56344
This is one of the wineries that wrote, and continues to write, the history of Barolo. In previous decades, Barolo here was aged first in wood and then in demijohns – great care was, of course, taken to avoid excessive oxidation – for several years before bottling. The approach enabled many enthusiasts to enjoy wines that, according to the Borgognos, had reached the "right" point of maturity after 30 or 40 years' ageing. As well as the standard-label Barolo, the cellar releases the Classico and Liste selections.

Giacomo Brezza & Figli
Via Lomondo, 4
Tel. + 39 0173 56191 - 0173 56354
A thriving restaurant and

hotel business does not distract the Brezza family – young Enzo in particular – from scrupulously looking after their 25-hectare estate. Average annual production is about 100,000 bottles, with the magnificently cellarable Barolo dominating the list. The Barolo selections released include Sarmassa, Bricco Sarmassa, Cannubi and Castellero.

Damilano
Via Roma, 31
Tel. + 39 0173 56105 - 0173 509187
After a period in the doldrums, Damilano seems to have got back into its stride under new management and is releasing some particularly attractive wines. Unsurprisingly, the flagship bottles are the basic Barolo and the Cannubi.

Marchesi di Barolo
Via Alba, 12
Tel. + 39 0173 564400
The are no more marquises but there is still plenty of history, for the Abbona family owns some plots that once belonged to Giulia Falletti, the woman who "invented" Barolo. The historic cellars are well worth visiting, especially the ones where the great vintages, some from the nineteenth century, are stored. The range includes most of Piedmont's registered designations, with some excellent Barolo selections at the top of the list: Brunate, Cannubi, Cannubi Valletta, Coste di Rose, Estate Vineyard, Millenium and Sarmassa. The array of nebbiolo-based products also includes Barbaresco Creja.

Bartolo Mascarello
Via Roma, 15
Tel. + 39 0173 56125
The erudite and articulate Bartolo Mascarello has wisely continued along the road mapped out by his father Giulio (see the relevant profile in the chapter on The Greats of Barolo). The only Barolo released is a blend of fruit from the estate's four plots, Cannubi, Rué and San Lorenzo in the municipality of Barolo, and Torriglione at La Morra. Shrewdly, Bartolo maintains that this way, he can ensure good consistency of quality for his Barolo, which is aged exclusively in large oak barrels.

E. Pira & Figli
Chiara Boschis
Via Vittorio Veneto, 1
Tel. + 39 0173 56247
To the natural elegance of the Cannubi soil, Chiara Boschis adds her sophisticated cellar technique to produce an aroma and fruit-rich Barolo

with a mouthfilling palate that foregrounds juicy fruit rather than tannins. The market has shown that this is a winning strategy and Chiara's 15,000 bottles of Barolo Cannubi are snapped up every year. All this is, of course, very different from the style of the great Luigi Pira, who passed away in 1980. He insisted that his labels should bear the proud boast, *pigiato con i piedi*, or "crushed by foot".

Giuseppe Rinaldi
Via Monforte, 3
Tel. + 39 0173 56156
The winery premises are in the former residence built just outside the town in the early 1920s. Wine was already being made there are the time. Until 1992, Beppe Rinaldi released a standard-label Barolo and a magnificent Riserva Brunate but from the following vintage, he decided to change tack and put the fruit from his four plots into two paired blends. Since then, his Barolos have been named after the resulting combinations, Brunate-Le Coste and Cannubi San Lorenzo-Ravera. Ageing is in large barrels of Slavonian oak after leisurely fermentation on the skins.

Luciano Sandrone
Via Alba, 57
Tel. + 39 0173 56239
Luciano Sandrone's outstanding abilities as a winemaker were obvious from the release of his first Barolo, bottled in1978. Throughout the 1980s, his was a name people mentioned in awe as one of the most exciting of the small producers who were emerging at the time. Luciano releases two selections, a Cannubi Boschis, from the vineyard of the same name, and a blend from various plots labelled Barolo Le Vigne.

Giorgio Scarzello e Figli
Via Alba, 29
Tel. + 39 0173 56170
Giorgio Scarzello's small and deservedly admired winery is going through a period of renewal. Not in the cellar, where large barrels and slow maceration are still the order of the day, but in the vineyards. From the 1999 vintage, production will increase from 5,000 to more than 12,000 bottles of Barolo a year. In addition to the standard-label Barolo, Giorgio makes a Vigna Merenda selection. In recent years, it has yielded spectacular results that are fully worthy of this fine vineyard adjoining Cerequio.

Tenuta La Volta
Località La Volta, 13
Tel. + 39 0173 56168
Nebbiolo is used for the flagship wines of this cellar, the Barolo Vigna La Volta and the Langhe Rosso Vendemmiaio blend. The winery itself is strategically located next to the Volta castle in the highest part of the town.

G.D. Vajra
Via delle Viole, 25
Frazione Vergne
Tel. + 39 0173 56257
Aldo Vaira, who has a degree in agronomy from Turin, is an intelligent, inquisitive and very competent winemaker. Aldo's wines reflect his constant striving to achieve a distinctive house style, an effort that since the early 1980s has made the G.D. Vajra label one of the most prestigious in this part of the Langhe. The attractive cellar with

its impressive windows has a modern, practical fermentation and maceration system that produces bottles very much in the traditional mould. As well as a standard-label Barolo, there are excellent Bricco delle Viole and Fossati selections to enjoy. The eagerly awaited new label is a selection from the La Volta vineyard.

WHERE TO SLEEP

Hotel Barolo
Via Lomondo, 2
Tel. + 39 0173 56354
Three stars, 31 double rooms with bathroom, television and telephone. Some rooms have spa tubs. The hotel stands among the vines at the entrance to the town and each room is named after a Barolo vineyard. Breakfast is especially good. The Brezza restaurant next to the hotel offers a typical Langhe menu, accompanied either by the very palatable house wines or the best labels in the DOCG zone.

EATING OUT

La Cantinella
Via Acquagelata, 4/a
Tel. + 39 0173 56267
We can only praise the initiative of offering three tasting menus, starting at around € 20.00, which means La Cantinella has an option for almost everyone's purse. The selection of local wines, especially Barolos, is reasonable.

Locanda del Borgo Antico
Piazza del Municipio, 2
Tel. + 39 0173 56355
Sophisticated cuisine, with a few unconventional proposals, warm hospitality and professional service.
Diners can select wines from two lists, one dedicated exclusively to Barolo, with all the finest labels in the DOCG zone. Your € 40.00, wine excluded, will have been well spent.

WHAT TO BUY

Enoteca Regionale del Barolo
Piazza Falletti
Tel. + 39 0173 56277
The lovely rooms of the castle house a range – with one or two gaps – of the finest Barolos made in the 11 DOCG municipalities.

Enoteca il Bacco
Via Roma, 87
Tel. + 39 0173 56233
Although you will find all the best labels here, Franco Cravero's shop has many other delights to offer, too.

Emilio Pietro Abbona

1877-1966

Commendator Emilio Pietro Abbona was born in Barolo in 1877, the third of nine brothers and sisters. From an early age, he was involving in the running of his father's winery, Cavalier Felice Abbona & Figli. Because of his father's ability and good fortune in having "estates of vineyards located on the Cannubio and other leading hills at Barolo" (as a document from 1914 tells us), the winery had already won many prizes all over Europe even before it had access to the cellars of the marquises. Awards included gold medals at the World Expositions in Vienna in 1873, in Turin in 1884, in Paris in 1901 and in Brussels in 1910. But it was from the 1930s onwards that the Abbonas' Barolo began to bear the label "Società Anonima Vini Classici del Piemonte" – with the additional words "già Opera Pia" ("formerly Opera Pia") adding historic and heraldic weight, that the cellar acquired international prestige, as can be seen from the orders received from the Italian Legations in Helsinki and Baghdad, to replace "the usual French wines" at table. Or the letter from the London-based William Standring company, which in February 1934 enquired about the price of the excellent Barolo served on board the motor vessel Rex. The letter mentions the two castles, Barolo and Serralunga, on the label to identify the wine.

A wise administrator and a genuine son of the soil, Pietro Emilio was assisted by his sisters Marina and Celestina, the latter an accomplished public relations manager *ante litteram* and a shrewd accountant, as may be deduced from the handwritten prices written on orders, which are sometimes corrected two or three times.

The winery was visited in 1949 by the legendary journalist Paolo Monelli, whose report in *La Nuova Stampa* on 29 April felicitously compared the work of an oenologist to that of an artist, going so far as to mention the eminent Bologna-born painter, Morandi. At the age of 76, Commendator Abbona was also visited by Ernesto Caballo for the *Gazzetta Sera* on his 1954 journey to discover the gastronomic delights of the Langhe, "...a self-taught master of his art, he has no need to taste or discuss to assess the qualities of a wine. For Abbona, it is enough to sniff the aroma from a distance and observe its colour". A further tribute to that marvellous wine – apart from the medals, awards and articles in the newspapers – is the cordial letter written by Luigi Carnacina, the prince of Italy's chefs, in 1962 to his "very dear" Commendatore, "Your enthralling Barolo 1953 has won my praise. It is peerless!". Carnacina continues, "I have written an article on food and wine which will be published by the Accademia della Cucina Italiana, and I have described this bewitching Marchesi di Barolo as the best wine in Italy! And it is the truth".

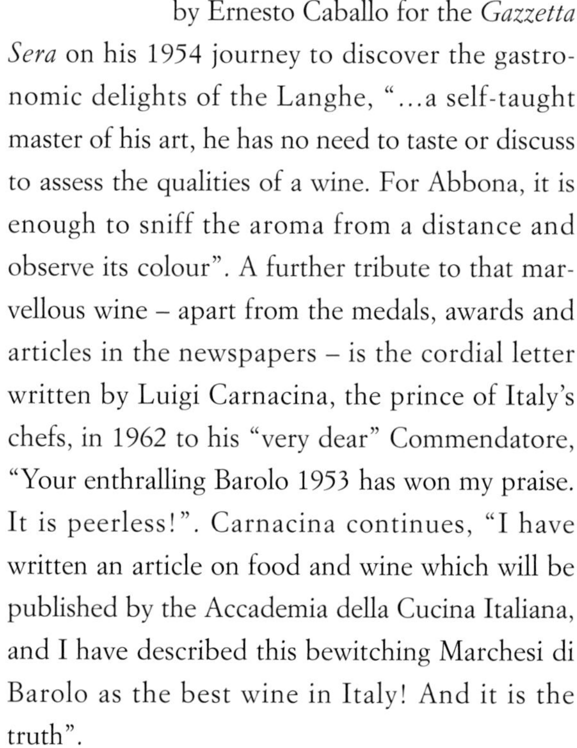

Emilio Pietro Abbona died in 1966. Three years later, his inseparable sister Celestina followed him. Neither ever married. There were no marital duties to distract them from their mission.

Cesare Borgogno

1900-1968

Cesare Borgogno was 15 when his mother Giulia brought him to Barolo to work in the vineyards. He had had to leave his boarding school in Mondovì following various youthful escapades. In fact, his father Giacomo Borgogno had also been forced to abandon his studies and take charge of the estate, entrusted temporarily to the less than careful and far from financially prudent management of the parish priest of Annunziata at La Morra. The Borgognos were a family of wine merchants but they were also growers and land-owners, already active in the area in the early nineteenth century. Cesare Borgogno was born with a vocation for making and selling wine.

The last of five children, he was born at Barolo on 28 April 1900. He lost his father at the age of 11 and was soon required to contribute to the family budget. Hard work in the vineyards taught the young Cesare the difficult art of viticulture, endowing him with knowledge that would prove useful for the rest of his life.

In 1920, he took over the company after his siblings decided to devote themselves to other activities. He increased sales and sold the company's wines all over Italy and beyond. The years after the First World War were hard ones when there was mass emigration from the Langhe to the New World. Then came the Great Crash and an economic crisis that cost many people their fortunes. During this crisis, Borgogno not only kept his head above water but also laid the foundations for future success.

The *annus mirabilis* for the company was 1937, when Cesare married Maria Chiavassa, who had recently come to teach at the town's primary school. The newlyweds set off in their brightly polished Balilla motorcar on an extended tour of France that soon turned out to be much more significant than most honeymoon trips. It was August 1937 when the couple crossed the Massif Central and arrived in Burgundy. In the vineyards of chardonnay and pinot noir, and in the ancient cellars of Beaune, Cesare Borgogno reached two conclusions that would remain his watchwords for the rest of his life, defining his winery's production. First, he became convinced of the superb quality of the nebbiolo grape and the extraordinary potential of Barolo wine. But the second, and much more important realisation, was that bottle ageing could enhance the prestige and quality of Barolo even further. If Burgundy's pinot noir could yield wine with such superb long-term prospects, then Barolo, with its generous tannins, good acidity and alcohol, should be even better able to stand the test of time. This was the beginning of Borgogno's glory days, interrupted only for a few years by the war and the partisan struggle in the Langhe hills. At that time, some young men from Barolo were arrested during a round-up. The German authorities threatened reprisals against the town and the rector of the Collegio, Father Massé, was imprisoned in Turin for having given shelter to a sick partisan. Cesare Borgogno

interceded, using his rhetorical skills and the occasional bottle of Barolo to plead his case. At the same time, between 14 and 17 July 1944, German troops combing the countryside for partisans accused the Borgogno winery of assisting the "bandits" and carried off 12,000 bottles of 1939 Barolo, as well as more than 6,000 bottles of Barolo Chinato. The episode is backed up by an application for compensation for war damage approved by the first post-Liberation mayor of Barolo, Giulio Mascarello.

After the Second World War, the cellar's prestige grew, in Italy and abroad in Argentina, thanks to local emigrants, and even in the United States and France. And it was in France that in 1955 the Institut des Appellations d'Origine took somewhat improbable legal action against Borgogno, claiming that the name was a form of unfair competition for the wines of Burgundy, or "Borgogna" in Italian. The court action, which seems ludicrous even today, was won by Borgogno in three successive judgements, partly thanks to a contract the winery presented as an exhibit to show that Giuseppe Borgogno, Cesare's grandfather, was supplying wine to the children of soldiers at the Racconigi college in December 1848.

The years of Italy's economic boom saw the winery expanding fast and production capacity more than doubled. But the underlying philosophy remained the same: careful selection of the fruit, blends from different vineyards, and tannin-rich, robustly structured wines, slowly aged in the bottle.

Cesare Borgogno was still working full-time when he died in July 1968, leaving his family to carry on his activities.

THE GREATS OF BAROLO

Giulio Mascarello

1895-1981

Giulio Mascarello was a significant, even emblematic, figure who deserves his place in this gallery of the great producers in the Alba area. His importance derives not so much from his undisputed international prestige as from his status as one of the first small, premium-quality, grower-producers, the winemakers that today are most representative of the Langhe.

Born in 1895 into a family of grape growers and the eldest of eight children, Giulio Mascarello was sent to work in a bakery in Genoa after he gave up his studies at the Convitto of the Opera Pia in Barolo. The intelligent, generous-hearted young man acquired his schooling in the workers' unions and the chamber of labour in Genoa. He learned a sense of justice and solidarity with the working classes but also a style and facility of expression that can be appreciated in his letters.

During the Great War, Mascarello was sent, and in a certain sense, relegated to the island of Sant'Antioco, along with other supporters of Italy's neutrality, anarchists and socialists. Mascarello's return to Barolo is described memorably in his words to Nuto Revelli, in the book *Il Mondo dei Vinti* (The World of the Vanquished). "In 1919, I was demobbed. I came back to Alba with a few pennies and hired a *break* (four-wheeled carriage) to take me to Gallo, then I continued on foot towards Barolo. When I smelled the hay, I was reborn. I walked into the house, where they were serving a delicious soup. I said to myself, 'Barolo is still the best place in the world'. I decided to stay in Barolo for ever and become a winemaker". The foundation of the cellar has a precise date, 1 January 1920. That was the day when a cousin gave Giulio Mascarello 10,000 lire. The loan was underwritten by Giulio's father, Bartolomeo, who was also the cellarman at the Cantina Sociale in Barolo for many years. The co-operative was in decline, like many others in the Langhe, because of the indifference of the central government, and this was the stimulus that prompted the young Mascarello to set up on his own. His first customers were from Genoa, thanks to the friends he had made during his years in the city. At that time, Barolo was normally sold to private customers who bought the wine in demijohns. Only about ten per cent of total output was sold in bottles. The producers supplied, along with the demijohn, labels, neck labels and bottling instructions. Relationships were maintained by visits during the year and on such occasions, the producers spoke of "going on a trip". Correspondence was more frequent and Giulio Mascarello was an assiduous letter-writer. We have one missive he sent in January 1926 to his friend Fantino at Monforte that shows the stylistic ability of this self-taught agricultural worker, not to mention his political insight. The letter discusses the induction courses that the Fascist party had decreed should be held for young men on the point of joining up. Mascarel-

lo's impression was that the "courses served no purpose except that of systematically filling the heads of the participants with the new, egregiously nationalistic, product, or in other words with disciplined stupidity... where discipline, currently so fashionable here, starts, logic and reason finish".

In the 1930s, the small winery expanded, acquiring two Piedmontese *giornate* in Cannubi, then in San Lorenzo and Rué. The new plots joined the smallholding at Monrobiolo, known as Bussia di Barolo, and the fruit from Torriglione grown by relatives. All went to make a very decent blend of Barolo. The technique of using grapes from a number of vineyards encouraged consistent quality, notwithstanding vintages that were dry or very wet. The great Barolo makers of the day exploited this approach to the full. Giulio Mascarello had a very high opinion of Dottor Cappellano at Serralunga, who at the time was the acknowledged leader of Barolo makers, and was a close friend of Cesare Borgogno. Unlike them, however, he continued to be a small-scale grower-producer with no ambitions to expand his business, although there were plenty of opportunities to do so. In the meantime, the close-knit agricultural world of Barolo enabled him to profess his socialist faith, to join the CLN, the partisan national liberation committee, and to be nominated the Liberation mayor.

After the war, Giulio's son, Bartolo, came into the business. Well instructed in his father's view of life, he helped to win for the Mascarello Barolo further prestige in Italy and abroad. In the mid 1970s, the proportions of the cellar's wine sold in demijohn and in bottle were reversed, with 90 per cent now released as bottled wine.

In 1981, at the venerable age of 86, the former baker's boy and personal friend of socialist leader Pietro Nenni, as well as an honest grower and skilled cellarman, passed away at home in Barolo, having charted a new path for the country people of the area.

Battista Rinaldi

1918-1992

Although he called himself "Giovan Battista", "Gibì" or "Giovanni Battista", for the registry office he was simply "Battista" Rinaldi, born at Barolo in 1918. And if he had been looking for a different name, then an appropriate one would have been "Colonnello" – or "Colonel", with "Captain" or "Commander" as variations – as his friends from the Alpini mountain troops referred to him. He had a very serious character and was little inclined to humorous remarks or banter. You could say that he was a gruff type, reluctant to comprise and frequently obstinate.

The Rinaldis came to Barolo from Diano d'Alba and in 1870 they and the Barales acquired the *cascina 'l Palas* from one of the Falletti's estate agents, the Boschis who was to add his surname to one of the finest locations in Barolo, Cannubi Boschis. It was here that Battista was born. He left it a few years later when his father Giuseppe moved away from the family to the lovely house that is still the home of the Giuseppe Rinaldi cellar.

Battista was the first resident of Barolo to graduate – top of his class – from the Oenological School at Alba. He began to make wine in 1944, soon finding himself alone in charge of the cellar when his father died in 1947.

As well as the winery, Battista inherited eight lovely hectares at Brunate, Le Coste and Ravera, which he extended with small purchases over the years, particularly in Cannubi San Lorenzo. He made excellent wines, especially the Riserva Brunate that he would age in large bottles. These stood in broad niches in the cellar for at least ten years before they were racked into individual bottles. In our memory, the vintages of 1958 and 1971 stand out for the absolutely spectacular results Rinaldi achieved. It does, however, have to be said that the quality of his vineyards and his no-nonsense cellar techniques produced superb Barolos with laudable consistency.

Battista was mayor of Barolo from 1970 to 1975 and at once was gratified by the realisation of his dream – the purchase of the castle by the municipal authority. This was made possible by a subscription by 92 families in the town, as well many former pupils of the Collegio Barolo.

Those were years of scrupulous adherence to statutory regulations by the local administration. There were few concessions for major building developments and work began on the creation of a public *enoteca* in the castle. The municipal *enoteca* was swiftly completed, opening in 1971, but the Enoteca Regionale del Barolo, representing all 11 DOCG zone municipalities, had to wait until 1982.

Battista was the first president of the Enoteca Regionale and in it saw the first part of a dream come true as Barolo assumed a leading role on the international wine scene, on a par with the most celebrated regions in France.

His life was deeply marked by his war experiences and his contribution in the Alpini, Italy's mountain troops. He remained close to his companions in the Alpini, even over the course of the long illness that was eventually to lead to his death.

Grafting nebbiolo

Bruno Boschis
known as *Brunone*
born 1910
grafter in Barolo

When I was a boy, I used to go to work in the fields, sometimes at Novello, other at Monforte. I'd change my employer every one or two years. In 1928, I worked for a whole year as a labourer for 1,500 lire, and in 1929 for 3,000 lire. Then in 1932, we moved to Aie Sottane and started to make our own wine. Before 1935, just after phylloxera, there were only fields. Then they started to plant vines again. We did the ripping by hand and we had to take the snow off to dig. Little by little, the vines returned but they were better laid out than they had been before.

Professor Ferrari and Professor Monticelli, who came to Barolo to hold meetings for the growers, had this heory, "If you want to fill the vats with good must, you've got to dig the vines in August". Now some people use herbicides. They haven't dug for ten years. Once, after the wheat was harvested, they'd apply 'water' (Bordeaux mixture) once or twice. Now, they never stop because the vines are producing all the time. The vines don't last they way they used to because they go over the vineyards with tractors. The soil is packed as hard as an asphalt road and the vines suffer.

I began grafting in 1939. Actually, we planted some new vines in 1935 on our land and I watched the man who was grafting. The following year, I tried and the scions took. Then I did a course of pruning and grafting. They examined us as the Oenological School and gave us a certificate that enabled us to do the job for other estates. I've grafted nearly all the vineyards in Barolo. When I got back in the evenings, there were always six or seven people waiting for me. "Well, then. When are you coming to my place?". One day, I went to Lu Monferrato to graft the grignolino vines. I did a thousand vines in a single day. I'd split the shoot, insert the scion, and a worker would come after me to bind the graft.

I used to graft 120 scions an hour but now I go a bit more slowly. Grafting went on from March to 8 May, nebbiolo, dolcetto, neirano and also merlot at Bene Vagienna.

I had a small nursery where I grew the cuttings on American wood. Before phylloxera, which arrived in Barolo in 1932, the cuttings were native. The grower would bend a shoot over, putting it underground, and the shoot would root. Generally, dolcetto vines were used and nebbiolo scions were grafted onto them. Nowadays, grafts are made by machine, using the whip and tongue method, and the cuttings are put in the rows. (*Spring 1990*)

Barolo in the early twentieth century

In 1919, the Opera Pia began to sell off the holdings that were least profitable. They say that it sold 2,000 giornate, or almost 800 hectares, for 3,500,000 lire. There were plenty of buyers. The Società Anonima Vini Classici, which would later become Marchesi di Barolo, purchased the largest part. The original estate went from Vergne through Cannubi, Brunate, Rocca, *cascina* Luciani and Batasiolo on one slope and on the other side reached as far as Serralunga and Castiglione.

My grandfather said that the Marchesa Colbert used to ride on an ox-drawn cart up to the Volta castle to be able to see all the Opera Pia's land.

The Alba-Barolo trolleybus had its garage at the first corner of the town, with an office, a shelter and a one metre high platform. The merchants used it to send demijohns, cases and barrels. As well as a passenger carriage, there was a goods wagon. I think it started working in 1910 and lasted until the war. The pylons for electricity ran alongside the road all the way to Alba, with a diversion that led to Fontanafredda.

Donato Camerano
born 1908
office worker in Barolo

In 1928, we paraded through Alba with an allegorical float representing the castle of Barolo and 70 participants. The set designers from Turin came to decorate the Savigliano cart with a score of marquises, pages and courtiers. The float was drawn by two oxen and their oxherds. There were heralds, standard-bearers and halberdiers. Alongside rode 18 horsemen. All the horses there were in Barolo! At the Fiera del Tartufo (truffle show) that year, we put on a great display and they awarded us the second prize.

In the (main) square (at Barolo), there was the Caffè-Ristorante Svizzero, so called because it was built between 1875 and 1880 like a chalet, with material left over from the restructuring of the castle. Below the café was the Cantina Sociale (co-operative winery). They set that up in 1902, I think. Then they closed it about 1930 when there was the depression. They weren't selling anything because no one had any money so lots of members started trading on their own.

The Cantina started out with eight members and by 1908 it had 36. The first president was Molinati and the last was Canonica. They only made Barolo, in first, second and third selections. For example, Brunate and Cannubi were first selections, Pugnane was a second, and over at Novello and Fava, the wines were third selections. I remember they employed a cellarman and an assistant.

At harvest time, the members helped out. They trod the grapes with their feet, starting after dinner, until they were falling asleep. (*Spring 1990*)

A lesson in viticulture

Once, the vines used to be planted closer together, about 70 or even 50 centimetres from each other, but the rows stood further apart. There might be five or six metres between the rows because they used to plant wheat, maize or broad beans.

Baldo Demagistris
born 1916
grower in Barolo

Today, the old vines are replaced with rooted cuttings but this is what they once did: they'd dig furrows with picks and then bend the old vine into it and cover it with earth, so the tops of the shoots were showing. They left them like that for two or three years so that they wouldn't vegetate and would get stronger.

On other occasions, they would graft nebbiolo

onto moscato, neirano, servavillano or dolcetto. Some growers made cuttings, but it was very rare. You can see from the wood whether a nebbiolo vine is good. It should be hard, red and not soft when you cut it, otherwise it's not a first-choice plant.

They didn't use much treatment on the vines. They cut the wheat and then applied water and sulphur, if it wasn't a very wet year. I remember we used to pick only two or three tubsful of nebbiolo a day during the harvest because the bunches were all discoloured by moths. Then the grapes were selected in the stable. Now, the grapes have a much better appearance.

The women came from the mountains and the flatlands for the harvest. There was a fine crowd of women at La Morra and Barolo. They slept in the stables or the barns. (*Spring 1990*)

Downy mildew

Teobaldo Prandi
born 1907
grower in Barolo

In 1915 – I was seven – the grapes weren't harvested. Downy mildew had destroyed the lot. The growers put on Bordeaux mixture without lime so it would have more effect. That year, it rained for 60 days without a break. My mother told me that, too. But then, hail was much less frequent. Nowadays, you get everything some years. When a storm comes from La Morra, there's always a chance of hail.

My father sold nebbiolo. He contacted the Barolo wineries without going to market. No one asked about the must weight. In autumn, you couldn't cross Piazza Savona in Alba because there were so many carts laden with barrels in the square. Most of the buyers were merchants and they tested the grapes. "How much will you take? Four *soldi* over the going rate?". The "going rate" was the market price for the day, or for the last few days. When you went into Alba, you had to pay a toll.

In 1922, my father didn't sell his grapes. "This year, we're making Barolo", he said. It was a year when there had been a terrible drought. In February, the wheat hadn't sprouted and we had already dug between the rows. In May, the vines had tiny buds. We harvested a barrel of grapes and made one of Barolo, which stayed sweet. It didn't turn dry. Pruning was easy that winter. The following autumn, in 1923, we had so much fruit we didn't know where to put it all. The 1924 vintage was an exceptional one. The ones after that were good until 1927, then the 1928 harvest was less good, and the 1929 one was good again. Phylloxera hit us in 1930-1931. It was total devastation. There had been phylloxera before that. It started in a very small area. "The vines seemed to go yellow", people would say. Then, as the years progressed, the vineyard slowly died. We had to rip out the vines and replant on American rootstock, which we went to get from a certain Signor Mazza in Alba.

Before phylloxera, all the vines were ungrafted. This is what we did. When we were pruning, we would cut some shoots and bury them underground so they would put down roots. The following year, we would plant them. The old vine could also be replaced by vegetative propagation. Part of a shoot would be planted so it would root and the following year it would be separated from the parent vine. I organised a downy mildew monitoring station for the whole town. If the humidity rose to 75 per cent, the situation was worrying. When the moment came, I rang the alarm bells. There were only a few days in which to apply Bordeaux mixture but it generally rained. (*Spring 1990*)

Women's work

Maria Alessandria
konwn as *Marianin*
born 1900
vine dresser in Barolo

At Ponte Rocca, there was the social club. I went there from Santa Maria to dance, when my father let me. One day, the priest at Santa Maria didn't want to let my mother take communion any more because she let us go dancing. So she wanted us to stay at home but I said, "Why can't we go dancing if my brother is with us?".

I met my husband at the social club, even though he didn't dance. He was the dance hall owner. After he had seen me, he heard us saying one day that we were going to visit relatives nearby and asked if he could come with us. I had already met quite a lot of young men but nothing had ever come of it. I was waiting for the right one. Bartolomeo was such a good boy! We married in 1926, in the spring, and I came to live here at the Rocca. He had no father or mother.

The social club was closed because there was Fascism at the time but it was great fun. There was dancing only on Saturdays and Sundays, with an automatic piano. You turned the handle and it played two or three tunes. Young people came from the hills round about.

Bartolomeo was born in 1894 and I helped him in the fields, doing women's work, like *scarsoré* (shoot thinning), *tòrse* (twisting) and harvesting the grapes. I raised my two children and looked after the house.

Don Merlo, the parish priest of Barolo, was terrible, a real old-fashioned cleric. I once had an argument with him because he wanted my children to go to Mass on Thursday mornings, when they didn't have school. The poor dears! They lived so far from the church! But I let them sleep on Thursdays and rest up a bit.

In December 1944, my son Michele took the priest from La Morra into Alba in the gig on some urgent business. Don Grasso later told this story in his memoirs and I found out that he was going to Alba to negotiate the exchange of two women and a partisan for three German soldiers. He aroused less suspicion by travelling with my son.

In those days, children were given *cherniele* (sweets made from sugared bread dough) for New Year. They came to sing *bondì, bon an, dene 'l Capdan* (good day, happy New Year, give us our New Year's treat).

However did I manage to get so old? How did it happen? (*Summer 1990*)

We lost the Barolo but we saved our boys

It was during the war and 240 wooden crates with 50 bottles each of 1935 Barolo were ready for delivery but at the last moment, we heard that the bridges on the roads had been bombed. Unfortunately, the Borgogno courtyard was small and couldn't stack all of them. It would have been a pity, as well as a weary waste of time, to unpack all the crates. Canonica had a large cellar. He didn't make wine any more and sold his grapes so we asked him if we could store the wine there, paying rent of course.

One day, a lorry full of Germans passed through Barolo looking for the road to Bra. All the villagers hid and a

Maria Chiavassa
born 1906
schoolteacher in Barolo

lady from Turin who was out walking her two dogs had to speak to them. At that time, the partisans had gathered here at Barolo with the idea of attacking the barracks in Alba. One of the partisans, who was probably frightened, fired some shots in front of our house, in the square, when he realised there were Germans in Barolo. The Germans returned the fire. Some of them were wounded and since they didn't know how many partisans there were, they retreated. They came back two days later to exact revenge for the incident.

They started drinking wine and then, drunk and angry, they began to loose off gunfire everywhere. As they raged through the town, they found the wine in the Canonicas' cellar. They arrived in the courtyard with their lorries and started loading up as much wine as they could. I could see them from the window of my room and I thought to myself, "I can't just stand here. What would I say to my husband? That I watched and did nothing?" So I went out in slippers to speak to the captain, who had an interpreter with him. I told him it was my wine, not the partisans'. My intervention was totally fruitless. And since they couldn't carry all of the wine away, they came back the following Monday. They came up to our cellar and I tried to humour them, telling them to come and get some rifles that their companions had left at our house. But they wanted to clean out the cellar where our wine was and in fact they carried off every single bottle.

A few days later, my husband came back and the first thing he asked me was whether I had asked the captain's name. Unfortunately, I had completely forgotten in all the excitement. We had a friend who had been an engineer at Lancia for more than ten years. He had been drafted during the war, although he wasn't in favour of it. His name was Engesten.

My husband thought that a word with Engesten might have enabled us to get back at least some of the stolen bottles. Thanks to our friend the engineer, we managed to find out the name of the captain, who unfortunately told us, "Nothing doing. The wine is spoils of war. If you want compensation, we can impose a tax on the residents of Barolo".

When he heard this, my husband said, "I don't want the people of Barolo saying they had to pay because of me. If I can rescue my life and the wine I still have in my cellar, I can carry on working". He did, however, ask the captain if it would be possible to release the prisoners from Barolo, who were young and innocent. They were huddled together on the floor of the cells in the Carceri Nuove, waiting to be sent to Germany. At a certain point, they saw my husband through the open door. "It's Borgogno! If that's Borgogno, then he's come for us!". (*Summer 1990*)

Castiglione Falletto

Located about 12 kilometres from Alba on the road for Monforte, Castiglione Falletto dominates the ridge of hills that runs through the heart of the Barolo DOCG zone. On one side, the view sweeps over the *grands crus* of the municipality – along the Grosso and Brunella roads – and beyond to the vineyards of La Morra and Barolo. The other side, which faces south east, looks out onto the vineyards of Serralunga and Monforte, with the splash of houses at Perno offering a contrast to the uniform shades of the rows.

Time has left little sign of its passage on Castiglione Falletto but the social history of the town has seen moments of turmoil and episodes of great cultural impact. The Cantina Sociale founded here at the end of the nineteenth century was a pioneering venture in a land of rugged individualists but it was followed by a second co-operative winery in the 1950s as well as the present Cooperativa Terre del Barolo. There was also Ferdinando Vignolo Lutati, a chemist and naturalist, who first defined the Barolo zone and by scrutinising the soil of the hills, compiled a Langhe herbal that is still a benchmark for botanists today.

The bishop's residence, now converted into a restaurant, looks onto the square where on holidays, the most popular sport in the Langhe, *pallone a pugno*, or *pallone elastico*, continues to be played. The square becomes an arena for contests between friends, districts and villages.

Look up and you can admire the austere mediaeval fortress with its three great cylindrical corner towers and massive keep. The castle is

documented from 1001 AD, when Otto III, the emperor of Germany and king of Italy, enfeoffed it to Odaldengo Manfredi, the count of Turin, along with other lands around Alba. In 1225, it passed to Bertoldo Falletti, who seven years later was nominated vicar of Monferrato by the emperor Frederick II. The castles of Castiglione, Serralunga, Barolo and Volta, at Vergne near Barolo, today bear witness to the centuries-long rule of the house of Falletti over these lands. Over time, the fortress became a residence and in 1860 was acquired by the noble Vassallo family from Castiglione.

However, the castle only acquires a certain perturbing fascination if observed from a distance as it rises above the *vigne del sindic*, or "mayor's vineyards" (so called because they once belonged to Arnaldo Rivera, the mayor of Castiglione) that seem to be scaling the slopes from the south. After an "olfactory" tour of Castiglione, whose lanes and cellars are redolent of fermenting must, it is time to leave the smell of the vats behind and explore the roads and lanes of wine. We might njoy the view from the Monforte provincial road over the vineyards of Meriondino and Serra, which face west are called *sorì d'la seira*, or "evening slopes". From the other side of the road, we can see the vineyards of Rocche, which break off where the grounds drops away down to the Rio Perno stream. This is a landscape where no corner has been left untouched by the diligent labour of man and his determination to respectfully shape the earth. The landscape is man-made to an unusual degree.

The great vineyards

There are 16 great vineyards in the municipality, all of which are included by the regulations in the Barolo DOCG zone. The vines stand on either side of a long ridge. To the west, they face Barolo and La Morra while to the east the rows look towards Perno di Monforte and Serralunga d'Alba. The former vineyards yield alcohol-rich, generously structured Barolos whereas those on the eastern slopes tend to be more aromatic and elegant.

Castiglione Falletto is a buffer zone between areas that produce wines with very different characteristics. It finds its own personality in a combination of the softness and elegance of the wines on one side and the full-bodied generosity of those on the other.

Most of the vineyard's own plants face west or south west, towards the municipality of La Morra. On the other slope, to the north of the residential area, we find the only significant exception in Pernanno, which faces east and south east. To the south of the village, the hill changes direction

DOC and DOCG	Total area under vine in hectares	% of area in municipality	% of area in zone
Barolo	**126.9446**	**57.36**	**10.16**
Dolcetto d'Alba	50.9055	23.00	2.72
Barbera d'Alba	28.8830	13,05	1.67
Langhe Chardonnay	6.7000	3.03	2.61
Other DOC zones	7.8620	3.55	
TOTAL	221.2951	100.00	
Other DOC zones			
Langhe Rosso	2.8450	1.29	4.04
Langhe Nebbiolo	2.1181	0.96	8.47
Langhe Freisa	1.8700	0.85	3.12
Langhe Bianco	0.6700	0.30	2.51
Piemonte Grignolino	0.3589	0.16	2.19

and turns towards Monforte, again acquiring a south-facing aspect that encourages nebbiolo to ripen fully.

The most famous of the vineyards is Rocche, a thin strip of land that a number of producers have attempted to extend, including grapes from other locations below the residential area of the town, as in the case of Pira and Rivera.

Much of the fruit is grown by small independent farmers who do not vinify their harvest, preferring to take their grapes to the Terre del Barolo co-operative winery, a genuine institution which is based at Castiglione Falletto on the flatlands near the boundary with Gallo Grinzane.

Production

There are 55 wineries in the municipality, with 127 hectares and a potential production of 7,083 hectolitres of wine a year, or 10 per cent of the entire Barolo DOCG zone.

THE GREAT VINEYARDS

BRICCO BOSCHIS
CODANA
FIASCO
LIPULOT
MERIONDINO
MONPRIVATO
MONTANELLO
PARUSSI
PERNANNO
PIRA
RIVERA
ROCCHE DI CASTIGLIONE
SCARRONE
SERRA OR BRICCO ROCCHE
VIGNOLO
VILLERO

BAROLO DOCG ZONE

GREAT VINEYARDS

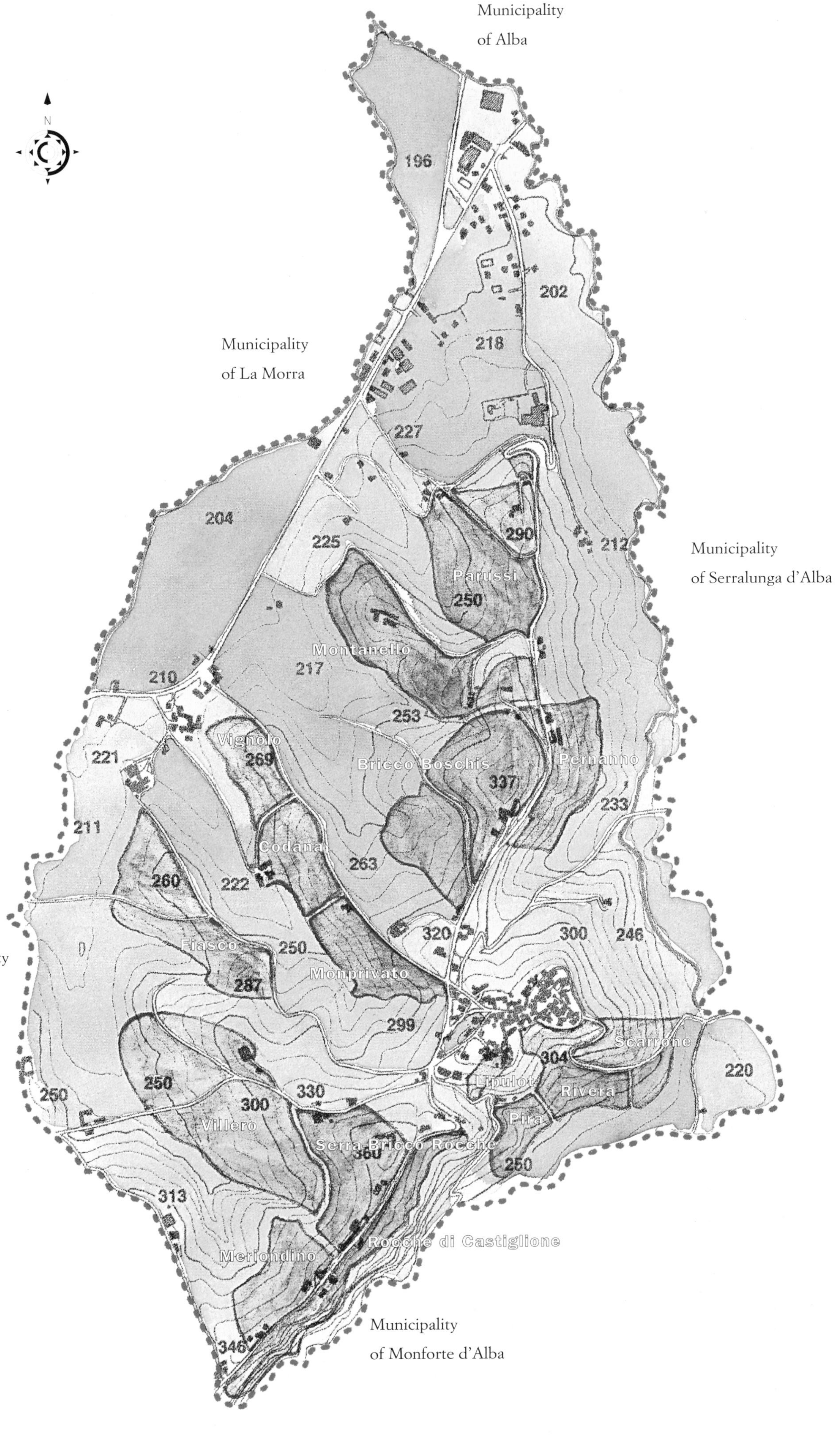

Municipality
of Alba

196

202

Municipality
of La Morra

218

227

204

290

225

212

Municipality
of Serralunga d'Alba

Parussi
250

Montanello

210

217

253

Vignolo
269

Bricco Boschis

Pernanno

221

337

233

211

Codana

263

260

222

320

300

246

Fiasco

250

Monprivato

287

Municipality
of Barolo

299

Scarrone

304

220

Lipulot

Rivera

250

250

300

330

Pira

Villero

Serra-Bricco Rocche

360

250

313

Rocche di Castiglione

Meriondino

Municipality
of Monforte d'Alba

346

Bricco Boschis

Seen from *cascina* Boschis, the vines here are stunningly beautiful as they descend to the valley, gradually turning from west to south west. The *bricco*, or peak, behind the *cascina* stands 340 metres above sea level and the nebbiolo vineyards are at about 300 metres. Bricco Boschis covers a large area, bordering to the north west on Montanello near *cascina* Ernestina and to the east with Pernanno at the Alba-Dogliani provincial road, which also forms the vineyard's southern boundary. The clay and limestone soil is fairly cool. It yields a Barolo with a good balance of alcohol and acidity, even in dry years.

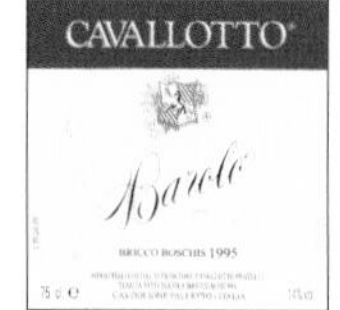

Main labels

*Barolo Bricco Boschis – Fratelli Cavallotto, Castiglione Falletto

Codana

Covering just over ten Piedmontese *giornate*, or about four hectares, Codana is the natural continuation of Monprivato. Opposite, a small road that cuts across the hill marks the border with Vignolo. In a small but very lovely valley in the lower part of the vineyard lies the village of Codana, a handful of houses facing the north slope of nearby Bricco del Fiasco.

Like Bricco Boschis, Codana faces almost entirely south west, at an elevation of around 250 metres. The white marly soil is similar to the rest of this hillslope. However, the lower portion has cooler, more fertile soil that is more suitable for dolcettos and barberas.

Main labels

*Barolo Codana – Cantina Terre del Barolo, Castiglione Falletto

*Barolo Codana in Castiglione Falletto – Giuseppe Mascarello e Figlio, Monchiero

Fiasco

Fiasco is located above the *cascina* Garbelletto Superiore, in the Altenasso vineyard, and is bounded to the north by the road that leads from the *cascina* to the centre of Castiglione. Nebbiolo is grown on just under half of this lovely hill, which is favourably aspected to the west and south west. The soil is largely comparable to that of the other hillslopes on the western side of Castiglione Falletto and belongs geologically to the celebrated calcareous Sant'Agata Fossili marls from the Tortonian epoch. The hill rises to an altitude of just over 250 metres and the best-aspected portion covers about 15 Piedmontese *giornate*, or less than six hectares. The lanes that link the Alba-Barolo provincial road to Castiglione are excellent walking routes for exploring the countryside.

MAIN LABELS

*Barolo Bricco Fiasco – Azelia, Castiglione Falletto

*Barolo Bric dël Fiasc – Paolo Scavino, Castiglione Falletto

Lipulot

Lipulot is a small but attractive vineyard that goes down from the last houses in the village towards the *cascina* Pira, where it borders the vineyard of the same name. The position is magnificent and the aspect ranges from south west to south east, on the border with the Rivera vineyard. The average altitude is about 300 metres. According to older growers in the village, the nebbiolos from Lipulot are every bit as good as those from nearby Rocche. For the time being, it is not possible to make a direct comparison as fruit from Lipulot has never been vinified as a single-vineyard selection.

Meriondino

The vines of Meriondino are the natural continuation of Serra on the western side of the main Alba-Dogliani road, almost at the limit of the municipality of Monforte d'Alba. The precise boundary is the *cascina* Fontana. Facing uniformly to the west, Meriondino is what is known in the Langhe as a *sorì d'la seira*, or "evening slope", that enjoys the last rays of the setting sun. The maximum altitude is about 300 metres and the traditional dolcetto vines are grown in the lower portion. On the ridge of the hill, the main road marks off Meriondino from the long, thin strip of Rocche di Castiglione at *cascina* Borgogno.

MAIN LABELS

*Barolo Mariondino – Armando Parusso, Monforte d'Alba

Monprivato

Monprivato is an exceptionally fine vineyard on the long strip of hillslope that descends from the village of Castiglione Falletto to the houses at Garbelletto Inferiore. All the vines face south west over an area of about 16 Piedmontese *gior-*

Monprivato

nate, or just over six hectares. The upper part of the vineyard has an average elevation of about 300 metres and is marked off by the Grosso road running behind the village cemetery. The road also runs through the neighbouring vineyards of Codana and Vignolo, offering a splendid panoramic view over the "Barolo valley". Cascina Nuova stands here at an altitude of 288 metres above sea level. The soil of Monprivato is similar to that of the other great vineyards on the western side of Castiglione and comprises mainly white and greyish marl.

The results from this vineyard have so far been excellent. The wines are well-structured but, at the same time, they offer elegance and intense aromas. The high quality of wines from Castiglione has been acknowledged for many years, as is shown by the fact that the proud residents of Barolo have always asserted that only the territories of the municipalities of Barolo itself and Castiglione Falletto could claim to produce traditional Barolo. More recently, Renato Ratti, in his *Carta del Barolo*, or Map of Barolo, put Monprivato in the first class as a subzone with outstanding quality characteristics.

The producer who has become most closely identified with Monprivato is Giuseppe Mascarello, who has been putting the name on his labels since 1970. From his Monprivato nebbiolo, Mascarello makes a Ca' d' Morissio selection in great vintages.

Main labels

*Barolo Monprivato in Castiglione Falletto – Giuseppe Mascarello e Figlio, Monchiero

Montanello

The magnificent Montanello winery was built in the heart of this vineyard in 1864. For many years, it was the home of the Langhe's first co-operative winery. At the end of the nineteenth century, the Cantina Sociale di Castiglione Falletto had 36 member growers in the municipality. If we glance through the list, we will find all the area's most famous names. They are the fathers and, in many cases, the grandfathers, of the present producers.

Today, the estate belongs to a single owner and is much more extensive that the vine-growing area. It goes right down to the valley floor, where there are small plots of woodland on the northern slope, facing the village of Parussi.

The vines face west, south west and south. The best nebbiolo-growing part is marked off by the country lane that links the Alba-Barolo provincial road with *cascina* Montanello. To the east, the vines surround the *cascina* Ernestina and climb up to the hilltop above, where there is another farm building known as *Tartifulot*. The altitude of this large, beautiful vineyard ranges from 250 to almost 300 metres.

*Barolo Montanello – Monchiero Fratelli, Castiglione Falletto

Parussi

Where the Castiglione goes down towards Alba, you will find the vines of Parussi. Behind the village of the same name, they form a gently sloping, natural amphitheatre that faces west and south west to Montanello. The vineyard's elevation lies between 250 and 300 metres. As you go down towards Alba, you will come to the main Alba-Barolo road. It is here that the Cantina Sociale Terre del Barolo stands. This co-operative winery, with its 500 member growers, is the most important example of collaborative effort in a land of individualists and first-quality wines.

MAIN LABELS

*Barolo Podere Parussi – Terre da Vino, Barolo

Pernanno

The vines of Pernanno – the name is sometimes spelled "Pernano" on labels – stand in an excellent position facing the morning sun. They run down a fairly

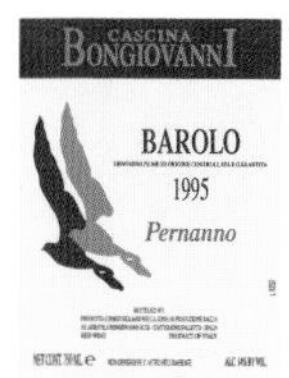

steep east and south east-facing slope. You can enjoy a fine view of Pernanno as you come up the road to Serralunga. The upper part is bounded by the part of the provincial road from Alba to Castiglione Falletto that goes from the junction for *cascina* Boschis and the Dellavalle winery.

An outstanding nebbiolo vineyard, Pernanno extends over nearly 15 Piedmontese *giornate*, or just over four hectares, at an altitude that varies between 250 and 300 metres.

Main labels

*Barolo Pernanno – Cascina Bongiovanni, Castiglione Falletto

*Barolo Vigneto Pernanno – Sobrero, Castiglione Falletto

*Barolo Pernano di Castiglione Falletto – Accademia Torregiorgi, Neive

Pira

Pira is a fine vineyard, and has been for some time, as a old countryman like Paolo Borgogno can testify. "Nebbiolo from *cascina* Pira is very good. I remember my father used to buy the fruit for Borgogno at Barolo. Borgogno always asked him if he could get the grapes from this vineyard".

To go down to *cascina* Pira, once called *cascina* Rocca, you take a country road that turns off the Alba-Dogliani provincial road. The vines below the cascina enjoy a good, almost entirely south east-facing position. In the lower part of Pira, which goes down to the Rio Perno stream, growers harvest good dolcetto and barbera.

Main labels

*Barolo La Rocca e La Pira – I Paglieri, Barbaresco

Rivera

The area takes its name from the vineyard owned by the Rivera family, one of whose members was Arnaldo Rivera, the much respected president of the Cantina Sociale Terre del Barolo (see the profile in *The Greats of Barolo*).

Even today, locals call this the *vigne del sindic*, or "mayor's vineyards". The vines are south-facing and descend from 350 to 250 metres.

Renato Ratti, in his *Carta del Barolo* map, lumps the three vineyards that lie under the castle walls, Pira, Rivera and Scarrone, with Rocche. For long, this view was widely accepted, although it does not reflect the actual terrain. In the higher parts, Rivera and Scarrone are similar to Rocche but it does not seem possible to bring them together in a single subzone.

If you want to get a full view of Rocche and the three vineyards that run downhill below the castle walls, you will have to go up the Perno road. Halfway along it, the Rocche vines rise majestically over the Rio Perno stream while Rivera and Scarrone stretch under the walls of the castle. Further down, you can see Pira and its well-aspected vines.
Note that the upper part of the vineyard, known as *Vigna della Mandorla*, is universally respected for the quality of its fruit.

MAIN LABELS

*Barolo Vigna Mandorlo – Giacosa Fratelli, Neive
*Barolo Rocche dei Rivera di Castiglione – Fratelli Oddero, La Morra

Rocche di Castiglione

The nebbiolo grown in the Rocche di Castiglione subzone has always been famous. Old-timers remember that merchants always paid more for them than they did for other grapes. This long, straight vineyard crowns the actual Rocche themselves, the cliffs that drop down to the Rio di Perno. The road that leads from Fontanafredda to Perno offers a superb view of the rows against the backdrop of the Alps. The upper part of the vineyard is closed off by the Alba-Dogliani provincial road. To either side, it extends from cascina La Tana to just into the neighbouring municipality of Monforte d'Alba. The slightly sandy, limestone-rich soil is relatively unfertile and loose-packed, with a medium consistency. Geologically, it is on the edge of the formation known as Diano d'Alba sandstone. Country people confirm the hardness of the substratum. "When we were ripping, which was done by hand with picks, we advanced three or four metres a day. Below, a metre under the surface, the ground was like rock. We had to take a forge with us because every evening we would have to resharpen the pick" (Paolo Borgogno). Ground like that does not retain water very well and in dry years, nebbiolo at Rocche suffers more than elsewhere.
This long, prestigious vineyard extends over about 20 Piedmontese *giornate*, less than eight hectares, almost all the vines face south east and the altitude ranges from 300 to 350 metres. When the members had a disagreement and the old co-operative winery moved from Montanello to the centre of Castiglione, it changed its name and became the Cantina Sociale Rocche di Castiglione, which shows how good a reputation the vineyard had at the time. "The Cantina Sociale Rocche di Castiglione only vinified nebbiolo from Rocche and Villero. They blended the two because they said, 'Rocche for fragrance, Villero for flavour'" (Sandro Zocca). Even more intriguing are the comments of Paolo Porello, "When there was the old Cantina Sociale, if the grapes from Rocche had a must weight of 20 degrees Babo, they were bought at the same price as fruit from Villero with 21. Rocche has a lower must weight but more aroma". It goes to show that quality

assessment in the old days wasn't just a matter of calculating must weights. he reports we have gathered agree with the valuable study published in 1930 by Professor Vignolo Lutati under the title, *Sulla Delimitazione delle Zone a Vini Tipici* (On the Delimitation of Typical Wine Zones). In the ampelographic map in the work, Lutati describes much of the terrain at Rocche as sandy and the nebbiolo grown here as being suitable for obtaining "a Barolo which may be slightly less alcohol-rich but which has a markedly aromatic nose that makes it outstanding, even when drunk at one year after the harvest".

Main labels

*Barolo Rocche dei Brovia – Fratelli Brovia, Castiglione Falletto

*Barolo Rocche – Cantina Terre del Barolo, Castiglione Falletto

*Barolo Le Rocche – Monchiero Fratelli, Castiglione Falletto

*Barolo Rocche di Castiglione – Fratelli Oddero, La Morra

*Barolo Rocche – Vietti, Castiglione Falletto

Scarrone

The Scarrone vineyard starts from the Scarrone road that winds down from the village at 350 metres above sea level to the 215 of the valley floor and carries on almost as far as *cascina* Gagliasso. South east-facing, Scarrone lies on the eastern part of the hill at Castiglione. For the purposes of this Atlas, the finest growing area, for location and aspect, is the part between the road and the point where the hill changes its orientation to east and north east-facing. The area that stretches in the direction of *cascina* Gagliasso is also in Scarrone but is better suited to barbera and dolcetto. Once, neirano was grown there. The best area for growing nebbiolo, which we have indicated on the map, borders with the Rivera vineyard on the far side of the road.

Serra or Bricco Rocche

Serra is wedged in between Rocche and Villero, extending over about 15 Piedmontese *giornate*, less than six hectares. This small vineyard includes the *cascina* Serra, some houses on the Alba-Dogliani provincial road and the Bricco Rocche winery, which stands on the 370 metre hill that is the highest point in Castiglione Falletto. From here, the west and south west-facing vines go down the slope overlooking the Barolo valley to form the natural continuation of Villero. From the part that faces Perno, to the road that bounds Rocche, the vines are aspected to south east. On Bricco, the soil is similar to that at Rocche but just below, as we continue to the west, it is resembles that of Villero. Bricco Rocche is a fine location from which to enjoy a view over almost the whole of Barolo territory. To the south, the vineyards of Serra border on those of Meriondino at two demarcating *capezzagne*, or country lanes.

Main labels

*Barolo Bricco Rocche – Bricco Rocche Ceretto, Castiglione Falletto

Vignolo

Located behind the houses at Garbelletto Inferiore, Vignolo is the final section of the hill that leads down from Castiglione. The area bears the name of the family that, for several years in the early twentieth century, owned this and many other plots, the Vignolo Lutatis. Only the upper part, with its 270 metre hilltop, is planted to nebbiolo. Lower down, in the part named Solanotto where the vines flank the road linking the villages of Garbelletto and Codana, stand the final rows of

nebbiolo as well as excellent dolcetto and barbera. Here, as at Codana and Monprivato, the vines face south west.

Main labels

*Barolo Vignolo Riserva – Fratelli Cavallotto, Castiglione Falletto

Villero

The technique of blending nebbiolo from several vineyards has always been practised in the Langhe. Until now, it has given excellent results. One classic blend, and a traditional match at Castiglione, is Rocche with Villero. It is a fine combination that can enhance the specific qualities of the two vineyards, ensuring good ageing potential even though weather conditions during the year may have been unpredictable. Villero covers an area of more than 15 hectares. The vines face south or south west and the compact soil is moderately clayey. More fertile than Rocche, it is also better able to retain water. Grapes from Villero are therefore of extremely good quality, especially in years when the weather is dry. Careful analysis and various studies, including the very valuable one by Professor Vignolo Lutati, have confirmed that there are three main types of soil that are suitable for viticulture: 1) white, grey and blue marls; 2) clayey soil; and 3) sandy soils. The Rocche has sandy soil but the great vineyards that face La Morra are mainly white or bluish marl. Interesting, in this context, is the statement we recorded from an elderly grower, Paolo Porello, who contrasted the two vineyards from the point of view of how they should be worked. "In Villero, the soil is more compact but when it rains, the earth gets hard. When we were breaking up the soil, you'd see it was almost black in some places. But at Le Rocche, the soil is white and loose-packed. If it rains, you can dig again the very next day, or just about". The wines from Villero grapes are a little less elegant, with more structure, tannins and alcohol than those from Rocche. It's not just a question of the soil but also of the magnificent location of the vineyard. Villero stands to the west of the Serra vineyard and is crossed by the local road to the cascina Brunella, in the heart of the vineyard, and by the road that leads to the village of Pugnane in the municipality of Monforte.

Main labels

*Barolo Villero – Silvano e Elena Boroli, Alba

*Barolo Villero – Fratelli Brovia, Castiglione Falletto

*Barolo Vigna Enrico VI – Giovanni ed Enrico Cordero di Montezemolo, La Morra

*Barolo Villero – Fenocchio Giacomo, Monforte d'Alba

*Barolo Villero di Castiglione Falletto – Bruno Giacosa, Neive

*Barolo Villero in Castiglione Falletto – Giuseppe Mascarello e Figlio, Monchiero

*Barolo Vigna Villero – Franco Molino, La Morra

*Barolo Vigna Villero – Fratelli Sordo, Castiglione Falletto

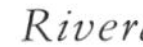

Rivera

Our selection

Population 614
Height 350 metres asl

INFORMATION

Town Hall
Via Cavour, 26
Tel. + 39 0173 62824

THE WINERIES

Azelia
Via Alba-Barolo, 27
Tel. + 39 0173 62859
This cellar came to the attention of Barolo enthusiasts with the 1982 and 1985 vintages but it has been making wine since the early twentieth century. In the past ten years, Luigi Scavino has made further changes, replacing more of the traditional large Slavonian oak barrels with French wood and initiating vinification of fruit from a new plot in the municipality of Serralunga. The result is his muscular Barolo San Rocco.

Cascina Bongiovanni
Via Alba-Barolo, 4
Tel. + 39 0173 262184
Youth and a consequent lack of experience have not stopped Davide Mozzone from becoming one of the most exciting newcomers to the Barolo scene. His enthusiasm, study and the research he continues to pursue, not to mention significant experience working at other wineries, carry him through. The three hectares of the family estate produce a standard-label Barolo and a remarkably elegant Pernanno selection.

Bricco Rocche
Via Monforte, 63
Tel. + 39 0173 282582
This magnificent Langhe cellar, which looks out onto all the great Barolo vineyards, releases the

Barolos that the Ceretto brothers label Bricco Rocche. Bricco Rocche from Castiglione Falletto, Prapò from Serralunga and Brunate from La Morra are the Barolos that have made the fortune of this cellar, one of the most important in the DOCG zone. As well as producing excellent wines, Bruno and Marcello Ceretto have stunned the world with their architectural initiatives. After restructuring the Brunate chapel, they put a glass cube on Bricco Rocche as a tasting room, with a 360 degree view over the vines.

Fratelli Brovia
Via Alba-Barolo, 54
Tel. + 39 0173 62852
The cellar is calmly heading towards its bicentenary, particularly now that Giacinto Brovia's daughters, Elena and Cristina, have joined the business. The link with history is underlined by the large barrels of Slavonian oak in the cellar but extension and restructuring work going on tell us that the winery is keen to improve even further. The Garblèt Sué, Rocche dei Brovia and Villero selections – the celebrated Monprivato is no longer released – have recently been joined by the Barolo Ca' Mia, from an estate-owned vineyard at Serralunga d'Alba.

Fratelli Cavallotto
Località Bricco Boschis, 40
Via Alba-Monforte
Tel. + 39 0173 62814
The entire Cavallotto family works industriously on the estate's 23 well-aspected hectares and on the vinification of the grapes, mainly nebbiolo, that they harvest. The cellar releases bottles that cellar superbly for 30 or 40 years, after ageing in the traditional manner in large barrels of Slavonian oak. In 1995, the Cavallottos started to rationalise their Barolo labelling. They no longer have the Colle Sud-Ovest and Punta Marcello, restricting the range to the more accessible Bricco Boschis and two riservas, the Bricco Boschis Vigna San Giuseppe and the Vignolo. Thanks to a laudable and long-established practice, it is possible to acquire bottles and magnums from the great vintages of the past at the winery itself.

Gigi Rosso
Via Alba-Barolo, 20
Tel. + 39 0173 262369
An historic name in Langhe winemaking, the Gigi Rosso cellar is a byword for Dolcetto di Diano d'Alba – especially Moncolombetto – and Barolo. The cellar releases the Arione selection from Serralunga and Sorì dell'Ulivo, from the same municipality.

Monchiero Fratelli
Strada Alba-Monforte, 58
Tel. + 39 0173 62820
For years, the Monchiero family ran the *cascina* Montanello, famous as the first home of the Cantina Sociale and for the prestige of the vineyard itself. Today, they make good selections of Barolo, Montanello and Rocche, which they release at consumer-friendly prices.

Paolo Scavino
Via Alba-Barolo, 59
Tel. + 39 0173 62850
Enrico Scavino has achieved international

fame thanks to his great skill in the vineyard and a carefully honed technique in the cellar. In addition to his standard-label Barolo, he releases under separate labels selections from three different municipalities. These are the Bric dël Fiasc from Castiglione Falletto, the outstandingly structured Barolo, produced since 1978, that made Enrico famous, Cannubi from Barolo, released since 1985 and remarkable for its aromatic profile, and the more exclusive Rocche dell'Annunziata from La Morra, a well-fruited and softly mouthfilling wine made since 1990. Fruit from other vineyards, including Rocche at Castiglione Falletto, goes into Enrico's Carobric, whose first release was the 1996 vintage.

Cantina Terre del Barolo
Via Alba-Barolo, 5
Tel. + 39 0173 262053
The meritorious Cantina Sociale Terre del Barolo has been – and continues to be – one of the most significant producers in the DOCG zone. Hundreds of growers contribute fruit to a cellar with a far-sighted, quality-oriented winemaking policy. The many selections, including Barolos from Castiglione Falletto, Castello, Rocche, Codana, Baudana and Monvigliero, are all made with excellent raw material and priced very competitively.

Vietti
Piazza Vittorio Veneto, 5
Tel. + 39 0173 62825
One of the historic names in Langhe winemaking, Vietti achieved fame with wines like the Barolo Rocche 1961 and the Barolo Villero 1971. Mario Cordero and Luca Currado carry on that tradition with great success, presenting long-lived wines of character and complexity. The recently restructured cellars release, in addition to the above selections, Brunate and Lazzarito Barolos and a well-made Barbaresco Masseria.

WHERE TO SLEEP

Albergo Residence Le Torri
Via Roma, 29
Tel. + 39 0173 62961
Le Torri offers eight apartments in a noble palazzo in the centre of Castiglione. Restructured a few years ago, it has four units with two bedrooms and living room, and four with one bedroom, living room and kitchen. Not long ago, two top floor apartments were opened. The views across the Langhe and Barolo vineyards are stunning.

Arnaldo Rivera

1919-1987

The autumn of 1959 was an important one for viticulture in the Langhe. At dawn one harvest morning, the presses of the Cantina Sociale Terre di Barolo completed their tests and went straight into action as the first cartload of grapes was waiting at the gates. That memorable day would never be forgotten by 40 year old Arnaldo Rivera, the tireless promoter and architect of the co-operative winery. Less than a year after its foundation, it was already working at full capacity. The Cantina Sociale was the future. It was a blow struck on behalf of the growers, who were no longer forced, in the late 1950s, to beg the best price they could for their grapes in the village squares. At the turn of the twentieth century, Castiglione Falletto had been the home of other co-operative wineries, which had closed ingloriously. That was why "Maestro Rivera", as he was universally known, knew that the road would be a difficult one. Nonetheless, he was convinced that "a social group, acting with democratic structures and sharing out income in proportion to the holding of each member, is a winning idea. We have to overcome the prejudice that men have been, and must always be, in conflict with each other in the name of privilege and the self-interest of individuals, castes or social classes" (from a speech for the twenty fifth anniversary of the Cantina Sociale Terre di Barolo, 11 September 1983).

Terre del Barolo grew and prospered, becoming a paragon, thanks in part to the thrifty management of its president, who warned the board not to try to run before the winery could walk. Rivera was life president of Terre di Barolo, simultaneously holding the chair of the Consorzio del Barolo e del Barbaresco from 1980 to 1983.

Arnaldo Rivera was born at Castiglione Falletto on 13 December 1919 and had recently gained his primary school teaching certificate when the Second World War broke out. He was a lieutenant in the Alpini mountain troops when, in the summer of 1943, he joined the partisans, enlisting with the 48.ma Brigata Garibaldi under the *nom de guerre*, "Arno". He took part in the defence of Alba and commanded the partisans who in October 1944 put plastic explosives on the Pollenzo bridge guarded by Kesserling's troops. On 1 November, he fought against the Fascists of the Tenth MAS who were attempting to encircle the partisans at Roddi. After the Liberation in April 1945, Rivera managed the Turin office for the assistance of Garibaldini partisans and was nominated provincial secretary for Turin of ANPI, the national partisans' association.

Rivera returned to Castiglione Falletto and his orig nal profession, teaching at the primary school from 1949 to 1977. He was also mayor of the town without interruption from 1951 to the year of his death. In this period, Rivera was also active in the Consorzio Acquedotto delle Langhe water company because while the land may be generous with its wine, water is scarce.

He was a shy man, who invariably put the interests of society before everything else. Although not a party member, he had leftwing sympathies and was also an excellent politician, in the truest sense of that word. Progress was his overriding aim.

THE GREATS OF BAROLO

Ferdinando Vignolo Lutati

1878-1965

First of all made a precise ampelographic map of the municipality (of Castiglione Falletto), marking and distinguishing, plot by plot, the nebbiolo vineyards from other varieties and noting the other crops in order to have a complete and accurate agricultural map of my town.

Thus wrote Ferdinando Vignolo Lutati in November 1929. Shortly before, in September 1927, he had made a map defining, for the first time in a comprehensive manner, the Barolo zone. They were years of impassioned debate in the defence of a great wine's typicity. Vignolo Lutati contributed with his studies, which he had been pursuing for a quarter of a century, as he recalled in his essay *Sulla Delimitazione delle Zone e dei Vini Tipici* (On the Delimitation of Typical Wine Zones), from which we have taken the opening quotation.

Who was this scholar and member of the Turin academy of agriculture and the academy of science, a man who was also well acquainted with the agricultural land of Castiglione Falletto and other areas? Ferdinando Vignolo Lutati was born on 17 March 1878 into an aristocratic family. His father Celestino, was one of the most famous doctors in late nineteenth century Piedmont and wanted Ferdinando to follow in his footsteps. In the end, they came to a compromise between natural sciences, which Ferdinando wished to study, and medicine. Ferdinando graduated in chemistry in 1900 and four years later, also gained a degree in natural sciences.

From 1908 to 1948, he taught product analysis at the faculty of economic and commercial science in Turin, where he was also dean. After his retirement, he drafted an annotated catalogue of all the species in the herbarium at the botanical institute. He died on 15 July 1965.

Vignolo Lutati was therefore a chemist, an expert in commerce and above all a botanist. He devoted every free moment to the study of flora.

In 1953, he published *Hieracia Pedemontana*, in which he described 182 species and 300 varieties of plants. He returned to the same subject in 1960 with a new work on *Hieracia delle Alpi Marittime*, also compiling a personal herbal with some 20,000 entries. He published widely, leaving us 91 written works. The most important of these from our point of view is undoubtedly *Le Langhe e la loro Vegetazione* (Langhe and Its Vegetation), the first volume of which was published in 1929, with appendices following in 1932 and 1960. The work is a veritable Bible of Langhe flora and a benchmark for later scholars, listing 1,703 plants. The result of meticulous research, it shows both Vignolo Lutati's scholarship and his love for the land of his birth.

The Vignolo Lutati family had their estate and *cascine* at Castiglione Falletto. From here, Ferdinando set out on his field trips for spontaneous flora, to record nebbiolo vineyards, to assay the soil and to carry out sensory analyses of the various Barolos.

This brief note taken from the biography written

by Arturo Cerutti is emblematic of Ferdinando Vignolo Lutati: "Until he died, he donated his entire salary to the Salesian institute, living on his own and his wife's incomes. She, too, was very devout and shared with her husband an intense spirit of charity and a refusal to countenance any compromise on matters of principle. He was not inclined to oppose the Fascist regime because in it he saw a defender of religion and ecclesiastical institutions from the extreme views of the left. He was profoundly affected when he realised that the birth of the Republic had changed, indeed swept away, the social hierarchy of the past. More than once, I even heard him complain about leftwing Christian Democrats". A conservative of the old school.

Memories of Castiglione Falletto

Paolo Borgogno
born 1925
grower
in Castiglione Falletto

The vineyards were ripped up, three or four metres a day, five or six rows a year. There was hard rock beneath. Once, we brought a forge into the courtyard to fix the picks because they were breaking so easily.

The first co-operative winery in Castiglione Falletto was at Montanello and had 30 or so members. They argued later and went into liquidation. Then they moved the co-operative winery to the carpenter's in the Borgogno district, with about 20 members. My father told me they sold the wine to a bishop from I don't know where. One year, they didn't have any Barolo and they sent him six or seven demijohns they bought from other producers. The bishop replied, "The Barolo is good, even if it isn't my usual one". The head cellarman was *Gioanin*, who could recognise the wine from each barrel.

Later, they moved the winery to the building on the corner. This was now 1925, the year I was born. My wife still has two bottles of the 1927, because that was the year she was born. They've got "Cantina Rocche di Castiglione Falletto" written on the label. But most people bought wine in demijohns. The customers put the labels on themselves. One of the members was the parish priest, Father Alario, who was always at the Cantina because he knew what he was talking about.

Vignolo was a professor of botany (see the profile in the chapter *The Greats of Barolo*). He would come to Castiglione every summer because his family was from round here. He walked everywhere, with an aluminium box on his shoulder, looking for plants.

The Vignolos were rich and had no children. The wife was a contessa. When they arrived on the coach from Turin, their tenant farmers invited them in to eat but the wife would always water the soup in case they complained that their tenants were eating too well. The tenants had money because the owners didn't keep a check on them. But they'd never have dared buy a radio because the Vignolos would have realised they were too well off. (*Winter 1989/1990*)

Recollections of a vine dresser

Once, they only used to put nebbiolo on the (south-facing) *sorì*. They would plant other varieties in the other plots. That meant that during the vintage, you had to harvest three or four times. The first time was for the dolcetto, then for the barbera and finally for the nebbiolo. You'd pick everything then in the evening at home, you'd select the fruit, discarding all the red, green or dry berries.

Few people made wine. Almost everyone sold the grapes. Those who made wine for the house used the discarded fruit, generally red or mouldy stuff. By carnival, there wouldn't be any left. You had to sell the grapes

to make ends meet but it was fun making wine. They'd run water over the bunches and get *picheta*, or thin wine. The money from the grapes was needed to pay off debts. The shop sold on credit.
Our vines (ungrafted, pre-phylloxera) propagated less. On the feast of Saint Anne (26 July), they put on Bordeaux mixture and sulphur and that was it. Nothing else. Now, with American rootstock, the vines yield more and for longer, partly because they use chemical fertilisers.
I remember the old Cantina Sociale. I used to have the accounts but I threw them away. There were 14 or 15 members who pressed only nebbiolo. They sold it the following year without ageing it.

Paolo Porello
born 1926
grower
in Castiglione Falletto

Apart from those 14 or 15 growers, everyone used to sell the fruit to Mascarello, Negro, Cappa at Dogliani and Bonardi and Prunotto in Alba. They used to come and inspect the grapes in the vineyard, or in the house if they had already been harvested, to decide the price. There were years when the barbera fetched a higher price than the nebbiolo. Barbera and dolcetto was mainly sold to private customers who came by horse and cart from the flatlands, from Marene or Cavallermaggiore. Few people wanted to buy nebbiolo here so they took the fruit to the grape market in Alba, held in Piazza San Paolo, three times a week, on Tuesdays, Thursdays and Saturdays. The buyers were private customers or *osterie*, like the Savonas, the Sinios and the Langhes. The agents – there's a tribe that will never die out! – bought on behalf of the merchants, who sat in the *osterie*. The agent would say to the merchant, "I'll go in the afternoon. Either they give us the fruit or they'll have to take it home". With private customers, you got a few pence above the market average per ten kilograms. The agent took two per cent, which was paid by the seller.
Once, I uncorked a bottle of 1808 Barbera at Vignolo's cellar. I also opened a bottled of Barolo that was a hundred years old. If the year is good, the wine will be, too. The cork was made out of corn cobs. (*Autumn 1989*)

Cheese with worms

Maria Prandi Zunino
born 1907
vine dresser
in Castiglione Falletto

I'm from Prunetto, a village in the upper Langhe. There were 14 of us in the family, five children, my father, mother and several aunts and uncles, including one uncle my age, who had been orphaned. At 38, my mother had already had eight children. Three died almost as soon as they were born, one from whooping cough.
My mother had five or six sheep. As each girl grew older, she'd start keeping an extra sheep. Early in the morning, we'd go to the meadow, then we'd make a bundle of grass, go back home, wash and go off to school. At about five in the evening, during the summer, we'd get in front of the animals to plough the fields after the harvest.
My mother made *tome marse*, small mature ewe's milk cheeses, in an earthenware bowl covered with a cloth. When you took it out, the *sattarin*, or worms, would jump out, too. You had to remove the *sattarin* with a

spoon, otherwise they would eat the whole cheese. The *tome marse* were used to make *bros*, a spicy spreading cheese. Every so often, you had to stir it with a stripped fig branch. In the winter, we'd take loaves of bread, cut them in half and spread some garlic and oil on the crust. On the other side, we'd spread the *bros*. Then, we'd toast the bread over the coals in the fireplace, or on the stove. The *bros* turned the colour of gold.

I married Basilio, who was from Saliceto and was ten years older than me. We bought this house in Castiglione and came to live here in 1935. I had two daughters, Argentina in 1938 and Graziella in 1943. I've always worked in the fields and vineyards.

It was tough during the war. One day, two partisans came to my house looking for my husband. I was suckling Graziella and Argentina was hanging onto my skirts. "My husband is here". "We want to see him". "But he's here. That's him", I said. At 35, Basilio already had white hair. "Give me your papers". They believed us. They took a look in the rooms and left. I went outside with them and fed the hens. One of the partisans wasn't well and I offered him some eggs. He said, "Not eggs. Give me some salt". Then he went up to the baby and asked whether it was a boy or a girl. "A girl", I said. He put a hand on my shoulder and said, "You're lucky she's a girl!" (*Summer 1990*)

How to be a Barolo maker

Violante Sobrero
born 1911
grower
and producer
in Castiglione Falletto

My grandfather Francesco had lots of holdings. He had one at *cascina* Pugnane, one at Villero, one at Codana and one at Valentin, as well as fields down on the plains. But he also had six children, four boys and two girls. When everything was split up, there wasn't much for my father. Then my father had seven children and didn't want to give them ordinary names. Here at Castiglione, everyone has their grandfather's name and there are lots of Giovannis, Giuseppes and Tonins (Antonio), sometimes with the same surname. It was sheer chaos when a letter arrived. So he called us Fiorito, Eider, Raffaele, Oscar, Violante, Elsa and Carmen.

Now only I, my brother Fiorito and my sister Eider still work the land. We've always made a little wine in the family but we sold most of our grapes. It was 1944 and there were partisans and republican troops. I was at home after escaping from the French front in 1943. You had to work the land without tools. I remember we used to make Bordeaux mixture with the copper from pans. You just muddled through. At harvest time, Signora Cappa came from Dogliani and wanted to buy the grapes. We sold the first at 190 lire for ten kilograms, then she came back and only wanted to give us 180. I said to my brother, "We're not going to sell her the grapes! Let's make wine. You'll see it's the right thing to do". We had a vat so we threw all the fruit in and trod it. We made the wine. The following year, we made a lot more money than we would have by selling the grapes.

I think the secret of making great wine is in the grapes, and to make good grapes you need sun. My brother Fiorito was born in 1903 and in my opinion he was a great farmer. He had a true passion. I've made some great wines – the papers have written about them – but I give the credit to my brother. He still followed the old traditions when he was harvesting the grapes. When we were harvesting, we only picked the berries that were perfect. We selected rigorously and any bunch that wasn't quite ripe didn't get accepted. We didn't want any bad berries. We used wooden tubs. Grapes are much better harvested in wood than plastic. Even if the fruit had to stand for a few days, it didn't suffer.

We began bottling in 1961 and the winery was called "Sobrero Filippo e Figli". In 1977, my brother died and the loss knocked the wind out of me. You can't keep on working to the bitter end if you've no one to fall back on so I decided to retire in 1982. I was dreadfully sad. you can't imagine how depressed I felt. Selling the vineyard was like a knife stabbing my heart. (*Summer 1990*)

Everyone sold the grapes

Once, there was less nebbiolo. You'd find barbera, dolcetto and neirano. The same vineyard might have six or seven varieties growing in it. They'd plant one grape on a plot of red earth, another one on white and so on.

Years ago, when nebbiolo began to be worth something, people planted it everywhere and the same thing happened with moscato. But if the position isn't good, nebbiolo doesn't do well. Nor does it thrive in extremely well-aspected sites. The main thing is to know how to prune. Instead of expecting a plant to yield ten kilograms, you make it give half that weight and then the grapes will be good. Once, nearly everyone sold the grapes. I remember when four buyers came from Dogliani. They'd arrive, load up and pay. If the grapes came from locations considered to be good, then they'd pay a little extra. There were agents who came to buy but they only looked after the interests of the large wineries. One or two looked after the growers, too. Once, one even told me how much to ask for my grapes.

Sandro Zocca
born 1908
grower
in Castiglione Falletto

At Castiglione, I grafted lots of vines after attending a course of pruning and grafting. In February and March, I'd work the season in several villages, grafting vines from Viganò to Barolo. It was at Barolo I was grafting a vineyard while other people were grafting in a neighbouring vineyard. We said to each other, "Let's see who's best at this game". When we went back to check, my vines had put out great long shoots but the others hadn't. It was the soil that made them take.

I could do 3,000 grafts a day and earned four *soldi* for each, guaranteeing they would take. If I made the cuttings and planted them, I earned ten *soldi* for each one, again with a guarantee that they would take. I also grafted buds. (*Winter 1989/1990*)

Cherasco

A few minutes' drive from Bra, before you reach the Fondovalle Tanaro road, you will come to Cherasco. A small portion of the municipality's territory lies in the Barolo DOCG zone but there are no great vineyards. The town has other treasures to boast and over the year has offered hospitality to many famous people in its noble palazzos.

Built in the fourteenth century to the plan of a *castrum romanum*, Cherasco changed its colours and rulers until the Treaty of Cateau Cambrésis in 1559, when it became one of the favourite residences of the Savoy court. After the D'Acajas, Angevins, Viscontis and Orléans, the Savoys redesigned and embellished the town, transferring their entire court to Cherasco during the outbreak of plague in Turin and many other parts of Piedmont in 1630. Later, after almost three centuries of Savoy rule, the town fell under Napoleon's spell. At every victory, the townsfolk hurried to the churches to sing the *Te Deum*. Cherasco in fact welcomed Napoleon before he became emperor. The mayor went out to meet him with the keys of the town and he was accommodated in Palazzo Salmatoris to dictate the conditions of surrender. The "Armistice of Cherasco" became a title of rank for the town and the date, 27 April 1796, was the beginning of a love affair that would last far beyond 1814, when the Savoys returned. The main flow of history then took other routes but the inhabitants of Cherasco refused to rest comfortably on laurels from the past. As usual, they were able to find a new role, discovering a passion for farming snails. The new activity was started in the early 1970s and today, Cherasco is Italy's snail capital.

The attractively fashioned gates of Cherasco's private houses hide many treasures that, unfortunately, are not

accessible. In the main thoroughfare, Via Vittorio Emanuele II, there are many historic buildings, including Palazzo del Carretto, which houses the Associazione Italiana Elicicoltori, or Italian Snail Farmers' Association, and above all the celebrated Palazzo Salmatoris, where in 1631 Vittorio Amadeo I signed the document that concluded the second war of Monferrato and where Napoleon signed the 1796 treaty. The interior is elegantly decorated with frescoes by the local artist, Sebastiano Taricco. Via Vittorio Emanuele II is closed to the south by the plain eighteenth-century Porta Narzole and to the north by Piazza del Comune, with its imposing 36-metre Torre Civica, and by the Arco del Belvedere, built to a design by Boetto as a votive offering after the 1630 plague that left Cherasco unscathed. Near the arch is the church of Sant'Agostino, again by Boetto, constructed in 1672 by the brotherhood of the Disciplinati Bianchi. Before you head for the outskirts of Cherasco, you will be able to visit other fine examples of ecclesiastical architecture, nearly all of them earlier churches restructured in the eighteenth century. San Pietro, San Gregorio and San Martino are all worth a detour. The church of Santa Maria del Popolo, consecrated in 1709, was actually built in the eighteenth century, as was Madonna delle Grazie, which reflects the charm of Vittoni's Santa Chiara in Bra.

After a look at the Visconti castle, restored, or rather completely rebuilt to plans by Alfredo D'Andrade, in the nineteenth century, it will be time to join the locals for a romantic stroll along the *Bastioni*, the town ramparts, to enjoy a marvellous view of the Langhe hills and the rivers Tanaro and Stura, which meet at the foot of the plateau.

The great vineyards

DOC and DOCG	Total area under vine in hectares	% of area in municipality	% of area in zone
Barbera d'Alba	11.5385	56.71	0.67
Dolcetto d'Alba	5.1871	25.49	0.28
Barolo	**1.8500**	**9.09**	**0.15**
Langhe Favorita	1.0800	5.31	1.08
Langhe Chardonnay	0.6900	3.39	0.27
TOTAL	20.3456	100.00	

Production

There is only one estate of 1.85 hectares, with a potential output of 148 quintals of grapes and 104 hectolitres of wine, accounting for 0.15 per cent of DOCG zone production.

Our selection

Population 2,967
Height 288 metres asl

INFORMATION

Town Hall
Piazza Umberto I
Tel. + 39 0172 489498

Tourist Information
Piazza Umberto I
Tel. + 39 0172 489382

Museum
Palazzo Salmatoris
Via Vittorio Emanuele II

WHERE TO SLEEP

Hotel Napoleon
Via Aldo Moro, 1
Tel. + 39 0172 488238
Three stars. A recently built hotel just outside the town on the road to Narzole. The restaurant offers an à la carte selection as well as a snail-based tasting menu for those who wish to sample Cherasco's most typical product.

EATING OUT

Osteria della Rosa Rossa
Via San Pietro, 31
Tel. + 39 0172 488133
Unfussy, traditional cooking. Cherasco's celebrated snails feature prominently on the menu. Wide-ranging wine list with an impressively large selection of Barolos.

La Lumaca
Via San Pietro
at the corner of Via Cavour
Tel. + 39 0172 489421
An excellent location for enjoying simple snacks with the wines of the area, which come straight from the cellars of the adjacent wine shop. Good value.

WHAT TO BUY

Enoteca La Lumaca
Via Cavour, 8
An interesting shop that sells not just wine but also many other premium-quality typical products from the area.

Diano d'Alba

A few kilometres beyond Alba, the spur of Diano d'Alba rises to a height of 500 metres above sea level to dominate the rolling landscape of the Langhe hills. To the west, the Langa del Barolo merges into the encircling Alps, joining the Roero hills on the right. As we continue in a clockwise direction, we note the Barbaresco hills and, to the east, the first rugged outcrops of the upper Langhe. Best-known for its Dolcetto – which has a DOC zone restricted to the municipality itself – Diano d'Alba also has a sliver of vineyards in Barolo territory, wedged between the bordering municipalities of Grinzane and Serralunga. Sorano is the most prestigious of the local vineyards.

Diano is divided into three very different areas, which have little in common. The first is the historic centre, where the earliest human settlement was located. Around it stretch the vineyards of Dolcetto di Diano. Then comes the Ricca district, where Diano's main industrial and commercial concerns are based. Finally, there is Valle Talloria, home of premium-quality Nebbiolo and other wines. The leading business activity here is Gallo Grinzane.

In over two thousand years of history, Diano d'Alba has enjoyed periods when it was a much respected political and military power. Now, however, little testimony remains of the glorious *Comitatus Dianensis* of Charlemagne's day. Once, the walls of the castle were the most redoubtable in the area, which was the scene of frequent clashes at the time of the Guelphs and Ghibellines. In the end, the castle was destroyed by the French general Colombier, when the Savoys became rulers of all Alba with the treaty of Cherasco (1631). Where once the castle stood, today visitors can admire the church of San Giovanni Battista, built between 1763 and 1770 to plans by the military architect, Carlo Francesco Rangone, Conte di Montelupo, who was evidently influenced by Filippo Juvarra. All that remains from ancient Roman times is the occasional inscription, fragments of bas-reliefs and the tiny temple carved into the rock at the entrance to the town. It appears that once, the temple was dedicated to the goddess Diana and it is the origin of the town's present name.

The great vineyards

DOC and DOCG	Total area under vine in hectares	% of area in municipality	% of area in zone
Dolcetto di Diano d'Alba	283.9884	67.78	100.00
Barbera d'Alba	52.3159	12.49	3.03
Nebbiolo d'Alba	26.1005	6.23	6.28
Barolo	**22.5905**	**5.39**	**1.81**
Langhe Chardonnay	17.1517	4.09	1.68
Other DOC zones	16.8390	4.02	
TOTAL	418.9860	100.00	
Other DOC zones			
Langhe Rosso	6.0450	1.44	8.60
Langhe Favorita	5.4100	1.29	5.40
Langhe Bianco	4.0590	0.97	15.22
Langhe Arneis	0.9150	0.22	2.22
Langhe Freisa	0.1600	0.04	0.27
Piemonte Grignolino	0.1600	0.04	7.07
Langhe Nebbiolo	0.0900	0.02	0.36

Production

There are eight wineries, with a total of 22.59 hectares under vine, producing 1,773 quintals of grapes with a potential output of 1,241 hectolitres of wine, or 1.81 per cent of the total for the Barolo DOCG zone.

Sorano

The thin strip of territory in the municipality of Diano d'Alba that protrudes into Barolo territory borders to the south with some outstanding vineyards in the municipality of Serralunga. However, Diano only embraces the north east-facing slopes of these fine vineyards, Gallareto, Gattinera and La Rosa. There is one exception, the vineyard of Sorano. Standing partly in Diano and partly in Serralunga, Sorano has an unbroken south eastern aspect that extends over about ten *giornate*, or about four hectares. The soil is fairly loose, clayey limestone running steeply down from about 310 metres above sea level to almost 270 metres. Sorano is a seriously good vineyard that deserves more attention. It is reached through the village of Sorano, part of the municipality of Serralunga.

Main labels

*Barolo Vigneto Sorano – Grimaldi, Diano d'Alba

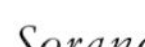

Sorano

Our selection

Population 2,967
Height 496 metres asl

INFORMATION

Town Hall
Via Umberto I, 22
Tel. + 39 0173 69403

THE WINERIES

Claudio Alario
Via Santa Croce, 23
Tel. + 39 0173 231808
Claudio Alario is one of the leading producers of Diano d'Alba. He made his name with the zone's signature wine, Dolcetto, and since 1995, he has also been releasing Barolo. Claudio obtains very few bottles of his estate-owned vineyard selection, Rive di Verduno.

EATING OUT

Langhet
Via Cane, 31
Valle Talloria
Tel. + 39 0173 69403
Langhet, which stays open until late, is also a wine bar and offers a good range of cheeses and salamis. The wine list is extensive and includes all the Dolcetto di Diano selections.

SORANO

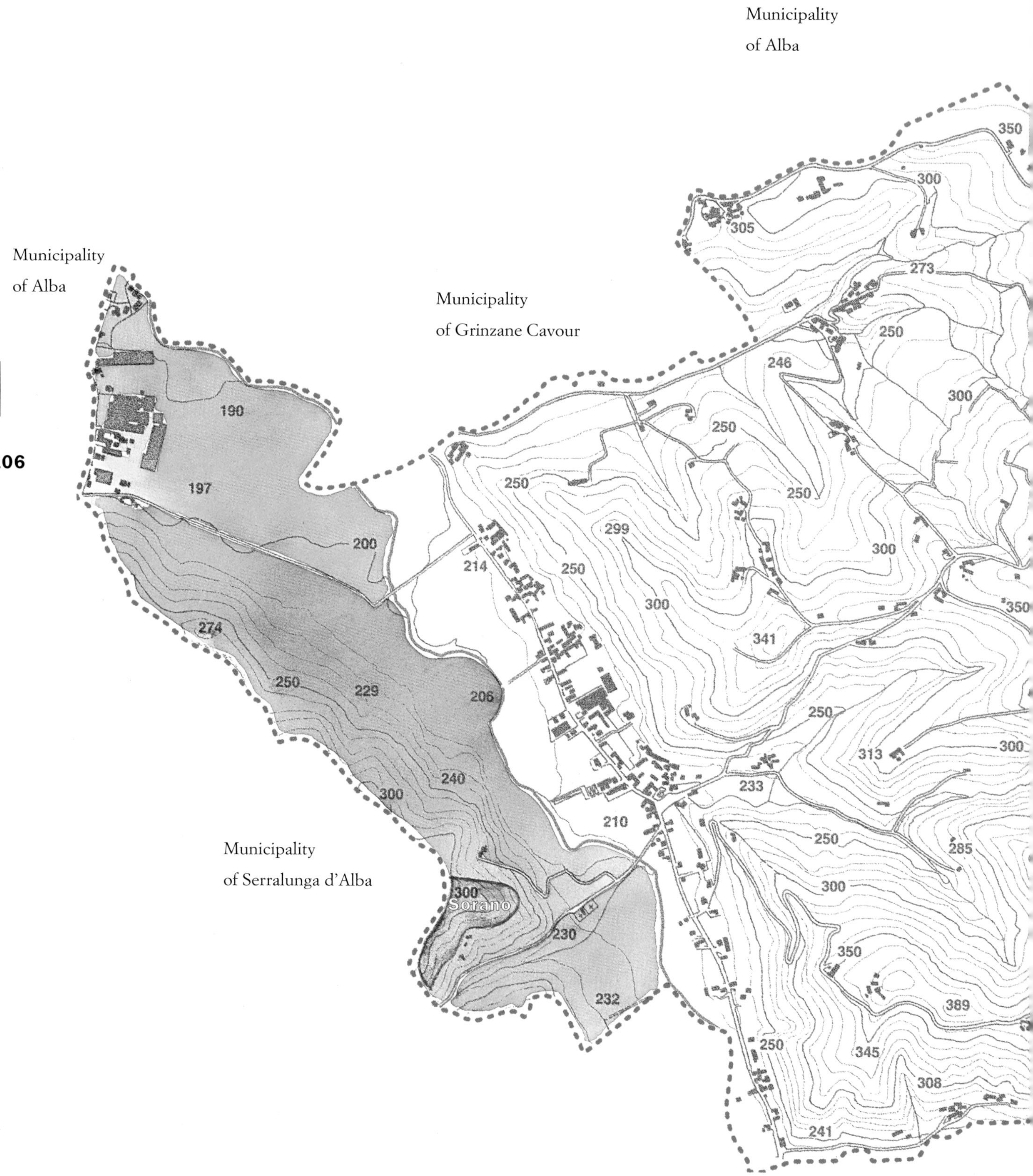

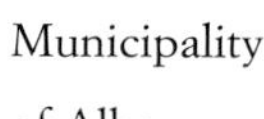

Municipality of Alba

Municipality of Grinzane Cavour

Municipality of Serralunga d'Alba

Sorano

Municipality
of Alba

Municipality
of Rodello

Municipality
of Montelupo Albese

BAROLO DOCG ZONE

GREAT VINEYARDS

Grinzane Cavour

The municipality of Grinzane Cavour has two centres: Gallo, on the Alba-Barolo provincial road, and Grinzane Cavour itself, a few kilometres further on. Gallo is the home of many craft and industrial activities, the best-known of which is making nougat. The residential area is undistinguished and more reminiscent of a big-city suburb than a Langhe village. Much more impressive is Grinzane Cavour's historic centre, which huddles around the castle near the municipality's only Barolo vineyard.

The castle's origins date back to the thirteenth century and the complex incorporates an earlier tower, which faces in a different direction. The imposing brick fortress has a quadrilateral-plan keep with four sections arranged in an irregular pattern around the cramped main courtyard. In the sixteenth century, two picturesque cylindrical towers were added. The Salone delle Maschere also dates from the same period. The caisson ceiling, its 157 panels painted with the crests of noble families, allegories, portraits and fantastic monsters, is an impressive sight.

The castle had a number of owners, including the Marchesi del Vasto, di Busca and del Monferrato, before it was acquired by Conte Camillo Benso di Cavour. He arrived in disgrace, having been sent by his very conservative and indeed reactionary father, who hoped that the leisure of the countryside would calm his liberal spirit. A "hothead" who had resigned from the army, Camillo Cavour was elected mayor of Grinzane – which since 1916 has owed part of its name to him – and was its diligent administrator for 17 years. He was also a shrewd, forward-looking owner of the castle estate, conducting winemaking experiments in the cellars with the assistance of the French oenologist, Oudart. When Cavour's great-niece and heir died in 1936, the castle became a young people's summer camp and was then left for many years in a state of neglect. Restored in 1961, it is today the Enoteca Regionale of Piedmontese wines and the headquarters of the Ordine dei Cavalieri del Tartufo (Order of the Knights of the Truffle), an association that promotes the food and wine of the Langhe. There is a restaurant on the first floor and the upper floors house a museum of country life, with reconstructions of seventeenth, eighteenth and nineteenth-century kitchens, shops and cellars. Country implements, weights and measures of wine, tools for working in the fields and Cavour memorabilia mingle with classical remains in a well-ordered, timeless display.

The great vineyards

DOC and DOCG	Total area under vine in hectares	% of area in municipality	% of area in zone
Barolo	**23.6143**	**35.07**	**1.89**
Dolcetto d'Alba	20.5530	30.52	1.10
Barbera d'Alba	18.1400	26.94	1.05
Langhe Chardonnay	2.5650	3.81	1.00
Other DOC zones	2.4660	3.66	
TOTAL	67.3383	100.00	
Other DOC zones			
Nebbiolo d'Alba	1.5460	2.30	0.37
Piemonte Grignolino	0.5000	0.74	3.05
Langhe Freisa	0.2600	0.39	0.43
Langhe Nebbiolo	0.0800	0.12	2.32
Langhe Rosso	0.0800	0.12	0.11

Production

There are 31 wineries in the municipality, totalling 23.61 hectares with a potential output of 1,889 quintals of grapes or 1,322 hectolitres of wine, representing 1.89 per cent of the Barolo DOCG zone.

Castello

The only major vineyard in the municipality of Grinzane Cavour, the *sorito*, or vineyard, of the castle itself, was mentioned by Fantini in the nineteenth century. It was described as lying at the foot of the Grinzane castle belonging to Conte Camillo Benso di Cavour and was aspected to the south west, south and south east. Most of this vineyard, which extended over roughly one Piedmontese giornata, or less than half a hectare, belongs to the provincial authority of Cuneo. It is cultivated by students at the school of viticulture associated with the Cantina Terre di Barolo. The castle is 269 metres above sea level and the nebbiolo vines run down the hillside to 250 metres. The soil is fairly compact clay and limestone. The wines obtained from this Barolo vineyard selection are extremely interesting thanks to the quality of the fruit and the aromas with which it imbues the wine.

MAIN LABELS

*Barolo Castello – Cantina Terre del Barolo, Castiglione Falletto

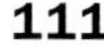

Our selection

Population 1,791
Height 183-310 metres asl

INFORMATION

Town Hall
Via dell'Asilo, 18
Tel. + 39 0173 262159

Castello di Grinzane
Via Castello, 5
Tel. + 39 0173 262159

EATING OUT

Trattoria Nonna Genia
Località Borzone, 1
Tel. + 39 0173 262410
The trattoria is located in a restructured farmhouse on the road that climbs from Gallo d'Alba into the Langhe. The Marengo family – Dario looks after front of house while his wife Renana runs the kitchen – offers local dishes prepared with a light, expert touch. Good wine list and decent prices.

Osteria La Salinera
Via IV Novembre, 19
Tel. + 39 0173 262915
Ever reliable home cooking. Bruno looks after diners and Luciana Manzone is in charge of the kitchen. This small trattoria adjoins a retail outlet for food, wine and typical local products. The menu is on the wall and bottles of wine can be selected straight from the shelves. Attractive prices.

WHAT TO BUY

Enoteca Regionale
Via Castello, 5
The impressive castle rooms host an eclectic but interesting selection of various local wines, chosen by the Ordine dei Cavalieri del Tartufo.

Distilleria Montanaro
Via Garibaldi, 6
For more than a century, the Distilleria Montanaro has made and sold grappas obtained mainly from Barolo and Barbaresco nebbiolo pomace.

THE GREAT VINEYARDS

CASTELLO

BAROLO DOCG ZONE

GREAT VINEYARDS

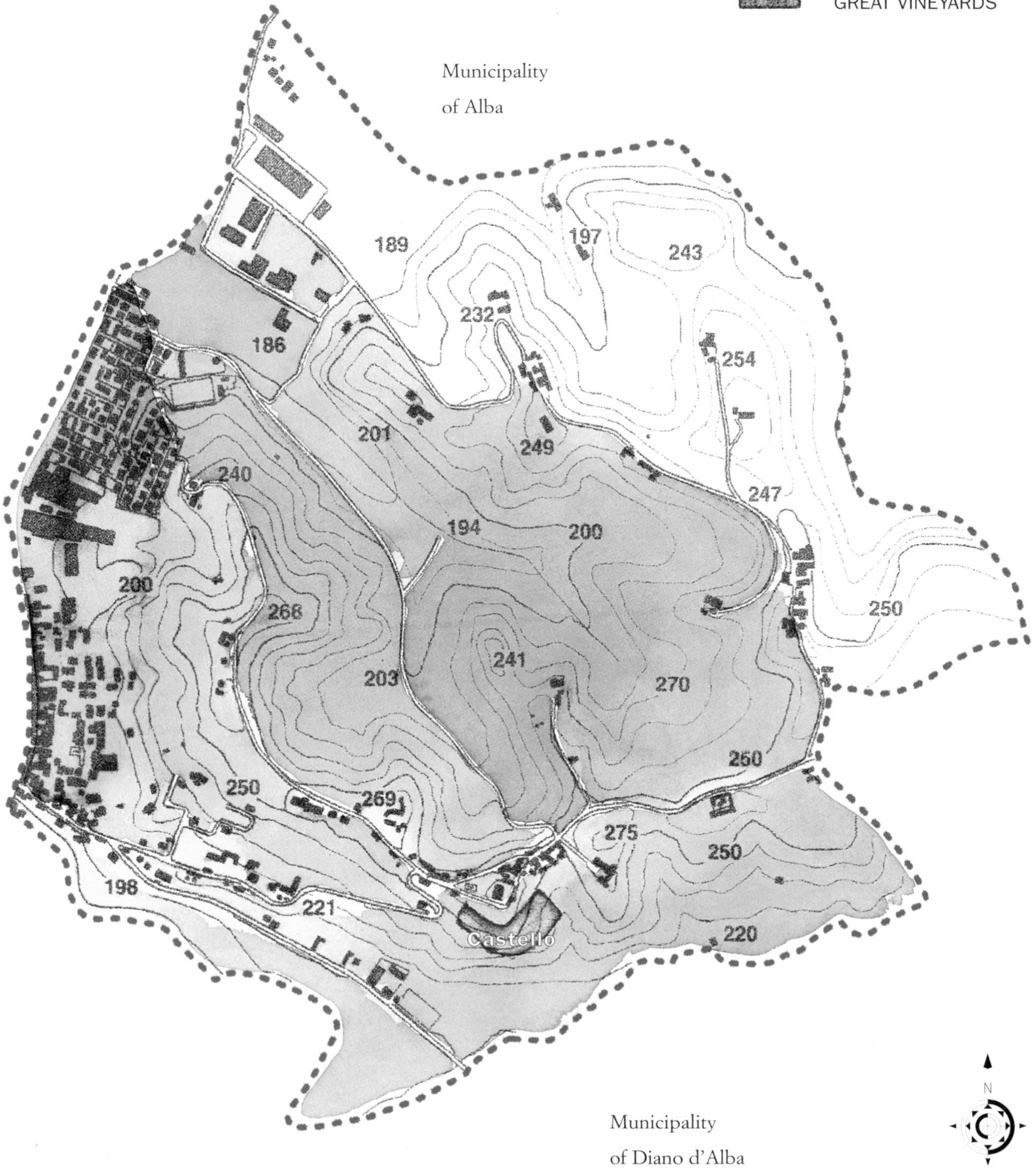

Municipality
of Alba

Castello

Municipality
of Diano d'Alba

BAROLO

La Morra

From its impressive hilltop location, La Morra dominates on one side the Po valley, extending to where the pyramid-like peak of Monviso adorns the Alpine chain. On the other side, the rolling vine-covered hills form a natural amphitheatre of rare beauty. The view from the town's high square is stunning. At 500 metres above sea level, Bricco del Dente has always formed a boundary and barrier towards the Barolo depression. In a sheltered position further down are the sorì of Brunate and Cerequio while to the left, beyond Rocche, is Monte dei Falletti, a gentle hill 300 metres high.

You reach La Morra from Bra through Pollenzo, crossing the bridge over the Tanaro and the district of Rivalta, or by way of Moglia, near Cherasco. Locals say that an emperor and a pope passed through La Morra. Julius Caesar wrote about La Morra on his return from Gaul but the mediaeval copy of his *Commentarii* that contained the phrase is no longer extant. Pius VII spoke of La Morra, when he stopped at Asti on his way to Paris and recalled his – unsubstantiated – noviciate at Annunziata di La Morra, "Morra, beautiful sky and good wine!" There is some doubt about the authenticity of these words. Nevertheless, they show that this Langhe town has always been famous enough to encourage the search for noble connections it never had and Roman origins that have never been proved. In fact, *Villa Murre* was founded in the early years of the second millennium. Its name hints at the main activity of the Alban community that resided here, for *murra* means "livestock pen".

In the second half of the twelfth century, La Morra, with Alba, was part of the domain of Charles of

Anjou. In 1269, it was enfeoffed to the knight Sordello of Goito and then sold in 1340 to Pietrino Falletti for 3,000 florins. In 1402, La Morra was granted the *Statuti* that regulated the life of the community. In the text, we find the first mention of *nebiolium*, proof of the town's ancient vocation for viticulture. In 1631, La Morra joined Cherasco under the Savoys.

The historic centre has conserved its typical mediaeval fan layout, which hinges on Piazza Castello. There is no trace of the ancient castle, except the foundation stones of the eighteenth-century bell tower, the town's symbol. Opposite the tower is the bronze grower's monument, by Antonio Munciguerra from Turin. The grower kneels next to the vine, almost becoming part of the plant. A short distance away, in Piazza del Municipio, is the municipal cellar, dominated by the Baroque bulk of the parish church of San Martino. Two eighteenth-century buildings face onto the square, the Palazzo del Municipio and the church of the Confraternita di San Rocco. If you continue along Via Roma, you will go down to the Borgo, where the chapel of Santa Brigida conserves frescoes from the fifteenth century.

In the district of Annunziata, you can visit the Romanesque and Baroque complex of the former Benedictine monastery of San Martino di Marcenasco, now the church of Annunziata, with its fifteenth-century bell tower and apse. Restoration has brought to light frescoes from various periods, ranging from the fifteenth to the nineteenth century, as well as a Roman plaque on the floor in front of the high altar and the original columns, whose stone columns are still visible. The cellars house the Museo Ratti dei Vini d'Alba.

The great vineyards

The best viticultural locations at La Morra are on the eastern side of the municipality. Here, the hills on which the town of La Morra stand shelter the great nebbiolo vineyards from the cold mountain winds. This broad expanse of vines can be divided into three distinct groups, Santa Maria, Annunziata and the vineyards around the hamlet of Cerequio.

Santa Maria and Annunziata are fairly different, both from the viticultural point of view and in terms of the organisation of production. The former is rich and fertile. Its vineyards are often over-exploited by management techniques that put quantity before quality. We want to highlight five excellent vineyards at Santa Maria, planted mainly to nebbiolo: Roncaglie, Bricco Chiesa, Roggeri, Capalotti and Rive. Unlike Santa Maria, the district of Annunziata is home to a high proportion of grower producers. Some of the best names in Barolo are to be found here. The Annunziata vineyards included in the Atlas are Rocche, Giachini, Conca dell'Annunziata, Manzoni, Gattera, Arborina, Bricco Luciani,

DOC and DOCG	Totale area under vine in hectares	% of area in municipality	% of area in zone
Barolo	**383.6390**	**56.37**	**30.70**
Dolcetto d'Alba	168.4500	24.75	9.01
Barbera d'Alba	98.4500	14.46	5.71
Langhe Chardonnay	17.0550	2.51	6.65
Other DOC zones	13.0281	1.91	
TOTAL	680.6221	100.00	
Other DOC zones			
Langhe Freisa	4.0656	0.60	6,78
Langhe Rosso	2.7370	0.40	3.89
Langhe Nebbiolo	2.6574	0.39	10.63
Langhe Bianco	1.7300	0.25	6.48
Langhe Favorita	0.6300	0.09	0.63
Verduno Pelaverga	0.5400	0.08	5.98
Piemonte Grignolino	0.3800	0.06	2.32
Nebbiolo d'Alba	0.2881	0.04	0.07

Gattera or Monfalletto

Bricco Rocche and Turna Longa. As may be seen, it is a fine collection of vineyards, arranged around the historic abbey of Annunziata, once dedicated to San Martino di Marcenasco. The ancient designation of this area was in fact Marcenasco, a name that Renato Ratti re-introduced when he began to make Barolo. Today, the ancient abbey is the home of the Museo Ratti of Alba wines, the most important exhibition of Langhe wines.

The third area, around the hamlet of Cerequio, is perhaps the finest concentration of great vineyards anywhere in the Langhe. Part of these vineyards is shared with the municipality of Barolo and the wines obtained possess very different tasting profiles from the other two areas.

Many of the vineyards in this municipality are mentioned in the invaluable mediaeval land registers from 1340 and 1477 conserved in the La Morra municipal archive.

Production

There are 227 wineries, totalling 384 hectares with a potential annual output of 21,288 hectolitres of wine, equivalent to 31 per cent of the entire Barolo DOCG zone.

THE GREAT VINEYARDS

ARBORINA OR ARBURINE
BRICCO CHIESA
BRICCO ROCCA
BRICCO SAN BIAGIO
BRUNATE OR BRINATE
CAPALOTTI OR CAPALLOTTI
CA' NERE
CEREQUIO
CONCA DELL'ANNUNZIATA
FOSSATI
GANCIA AND LUCIANI
GATTERA OR MONFALLETTO AND TURNA LUNGA
GIACHINI OR GIACCHINI
LA SERRA
MANZONI
RIVE
ROCCHE DELL'ANNUNZIATA
ROGGERI
RONCAGLIE

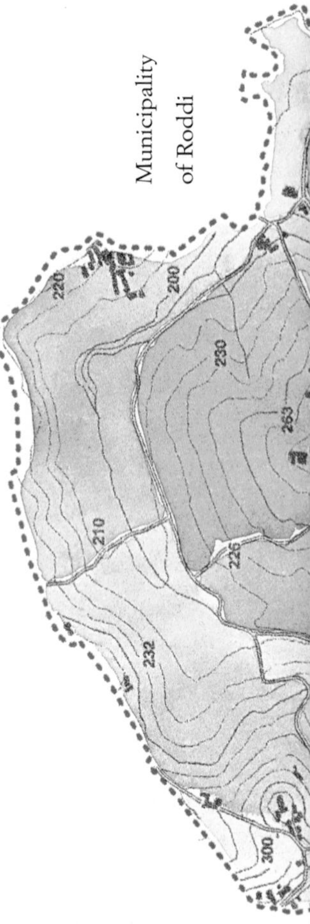

BAROLO DOCG ZONE

GREAT VINEYARDS

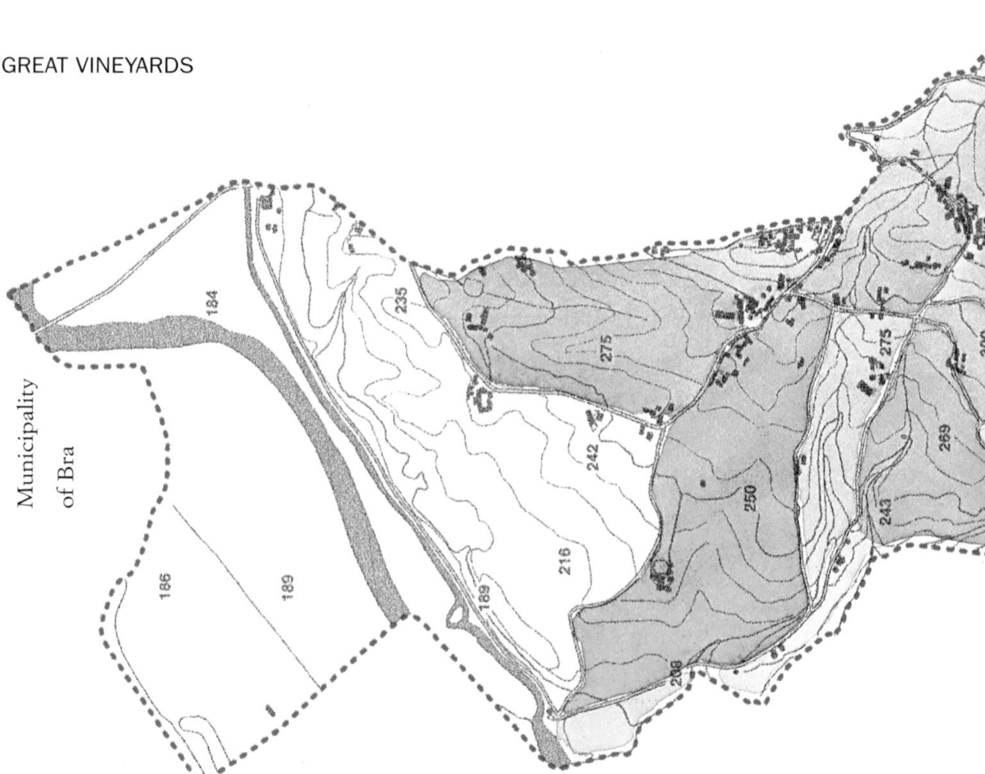

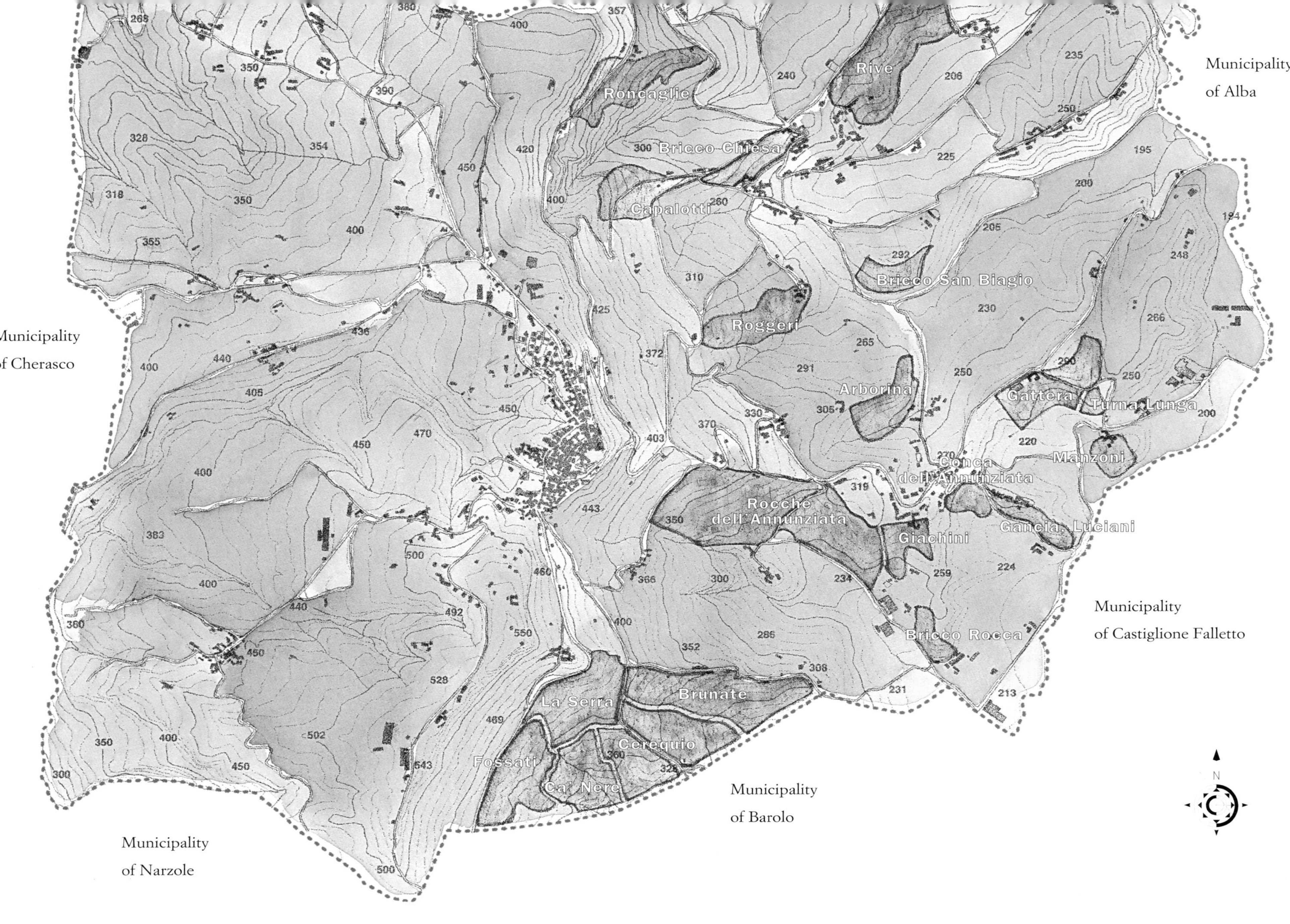

Municipality of Alba
Municipality of Castiglione Falletto
Municipality of Barolo
Municipality of Narzole
Municipality of Cherasco
N
Rive
Bricco San Biagio
Gattera
Turna Lunga
Manzoni
Conca dell'Annunziata
Gancia
Luciani
Bricco Rocca
Giachini
Arborina
Rocche dell'Annunziata
Roggeri
Bricco Chiesa
Capalotti
Roncaglie
Brunate
Cerequio
La Serra
Case Nere
Fossati

Arborina or Arburine

The Arborina vineyard runs round a hill aspected first to the east and south east at the village of Ciotto and then to the south in the part that faces Annunziata.

At the top of the hill is a flat vineyard called *La Buta*, which in the Piedmontese dialect means "the bottle". The vineyard can be reached from the hamlet of Pozzo through Cascina Nuova, or from the village of Ciotto, located below the vineyard itself. It is clearly visible from the Gattera vineyard. The average altitude is around 270 metres and the total area is about ten hectares. This is a nebbiolo-growing zone and the grapes, until a few years ago, were sold to the historic Barolo-making cellars or sent to the Cantina Sociale. Today, the few growers at Arborina are showing that they can produce a premium-quality Barolo, promoting a vineyard that is becoming better known with each vintage.

MAIN LABELS

*Barolo Vigneto Arborina – Elio Altare, La Morra
*Barolo Vigneto Arborina dell'Annunziata – Gianfranco Bovio, La Morra
*Barolo Vigneto Arborina – Giovanni Corino, La Morra
*Barolo Vigneto Arborina – Mauro Veglio, La Morra

Bricco Chiesa

The church of Santa Maria della Neve is just over a century old but it stands on the site of an ancient chapel dedicated to the Vergine in Plaustra. "Plaustra" derives from *plaustrum*, meaning a farm cart, the symbol and emblem of this especially fertile valley. From the top of a hill to the south of the church, the vines of Bricco Chiesa descend to the houses at Tetti, marked off to the east and north by the provincial road that goes down to Gallo Grinzane. The aspect varies from south east to south-facing. The plots in the central area are called Le Turne, and it was here in the 1940s and 1950s that the celebrated Dottor Cappellano from Serralunga came to buy his nebbiolo. The Bricco itself is 287 metres high while the vineyard extends over about five Piedmontese *giornate*, or two hectares.

MAIN LABELS

*Barolo Bricco Chiesa – Silvio Alessandria, La Morra

Bricco Rocca

On the border with the municipality of Barolo, there is a small road that leads up into La Morra at Ponte Rocca, where the Crosia road meets the Alba-Barolo

highway. This minor road forks left to Brunate and continues towards Torriglione, skirting the *cascina* Rocca. Behind the *cascina* is a round-topped, well-aspected hill, covered in vines.
This small vineyard has an average altitude of 312 metres and enjoys a good reputation among growers in the area, as well as with the producers who buy its grapes.

MAIN LABELS

*Barolo Bricco Rocca – Cascina Ballarin, La Morra

Bricco San Biagio

Bricco San Biagio is a steep hillock that stands between Annunziata and Santa Maria. It has an excellent, mainly south-facing, position, although at some points the vines look south west. The location is noted for having been the home of a small community of friars since the Middle Ages. The area under vine is less than three hectares.

Brunate or Brinate

The original name, and certainly the one used most often by the residents of La Morra and Barolo, is Brinate. The first mention of the vineyard is in the mediaeval land register in the municipal archive of La Morra, dating from the fifteenth century. The name used is *Brinatam*. We find the variant "Brinate" in nineteenth-century documents and it is only in the twentieth century that the version "Brunate" appears. Brunate is a Langhe *grand cru* and plots here are much sought-after.

The Fontanazza road, which leads down from the centre of La Morra, marks off Brinate at the top of the hill, going down to the Ponte Rocca area on the Alba-Barolo provincial road. It is one of the loveliest panoramic roads in the Barolo DOCG zone. The two *cascine* of Fontanazza Soprana and Fontanazza Sottana stand on the road, as does the modern Ceretto distillery with its colourful chapel. On the slope opposite Brunate grow excellent barbera and dolcetto grapes. The plots below Brinate belong to the municipality of Barolo and are wedged into the holding of the *cascina* Zonchera, or Zonchetta. A small stream is the boundary to the south with another great vineyard, Cerequio.

The vines enjoy magnificent positions, facing south at *cascina* Brunate and south east further up the slope. The altitude variety ranges from 239 metres at *cascina* Zonchetta to 353 metres at Fontanazza Superiore. The overall area of Brunate is about 25 hectares, equivalent to almost 60 Piedmontese *giornate*. The vineyard

Brunate

includes several plots with their own designations, owned by the some of the most celebrated names in Langhe winemaking.

Barolo from Brunate is exceptionally well-balanced. Its broad, intense, pervasive nose is complemented by generous structure and a body with well-gauged tannins and good alcohol. It is a delightfully rich and complete Barolo. In exceptional vintages, there is a hint of truffle on the nose that mellows over time into a vibrant note of tar.

Main labels

*Barolo Brunate – Elio Altare, La Morra
*Barolo Brunate – Enzo Boglietti, La Morra
*Barolo Brunate – Bricco Rocche Ceretto, Castiglione Falletto
*Barolo Brunate – Michele Chiarlo, Calamandrana
*Barolo Brunate – Marcarini, La Morra
*Barolo Brunate – Mario Marengo, La Morra
*Barolo Brunate – Vietti, Castiglione Falletto
*Barolo Brunate – Roberto Voerzio, La Morra

Ca' Nere

In the middle of Ca' Nere, there is a clump of acacias where you can still see the ruins of the houses that local legend claims burned down long ago in a great fire. They could be the origin of the vineyard's name – it means "black houses" – but there is another theory. The houses are also said to have been destroyed in a landslip for here, we are in one of the least stable parts of the Langhe. Beyond the lower part of the vineyard is a small wood, at an altitude of nearly 350 metres.

Ca' Nere borders on Cerequio, La Serra and Fossati. The vines face south east and cover an area of just over 20 Piedmontese *giornate*, or almost eight hectares. The quality of the fruit is in no way inferior to that grown at its more celebrated neighbours.

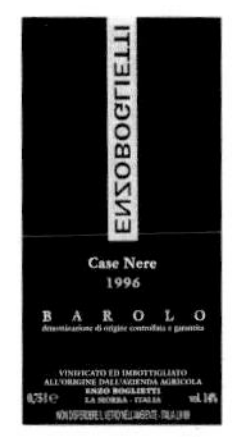

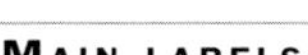

*Barolo Vigne Case Nere – Casetta, Vezza d'Alba

*Barolo Case Nere – Enzo Boglietti, La Morra

Capalotti or Capallotti

Situated north of the hamlet of Capallotti, the vineyard embraces 25 *giornate*, or just under ten hectares, benefiting from the morning sunshine on its position facing Santa Maria. Here, growers obtain nebbiolo, and also a little barbera, that goes into wines much appreciated by even the most demanding producers at La Morra.

We are in the territory of Santa Maria di La Morra. Too often, the quality of the vineyards here has been the target of disparaging generalisations. We believe that the Capalotti vineyard should not be written off too quickly and recent selections from the cru have backed up this positive evaluation.

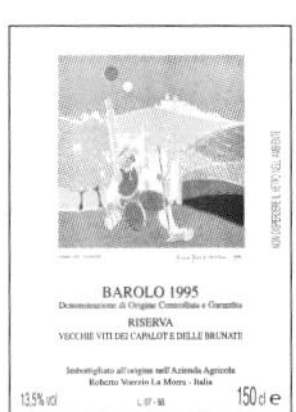

MAIN LABELS

*Barolo Capalot – Crissante Alessandria, La Morra

*Barolo Vigneto Capalot – Aldo Viberti, La Morra

*Barolo Vecchie Viti dei Capalot e delle Brunate – Roberto Voerzio, La Morra

Cerequio

Cerequio is another vineyard La Morra shares with Barolo: another *marcaleone*, as they say around here about anything of superb quality. The vineyard is crossed by the steep road from Barolo and in the middle, there is a group of houses where 30 or 40 people used to live before the Second World War. Today, the buildings stand abandoned yet their charm lingers on. Set in a superb frame of vineyards, they offer a panoramic view of the Langhe of Barolo, Castiglione Falletto and Monforte.

The most important building is known as *'l Palas*, or the Palace, and until recently belonged to the Averame family from Genoa. The terrace still bears a plaque recording the 18 partisans that German troops lured to their deaths here. Below the houses runs the boundary with the municipality of Barolo, on whose territory a small part of the vineyard stands. The other adjacent vineyards are La Serra, Brunate and Ca' Nere.

The soil is fairly loose-packed and the vines face south or south east on roughly 19 hectares. The hamlet lies 355 metres above sea level. The part of Cerequio to the east of the steep road from the houses borders on Brunate. It faces east and south east.

Compared to the Brunate version, Barolo from Cerequio is slightly more tannic and structured. Over time, it develops rich, complex aromas with liquorice, tar, dried roses and truffle discernible.

Main labels

*Barolo Cerequio – Michele Chiarlo, Calamandrana

*Barolo Cerequio Tenuta Secolo – Giuseppe Contratto, Canelli

*Barolo Cerequio – Roberto Voerzio, La Morra

Conca dell'Annunziata

As you reach the first bends on the road from Annunziata down to the Alba-Barolo provincial highway, you pass on your right a small depression covered with well-tended vines.

It is a sheltered spot with a favourable site climate and good, south east-facing positions. In season, a rare flower can be found growing among the vines, the red crown anemone, which might serve as the vineyard's proud emblem. If we calculate that the abbey of Annunziata is at 275 metres above sea level, the vines here are at about 240 metres.

Main labels

*Barolo Conca – Renato Ratti, La Morra

*Barolo Vigna Conca – Mauro Molino, La Morra

*Barolo Vigna Conca – Fratelli Revello, La Morra

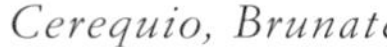

Cerequio, Brunate

Fossati

The provincial road from Barolo to La Morra skirts the Fossati vineyard, a small portion of which lies in the municipality of Barolo. The vines stand on a classic, east and south east-facing "morning slope" at an altitude of between 370 and 420 metres, covering about 30 Piedmontese *giornate*, or almost 12 hectares. This part of the hill country is subject to landslips, as can be seen not only at Ca' Nere but also at the old *cascina* Fossati. Fossati is a good area for nebbiolo but also has a long tradition of growing barbera that has a tendency to resemble Barolo with age, a characteristic the nature of the soil encourages. The vineyards closest to Fossati are La Serra and Ca' Nere. On the far side of the provincial road, the hill rises up to Bricco del Dente. Its 515-metre summit offers a stunning panorama over the Langhe side and on the Monviso side.

Main labels

*Barolo Fossati – Enzo Boglietti, La Morra

*Barolo Fossati – Dosio, La Morra

Arborina

Gancia and Luciani

This is a narrow strip bounded below by the road leading from Annunziata down to Alba. Bricco Luciani, the peak above, should be included in the vineyard. The first of these two small plots takes its name from the hamlet of Gancia above while the other, Luciani, is named after the *cascina* below. Each is the continuation of the other. South-facing, they extend over a total of about ten Piedmontese *giornate*, or less than four hectares, at an average altitude of 250 metres.

The soil is fairly compact and the grapes harvested here have always yielded well-structured, aroma-rich wines. *Cascina* Luciani was actually once a convent. Pius VII is supposed to have stayed here on his way to Paris to crown Napoleon. The name Gancia comes from the general of that name whose family in the nineteenth century owned the *cascina* on top of the hill.

Main labels

*Barolo Bricco Luciani – Silvio Grasso, La Morra

*Barolo Vigna Gancia – Mauro Molino, La Morra

*Barolo Bricco dei Gancia – Angelo Veglio, La Morra

Gattera or Monfalletto and Turna Lunga

We have included both of these designations although the former, Gattera, often indicates the area to the west of the Gattera road, which is not an outstanding position for nebbiolo. The other area, Monfalletto, indicates the *cascina* and hill dominated by a majestic cedar tree.

The name of the hill – Monfalletto – derives from the ancient *Mons Fallettorum*, then *Mont Fallet*, or "Mount of the Falletti family". The summit offers a panoramic view from about 300 metres above sea level of the entire Barolo area.

Paolo Cordero di Montezemolo wrote, "The tree is part of the history and heritage of the area. It was planted by Costanzo Falletti from Rodello and Eulalia Della Chiesa from Cervignasco when they were married in 1856 as a symbol of their love for the land".

The vineyard can be considered as having three distinct levels. The upper part, Monfalletto in the strict sense, faces south west. The central area around the *cascina* has a position that ranges from east to south-facing. Finally, the lower part, which looks onto the hamlet, has a small vineyard called Turna Lunga, which enjoys a splendid south-facing location. Overall, Gattera covers an area of about 20 hectares. The best view of the vineyard can be had from nearby Gancia.

Main labels

*Barolo Vigna Gattera dell'Annunziata – Gianfranco Bovio, La Morra
*Barolo Monfalletto – Giovanni ed Enrico Cordero di Montezemolo, La Morra
*Barolo Vigna Gattera – Fratelli Revello, La Morra
*Barolo Vigneto Gattera – Mauro Veglio, La Morra

Giachini or Giacchini

Today, cascina Giachini at Annunziata is surrounded by modern housing but it has long lent its name to the surrounding vines. The area we are reviewing is planted to nebbiolo. It borders on the superb Rocche vineyard near a cascina called Ciabot d' Can, where the vines face south east. Continuing to the east from here, Giachini forms a small hollow with a fine south-facing position before it rises into a long hill overlooking cascina Gallinotto. The vineyard includes about nine Piedmontese *giornate*, or three and a half hectares. For centuries, religious orders owned the territory. It was part of the estate of the Benedictine abbey of San Martino di Marcenasco and bears witness to the monks' efforts to safeguard viticulture in the area.

The grapes grown at Giachini, and they wine they yield, are similar to those in the neighbouring Rocche vineyard.

The vines stand on fairly steep slopes at 240 to 275 metres above sea level. The Fontanazza road along the ridge of the Brunate hill offers a view of the entire vineyard.

MAIN LABELS

*Barolo Vigna Giachini – Giovanni Corino, La Morra

*Barolo Vigna Giachini – Fratelli Revello, La Morra

La Serra

The vines of La Serra lie above Cerequio and Ca' Nere: To the south west, they border on Fossati while the Cerequio local road to the east separates them from Brunate. Behind the vineyard, which faces east and south east, stands the hamlet of Croera, a superb spot from which to enjoy a view over the Barolo area. The vineyard is planted to other varieties, as well as nebbiolo. It yields excellent barbera, demonstrating that the variety has always been cultivated around Alba. La Serra extends over almost 38 Piedmontese *giornate*, or 14 hectares, and the average height above sea level is about 400 metres. La Serra does not enjoy the reputation of Brunate or Cerequio, although the Barolo obtained from its grapes is very similar to those from the two neighbouring *grands crus*. The outstanding sensory characteristic of Barolo La Serra is its vibrantly intense nose.

MAIN LABELS

*Barolo La Serra – Marcarini, La Morra

*Barolo La Serra – Egidio Oberto, La Morra

*Barolo La Serra – Gianni Voerzio, La Morra

*Barolo La Serra – Roberto Voerzio, La Morra

Manzoni

The Manzoni vineyard lies behind the hamlet of the same name and is clearly visible from the Alba-Barolo provincial road. This attractive peak includes about eight Piedmontese *giornate*, or three hectares, under vine. The upper part of the hill is about 275 metres above sea level. Its best plots, those suitable for nebbiolo, face south or south east and the rows reach the middle of the slope. However, the most interesting feature of Manzoni is *Ciabot dij Preve*, or the "priests' cottage", a small brick building where two brothers, both ordained and who both died in 1869, are buried. Giacomo, the older brother, was prefect of studies at Alba, canon of the cathedral and a knight of Saint Maurice and Saint Lazarus, the Savoys' highest honour.

Main labels

*Barolo Manzoni – Fratelli Ferrero, La Morra

*Barolo Ciabot Manzoni – Silvio Grasso, La Morra

Rive

As you go along the provincial road from Santa Maria to Gallo Grinzane, you can see the long, lovely Rive vineyard to your left, just after the hamlets of Rusconi and Alessandria. At the end of the nineteenth century, it belonged to Cavalier Parà, an historic figure in Langhe oenology, who vinified fully 300,000 kilograms of grapes at his *cascina* Bettolotti. For local residents, Cavalier Parà is a legend. Stories abound of his at times over-enthusiastic gallantry and he is said to have hired all the horses in the area to draw long convoys of carts laden with barrels of his wine to the railway station at Alba on their way to Britain. The Rive vineyard still has as its emblem a symbol of its former owner, the little tower from which the eccentric gentleman used to shout his orders to the workers in the vineyards.
The upper part of Rive is marked off by the Bettolotti road as far as the hamlet of Muratori. From here, a small lane leads down to the hamlet of Onorati. The vines face south and the other details of the vineyard are as follows: an average altitude of about 230 metres and an area of almost 20 hectares.

Rocche dell'Annunziata

A highly prestigious vineyard, which Renato Ratti classified as a first growth, Rocche dell'Annunziata is part of the territory once known as Marcenasco, which fell under the jurisdiction of the Benedictine abbey of San Martino. The place name *Marcenascus* is recorded in a document from 1194.
This great vineyard extends over about 30 hectares in the small valley where the hamlet of Torriglione stands. At Rocche, many of the plots carry the names of their former or present owners. Some of the plots came to be called Rocchette and another small area bears the delightful name of Cuore, or "heart", but the whole vineyard is referred to as Le Rocche.
The local road from Pozzo to Torriglione passes through the middle of this vineyard. The vines themselves enjoy two differently aspected positions. One faces south east in the area that goes down from the Boiolo road and Costamagna and the other looks south and south west in the zone facing Torriglione. The latter is a particularly sheltered location. At the top is the *cascina* known as *Ciabot d' Can*,

Brunate

or "dog's cottage". Since Rocche extends over a wide area, we will report the altitude at several points: the Boiolo road is at 371 metres, the hamlet of Torriglione is at 290 metres, *Ciabot d' Can* stands at 320 metres and the area below the *Ciabot d' Can* is 250 metres above sea level.

Barolo from Rocche dell'Annunziata is graceful and richly scented. The importance of the vineyard is clear from the number of major Barolo-making names that have purchased, or are about to purchase, plots here. The latest arrival is Roberto Voerzio.

Main labels

*Barolo Rocche – Giovanni Accomasso & Figlio, La Morra
*Barolo Vigneto Rocchette – Giovanni Accomasso & Figlio, La Morra
*Barolo Rocche – Renato Ratti, La Morra
*Barolo Vigneto Rocche – Giovanni Corino, La Morra
*Barolo Vigna Rocche – Erbaluna, La Morra
*Barolo Rocche dell'Annunziata – Franco Molino, La Morra
*Barolo Vigneto Rocche – Andrea Oberto, La Morra
*Barolo Rocche dell'Annunziata – Fratelli Revello, La Morra
*Barolo Rocche dell'Annunziata – Rocche Costamagna, La Morra
*Barolo Rocche dell'Annunziata – Paolo Scavino, Castiglione Falletto
*Barolo Rocche – Aurelio Settimo, La Morra
*Barolo Vigneto Rocche – Mauro Veglio, La Morra

Roggeri

The approach to Roggeri is along a lane from Santa Maria through the hamlet of Tetti. The vineyard itself rises above the hamlet of Roggeri towards the Santa Maria-La Morra provincial road and extends over about 18 Piedmontese *giornate*, or almost seven hectares.

The vines lie 264 metres above sea level and are almost entirely south east-facing. The soil, relatively clayey and fertile, has always been planted to nebbiolo. Roggeri is considered part of Santa Maria but in fact stands halfway between Santa Maria and Annunziata.

In the upper part of the vineyard is a ruined house called *Ciabot d' Berton*, where a certain Bertone produced handmade fireworks in the nineteenth century. Predictably enough, an accidental explosion removed the roof.

*Barolo Roggeri – Crissante Alessandria, La Morra

*Barolo Roggeri – Ciabot Berton, La Morra

Roncaglie

The Roncaglie vineyard is crossed by the Silio municipal road. Known since the thirteenth century as *Ronchalia*, it bears the name of the two *cascine* that mark off its upper (Roncaglia Soprana) and lower (Roncaglia Sottana) boundaries. Already deservedly famous in the 1800s, Roncaglie is one of the most important vineyards at Santa Maria. In the nineteenth century, much of the vineyard belonged to the Opera Pia Barolo. It was only in the early twentieth century that the vines were split up among a large number of small growers. We feel obliged to report that doubts have been expressed about the suitability of Santa Maria for growing nebbiolo. In our opinion, these objections are inappropriately framed and, in any case, generalisations are unhelpful to an understanding of a territory that includes some excellent vineyards. Roncaglia is one of these, not just for its excellent south east-facing position but above all for its soil, which is medium-packed and fairly clayey.

The altitudes of the two *cascine* at Roncaglia are respectively 379 and 276 metres above sea level. Further down, beyond Roncaglia Sottana in the direction of the municipality of Roddi and the hamlet of Ciocchini, there is a fertile and very lovely valley that usually escapes the attention of the tourists who flock to the Langhe, especially in spring and autumn.

MAIN LABELS

*Barolo Roncaglie – Braide di Viberti, La Morra

Our selection

Population 2,607
Height 513 metres asl

INFORMATION

Town Hall
Via San Martino, 1
Tel. + 39 0173 50105

Museo Ratti dei Vini d'Alba
Abbazia dell'Annunziata
Frazione Annunziata
Tel. + 39 0173 50185

THE WINERIES

Giovanni Accomasso & Figlio
Via Annunziata, 34
Tel. + 39 0173 50843
Lorenzo Accomasso releases only 13,000 bottles each year. Luckily Barolo, from the Rocche vineyard at La Morra, makes up the lion's share. The special characteristic of Lorenzo's wines is their fresh, spice-rich aromas, set against a very traditional backdrop of liquorice and tar. The cellar offers two selections, a Barolo Rocche and a Rocchette.

Elio Altare
Cascina Nuova, 51
Frazione Annunziata
Tel. + 39 0173 50835
Justly considered a symbol of the new wave of winemaking in the Langhe, Elio Altare cossets his vines with incredible care, striving to obtain the very best from each bunch. A great admirer of Burgundy and barriques – one of his favourite phrases is the celebrated "*Signori, la barrique non è una moda!*", or "Gentlemen, the barrique is not a fad!" – Elio has won international acclaim for his standard-label Barolo and his Vigneto Arborina selection. The 1995 vintage enabled Elio to make a 20 year old dream come true when he released a Barolo Brunate.
His exquisitely made

Gattera

Langhe Arborina is also nebbiolo based and the Altare Langhe La Villa, which also contains barbera, is uncommonly elegant.

Renato Ratti
Frazione Annunziata, 7
Tel. + 39 0173 50185
Renato Ratti, a man whose story we tell in detail in the chapter on *The Greats of Barolo*, created this winery more than 30 years ago, bringing to it his uniquely great winemaking skills. The winery is magnificent and the estate comprises about 30 hectares under vine. Annual production is around 150,000 bottles. There are three Barolos, Marcenasco, Conca and Rocche.

Batasiolo
Frazione Annunziata, 87
Tel. + 39 0173 50130
With over 100 estate-owned hectares under vine and a couple of million bottles sold each year, Batasiolo is one of the zone's leading wineries. The best in the range of interesting Barolos – Bofani, Boscareto and La Corda della Briccolina as well as a standard-label wine – is probably the last of these, thanks to a sophisticated cellar technique and the structure that comes from an excellent plot at Serralunga.

Enzo Boglietti
Via Roma, 37
Tel. + 39 0173 50330
This winery has been active for more than a decade, producing just over 40,000 bottles a year. It has enjoyed success thanks to a range of well-structured and exceptionally elegant wines. There are two Barolos on the list: Case Nere, which ages in small French oak barrels, and Brunate, matured in larger barrels.
The Langhe Rosso Buio also has a substantial proportion of nebbiolo in the blend, which also contains barbera.

Gianfranco Bovio
Borgata Ciotto, 63
Frazione Annunziata
Tel. + 39 0173 50190
Not content with the success of his Belvedere restaurant, Gian Bovio has built up over the last few years an exciting *enoteca* in the stupendous rooms below his dining rooms. Having completed this temple to food and wine, he has turned his attention to the cellar, now being refurbished so that it will be more practical and productive. The wines were good

before and look as if they will get even better, given the commitment of the owner and his collaborators. Form the two fine positions he shares with other outstanding La Morra producers, Gianfranco Bovio obtains Barolo Vigneto Arborina dell'Annunziata and Barolo Vigneto Gattera dell'Annunziata.

Giovanni ed Enrico Cordero di Montezemolo
Frazione Annunziata, 67 bis
Tel. + 39 0173 50344
This winery has a deservedly important name as it was established by Paolo Cordero di Montezemolo, a profile of whom we have included in the chapter *The Greats of Barolo*.
The cellar releases two Barolos. The Monfalletto, from the magnificent natural amphitheatre around the winery, is generally smoother while the Enrico VI, made with fruit from Villero in the municipality of Castiglione Falletto, has more structure and greater ageing potential.

Giovanni Corino
Frazione Annunziata, 24
Tel. + 39 0173 50219
The turn-round in this estate's fortunes took place in the mid 1980s, when Giovanni Corino and his young sons, all highly skilled growers, decided to take the plunge and release wines under their own label. The results were encouraging, starting with a Barolo Vigna Giachini that was one of the best in the DOCG zone even in the less than memorable 1987 vintage. Over the years, the range grew steadily and there are now two more excellent Barolos, the Vigneto Rocche and the Arborina. In a few years' time, a new estate-owned nebbiolo vineyard at Roncaglie will come onstream.

Dosio
Regione Sarradenari, 16
Tel. + 39 0173 50677
The estate's flagship wine is Barolo Fossati. Dosio is an interesting producer with a good range of traditional-style wines.

Gianni Gagliardo
Borgata Serra dei Turchi, 88
Frazione Santa Maria
Tel. + 39 0173 50829
A winery with many strings to its bow, Gianni Gagliardo produces a fine range of Roero wines, notably Favorita, as well as the Langhe classics. The innovative Barolo Preve is very successful.

Silvio Grasso
Cascina Luciani, 112
Frazione Annunziata
Tel. + 39 0173 50322
The Grasso family from Annunziata began bottling on the estate in the mid 1980s, to immediate critical acclaim. Since then, their activities have prospered and they now release 40,000 bottles a year. The house style focuses on sophisticated modern wines without laying too much emphasis on oak. There are three in the range, a standard-label Barolo, the Bricco Luciani and the Ciabot Manzoni.

Gromis
Via del Laghetto, 1
Tel. + 39 0173 50137
In 1995, Angelo Gaja acquired a cellar – in-

cluding a number of wines from previous vintages – that had already distinguished itself by releasing an excellent Barolo from Cerequio. Quality and commercial success have been kept up and now there are plans to increase the area under vine with the acquisition of new plots at Santa Maria di La Morra. The cellar's wine is Barolo Conteisa Cerequio.

Marcarini
Piazza Martiri, 2
Tel. + 39 0173 50222
The Marcarini name has special significance, thanks to a Barolo Brunate that has been the talk of winelovers abroad since the 1961 vintage. Since then, quality has been consistently high, thanks to scrupulous cellar management and the well-aspected estate plots, which total just over 12 hectares. The Brunate is, of course, superlative but the Barolo La Serra, too, is often outstanding.

Mario Marengo
Via XX Settembre, 32
Tel. + 39 0173 50127
Until only a few years ago, Mario Marengo was better known as an ironmonger than a producer. Today, he and his son Marco have established themselves as serious contenders in the world of Langhe wine. Nor should we forget that the cellar obtains its grapes from one of La Morra's historic vineyards, Brunate.

Mauro Molino
Borgata Gancia, 111
Frazione Annunziata
Tel. + 39 0173 50814
Mauro Molino first bottled in 1985 and since then, things have gone from strength to strength. Scrupulous attention to quality is the watchword that informs Mauro's considerable skills in both vineyard and cellar. The cellar releases a total of 40,000 bottles a year, with the Barolo Vigna Conca and the Barolo Vigna Gancia as standard-bearers. Some of the nebbiolo fruit joins the estate's barbera in the excellent Langhe Rosso Acanzio.

Andrea Oberto
Via Marconi, 25
Tel. + 39 0173 509262
This cellar began quietly bottling wine in the late 1970s, when a young Andrea decided to see what he could do with the estate-owned plot at Rocche dell'Annunziata. A small proportion of the nebbiolo, together with barbera, goes

into the Langhe Fabio. The two estate Barolos are the Vigneto Albarella and the Vigneto Rocche. The former evolves fairly quickly while the Vigneto Rocche is an impeccable expression of the vineyard's complexity.

Fratelli Oddero
Frazione Santa Maria, 28
Tel. + 39 0173 50618
This is quite a large winery in Langhe terms. The estate has more than 50 hectares under vine, scattered across some of the finest vineyards in the Barolo DOCG zone.
As well as a Barbaresco, of which about 10,000 bottles are produced each year, the Odderos release four Barolos: a standard-label wine; Mondoca di Bussia from Monforte; Rocche dei Rivera from Rocche di Castiglione Falletto; and Vigna Rionda from more than two hectares in the celebrated Serralunga d'Alba vineyard of that name.

Fratelli Revello
Frazione Annunziata, 103
Tel. + 39 0173 50276
After only ten years' making wines, and having immediately shown their prowess as growers, the Revellos have also proved over the past few vintages that they are expert cellarmen. Almost 40,000 bottles a year come out of the winery, including the standard-label, Giachini, Vigna Conca, Vigna Gattere and Vigna Rocche Barolos.

Rocche Costamagna
Via Vittorio Emanuele, 8
Tel. + 39 0173 509225
A well-established winery whose fortunes are founded on the exceptional Annunziata vineyard, Rocche. The Locatelli family's range is completed by a good Barbera, again from Annunziata, and the Bricco Francesco, another Barolo selection.

Aurelio Settimo
Frazione Annunziata, 30
Tel. + 39 0173 50803
The Settimos have tied their name to one of Annunziata's leading vineyard, Le Rocche. The standard-label and vineyard selection Barolos are joined on the list by a Barbera and a Dolcetto d'Alba.

Mauro Veglio
Località Cascina Nuova, 50
Frazione Annunziata
Tel. + 39 0173 509212
Only a decade or so after he began bottling, Mauro Veglio is one of the leading producers of Barolo and now releases almost 50,000 bottles of fine wine each year. This is the result of acquisitions in La Morra's leading vineyards, such as Gattera, Arborina and Rocche dell'Annunziata, from which the cellar obtains its Barolo selections. The 1996 vintage saw the release of a new Barolo label, Castelletto, from the vineyards at Castelletto in Monforte d'Alba.

Eraldo Viberti
Borgata Tetti, 53
Frazione Santa Maria
Tel. + 39 0173 50308
Eraldo Viberti's small cellar continues to produce about 25,000 bottles a year of admirably consistent quality from the estate's five hectares.
Since nebbiolo from a number of plots is avail-

able, the cellar has sensibly decided to release only one Barolo, with no indication of the vineyard, to avoid spreading its production too thinly.

Gianni Voerzio
Regione Loreto, 1 bis
Tel. + 39 0173 509194
The cellar has been releasing wine under the present label since 1986, extending a family business that had previously focused on the vineyard. With a style that is distinctly modern, thanks to the use of French oak and stainless steel, the Gianni Voerzio winery has been steadily enhancing its quality and with it, the range's reputation among wine-lovers. The house Barolo comes from the La Serra vineyard, after which it is named. Part of the nebbiolo goes into the Langhe Nebbiolo Ciabot della Luna and the exquisite Langhe Serrapiù.

Roberto Voerzio
Regione Ceretto, 1
Tel. + 39 0173 509196
Roberto Voerzio immediately attracted critical attention with his sophisticated, mouth-filling wines whose richness and structure are achieved by scrupulous, intelligent work in the vineyard. For almost two decades, he has been crafting great wines that have brought him well-merited respect around the world. Ferocious selection of the bunches from four magnificent estate-owned plots enables the release each year of a few thousand splendid bottles of Barolo Brunate, Cerequio, La Serra and Vecchie Viti di Capalot e Brunate. Soon to be released is a new Barolo selection from a recently acquired plot at Rocche dell'Annunziata.

WHERE TO SLEEP

Azienda Agrituristica Ca' Bambin
Frazione Santa Maria
Borgata Crissante, 68
Tel. + 39 0173 50785

Azienda Agrituristica Cascina Ballarin
Frazione Annunziata, 115
Tel. + 39 0173 50365

Azienda Agrituristica Erbaluna
Frazione Annunziata
Borgata Pozzo, 43
Tel. + 39 0173 50800 - 0173 509336

Azienda Agrituristica La Cascina del Monastero
Frazione Annunziata, 112/a
Tel. + 39 0173 509245

Azienda Agrituristica Il Gelso
Borgata Croera, 34
Tel. + 39 0173 50840
Five reliable addresses for those who are looking for somewhere comfortable to stay in the heart of the Langhe vineyards. They are ideal starting points for walking, cycling or driving excursions around the area's most interesting sights. All offer cooking facilities and generous meals featuring local produce. Mountain bikes are available for hire at most centres. Attractive prices.

EATING OUT

Belvedere
Piazza Castello, 5
Tel. + 39 0173 50190
It is highly likely that without the Belvedere and Gian Bovio, much of the La Morra legend

would simply not exist. The restaurant is part of local history and indeed of the Langhe heritage. For more than 50 years, professionalism and tradition have been the keynotes of this locale, with its stunning panoramic view. Make sure you visit the cellars and the adjoining tasting room, where you will find great labels from the Langhe and beyond, as well as a long list of Barolos and Barbarescos. Expect to spend around € 40.00 without wine.

Osteria del Vignaiolo
Frazione Santa Maria, 12
Tel. + 39 0173 50335
In this small, cosy restaurant, Luciano Marengo serves a range of well-prepared and presented dishes. The wine list highlights Barolo and Barbaresco. You will spend € 25.00 to 30.00 without wine.

Azienda Agrituristica Fratelli Revello
Frazione Annunziata, 103
Tel. + 39 0173 50276
This is an *agriturismo*, or farm holiday centre, where you can sample the entire gamut of Langhe cooking. The traditional delights are delightfully prepared and you will find *vitello tonnato all'antica*, *ravioli del plin* and *finanziera* prominent on the menu. The excellent wines served are the ones produced by the Revello cellar. There are also two guest rooms for those who wish to stay for the night. Around € 25.00, wine not included.

Osteria Veglio
Frazione Annunziata, 9
Tel. + 39 0173 509341
The long-established Osteria Veglio has at last re-opened, thanks to the efforts of a young, skilful team and the guiding hand of chef Franco Gioelli. There is a good wine list, with all the best Annunziata vineyards represented. The atmosphere is relaxing and in the summer, the terrace dining area offers a fine view over the Langhe del Barolo. Expect to spend about € 30.00 without wine.

WHAT TO BUY

Cantina Comunale
Via Carlo Alberto, 2
This very professionally run cellar has wines from 44 La Morra producers.

Bacco e Tabacco
Via Umberto I, 32
Local wines, typical products, guides and books on food and wine.

L'Enoteca
Via Roma, 19
A good selection of local wines and foods, from sweets to mushrooms conserved in oil. Purchases can also be made through the website.

Enoteca Gallo
Via XX Settembre, 3
There is a long list of prestigious labels from the Langhe and, occasionally, other regions of Italy, a good choice of local gastronomic delights. Then shop has an attractively decorated ceiling and panelled boiserie walls.

Vineria Sangiorgio
Via Umberto I, 1
A charming wine shop on several floors of a lovely eighteenth-century building. An excellent place for a light snack, it offers an extensive selection of Langhe wines.

Paolo Cordero di Montezemolo

1920-1987

In the history of Barolo, there have been men who started out with a solid family fortune, albeit perhaps not one accumulated by viticulture and wine, then worked hard, acquiring vineyards and castles, trading and emerging to become leading figures in the world of early twentieth-century agriculture and winemaking.

In some respects, Paolo Cordero di Montezemolo was more fortunate. He already owned fine growing positions that he inherited from the Falletti family. In other respects, however, rampant middle-class entrepreneurialism suffocated him, even though he was attentive to all he new developments in the sector, especially those arriving from France. He thought of himself as a "man of the country", or rather a gentleman. *Honneur et Fidélité* is his family motto and never did words fit the man so well. Those were days when land was cheap and quality wines struggled to gain acceptance. Paolo was a firm believer in viticulture, replanting his vineyards and tending them as if they were private gardens. He regarded those who worked the land with the highest respect. The *Cont d'la Mora*, or Count of La Morra, and his tenants and employees shared the highest mutual esteem.

Paolo's approach to viticulture, which bucked the trend of the day, may have looked destined to failure but in the long run it proved successful. It was a success he may have aspired to but never openly pursued for his reserve was legendary. One day, however, success knocked at his door. There were no headlines or photographs in the newspapers, just a universal acknowledgement of the quality of his wine, and of the scrupulous, almost obsessive, work he applied to vineyard and cellar. Paolo Cordero's estate was already a symbol of excellence, perhaps not in the distant past but certainly in an age before the recent rediscovery of premium-quality wines. His was one of the leading Langhe estates, on a par with some of France's finest *domaines* and *châteaux*.

Paolo Cordero di Montezemolo was born on 24 January 1920. Six days earlier, his father, a navy lieutenant also called Paolo, had died. His mother, Maria Lidia, was the daughter of Luigia Falletti, the last scion of that noble house, from the Rodello and La Morra branch. When his grandmother Luigia died in 1941, Paolo inherited the Falletti estates at La Morra that had passed from father to son since 1340 for 16 generations. Over the centuries, however, the ancient holdings at Rodello and La Morra had been whittled away by the course of events, financial adversity and not least by the exchange of some hillslope plots for land in the well-watered plain between Savigliano and Costigliole.

Nevertheless, the *Mons Fallettorum* itself, now known as Monfalletto, was jealously conserved. Standing 299 metres above sea level, it has on its summit the cedar tree planted by Costanzo Falletti on his wedding day in 1856.

It was Giacinto Massimiliano who first started timidly to sell wine produced on the estate. The widow of his son Costanzo, Eulalia Dalla Chiesa, expanded both the vineyards and the cellars. None was sold outside Savoy. Then came another woman, her daughter Luigia Fal-

letti, to bring new drive and dynamism to the winery. From 1938, she was assisted by her grandson, Paolo.
Thus the year 1938 marked the official entry of Paolo Cordero di Montezemolo into the world of wine and three years later, he took charge of the winery itself. In 1943, Paolo married Anna Dumontel, who came from a long-established business family from Lyons. They were to have six children. Two, Giovanni and Enrico, assisted Paolo from 1975.
The winery released one of the first La Morra Barolos, vinified in the cellars of the noble palazzo in Via XX Settembre, under the name "Nebiolo" in large letters and "Barolo" written in smaller characters, as may be seen in a label from the time.
Another famous label was the one Paolo Cordero esigned in the early 1960s. It is octagonal, or rather rectangular with cut-off corners, because in that way, to quote Cordero, "it coincides with the field of vision on a champagne bottle".
From 1941, Cordero designed all the labels. This is unsurprising, since his ancestors included men who had promoted graphics and publishing in the Savoy kingdom. He applied the same scrupulous care to the replanting of the Monfalletto vineyards in 1945. As well as dolcetto, Cordero set aside plenty of space for nebbiolo, even though at the time there was little demand for the grape. Cordero planted his nebbiolo on east-facing and south east-facing slopes that were "bowl-shaped, like parabolic mirrors" – his very words.
In 1965, Cordero acquired the Enrico VI vineyard at Villero in Castiglione Falletto. Later on, Paolo and his sons built the cellars at Gattera, at the foot of *Mont Falet*.
Even in those years, around 40 per cent of the estate's Barolos were exported all over Europe, to America, Japan, New Zealand and Australia.
We would like to conclude this short biographical note with a passage from Paolo's last writings, dated December 1987: "It is my opinion that exceptional wines can only be obtained from outstanding grapes, and these can only come from supremely good soil that is in a class of its own... Many people say that great wine is a work of art yet it is actually a work of nature, of the sun, of the climate, of the soil type and so on".

Luigi Parà

The pioneers of Barolo at La Morra were men like Giuseppe Tarditi, the father of Oddero, and the Costamagna family, as well as more recent figures, such as Paolo Cordero di Montezemolo and Renato Ratti. But the town can also boast others whom it would be unfair to call "lesser" personalities. The reason we are unable to reconstruct their biographies in full is simply that we lack written or oral sources. Cavalier Luigi Parà of Santa Maria La Morra, who was originally from Cherasco, is only a partial exception.

Taking advantage of the 1867 law that put up for auction vast areas of church-held estates, Luigi Parà acquired from the bishopric of Alba an almost completely uncultivated property of 50 hectares in the district known as Bettolotti di Santa Maria In a few years, he transformed it into a model estate that attracted the academic attentions of Professor Domizio Cavazza, the principal of the Scuola Enologica in Alba. Lorenzo Fantini, in his Monografia sulla Viticoltura ed Enologia della Provincia di Cuneo (Monograph on Viticulture and Oenology in the Province of Cuneo), writes extensively about the recently experimented "Parà planting system", calling it "bold, new and economical". It was bold and new because "it does not use cuttings but shoots alone" and was economical because "in less than two years, Parà has planted half a million vines on 50 hectares", spending much less than is usually necessary in the Barolo area. This was going on around 1870.

Cavaliere Parà had seven cascine, from Arnulfo to Toetto at Roddi, and in his cellars at Bettolotti, pressing went on for days and an endless line of carts took the wine, destined for Britain, to the station in Alba.

In a 1990 interview, Edmondo Adriano gave us a very interesting description of Parà. "I didn't know Cavalier Parà personally because he died before I was born but my father often used to tell me about him. He had a cascina at Bettolotti of more than 100 Piedmontese *giornate*, with vines on two hillslopes facing east and west. He had had a tower built, an observatory from which he could keep an eye on the workers. It's still there. If the men weren't pulling their weight, he would call them by name using a long megaphone that I found in one of the attics when I was working there as a boy. He had a *cascina* of 60 or 70 *giornate* on the flatlands at Biglini and also owned others, at Toetto, Arnulfo and elsewhere. When Vergiati, the Alba-trained wine technician from Sale Tortonese, was taken on by Parà, he spotted the main chance and married one of Parà's three daughters. That's how he came to own Bettolotti. Then, Vergiati's daughter married Captain Comin, from the Veneto, who was stationed at the primary school in La Morra during the 1915 war.

The 100 *giornate* passed to Comin, although about 20 had been sold in the meantime. During the Second World War, the Germans came to Santa Maria and wanted to arrest Comin, who had been promoted and was a colonel by then. But Comin could see there was trouble brewing and had already left. The Germans then decided to take his wife, Eugenia. At that point, the wife of Tantin, the tenant farmer, stepped in, saying, "Take me". Comin gave Tantin 20 *giornate* then sold the rest to the Odderos".

Renato Ratti

1934-1988

When, in September 1988, the aristocracy of winemaking from Piedmont and beyond met in the village of Mango to pay a final tribute to Renato Ratti, those present were painfully aware of the loss his death represented. The respect won by Ratti, both for his intense professional activity, especially for his studies and publications on the history and culture of wine, is without equal in viticulture at Alba. Ratti was neither an academic nor a scholar aloof from the problems of the market. He was a man of great culture who accepted the challenge of new developments in the sector, starting from the French model of promoting wines and their territories, which he attempted to transfer to the Langhe. The enterprise was arduous, not to say impossible, if we bear in mind the traditionally stubborn individualism of many at Alba and the petty deceptions characteristic of an environment unused to dealing with the outside world. Despite all this, Ratti took up the challenge, convinced that determination would in the long run win the day. He may have inherited his tenacity from his maternal grandfather, Cesare Francia, a doctor from Racconigi who was forcibly moved to the poor practice of Villafalletto for his strongly held libertarian ideals. It was at Villafalletto that Renato Ratti was born on 23 October 1934. He spent his childhood there and after a short stay in Turin, he moved into his grandparents' home at Mango when his father died in 1948. He enrolled at the Scuola Enologica in Alba, graduating in 1953 as a wine technician and also winning a medal for herbal studies. In the same year, he enrolled at the faculty of agriculture in Turin, abandoning the university for ever in 1954 to seek employment, first at the Canelli-based Contratto winery then at Cinzano in Santa Vittoria d'Alba. Ratti was barely 21 years old when the influential spumante makers offered him the opportunity to move to Brazil to the Cinzano facilities at San Paolo and Recife.

It was the beginning of a great adventure for the young wine technician from Mango. In July 1955, Ratti boarded the Giulio Cesare, owned by the Compagnia Italia, bound for Brazil. In that vast land, he implemented a project that in some respects resembles science fiction and for which he is still remembered in the Sertão region. Ratti planted vineyards in a desert area 500 kilometres from Recife, using the waters of the Rio San Francisco to irrigate it after consulting Israeli experts who had already converted deserts in their own land into wine country. The results were swift to arrive. The vines gave two harvests a year and Cinzano was able to stop shipping in grapes from the southern state of Rio Grande do Sul hundreds of kilometres away. At only 24, Ratti was technical director of Cinzano in Brazil.

Those were years of intense activity. The exciting new world offered endless opportunities. At Mailaschi, 50 kilometres from San Paolo, Ratti set up his own modest winery, the Azienda Vitivinicola Piemonte. In the meantime, he had married Beatrice Sitia, the daughter of a family of friends from Genoa. When Cinzano found out about the new winemaking venture, Ratti was transferred at once to Santa Vittoria d'Alba. He returned to Italy in January 1965.

After a very instructive visit to France in 1961, and purchasing wine through his friend Gigi Rosso in 1962,

Ratti had begun to think about investing in the Langhe. When he left Cinzano in 1965, he had already signed a contract to rent premises in the abbey at Annunziata in La Morra. A new Barolo maker had come into being. Ratti released his first wines in 1965 and three years later expanded the cellar. In 1969, Renato's nephew Massimo Martinelli, also a wine technician, joined the company. The partnership was to last for the rest of Renato's life. There can be no doubt that Martinelli's contribution enabled Ratti to devote much of his time to the methodical documentary research that underpinned his publishing and academic activities. In 1971, his book *Della Vigna e del Vino dell'Albese* (On Vines and Wines around Alba), the finest research work ever done on the area, was published by the Cavalieri del Tarufo e dei Vini d'Alba, a food and wine association of which Ratti was a founder member. It was followed in 1973 by *Civiltà del Vino* (The Culture of Wine) and in 1974 by *Manuale del Saggio Bevitore* (The Wise Drinker's Handbook). Ratti's style is sober and instructive: he has an ability to draw the lay reader into the fascinating world of wine. There is nothing arrogant about his expertise. Instead, we note a genuine desire to inform and communicate knowledge. Ratti brought the same spirit first to the Consorzio del Barolo e del Barbaresco, then to the equivalent body for Asti Spumante. He founded the Associazione per la Bottiglia Albeisa and, on the premises of the abbey, created his masterpiece, the Museo Ratti dei Vini d'Alba.

Ratti continued to publish. In 1977, the *Guida dei Vini del Piemonte* (Guide to the Wines of Piedmont) appeared and in 1981 he published *Come Desgustare I Vini* (How to Taste Wines) then, in 1985, there came *Conoscere I Vini d'Italia* (Getting to Know Italy's Wines).

In the decade before his death, Ratti travelled far and wide. His reputation as a wine intellectual was by now firmly established in Italy and abroad.

Ratti's name crops up frequently in this *Atlas*. His *Carta del Barolo* (Map of Barolo), the document that first traced the location of the great Langhe vineyards, is given due prominence. Without Renato Ratti, our work would have been very much more difficult.

Giuseppe Tarditi

1836-1919

The recipe for Barolo vermouth was created in the old chemist's shop in what was then Via Portamercato at La Morra, in the early nineteenth century. The herbalist Giovanni Andrea Tarditi sold his precious elixir in a lovely bottle with a blue and gold label that bore the somewhat pretentious message, *Tarditi Padre e Figlio* (Tarditi Father and Son) after Giuseppe was born in 1836. The noble residence, situated between the Battuti Bianchi church and the Osteria Belvedere in Piazza Castello, was part of the dowry of Giovanni Andrea's wife, the last female descendant of the Roggeri family, as well as other properties near Rivalta di La Morra. On the advice of her guardian, the young orphan had sold to king Vittorio Emanuele II the estate at Fontanafredda that would later be the home of *Bela Rosin*, the king's morganatic wife. The young Roggeri then married Giovanni Andrea, from Novello, and they had set up home together at La Morra. As well as dabbling in aromatised wines, the herbalist Tarditi was also a cellarman. In fact, the wine trade was starting to become lucrative, thanks partly to the efforts of Giulietta Colbert at Barolo and Camillo Benso at Grinzane. Tarditi's son Giuseppe grasped the significance of this development and after graduating in pharmacy in 1857, set to one side his degree certificate and forgot his thesis, entitled *Cenni intorno ai Glucosidi ed in Particolare della Salicina* (Comments on Glucosides and on Salicin in Particular). An appendix contains the formulary of preparations that graduating pharmacists had to make, including the Gaus elixir. But Giuseppe was not distracted by pharmacy He began to look beyond the family estate, buying fruit from growers, who were happy to sell because he paid cash on the nail. The Tarditi winery was a jewel of technology and in fact was mentioned, with a drawing, in Fantini's 1881 monograph, which shows the vats in the upper courtyard and the racking and ageing cellars in the lower section. After alcoholic fermentation, the wine was gravity-fed into the barrels without the use of pumps.

Some older residents tell the story of how Tarditi was wandering around the cellar with a worried look one autumn day. When asked what was the matter, he replied, "I have 100,000 lire's worth of fruit bubbling away in the vats". Quite a sum for the time.

Giuseppe married young and was widowed at only 26. He had three sons.

For many years, Tarditi was the mayor of La Morra and in 1881 he was honoured, acquiring the title of cavaliere. The nomination states among other things that he was "an oenologist and founder of the La Morra Workers' Mutual Aid Society".

Tarditi was a liberal and Teobaldo Calissano, the member of parliament for Alba, was often grateful for the votes his influence swayed in the constituency of Cherasco.

During the First World War, the elderly Tarditi, now alone, could no longer pursue his business. He sold the winery to Camerano from Barolo, who moved it to Via Garibaldi.

The aged herbalist, mayor and oenologist who in 1884 made twice as much Barolo as the Opera Pia Barolo, finally passed away in 1919.

The benefits of blending

My grandfather was from Toetto and he married at Santa Maria. He "hung up his hat", that is settled down, thanks to his wife's property. He restructured the winery and built a vat cellar three metres higher than the cellar itself so that the after crushing, the must would be gravity-fed into the barrels. They were oak, but local wood, not Slavonian. Once, the grapes used to be put in the vats and soft-crushed, a little at a time, so that the bunches were always under the must. When the vat was full, it was covered with boards jammed in place by rakes or poles resting against the ceiling. If the skins didn't stay completely submerged in the must, it went vinegary. The vats were left like that for six or seven days and sugars were checked. Then the must was run off and the real pressing began. A sieve was used to separated the stalks from the skins, which were put in the barrels with the must. So the stalks weren't there during fermentation and my grandfather, Giuseppe Adriano, used to rack when all the sugar had been transformed. My grandfather died in 1912. Before he passed away, he said to me, "If you want to make a good Barolo, don't restrict yourself to one plot". He used to press his grapes from Santa Maria and buy more from Torriglione, Cannubi, Cerequio and Castiglione. He made a blend, what they call an *assemblaggio* these days. We have good yields here at Santa Maria, Cannubi has aroma but there's more tannin at Cerequio and so on. Blending gives you great results. That's what my grandfather thought and he was an expert taster. (*Summer 1990*)

Edmondo Adriano
born 1900
grower and cellarman
in La Morra

When there were harps in the Langa

I remember Cavalier Tarditi, who had a fine cellar on the road that goes to Piazza Castello. They'd park the cart in the middle of the road, on a downhill slope, and then roll the barrels of wine on and take them to the station at Cherasco. At that time, almost all of the wine was sold unbottled, in barrels or demijohns. I was at school then and I remember that Cavalier Tarditi, who had been mayor for 40 years, put a bucket of water and a packet of sugar outside the door so we could drink sugared water. He had plots at Brinate, Pria and in other vineyards. He also bought in grapes. In those days, the other cellarmen in La Morra, the Costamagnas and the Genesios, bought in very little fruit. They pressed the grapes from their own estates.

But Napolin Ravinale was a wine merchant. He pulled a fast one on me! One day, when I was still a lad, I was shovelling snow in the street. Napolin came up to me and said, "Can you give me something to drink?" My father, who was a clerk in the town hall, had 22 *brente* of Barbera to sell and wanted to get 22 lire, because the wine was very good indeed. Napolin took a sip and went on his way. He went to my father and said to him, "How much do you want for the Barbera?" "Twenty-two lire, not a penny less". "I'll buy it". "What, without even tasting it?". Napolin replied, "I'll take your word for it". Ravinale had a wine warehouse in Turin and set up a stall in Piazza Carlina during Carnival. The Barbera, which came from the Pria vineyard, won first prize for him.

Giuseppe Gambera
born 1905
grower in La Morra

The Cameranos, the Piras and Borgognos used to come from Barolo to buy our grapes. My father sold fruit to Francesco Burlotto from Verduno. Our family had a plot at Rocche, another at Fossati and another below the village. I've still got the last one. One year, I sold some nebbiolo to a winery in Barolo. The owner took the only two bunches that weren't particularly good-looking and threw them away before he weighed the fruit. I lost my temper. The following year, I was harvesting the grapes and he was out hunting. He came over and asked me, "Why haven't you offered me any more nebbiolo?". "I'd cut down the vines before I sold anything to you".

I didn't like going to the market in Alba. I only ever went once, the time when uncle Gioanin lost 30 *soldi* because he insisted on being stubborn. In the morning, he refused to sell at 12 lire and in the evening he had to sell to Rinaldi from Barolo at a lower price. And he had to deliver the fruit himself.

Sometimes, we would barter with the people from the flatlands. In May, we gave them wine and they gave us hay. On the plains, you could sell off wine that had gone vinegary but that was in June. They'd dilute it with water to give the harvesters something cheap to drink.

Once, the wineries bought on the basis of position, not sugar content. That is, they wanted to know where the grapes had grown. And once they only used chestnut poles in the vineyards. They'd come from Ceva by train. I went to get them from the station at Narzole for two *soldi* for ten kilograms. It wasn't much, when you bear in mind the work, especially when it snowed. So I made an agreement with the other carriers to ask for six. For taking grapes to Savigliano, they gave me 20 *soldi* per ten kilograms because I had to pay for haulage up the Roreto hill. It was three or five lire for an ox or horse to help my mule to draw the cart. Some *cascina* owners who did nothing else during the winter.

I also took wine to Turin. The journey took three days. I took the demijohns to the Gran Mogol, working for *Cichin* (Francesco) Oberto. At night, I slept in the cart, under the portico of the Carignano stables. There were too many people in the stables and I didn't like the atmosphere. And it was the early months of the year. When we got back from Turin, there were lots of unsavoury types waiting for us in Via Lagrange but I went straight past them.

I also carried the heaviest instruments for the conscripts' orchestras, the piano, drums and harp. Once, I took them from La Morra to Rivalta, then from there on the following Saturday to Pollenzo, and then to Neive. All that work for 30 lire. This was during the 1920s. (*Spring 1990*)

When people went hungry

My father and uncles had several *cascine*. The one at Simane belonged to my father. It had 40 Piedmontese *giornate* in a single plot. There was the farmhouse, the tenant's house, a big stable and a huge portico. Sometimes, my father would stay working there all week. My mother and elder sisters used to take him food. I hurried over there on Thursdays, when there was no school, because I loved going to the meadows with the tenant's daughters. In our house, there were seven girls and one boy. I went to secondary school at Mondovì. In 1927, I started teaching at primary school and I retired in 1967. It was difficult at first, as a supply teacher. I ended up in schools out in the woods, where there were no roads and no janitors. I would light the stove in the classroom in the morning, ring the bell and clean, not to mention teaching the first three classes all together. Sometimes, I had the fourth as well. Out in the country, there was accommodation, the teacher's room, next to the classroom. Those multiple classes were very large, up to 40 children, and the ones in the first class only spoke dialect. In the countryside and mountains, I saw such terrible poverty. I was a godmother at Piasco and at Cherasco. When poor people, tenant farmers, ask you, it's difficult to say no. The tenants at Cherasco didn't even have enough to eat. Every week, the travelling salesman's gig came to the village. I would buy some coffee or sugar or something else for the family. Once, the mother took to her bed ill and I ran off to get a doctor. The poor woman didn't even have a change of underwear. I gave her mine.

Radegonda Oberto
born 1904
schoolteacher
in La Morra

In La Morra, there were schools in all four districts and In La Morra itself. Children who came from the countryside had to walk, come rain or shine. The students would bring something to eat at lunchtime. Then they set up the charitable foundation with hot food. (*Summer 1990*)

There wasn't much money around

Some shoppers put their purchases on the slate while they were waiting to sell their wheat, or grapes, or calf or silkworms. They'd pay when they had the cash. Or they'd bring me flour or eggs in payment. I would then take the flour to Gallo Grinzane, where there was a man who made pasta. But I bought the best past from the travelling salesman. There was a family from Barolo who had run up quite a bill. They just couldn't find a buyer for the calf they needed to sell to pay me. One day, I went to see them and ran away in despair. They were in a dreadful state. The woman was pregnant and had three young children. The stove was smoking and needed fixing. They had nothing to eat. I felt I ought to be giving them money, not asking for it!

I took over the shop in 1932 and kept it until about 1980. I won two gold medals and they even wanted to give me a gold eagle but I refused. At that time, the shop opened at six in the morning and closed at ten at night every day, including Sundays. When people were cutting hay or harvesting the wheat, at six in the morning they were already waiting to buy vegetables to dress with oil and cheese for the workers' midday meal. Or they'd come to buy all the stuff for the wheat-beating (threshing) meal. Customers came from the *cascine* and filled their baskets. Apart from these big occasions, people didn't usually buy much at a time. They made small purchases of two or three hundred grams of sugar, 50 grams of coffee or 100 grams of butter. There wasn't much money around and there weren't any fridges, either. Country women came after early Mass. During the month of the Heart of Jesus, in January, the shop was always full.

Colombina Stroppiana
born 1912
shopkeeper
in La Morra

In 1933, there was a big celebration at La Morra. I set up the grape stall outside the shop. There were four of us serving. In the morning, the officers from the town hall came and told me, "It's very nice but where's the portrait of the Duce, Mussolini?". So, I shoved it in with the grapes and won the prize. There were lots of grape stalls in the streets that September Sunday. In Piazza Castello, there were wine stalls selling wine by the glass or in little souvenir bottles. A special train sent by the newspaper, La Stampa, came from Turin. There was a long procession of people walking up from the station at Cherasco. They closed all the streets in the town and set up a mandatory route. Of course, the *osterie* were full to bursting. The Albergo dell'Angelo, famous for Maria d'l Angel's *tajarin* (tagliatelle), the Belvedere, the Trattoria delle Indie, the Trattoria Italia and even the Osteria dei Tre Carlin were all packed. And there were masses of people picnicking on the grass, drinking or dancing on the three dance floors. (*Summer 1990*)

Monforte d'Alba

Monforte d'Alba is the final spur of the Langa del Barolo. Stunningly situated, the village has an older part where the houses back onto a steep hill, piled one on top of another. The extensive municipal territory includes the hamlets of Bussia, Manzoni, Ornati, San Sebastiano, Sant'Anna, San Giuseppe, Ginestra, Perno and Castelletto, many of which are outstanding areas for Barolo. Lying halfway between Alba (via Gallo) and Bra, Monforte is reached from the latter along the Fondovalle Tanaro, turning left at Monchiero.

Monforte was once *Pagus Romanus* and, subsequently, a Lombard feud. Then during the Carolingian era, it was a "minor feudal county". The ancient castle was demolished and burnt in 1028, in the course of a crusade by the Signori of the Langhe against what had become a stronghold of Manichaean heretics. The leaders of the sect were Girardo and the Contessa Berta, Rodolfo il Glabro and Lamberto Seniore, who were led in chains – with nobles and commoners – to Milan, by order of the archbishop Ariberto d'Intimiano. The defeated Cathars, as the heretics were called, were burnt at the stake and the purificatory fires continued to blaze for many days in the district of Milan known today as Monforte. For years after this slaughter – when only a single tower of the castle remained – the fortress of *Mons Fortisi* lay abandoned. In 1819, the poet Giovanni Berchet wrote this unfinished verse on the story of the Cathars, "From Monforte no one comes, / to Monforte no one goes".

Rebuilt in the seventeenth century, the castle was sacked by the armies of the Austrian emperor and then by the troops of Duca Vittorio Amedeo of

Ginestra

Savoy. Thereafter, it was occupied on several occasions, each time suffering the devastation and destruction that followed capture. The castle was finally given to the Del Carretto family by Carlo Emanuele III of Savoy, who was solemnly invested as feudal lord in 1733 by the emperor Charles III. Currently, it is the residence of the Marchesi Scarampi del Cairo. The present castle was constructed in several stages after 1706 on the walls of the ancient feudal residence. The architectural complex dominates the old village and includes a thirteenth-century Romanesque bell tower and two churches, the church of the Confraternita delle Umiliate and the fourteenth-century church of Sant'Agostino. From the top of the hill, there is a fine panoramic view over the village and beyond, to the entire semicircle of the Alps, from the pass of Cadibona to the massif of Monte Rosa. The little square has been converted into an unusual auditorium dedicated to the pianist Horszowski, who inaugurated it in 1986. When you leave Monforte, you are well advised to visit Perno, which was once itself a municipality, and Castelletto. This will take you round a ring a few kilometres long through vineyards, castles and chapels. On a hill overlooking the Rio Perno stream, you can admire the lovely Romanesque apse of a now deconsecrated chapel. It is probably a relic from the eleventh-century parish church dedicated to Saint Stephen and stands on the site where once there was a village razed to the ground by the Cathars, who on this occasion were persecutors rather than persecuted. They were exacting their revenge on the villagers who did not embrace their heresy.

The great vineyards

The great vineyards of Monforte d'Alba are concentrated in the north east of the municipality and can be divided into two large strips, with a small central zone including the vineyards of Santo Stefano di Perno and Gramolere.

To the west, as you turn to Barolo, you will find the vineyards of Bussia. Further south lie Dardi, Pianpolvere, Visette and Arnulfi, in a lovely valley sheltered by the hill of San Giovanni. To the east is a long series of parallel vineyards that crown the valley of the torrential Talloria di Castiglione stream, known in the local dialect as the *Taloria fausa*, or "false Talloria". On the opposite slopes to these lovely plots are the great Serralunga vineyards. Like them, they produce well-structured, tannin-rich Barolos.

Monforte is a generous territory, not just for the quality of its Barolo but also for the range of nuances the wine expresses.

Bussia is an area that embraces two separate villages, Bussia Soprana and Bussia Sottana. Considered as a whole, Bussia includes some

DOC and DOCG	Total area under vine in hectares	% of area in municipality	% of area in zone
Dolcetto d'Alba	336.2234	46.08	17.99
Barolo	**208.3518**	**28.55**	**16.67**
Barbera d'Alba	140.3541	19.24	8.14
Langhe Chardonnay	17.3800	2,38	6.77
Langhe Rosso	10.6600	1.46	15.16
Langhe Freisa	8.2500	1.13	13.76
Nebbiolo d'Alba	4.3050	0.59	1.04
Other DOC zones	4.1500	0.57	
TOTAL	729.6743	100.00	
Other DOC zones			
Langhe Nebbiolo	1.8100	0.25	7.24
Langhe Bianco	1.6400	0.22	6.15
Langhe Favorita	0.7000	0.10	0.70

outstanding plots that produce wines with superb sensory profiles, beginning with their very fresh, intense aromas.

The great vineyards in this Atlas include Munie and Pugnane at Bussia Sottana, as well as the vineyard that surrounds the hamlet itself and from which it takes its name.

Similarly, the vineyard below the houses at Bussia Soprana is named after the little village and ranks in quality alongside the celebrated Colonnello, Bricco Cicala, Romirasco and Gabutti della Bussia vineyards.

Production

There are 122 wineries, totalling 208 hectares with a potential annual output of 11,468 hectolitres of wine, equivalent to 17 per cent of the entire Barolo DOCG zone.

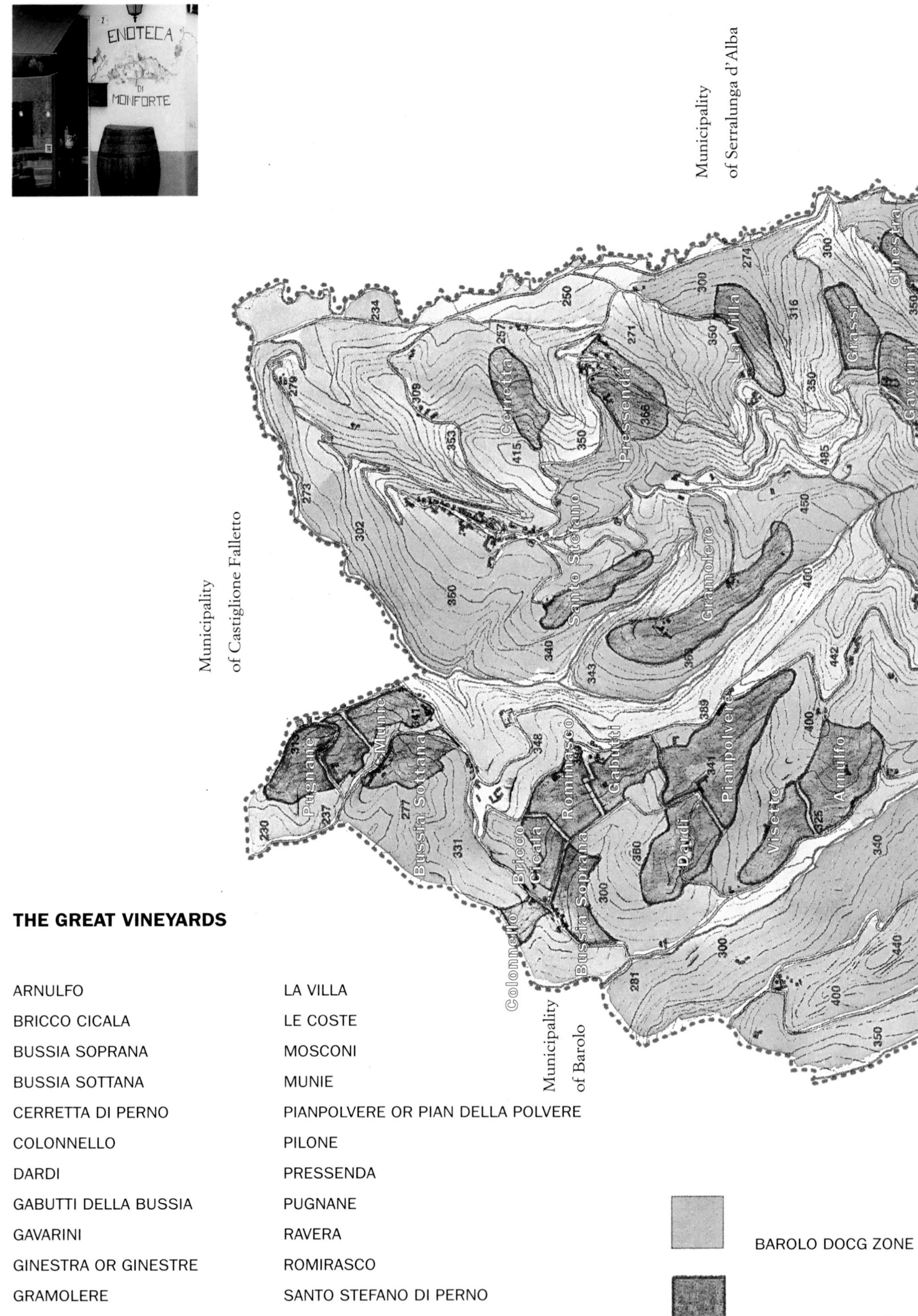

THE GREAT VINEYARDS

ARNULFO
BRICCO CICALA
BUSSIA SOPRANA
BUSSIA SOTTANA
CERRETTA DI PERNO
COLONNELLO
DARDI
GABUTTI DELLA BUSSIA
GAVARINI
GINESTRA OR GINESTRE
GRAMOLERE
GRASSI
LA VILLA
LE COSTE
MOSCONI
MUNIE
PIANPOLVERE OR PIAN DELLA POLVERE
PILONE
PRESSENDA
PUGNANE
RAVERA
ROMIRASCO
SANTO STEFANO DI PERNO
VISETTE

BAROLO DOCG ZONE

GREAT VINEYARDS

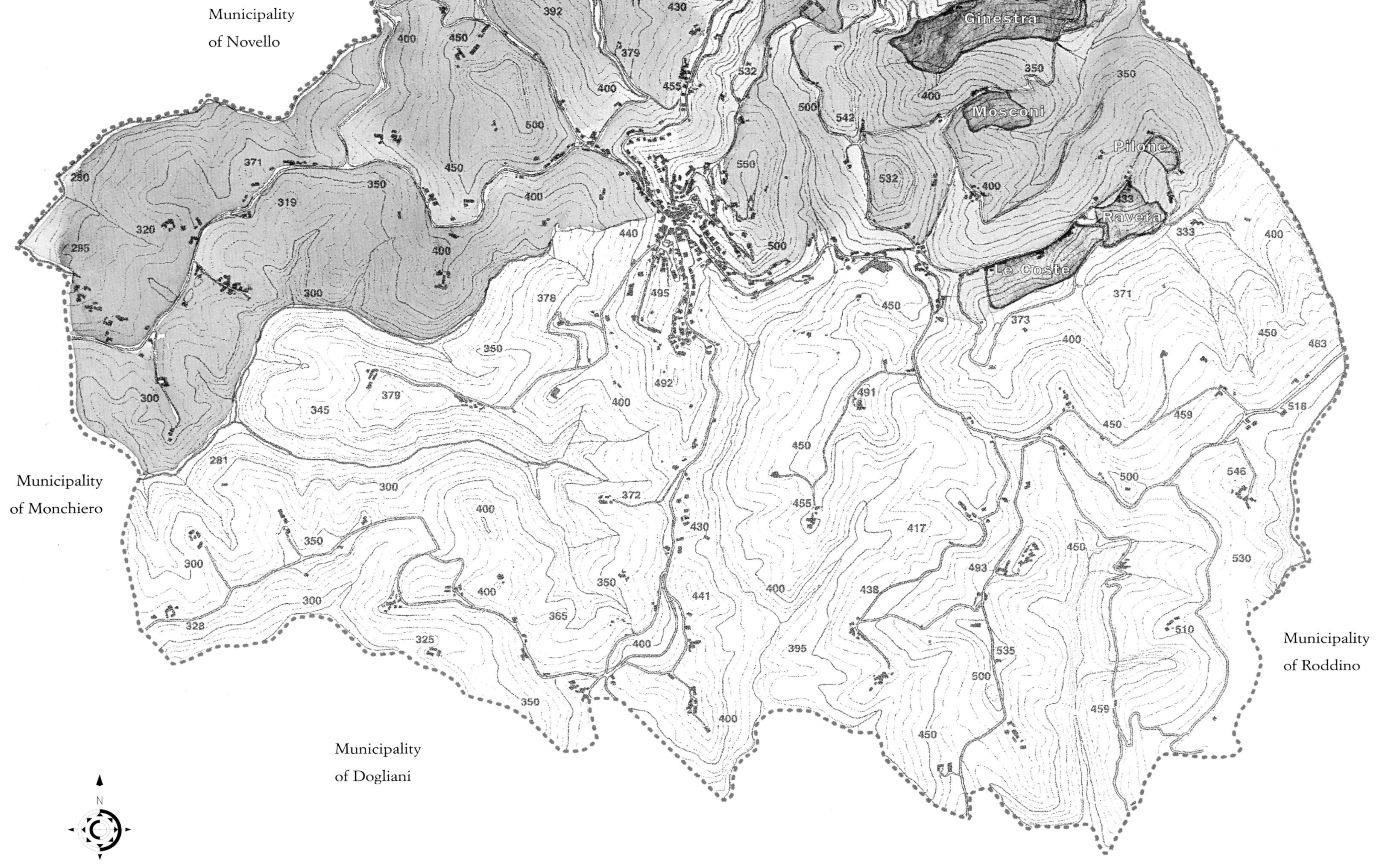
Municipality of Novello
Ginestra
Mosconi
Pilone
Ravera
Le Coste
Municipality of Monchiero
Municipality of Roddino
Municipality of Dogliani
N

Bussia

Arnulfo

It was in the year 1874, on 24 February, that pharmacist Carlo Arnulfo and his son Luigi, resident at Cherasco, signed the papers for the purchase of the *cascina* known as *dei Bertoloni* in the municipality of Monforte. It took only a few years for the commitment of the Arnulfos to bear fruit for they won prizes and medals at major exhibitions, in Turin in 1883 and in Paris in 1892. As is often the case, the name of the enterprising owners came to indicate a subzone, in this case in the plural – the *Arnulfi*. The growing area of Arnulfi borders to the north with Visette, and to the west and south with the local Bovi road. The elevation of the vineyard ranges from 250 to 320 metres and the vines face south or south west, moving round to the west in the lower section. Quite rightly, Ratti classified the subzone as one of the historic Barolo vineyards and the Arnulfo family may well have known this when they acquired the property from the Zabaldano brothers.

Bricco Cicala

Bricco Cicala, or *Bricco della Cicala* as it is often called in this part of the Langhe, is a delightful vineyard overlooked by woods. The vines form a bowl with aspects

that move round from south east, to south, and on to south west. This *sorì*, or slope, is sheltered from the wind and located in the upper part of the Bussia Soprana valley.
A few years ago, the denomination "Gran Bussia" was widely used to indicate that a wine contained a proportion of fruit from these vineyards. Ratti also uses the term in his *Carta del Barolo* (Map of Barolo). The name Gran Bussia has a basis in fact, thanks to the uniform quality of the grapes and the special mesoclimate of this lovely valley, protected by the high hillside running from the village of San Giovanni di Monforte to Boschetti at Barolo. Halfway up the hill, a road runs along the valley to the next hill, where the vineyards of Dardi and Pianpolvere are located. Between this road and Bricco Cicala is the Briccotto vineyard. To the south, the vineyard borders Bussia Soprana and to the east Romirasco, all of which belong to the Gran Bussia subzone.

Main labels

*Barolo Cicala – Poderi Aldo Conterno, Monforte d'Alba

Bussia Soprana

This is a separate village that bears the name of the prestigious Bussia subzone. Although there are two groups of houses, locals have always used the name Bussia to indicate the entire area.
Over time, broader or narrower interpretations of the name have grown up. We shall take our lead from an old grower from the subzone who told us, "Once, *Bussia* meant the road that goes from Bussia Soprana to Bussia Sottana. Some people still said *Gabutti della Bussia*, but not *Pianpolvere della Bussia*". Having noted this, we shall concentrate on the stupendous vineyard that spreads out below the houses in a little amphitheatre, aspected to the south east, south and south west.
There are about four hectares under vine, which have always produced superb grapes. Barolo from Bussia generally has excellent structure and crisp, clean aromas that evolve over time into notes of *goudron*, or tar. The prominent tannins merge with the other elements to produce a wine of outstanding character.
The lane that leads from the village to Pianpolvere separates the vineyard to the north from two other exceptional plots, Bricco Cicala and Colonnello.

Main labels

*Barolo Bussia – Bussia Soprana, Monforte d'Alba
*Barolo Bussia – Poderi Aldo Conterno, Monforte d'Alba
*Barolo Bussia – Giacosa Fratelli, Neive
*Barolo Mondoca di Bussia Soprana – Fratelli Oddero, La Morra
*Barolo Bussia – Prunotto, Alba

Bricco Cicala

Bussia Sottana

The vineyards of Bussia Sottana descend from the Alba-Dogliani provincial road towards the village itself. South west-facing, they have an elevation of between 280 metres, at Bussia Sottana, to 340 metres at the *cascina* of Rovella. The local road that leads down to Barolo marks off other south-facing vineyards that are sheltered by the hill. On the other side are the excellent vineyards of Castellero and Vignane in the municipality of Barolo.

At Bussia Sottana, there is a hollow that is well-protected from cold winds. The site climate here is very favourable and encourages excellent quality fruit.

Renato Ratti, in his *Carta del Barolo* (Map of Barolo), classified Bussia Sottana as a subzone with exceptional characteristics. Today, the houses of the village, like those at Bussia Soprana, clearly show the fall in population the Langhe area has suffered over the past half century. "Bussia used to have 75 families. Now, there are scarcely 75 people. In the 1930s, phylloxera devastated everything. People began to leave because there was so much poverty. Many went to America" (Francesco Alessandria, known as *Cichin*).

MAIN LABELS

*Barolo Bussia – Barale Fratelli, Barolo

*Barolo Bussia – Giacomo Fenocchio, Monforte d'Alba

*Barolo Bussia – Cascina Ballarin, La Morra

Cerretta di Perno

Seen from the road that leads from Castelletto to the hamlet of Capalotto, Cerretta, or in the Piedmontese dialect *Srea*, is a majestic vineyard overlooking the valley and facing south to south east. Surrounded as it is by vegetation, Cerretta is by no means easy to reach and it is also very difficult to cultivate. Nevertheless, it is an outstanding vineyard and, with Santo Stefano, represents the viticultural heritage of the village of Perno.

The soil is tufaceous but at the same time made of red earth. Since it is steep and hard to tend, the vineyard was for long left uncultivated. Today, nebbiolo is again grown here and the finest growing area extends over 20 Piedmontese *giornate*, or almost eight hectares. "There was always nebbiolo in the Cerretta vineyard but they're old vines and they yield very little fruit. There was a plot in the middle of Cerretta that was called San Giovanni. It was a marvellous place but it was left uncultivated. It was all nebbiolo there. You can still see the vines among the acacias" (Carlo Rapalino).

To get to this wonderful plot, you had to take the road from Perno to Disa and turn off towards the *cascina* Belvedere. Cerretta is almost unknown and should certainly be promoted.

Colonnello

The Colonnello vineyard, or Bricco del Colonnello, dominates Bussia Soprana and extends to the border with the municipality of Barolo in the subzone known as Monrobiolo. Careful research has failed to identify the origin of the name *Colonnello*, which means "Colonel".

This small vineyard is aspected to the southwest and basks in the sun's rays until nightfall. To the north, it borders on the municipality of Barolo while its southern edge is marked by the local road that links the village of Bussia Soprana with Bussia Sottana. Colonnello opens the long line of vineyards that spread out around Bussia Soprana. The wine has all the elegance and harmony of Barolo from the municipality of Barolo but also reveals the structure and power of the

Serralunga version. Bussia, of which Colonnello is part, is a buffer subzone that in the distant past, tended to look more to Barolo than to Monforte. In the week of the feast of the Ascension in mid August, the village holds one of the finest country fairs in the Langhe.

Main labels

*Barolo Vigna Colonnello – Bussia Soprana, Monforte d'Alba
*Barolo Colonnello – Poderi Aldo Conterno, Monforte d'Alba

Dardi

Today, Dardi is almost entirely abandoned but in the early twentieth century, more than 30 people lived here and the surrounding vineyards have always produced excellent nebbiolo grapes. Calissano, Pio Cesare and Prunotto – historic names in Langhe winemaking – for many years bought grapes from this vineyard to the north west of Pianpolvere, with which it forms a broad hillside front.
The best plots are above the village. Nebbiolo has always been grown there, even in the 1930s when poor prices for the variety led to its substitution with the more profitable barbera.
The peak of the vineyard is known as Mondoca, whereas the part that faces Bussia is a *sorì di mezzanotte*, or north-facing "midnight" hillslope unsuitable for nebbiolo. Most of the vineyard is aspected to south west and the total area is about seven hectares.

Main labels

*Barolo Vigna dei Dardi – Alessandro e Gian Natale Fantino, Monforte d'Alba
*Barolo Dardi Le Rose Bussia – Poderi Colla, Alba

Gabutti della Bussia

This vineyard is known as Gabutti della Bussia to distinguish it from Gabutti di Serralunga. It lies alongside the village of the same name and borders the vines of Romirasco. Gabutti closes off the natural amphitheatre of vineyards that runs from Bussia Soprana up to Bricco Cicala and Romirasco.
The vines vary from south west to west-facing, or what Langhe growers call a *sorì d'la seira*, or "evening" hillslope. The west-facing plots are highly prized because they are sheltered and warm enough for nebbiolo to ripen fully.
Gabutti is the pivotal area that links Bussia to the vineyards of Pianpolvere and Dardi. The village lies 395 metres above sea level and the vines go down to 350 metres, over an area of about five hectares.

Gavarini

Gavarini

The majestic sweep of the Gavarini vineyard is best admired from Ginestra. Located under a steep cut in the hillside and overlooked by woodlands, Gavarini lies around the *cascina* of the same name, exposing its vines to the rays of the morning and midday sun. The soil is particularly sandy. The *cascina* at Gavarini can be reached along a road that skirts the municipal cemetery or along a side road that leads off the Monforte-Perno road through a delightful, cool wood.

For over a century, the Grasso family has owned this farmhouse in the centre of a vineyard where nebbiolo and barbera reign supreme. Gavarini's grapes were long sought after by the Langhe's leading producers for their universally acknowledged quality.

Today, these plots can be cultivated mechanically. Once, however, they had to be worked by hand so it is easy to understand their importance for, and the effort required from, the generations who handed this heritage on from father to son. Nebbiolo was already grown at Gavarini in the early twentieth century and it was here that the first new rootstock was planted after phylloxera. The vineyard covers almost six hectares and borders on Grassi, another exceptionally fine cru.

Barolo obtained from the grapes grown here opens very slowly on the nose and is less immediately attractive than wine from Ginestra but it does have impressive power and structure. In great vintages, it has excellent ageing prospects.

MAIN LABELS

*Barolo Gavarini Vigna Chiniera – Elio Grasso, Monforte d'Alba

*Barolo Rüncot – Elio Grasso, Monforte d'Alba

Ginestra or Ginestre

The best sited parts of the Ginestra vineyard can be divided into two sections. The first is broad and even, starting at Rodoli and descending to Ginestra to continue towards Serralunga. The second, and smaller, plot lies at the Pajana *cascina* and faces south east. The larger plot also faces south east, with the exception of the central section, below Ginestra, which is south-facing.

Ginestra

Ginestra can be considered a historic Barolo vineyard as it was already cited, together with Bussia and Pugnane, in the late nineteenth century by Fantini as a part of Monforte that could yield Barolo of "superior excellence". The central section, called *Sorì* has a more compact soil type than the sand and greyish marl of the area that overlooks the Tallerio di Castiglione stream.

Ginestra della Pajana, which covers about six Piedmontese *giornate*, or just over two hectares, was purchased in 1996 by Renzo Seghesio. From Pajana, which was made famous by Clerico, you have a superb view of the imposing vineyards of Grassi and Gavarini.

Greater Ginestra extends over about 40 Piedmontese *giornate*, or 15 hectares, and the altitude of the entire vineyard ranges from 300 to 400 metres. The access road to Ginestra runs past the cemetery of Monforte, rising up to a high hill that overlooks the great vineyards of Monforte and Serralunga. As you descend towards Ginestra, you can admire a panorama of breathtaking beauty.

This is a valley of long-lived, superbly structured Barolos, which for decades was the hunting ground of the great winemakers as the grapes from the area give the body required to make an outstanding wine.

Main labels

*Barolo Ciabot Mentin Ginestra – Domenico Clerico, Monforte d'Alba
*Barolo Pajana – Domenico Clerico, Monforte d'Alba
*Barolo Ginestra – Paolo Conterno, Monforte d'Alba
*Barolo Sorì Ginestra – Conterno Fantino, Monforte d'Alba
*Barolo Ginestra Vigna Casa Maté – Elio Grasso, Monforte d'Alba
*Barolo Pajana – Pajana di Renzo Seghesio, Monforte d'Alba

Gramolere

Gramolere extends over a long strip of hillside, descending from 450 metres, near the cascina Pemollo, to the plots below the hamlet of Gramolere Sottane, at 350 metres above sea level. Aspects vary from west, to south west, and south.

Once, this area came under the municipality of Castelletto, now suppressed.
The vineyard has always been highly regarded by local growers, not just because of its orientation but also because of the soil. "Gramolere, land of *gramun* (couch grass) and *pere* (stones)", say the old timers. Another saying goes, "Where couch grass grows, the wine is good".

People can remember nebbiolo from here with robust must weights, as well as excellent barbera fruit. In fact once, it was common practice to add a little barbera to the nebbiolo that went into Barolo. The results were impressive.

This vineyard, which deserves to be reassessed and more widely known, extends over roughly 35 Piedmontese *giornate*, or nearly 14 hectares.

Main labels

*Barolo Gramolere – Giovanni Manzone, Monforte d'Alba

*Barolo Gramolere Bricat – Giovanni Manzone, Monforte d'Alba

*Barolo Cascina Gramolere – Pressenda, Monforte d'Alba

Grassi

Once, Grassi stood on edge of the municipal territory of Monforte d'Alba, as the present-day districts of Perno and Castelletto formed a municipality of their own. Here, too, over the years, the population has fallen steadily.
The vineyard lies between 400 and 300 metres above sea level and faces south, looking onto the Ginestra vineyard, and south east where it descends to the Talloria di Castiglione river, in the direction of Serralunga. The best growing area extends over roughly seven hectares.
Grassi is a natural extension to the east of Gavarini but the soil is more compact and less sandy, especially in the lower part of the vineyard. The northern border of the vineyard is the Grassi local road, which descends through a wood from the Monforte-Perno municipal road. The eastern boundary is in the vicinity of the old *cascina* Roggeri.

La Villa

La Villa is a vineyard with a superb south-facing aspect that links the hamlet of Villa with the Assunta area. Here, you will find a lovely country church that boasts a superb fifteenth-century fresco of the Virgin and Child. Beside the church is a small cemetery that, until a few years ago, was surrounded by trees. These were then cut down to make way for new vine plantings. But the finest part of the vineyard, where nebbiolo is grown, lies in front of the Grassi farmhouse. To the north, it is marked off by the lane that leads to Assunta and the vines descend from an average elevation of 370 metres to about 300 metres. The Rio dei Grassi stream flows at the foot of the vineyard. To the east, the hill turns away and the vines are aspected from south to south east, opposite the hamlet of Collaretto in the municipality of Serralunga d'Alba.

Main labels

*Barolo Vigneto La Villa – Fratelli Seghesio, Monforte d'Alba

Mosconi

Le Coste

The long road from San Giuseppe to the houses at Ravera marks off this vineyard to the north. It descends, with a south or south east-facing aspect to the minor Tetti road, its southern boundary.

But this is also the border of the Barolo zone, and it is no coincidence that the vines here, even though they are slightly exposed to the wind, have been included in the DOCG zone.

The vineyard known as Castlé is particularly highly regarded, with its marly white, tufaceous soil, which is similar to that on the rest of the hillslope.

It was with grapes from here that Giacomo Conterno vinified the first Monfortino.

For as long as anyone can remember, nebbiolo has been grown at Le Coste. The total area is about 20 Piedmontese *giornate*, or just under eight hectares.

Main labels

*Barolo Le Coste – Ferdinando Principiano, Monforte

Mosconi

Here we have a small group of farm buildings at the respectable elevation of 420 metres above sea level and a steep, south-facing vineyard opposite the long line of houses at Le Coste. The white tufaceous soil has always been planted to nebbiolo, which thrives here. The wine obtained is a robustly structured Barolo with generous tannins. In the cellar, it develops with remarkable austerity and a rich abundance of aromas.

Mosconi has always yielded Barolos of distinction but its Barberas are equally impressive. Winemakers like Prunotto, Conterno and Basso were well aware of these virtues and were only too happy to purchase fruit here.

Until the Second World War, there were three separate Moscone families resident here, cultivating roughly three hectares of vines. The road that leads from San Giuseppe to Mosconi skirts the hamlet of Conterni, where we should also mention a small south-facing plot that has an excellent quality profile.

MAIN LABELS

*Barolo Mosconi – Bussia Soprana, Monforte d'Alba

Munie

The Pugnane road, which leads down from the Alba-Dogliani provincial road to the *cascina* Pugnane, marks the border between the municipality of Monforte d'Alba and that of Castiglione Falletto. It is also the boundary of the Munie vineyard, whose name means "nuns" in the local dialect. Munie extends across about 30 Piedmontese *giornate*, or about 11 hectares, and faces from west to south west.

The altitude ranges from 330 metres down to the 250 metres of the *cascina* Conterno, better known as *cascina* Sciulun. Beyond this plot, the Pugnane vineyard begins.

In the lower part of Munie is the singular *cascina* Lanza, also known as Bofani. Here, many years ago, the Bussia fair was held in the meadow. People came from Barolo and Castiglione to take part. In the upper part of the Pugnane road is the *cascina* Funtanin, run by the Fontana family for five generations. An excellent nebbiolo area, Munie yields wines of great elegance and finesse.

MAIN LABELS

*Barolo Vigneto Bofani – Batasiolo, La Morra

*Barolo Bussia Munie – Sciulun, Monforte d'Alba

*Barolo Bussia Vigna Munie – Armando Parusso, Monforte d'Alba

Pianpolvere or Pian della Polvere

The origin of the name Pianpolvere, or Pian della Polvere, is much debated. The story goes that Napoleon's army stored gunpowder (*polvere da sparo*) in the area. Once, *cascina* Pianpolvere belonged to the bishop of Alba, its fields and vineyards covering more than 80 Piedmontese giornate, or over 30 hectares. The village of Dardi and the *cascine* of Visette and Maniscot were all part of the estate. When the Siccardi law was passed and the state expropriated church holdings, this large estate was put up for sale. As excommunication was the fate reserved for those who acquired former ecclesiastical property, the entire estate was purchased by Jews, who were unconcerned about such threats. Subsequently, the purchasers did excellent business selling off the land in small plots.

The vines of Pianpolvere now cover more that 16 hectares, embracing the *cascina*, a fine example of rural architecture, the *cascina* known as Brichet and the vineyards of Pianpolvere Soprano, with their building. The average elevation is 350 metres and at the *cascina* Brichet rises to 400 metres From here, it is possible to admire the vines of Pianpolvere and Dardi, separated first by the local road leading down from the Alba-Monforte highway and then by a long *capezzagna*, or unsurfaced lane. The provincial road forms the eastern border of this historic vineyard, classified by Ratti as a subzone with remarkable quality characteristics. The aspect is almost entirely uniform, with the rows facing south west.

Main labels

*Barolo Pianpolvere Soprano Bussia – Pianpolvere Soprano, Monforte d'Alba

Pilone

This vineyard does not have a uniform aspect but most of it can be regarded as a good *sorì*. Here, there is a *cascina* with a votive pillar, or *pilone*, dedicated to the Virgin. This side of the hill, which also includes Ravera and Le Coste, is the most southerly point of the Barolo DOCG zone. It looks onto the higher hills of Roddino, which herald the beginning of the Upper Langhe. The vine-growing area covers about two and a half hectares, running down to a small but very lovely valley crossed by the Talloria di Castiglione stream.

Pressenda

Mentioned by Fantini, the Pressenda vineyard is situated around the houses of Pressenda, through which runs the road that goes down from Castelletto to Molino di Perno. Directly opposite, on the far side of the Talloria di Castiglione stream, rises the impressive castle of Serralunga surrounded by its village and its magnificent vineyards. The growing area at Pressenda covers about 18 Piedmontese *giornate*, or nearly seven hectares. Most of the rows face south east and the altitude ranges from 300 to 350 metres above sea level. The area is part of the village of Castelletto, which was once a separate municipality.

MAIN LABELS

*Barolo Söri Pressenda – Giovanni Pira, Monforte d'Alba

Pugnane

Pugnane is the natural continuation of the hill that descends from the Munie. Like that area, it faces west or south west. The soil is richer than that of Munie, especailly around the *cascina* Pugnane, at 264 metres above sea level. At Pugnane, the municipality of Monforte is wedged in among those of Barolo, La Morra and Castiglione Falletto.

The hills here run parallel so the vineyards face in the same direction and the soil types are pretty much the same. In the nineteenth century, Pugnane was already known as a choice location in which to grow nebbiolo. Naturally, the area we are interested in is the one facing the municipality of Barolo, overlooking the local Bussia Sottana road. On the other slope grow the lesser nebbiolo vines and other crops. The vineyard covers an area of nine hectares.

Ravera

This vineyard takes its name from the Ravera family. In the early twentieth century, Sabino Ravera was noted for his education and skill as an administrator of agricultural estates. From the houses, which once belonged to the Raveras, the vines descend the rather steep slope to the Pian Romualdo road, which marks their southern boundary. The same road forms the western boundary with Le Coste. The higher vines face south west then the vineyard goes down to two attractive plots, Grafion and Barcalin, that face due south and enjoy a favourable site climate.

Romirasco

Cascina Romirasco stands on a ridge at 400 metres above sea level. The view from up there takes in the *Bussia* subzone, the village of Perno and, further off,

Castiglione Falletto. Behind the *cascina*, in a sheltered position, the splendid rows of nebbiolo cover the hillside between Bricco Cicala and the vines of Gabutti. The upper part of the vineyard was once crossed by a road, which has now disappeared. It linked the hamlet of Gabutti with the school at Bussia. But we shall return to Romirasco, which has the following vital statistics: an area of nearly 18 Piedmontese *giornate*, or just under seven hectares, aspected almost entirely to south west, and a single owner, Aldo Conterno, who nurtures the vines to produce a Barolo with an outstanding sensory profile.

MAIN LABELS

*Barolo Gran Bussia – Poderi Aldo Conterno, Monforte d'Alba

*Barolo Romirasco – Poderi Aldo Conterno, Monforte d'Alba

Santo Stefano di Perno

As you go down from Monforte to Castiglione, you can admire, when you come to the village of Gabutti, the lovely vineyard of Santo Stefano on the far side of the Rio delle Gramolere. The fine ridge is dominated by a delightful twelfth-century Romanesque chapel, whose attractive apse was restored a few years ago. The chapel is dedicated to Saint Stephen the Martyr.

Until recently, the vines around the chapel belonged to the diocese of Alba but the plot has always been known as the *Vigna del Parcu* (the parish priest's vineyard).

Once, the nearby hamlet of Perno was a separate municipality and older, wiser heads have always looked on Santo Stefano as an excellent location. "Santo Stefano di Perno is the best place. There are lots of good sites but the grapes from Santo Stefano, in the part where it looks onto Bussia, are better than all the rest" (Carlo Rapalino).

Borgogno used to say, "They can say what they like but you won't find any Barolo as good as the parish priest's" (Francesco Alessandria, nicknamed *Cichin*).

All the reports agree but the very nature of the soil and the excellent location confirm that this is a superior vineyard. It extends for about 15 Piedmontese *giornate*, or less than six hectares, at an average height of 360 metres above sea level. The tiny chapel on the hilltop stands at 390 metres. Should anyone ever venture to draw up a Barolo "league table", Santo Stefano would certainly deserve a leading position, for the quality of both its grapes and the wine they yield.

MAIN LABELS

*Barolo Santo Stefano di Perno – Giuseppe Mascarello e Figlio, Monchiero

*Barolo Vigna Cappella di Santo Stefano – Podere Rocche dei Manzoni, Monforte d'Alba

Visette

The parallel hills create small valleys and vineyards with good sunlight, the *sorì*. On the opposite slopes are the less fortunate vines, the *uvé*. We find the two terms, in an Italianised form, in a number of notarial deeds from the nineteenth century, as *sorito* and *uvaro*. Here, too, at Visette, the *uvaro* faces north to Dardi and Pianpolvere while the *sorito*, the area we are interested in, extends from *cascina* Visette, at 340 metres, to the Bovi local road, which forms its border to the south and west. To the east, Visette borders on Arnulfi. The vineyard is south to south west-facing and extends over nearly 15 Piedmontese *giornate*, or almost six hectares.

From cascina Visette, there is a fine view of the vines of Dardi and Pianpolvere. To get a really good view of Visette and Arnulfi, you can take the San Giovanni local road. Looking down, you can clearly distinguish the features and borders of these two lovely subzones.

Main labels

*Barolo Bricco Visette – Attilio Ghisolfi, Monforte d'Alba

Ginestra

Our selection

Population 1,926
Height 480 metres asl

INFORMATION

Town Hall
Piazza Monsignor Dallorto
Tel. + 39 0173 78202

THE WINERIES

Gianfranco Alessandria
Località Manzoni, 13
Tel. + 39 0173 78576 - 0173 787222
Having started off quietly in the 1990s with just over four hectares under vine, Gianfranco Alessandria quickly drew the attention of winelovers with an outstandingly elegant Barolo. The fresh, spicy aromas of his 1993 set the critics talking. Since 1995, Gianfranco's standard-label Barolo has been joined by the San Giovanni, a seriously stylish wine with a tad more structure.

Bussia Soprana
Località Bussia Soprana, 87
Tel. + 39 039 305182
After spending a considerable number of years distributing fine wines around Italy, Silvano Casiraghi decided to find a vineyard where he could make premium wines himself. That being the case, he was bound to fall in love with the fragrances of Barolo from Bussia. Soon, the Bussia Soprana winery was turning out its bottles, thanks to assistance from Silvano's partner in the enterprise, Guido Rossi. From the Bussia plots, the pair make Barolo Bussia and Vigna Colonnello. Not long after they started, the estate acquired vines in Mosconi, one of Barolo's historic names.

Domenico Clerico
Località Manzoni Cucchi, 67
Tel. + 39 0173 78171
Domenico Clerico is one of the great names of the Langhe, a reputation gained for his astounding consistency of quality. He gained attention with his Barolo Ciabot Mentin Ginestra from the 1982 vintage and, the following year, began to release the enormously successful Arte, a blend of 80-90 per cent nebbiolo with separately vinified barbera. Next came Barolo Pajana, a fresh-tasting, modern wine aged in barriques for two years. The 1990 version was in a class of its own. The 1995 vintage saw the first release of Barolo Cristina, from a plot at Mosconi.

Poderi Aldo Conterno
Località Bussia, 48
Tel. + 39 0173 78150
Gran Bussia is universally acknowledged as one of the finest interpretations of Barolo. Created in 1970 from a selection of the estate's best grapes, Gran Bussia – released only in the best vintages – has shown how it is possible to achieve a perfect marriage of aromas and flavour with unhurried cellaring. Recent tastings of all the vintages have confirmed the staying power of the wine, which exalts the majestic nose of nebbiolo while offering a palate that becomes increasingly velvety with the passing years. The other Barolo selections released are Bussia Soprana, Romirasco, Cicala and Colonnello. The last two, in particular, have shown that they can frequently scale the heights of quality, coming close to the dizzy peak of Gran Bussia. Another wine worth noting from this cellar is Favot, a monovarietal Nebbiolo.

Giacomo Conterno
Località Ornati, 2
Tel. + 39 0173 78221
Wine has been made here since the end of the eighteenth century and that may be why Giovanni Conterno is acknowledged by everyone as one of the leading representatives of the great Barolo tradition. He is not, however, celebrated merely for historical reasons, or because Monfortino – it was not yet called Barolo – has been bottled and labelled here since 1915. It is a wine that combines the strength of the territory at Serralunga (the Francia subzone) with impeccably painstaking vinification and leisurely ageing, first in large barrels and then in bottle. The 7,000 bottles released have become famous all over the world, in part because of a cellaring potential that can exceed half a century.
This oenological pearl is joined by Barolo Cascina Francia, also available in a Riserva version.

Paolo Conterno
Via Ginestra, 34
Frazione Ginestra
Tel. + 39 0173 78415
Located in the very heart of Ginestra, this winery oversees seven hectares under vine, making it a leading player in the subzone. About 25,000 bottles are released each year of Barolo Ginestra, aged in large barrels of French oak. It is a per-

fect example of the vineyard's characteristics of power on the palate and finesse on the nose and, in the best vintages, those virtues are exalted in the Barolo Ginestra Riserva.

Conterno Fantino
Via Ginestra 1
Località Bricco Bastia
Tel. + 39 0173 78204
Winemaking in the Langhe received a boost in the 1980s when many growers decided to become producers and proudly released bottles with their own names on the labels. The Conterno Fantino cellar was one such and quickly established itself as a leading estate, capable of achieving the highest levels of quality and maintaining them. Guido Fantino – competently assisted by the entire family – demonstrated his skills with his 1982 Barolo Sorì Ginestra, a vineyard with one of the most fascinating aromatic profiles in the subzone. Three years ater, he released one of the Langhe's most celebrated blends, the Monprà, obtained mainly from nebbiolo and barbera. The other estate selection is called Vigna del Gris. The success is well-deserved and founded on painstaking work in the vineyard, followed up in the rooms of the superbly equipped, panoramically sited cellar.

Alessandro e Gian Natale Fantino
Via Silvano, 18
Tel. + 39 0173 78253
You have to walk along the rows of the Dardi vineyard to realise how much commitment and respect the Fantinos have for their grapes and for the natural environment. Chemical intervention of any kind is banned. The success of the harvest lies entirely in the hands of the workers and the animals – whether airborne or earthbound – that collaborate and contend in the search for biological equilibrium. Those efforts are completed in one of the smallest and most beautiful cellars in the Langhe, in an historic building in the centre of Monforte.
In addition to the Barolo Vigna dei Dardi, nebbiolo-based wines include 1,500 bottles of Passito with an understated sweetness and powerful impact on the palate.

Attilio Ghisolfi
Cascina Visette, 27
Località Bussia
Tel. + 39 0173 78345
The estate is a small one and no more than 30,000 bottles are released each year but in little more than a decade, the name Ghisolfi has become well-respected by lovers of Barolo. This is thanks to the vineyard experience of Attilio and the commitment of young Gian Marco, a skilful cellarman who knows his way around the French barriques and Slavonian barrels. The picture is complete if we add the well-placed plot at Visette, where the grapes easily acquire good concentration and ripen well. This is where Barolo Bricco Visette comes from.
A small proportion of the nebbiolo joins the freisa in the unusual and very attractive Langhe Rosso Carlin.

Elio Grasso
Località Ginestra, 40
Tel. + 39 0173 78491
In the late 1970s, Elio Grasso set himself a challenging, but rewarding, objective: to make premium Barolo and go back to live and work on the family *cascina*, in one of the finest locations in the entire Barolo DOCG zone. Achieving that goal has not been easy but as you taste the wines in the new cellar, you can have no doubt about the outcome. Elio gained a reputation as a producer with his Barolo 1988 and since then – vintage permitting – the name Elio Grasso has become increasingly well-known as one of the Langhe's top producers. His nebbiolo vines are planted in two magnificent locations on the 13-hectare estate and go into the Barolo Gavarini Vigna Chiniera and Barolo Ginestra Vigna Casa Maté. In outstanding years, Grasso makes a special selection called Rüncot with the finest fruit from Gavarini.

Giovanni Manzone
Via Castelletto, 9
Tel. + 39 0173 78114
Giovanni Manzone has always been a keen viticulturist. He has concentrated on nebbiolo but he also grows less well-known varieties, always with excellent results. He has recently acquired a cellar that lets him vinify they way he wants to so we are hoping for even better results in the near future. But the two Barolos Giovanni has released in recent years, the Gramolere and the Gramolere Bricat, are already outstanding. Part of the estate's nebbiolo goes into the Langhe Rosso Tris, together with dolcetto and barbera.

Monti
Località San Sebastiano, 39
Frazione Càmia
Tel. + 39 0173 78391
Pier Paolo Monti is a young builder from Turin. In 1996, he acquired this lovely estate, immediately putting the emphasis on quality, and the results have been very satisfactory. The first wine released, a cask-conditioned Barbera d'Alba, was very well received. The winery is steadily expanding and in 2003, the first bottles of Barolo Bussia will emerge.

Armando Parusso
Località Bussia, 55
Tel. + 39 0173 78257
At Marco Parusso's cellar, you can touch – and taste – the differences in the sensory profiles of vineyards that are near to each other and apparently very similar: Marco bottles three separate Barolos.
They are the Barolo Bussia Vigna Munie, Barolo Bussia Vigna Rocche, both in the municipality of Monforte, and Barolo Mariondino from Castiglione Falletto. Soon, the comparative tasting options will be increased with the release of the Barolo Bussia Vigna Fiurin 1998.

Pianpolvere Soprano
Località Bussia, 32
Tel. + 39 0173 78335
Valentino Migliorini's new investment is now onstream after he increased his holdings in Monforte by acquir-

ing this historic winery, once the property of the Fenocchio family. Today, you will find in the shops the Barolos that came with the sale but 2005 will see the release of the new 1999 Barolo Pianpolvere Soprano Bussia Riserva, vinified Valentino's way.

Ferdinando Principiano
Via Alba, 19
Tel. + 39 0173 787158
Having hit the headlines with his surprising Barolo 1993, young Ferdinando is pursuing a policy of gradual expansion of the estate vinestock. He started with only 1,300 bottles from the lovely Boscareto vineyard at Serralunga. The 1996 vintage saw production begin from another small plot at Le Coste in Monforte.

Flavio Roddolo
Località Sant'Anna, 5
Bricco Appiani
Tel. + 39 0173 78535
Here is another rising star in the Barolo firmament. After years as a grower, Flavio Roddolo decided to bottle his own wine ten years or so ago and the results were greeted with enthusiastic appreciation. His first Barolo, with grapes from Le Coste, came from the 1993 harvest and since then, production has been rock steady, in a style that exalts the contribution of the fruit over the wood. The cellar also releases a few hundred bottles of exquisite Langhe Nebbiolo.

Podere Rocche dei Manzoni
Località Manzoni Soprani, 3
Tel. + 39 0173 78421
Valentino Migliorini arrived in the Langhe in the 1970s with clear ideas, determined to build up a good-sized, top-quality cellar. His dream came true and today, Rocche dei Manzoni is one of the most important and prestigious wineries in the Langhe. It is also destined to expand, if we are to judge by the investments being made in the vineyard and the cellar. Vigna Big at Mosconi, Vigna Cappella at Santo Stefano di Perno, Vigna d'la Roul and Ciabot d'Agust at Ginestra and Madonna della Assunta and La Villa di Castellero are some of the finest sites in Monforte and they enable Valentino to produce five magnificent Barolo selections. Part of the estate's nebbiolo goes into the Bricco Manzoni, one of the first Langhe wines to be aged in barriques, as well as into the Langhe Rosso Quatr Nas.

Podere Ruggeri Corsini
Località Bussia Corsini, 106
Tel. + 39 0173 78625
Loredana Addari and Nicola Argamante of the Podere Ruggeri Corsini are two exciting newcomers to Monforte. Their wines are exciting and have already gained admirers among lovers of Barolo. Taste the recent addition to the list, Barolo Corsini.

Fratelli Seghesio
Frazione Castelletto, 20
Tel. + 39 0173 78108
Brothers Aldo and Riccardo Seghesio are dedicated winemakers whose vines are in the La Villa vineyard at Castelletto. Their eight or so hectares are all in La Villa and the pair release

Santo Stefano di Perno

about 50,000 bottles each year of premium-quality wines, from Dolcetto to Barbera and including a blend of local grapes with varieties from Bordeaux. But the Seghesios' strong suit is their Barolo La Villa. The roughly 20,000 bottles released each year are every bit as good as many wines from much more celebrated vineyards.

WHERE TO SLEEP

Giardino da Felicin
Via Vallada, 18
Tel. + 39 0173 78225
Three stars. Quiet, well-furnished and very comfortable rooms with a panoramic view over the hills are the main attractions of this delightful country hotel, an ideal place to rest and enjoy good food. Breakfast is particularly memorable, served in a room with a terrace looking onto the valley.

Villa Beccaris
Via Bava Beccaris, 1
Tel. + 39 0173 78158
Three stars. The Villa Beccaris hotel stands in the upper part of the village, in a pleasant building on the edge of the historic centre. The rooms are elegantly furnished with period furniture and upholstery. The long-established gardens offer shade in summer and a climate-controlled gazebo is available in winter.

EATING OUT

Giardino da Felicin
Via Vallada, 18
Tel. + 39 0173 78225
For three generations, the Giardino da Felicin has been a mandatory stopping point for tourists, particularly from abroad. Its menu offers an elegant array of Langhe cuisine. The cellar is extraordinarily beautiful and equally well-stocked. A full meal in one of the Langhe's most prestigious eateries will cost around € 50.00, without wine.

La Salita
Via Silvano, 4-6
Tel. + 39 0173 787196
Part *osteria* and part wine bar, La Salita proposes a limited range of expertly prepared dishes, accompanied by the great wines of the Langhe from its truly monumental wine list. A branch of the ARCI organisation, La Salita also welcomes those who merely want to enjoy an excellent bottle of wine. Prices are attractive, for the food and for the wines, which are not burdened by excessive mark-ups.

Trattoria della Posta
Località Sant'Anna, 87
Tel. + 39 0173 78120
The Trattoria della Posta has moved to new and more comfortable surroundings in borgata Sant'Anna but the cuisine and the ambience have remained the same. The classic Langhe dishes are always available, *tajarin* (Piedmontese pasta) and *muscolo al Barolo* (beef in Barolo) at the top of the list. The wine list is extensive and balanced, with all the great Barolo vineyards represented.

WHAT TO BUY

Enoteca di Monforte
Via Palestro, 2
A carefully considered selection, put together with skill and commitment.

THE GREATS OF BAROLO

Giacomo Conterno

1895-1971

As you retrace the story of Giacomo Conterno, it is impossible not to be entranced by the saga of this Langhe family and the role it has played in the world of wine at Monforte.

Giacomo Conterno was born in 1895 at Tucuman in Argentina, where his father Giovanni had emigrated. In the early twentieth century, the family returned to Italy and settled at the *cascina* belonging to Giacomo's mother at Le Coste. In 1908, Giovanni Conterno and his second wife, Marietta Vivaldo, opened an *osteria* at the village of San Giuseppe and began to make wine. Giacomo, his brother Franco and their sister Annetta all helped with the family business, then Giacomo was called up in the Great War of 1915-18, when he served as a mountain artilleryman on the Karst front.

When he came back home, the Conterno cellar began to produce substantial quantities of wine that was sold in casks, not just in Piedmont and Liguria but also in the Americas. The Oreste Benvenuto forwarding agency in Genoa sent Langhe wines to Argentina for Piedmontese emigrants, thanks to the efforts of uncle Ernesto Conterno, who lived there.

These were difficult years for the agricultural economy of the entire zone. The division between growers and the winemaking industry grew increasingly clear-cut. There were no small grower-producers.

In those days, discussions between father and son were principally on what containers to use for transport. Young Giacomo preferred glass demijohns to the customary wooden casks. The Conternos did, however, agree on the need to meet the demands of a market that was now ready for a great Barolo. It would be a Barolo made only in outstanding vintages, with long fermentation, so that it would have great ageing potential. They started by bottling a 1920 Riserva and that was how Monfortino was born.

Giacomo Conterno was now a fully-fledged producer, visiting customers personally to consolidate his position in the markets of Turin and Genoa. Most of the wine was still sold unbottled but the bottled version was beginning to acquire admirers. The Conterno advertising slogan for the tenth Fiera del Tartufo in 1938 was, *Conterno Giacomo - Produttori Vini - Specialità Super - Barolo - Monfortino* (Giacomo Conterno - Wine Producers - Super Specialties - Barolo - Monfortino).

When Italy went to war in 1940, Giovanni had been dead for six years. Giacomo continued to run the cellar and the small Osteria del Ponte, where for some time his wife Antonia had been working alongside the legendary "Marietta del Pont". Many partisans still remember them, their generosity and their considerable courage in running the risk of serious reprisals. It is, perhaps, in this willingness to help others, this sociable personality, that we can find one of the main characteristics of Giacomo Conterno. He shared the esteem and friendship of every-

Ginestra, Mosconi, Gavarini

one, from Cappellano at Borgogno, Giulio Mascarello at Bressano of Fontanafredda, Scarzello of the Opera Pia to the many growers who supplied his grapes. Conterno always advised growers to buy cement vats so they could vinify their own fruit. That way they would not be forced to sell off their harvest. "You have to sell grapes in ten days but you've got a whole year for wine", he used to say to encourage growers who wanted to start vinifying on their own.

After the war, market pressure to bottle was decisive for the Conterno estate, in part because of the prestige that Barolo was beginning to acquire. We should remember the importance at the time for Barolo sales of Christmas purchases. Before Champagne became popular as a status symbol, families and companies in Italy used to give Barolo as a prestige wine gift. Theססnternos, like many wineries around Alba, reaped the benefit of this custom and there were substantial orders from large companies like FIAT, RIV and Pirelli.

When Giacomo Conterno handed over to his children in 1961, the Cantina Conterno was a thriving enterprise. Until his death in 1971, Giacomo was to maintain his firm view of Barolo, "A wine will be acknowledged and respected when everyone makes it well". We can only note that this is an important message in a land of individualists, often split by senseless personal feuds. Giacomo's words anticipate modern marketing. Only widespread premium-quality production can bring prestige to the Langhe and its wines. That was Giacomo Conterno's conviction.

When the grapes were trod, not pressed

Among the people who came to Bussia to buy grapes were Maiocco from Asti, Calissano from Alba and others. They set the prices, as the buyers do now. From 1928 to 1940, Barolo went through a crisis. Instead of nebbiolo, we planted barbera, which had a higher yield and commanded a better price.

After 1930, phylloxera hit us. It wiped out entire vineyards. We had to replant, grubbing up the soil with picks. There weren't any tractors, then. There was plenty of labour, though, and we worked from dawn till dusk. Families were large back then. At Bussia, there were 75 electricity meters, one for each household. I doubt if there are 75 people today.

In the 1930s, there was a lot of poverty and many left to seek their fortune in America and elsewhere. But I built this house in 1932, paying five *soldi* for ten kilograms of bricks and four *soldi* for ten kilograms of pine trunks to make the roof. A *soldo* was five hundredths of a lira.

My father had a bit of money set aside. He got by. He was a driver who took stuff to Turin with two mules and did the trip in three days. I went with him. In the evening, he'd stop off in Bra and we ate for 17 *soldi*. There were 60 or 70 drivers. Afterwards, those who could afford to smoked a cigarette.

If you didn't have any land, you became a tenant farmer or a casual labourer. The grapes always found buyers. We'd use the worst of the crop to make a little wine for the family. There were some tenant farmers who had no wine at all left by the springtime.

The Cantina Sociale at Castiglione Falletto, the one founded around 1911-12, had a vat that could hold 7,000 kilograms of grapes. Six of us, all boys, used to tread the fruit from the evening to the morning. I was about 16. Over the cellar was a large hall where people danced, put on theatre performances and puppet shows. It was also a wine bar. (*Winter 1990*)

Francesco Alessandria
known as *Cichin*
born 1900
grower in Monforte

Wine and gambling

I bought and sold a few grapes and a little wine but my main occupation was as an innkeeper. I went out into the vineyards to test the berries and if the grapes had a high enough sugar content, I would buy the whole lot and pay a little extra. When I saw vines overloaded with fruit, or the grapes didn't have a high enough must weight, then I wouldn't buy them, even if they came from a good zone. The winemakers who bought from me wanted the grapes to be picked late, when they were properly ripe. The problem with many growers was that they harvested too soon. You'd start buying in the best vineyards at Monforte, then go up the hillslopes to Cerretto Langhe, where the fruit ripened later. Out in the rows, you'd test the sugar, the acidity, everything. But I'm talking about 20 years ago.

Lots of *cascina* owners sold part of their fruit straight away for cash and then filled their cellars with wine. When we'd finished loading the grapes, we'd go to the weighbridge and there, or in my *osteria*, we'd conclude the deal. Load it and pay for it. Then came the big companies from outside the area that paid at two or three months. I'd telephone and get them to leave something on account for the farmers.
I was a grape agent for one month, during the harvest, and then for the rest of the year I sold the new wine. I took two per cent and the seller paid me. Wine merchants would often come. Sometimes, on market day, there were 15 or 20 at my place in the upstairs room. They tasted all the samples and selected the wine, which was sold by the barrel. Nowadays, you can't find a barrel for love nor money. One producer had a 60-*brenta* barrel (3,000 litres) that tasted of wood, of sawdust. I told him every year, for ten years, "Break up that barrel. It's got woodworm". He was convinced the wine was good but he never got very much money.
This area was very good for barbera and dolcetto. They pressed a bit of nebbiolo, too, but it wasn't considered to be top quality. The Meneghinis, the Sardos and the Cappas from Dogliani came to buy fruit here. All this was before the Second World War.
For my *osteria*, I used to buy an average of 120 to 130 *brente* each year. I bought Barbera, Dolcetto, Freisa and sometimes Barolo, too. And we bottled the lot because wine should always be served at table in a bottle, never in a carafe. In 42 years, I never had a bottle of white wine in the house because no one ever asked for it. I waited for the Monforte fair on 21 November to buy wine for the whole year, which we would then bottle a little at a time. On the day of the fair, people drank five or six *brente* of wine. The evening before the fair, carts laden with cabbages and leeks came in and put up at the stables of the Cannon d'Oro. From early morning, the tables began to fill up with people playing *tressette*, who would not get up all day. At midday, I'd bring them tripe and a half bottle each, then they'd go back to their cards and their bottles and play all night long. They sang and they drank. In 42 years, I never closed and never took a holiday.
In the square in front of my *osteria*, they played *pallone elastico*. And bet on the results. When you haven't got much money, you try to take some off people who have. One day, the game wouldn't finish because they were betting so much on it. It went on for another two or three days. Where there's poverty, people like to bet, to gamble. Some evenings, there were 60 or 70 people playing cards upstairs here. I made more money upstairs than downstairs in the bar. Then at six in the morning, I turned them out in case the Carabinieri paid a call. They gave me a tip for every win. Some nights, I could get as much as 10-15,000 lire. They often used to play the game called *nove*. Then there were the professional gamblers, the card sharps, who were looking for victims. On workers' day – it got its name because on that day in December the wage-earning labourers received their pay for the year – well, that evening there were always six or seven professionals waiting for them. In a single night, they took the money the men had earned in a year. One day, two women arrived complaining that their husbands had lost 100,000 lire, one of them, and 70,000 the other. "If they've been gambling, I can't do anything", I told them. But they said, "They were in your *osteria*, and so on and so forth ... so let's go to the Carabinieri". We put some money together and gave them 30 or 40,000 lire each. Then when the husbands came back, we banned them from the upstairs room. They gambled on market days in particular, on Mondays. (*Spring 1990*)

Sabino Massolino
born 1929
grape agent and
innkeeper in Monforte

If I live to be a hundred

Carlo Rapalino
born 1892
farmer
in Monforte

On 25 January 1992, I'll be one hundred years old. The mayor and the parish priest have promised me they'll hold a big party in my courtyard. They told me, "We'll take care of everything". All I've got to do is supply the wine. I've always worked the land. We had grapes that we pressed to make wine. I sold it to the *Narzolini*, the bottlers at Narzole.

I came to live here at Perno when I got married, in 1922. My wife was called Giuseppina Monchiero. She passed away in 1970 so I live with my son, Luigi, who also works on the land. Last year, we sold the vineyard, ten *giornate* – almost four hectares – of the very best land because we couldn't look after it any longer.

At Perno, the best plots are at Santo Stefano and Cerretta, where you don't need a pick to plant your vines. That's how crumbly the soil is. Santo Stefano di Perno is best of all. There are other good areas but the grapes from Santo Stefano, in the part that faces Bussia, are better than any others. There's always been nebbiolo in Cerretta but the vines are old and give very little fruit. There used to be a plot in the middle of Cerretta called San Giovanni. It was a superb site but it's been left to run wild. It was all nebbiolo there. You can still see the vines in among the acacias. We've always had well-aspected plots. I would shout over to my son on the other side of the hill. When they had a Shouting Fair at Monforte, I won first prize because I had plenty of training. My shout was louder than anyone else's. (*Summer 1990*)

We had a hired worker

Palmira Benevelli
born 1917
vine dresser
in Monforte

I was born at the Ca' Bianca on Bricco Ravera. I went to live in my aunt's house – she was childless – in 1929. It was on Bricco Ravera, too, and I stayed there until 1989, for 60 years. Now I'm in this home because my legs won't carry me any longer. The doctors say it's "arthrosis". I don't want to go back to Bricco Ravera. I couldn't face it. The dog and cat are still there. The people from the next *cascina* look after them for me. There's a baker's as well. Until last year, I kept it fired but now someone else is looking after it. I got up at two in the morning to knead flour, water, salt and yeast in the kneading trough. While the dough was rising, I heated the oven and then put the bread in. In winter, it was still dark when I finished. Then other people arrived to bake their bread. Everyone had their own particular time. Every Friday.

One night, they came from Bra to "sing the eggs". At three in the morning, they wanted some of the bread and then they made *soma d'aj* (crusty bread with garlic, oil and salt).

I would make ravioli and tagliatelle with a rolling pin on the kneading board. About once a week, my mother made rabbit, with lots of gravy because we were a large family. My three sisters and I got the small pieces,

Santo Stefano di Perno

with plenty of bread to dip into the gravy. On Sundays, there was boiled beef or boiled chicken. We only ate the broth in the evening, though, because at midday there were tagliatelle or, on holidays, ravioli. Our family was reasonably well off. We had a hired worker.

When I went to stay with my aunt and uncle at Bricco Ravera in 1929, you huddled round the fireside to keep warm. Then the following year, my uncle bought two stoves. There was a big one for the kitchen – it's still there – and a small one for the living room. But the stove, or fireplace, was only lit in the morning, at midday and for the evening meal. For the rest of the day, you had to go to the stable to get warm. The bedrooms were cold and the beds weren't warmed. That's what we were used to. We bought a copper bedwarmer when my uncle fell ill. It was only towards the end of my time there that I used the bedwarmer before going to bed.

In the stables, the women used to knit and them men prepared wicker to bind the vineshoots, or did nothing at all. In the evening, they played cards. We had oil lamps and when the oil ran out, we used acetylene or carbide. Electricity arrived in Ravera in 1943.

In 1970, only my sister and I were left. She died in 1979 and now I'm on my own. She was younger than me. I've always worked in the fields. I used to give my uncle's tenants a hand. In the contract, it said they could keep two sheep for their own use. And so every now and then they would give me a *toma*, or small ewe's milk cheese, in exchange for my work.

I was one of the first women in Monforte to get my driving licence but my aunt didn't want me to drive a car, so we didn't buy one. I've always read a lot, especially the newspapers they gave me, the *Coltivatore Cuneese*

and the *Gazzetta d'Alba*. We never had a television in the house, or a radio, or a tagliatelle machine or even drinking water because we had a tap in the courtyard, and also a well.
My uncle and aunt had about 23 *giornate*, or nine hectares, of vineyards, fields, meadows and woodland. They had a tenant, whom they kept on until 1961.
I didn't like parties and never went dancing. And my aunt didn't want me to, either. I used to go to early Mass because then there was still time to work afterwards. I also went to the processions, including the one every seven years for Saint Anne, with the people from La Morra who came to Monforte to thank the saint for a miracle many years earlier. I always went to vespers as well. For the processions, I would put on my white dress of the Daughters of Mary. Then there were the Luigini, that is the boys of marriageable age, the Battuti Bianchi and the Umiliate with their yellow dress. Men at Monforte have never been great ones for processions. (*Spring 1990*)

They gambled their money away

On 21 November, they held the fair and the square was full of oxen. People from Monforte have always been proud of their oxen. Instead of yoking an ox to the plough, they'd dig the fields themselves or get their workers to do it. When it was time to load the hay, then *Cin d' Montagnarot* put some onto the wagon but the rest went home on the back of the worker. In San Giuseppe alone, there were eight or ten farm workers. After the meal on Boxing Day, the master paid them for the whole year, if they were still entitled to anything. There was always someone who came asking for an advance, especially the ones who gambled everything away. In the days towards the end of the year, you might hear someone say "Oh, what a coincidence. I haven't seen you for a while! Come on, let's have a game of cards. Don't you feel like a game?" And a year's pay vanished before the new year had even come in.

Francesco Benevelli
known as *Cichin*
born 1906
grower in Monforte

Then there were the *giogarela* (semi-professional gamblers) who left on Mondays and came back on Saturdays. When he was young, Basarisch was one of them and Tranta was another. If all went well, they brought a couple of cakes for the farm worker when they came back. Basarisch never let his family go without anything. He didn't fritter away the money he earned in America at cards. He brought two parrots back from America. Everyone went to gape at them and get them to talk.
People gambled anywhere, in the bars, at Settimo's in the square and at Sapai. One day, the Carabinieri surprised a group of gamblers and took them off to prison. When they came out, one said, "If you knew how good it feels to get out, you'd all want to do some time!"
Workers arrived from Gorzegno, Cortemilia and villages where the families were large. They were fairly young, about 20 years old. They stayed with the family and slept in the barn, or in the winter in the stable. But theeldest children of large families also bedded down in the hay or straw. I never had to but my father did.
The workers did the heaviest jobs. They watered (sprinkled the vines with Bordeaux mixture), dug the rows and cut the wood. Hay and wheat was cut by hand with a scythe. You went into the fields in wooden clogs, using straw for socks. Some people still do. When the wheat was cut, either in the morning or the evening to

avoid the heat of the day, the sheaves were tied into stacks. The first mechanical harvester I remember belonged to Nando at Mosconi, in 1915. During the war, the coal-fired machine was replaced by an electric one because there was a coal shortage. We got electricity from the tenant farmer's house with a cable as thick as your wrist. Electricity was generated at the mill in Monforte then, after the war, diesel engines arrived. With what we got from the tenant, and with wine at 18-20 lire for a *brenta* and the 150-200 *brente* we received, there wasn't enough to pay the taxes and cover our costs. We made ends meet with wheat, maize and silkworms. (*Spring 1990*)

One baby after another

I came to work in Monforte in 1925. My family was from Cerretto Langhe. I was a *serventa*, or maid, in the hotel in the square and I met my husband. We saw each other for five or six months and in the end we got married. At the time, he was a *caglié* (cobbler) and I was in service in the houses. But we had one baby after another. I had five of my own and I was wetnurse to five more. I had lots of milk and I kept the babies for four or five months. Then the families paid me and took the children back.

I had a very hard life until after the war, when we opened this *osteria* in 1948 with my husband as cellarman. It was known as the Osteria della Posta because the letterbox was there once. My husband's sister was an excellent cook so I took her on and we worked together for many years. Her husband was a wine agent. He had a room near the *osteria* where he sold grapes and wine. He brought us lots of customers. His name was Settimo Passone and he had an amazing palate. Everyone knew him and people came from Turin, from Savona and even from the mountains to buy from him. He was a fair man and knew his wine. In our family, and at this *osteria*, we have always bought and sold grapes. Wine has always been traded here.

We always got on well with everyone. Antonia, the wife of *Giacolin del Pont* (Giacomo Conterno), was like a sister to me and I also knew her *madona* (mother-in-law), *Marieta*. *Felicin* (Felice Rocca, the well-known restaurateur) was my brother-in-law and a very hard worker. He would turn his hand to anything. He cooked, he washed up and when he had to he could also sing. Working with him was never dull. He was an important man. They still talk about him. (*Summer 1990*)

Metilde Rinaldi
known as *Tilde*
born 1904
cook in Monforte

Novello

Novellum Albensium Pompeianorum, or "Novello of the people of Alba Pompeia", is the ancient name of this town. It is thought to derive from the *novae villae*, or new towns, built here in the early centuries of the second millennium. Nevertheless, the original settlement is much older, dating back to Roman times, if not before.
Situated a few kilometres from Barolo, modern Novello is a cluster of houses perched on a ridge that plummets down into the Tanaro valley. Access to the town is through a mediaeval gate surmounted by a squat, robustly built clock tower. Its double-headed eagle was chiselled off during the Risorgimento because it was believed to be the symbol of the Habsburgs. In fact, this blameless and very Piedmontese bird was the emblem of the Del Carretto family. Adjacent to the tower is the eighteenth-century parish church of San Michele Arcangelo. It was built to a design by Francesco Gallo, although the thrusting brickwork façade in the neoclassical idiom diverges from the Baroque style so beloved of the architect from Mondovì. The interior, however, is majestically expansive, rising 34.5 meters to the summit of the dome. Next to the parish church is the church of the Confraternita di San Giovanni, which boasts and exquisite façade. In this case, Baroque art has maintained its sense of proportion.
At the edge of the town, the castle dominates the entire area from its lofty position. For centuries, it was the home of the Marchesi Del Carretto, a family plagued by a chain of killings and tragedy whose cause was known to everyone. On the night of 22 May 1340, Marchese Manfredo Del Carretto

was butchered in the rooms of the castle by his son, Malefatto. Since then, first at the instigation of the murdered nobleman's wife, Alasia di Savoia-Acaja, then in an inexplicable concatenation of apparently fortuitous accidents, there began a terrible sequence of violent deaths. In the seventeenth century, the Del Carretto family suffered 18 deaths. Shaken by this bloody turn of events, Marchese Giovanni Battista Del Carretto relinquished the feud of Novello and took his family to holding of Camerano, near Asti, which he purchased for 10,000 lire.

It is a great pity that there is no trace of the ill-starred noble residence today. On the site, there now stands a new castle, completed in 1880 to a design by the architect from Dogliani, Gian Battista Schellino. Closely related to the plans for Pollenzo, drawn up for the court of Carlo Alberto of Savoy, the new castle has all the features of the neo-Gothic style so popular at the time, its eclectic air resonant with mediaeval grace notes. The excesses of its brickwork façade, the crenellated towers, the profusion of pointed windows and arches, and the white marble staircase have prompted commentators to compare it to the set for a Wagner opera or, equally appositely, a Walt Disney cartoon, Herod's palace in nativity scenes or a stereotypical wedding cake. Three of the rooms can be visited, the hunting room, the Venetian room and the bridal suite, all lavishly decorated and embellished with antique furniture.

In the garden is the *foresteria*, or guest quarters, with a central arch and first-floor loggia that are the only surviving parts of the original mediaeval complex.

The great vineyards

DOC and DOCG	Total area under vine in hectares	% of area in municipality	% of area in zone
Dolcetto d'Alba	63.0842	40.72	3.37
Barolo	**52.3005**	**33.76**	**4.18**
Barbera d'Alba	34.9158	22.54	2.03
Other DOC zones	4.6040	2.97	
TOTAL	154.9045	100.0	
Other DOC zones			
Langhe Chardonnay	1.1450	0.74	0.45
Nebbiolo d'Alba	0.8200	0.53	0.20
Langhe Nebbiolo	0.7700	0.50	3.08
Langhe Freisa	0.6640	0.43	1.11
Piemonte Pinot Nero	0.6550	0.42	8.41
Langhe Bianco	0.3500	0.23	1.31
Langhe Rosso	0.1600	0.10	0.23
Langhe Favorita	0.0400	0.03	0.04

Production

There are 44 wineries in the municipality, with 52.30 hectares and a potential production of 4,159 quintals of grapes and 2,911 hectolitres of wine, corresponding to 4.18 per cent of the Barolo DOCG zone.

Ravera

The Ravera vineyard is the area in the municipality of Novello that borders on Barolo. It includes three *cascine*, all called Ravera. The territory we have identified as the Ravera vineyard does not extend over the whole area and in fact covers about five *giornate* (two hectares). It is a south-facing vineyard that runs along the Ravera municipal road descending from Novello, near the church of San Rocco, to the Panerole municipal road. The vines stretch away from the Ravera road along the slopes of a hill whose peak is known as Bric delle Pernici. The soil here is fairly loose-packed and comprises mainly whitish-coloured marl. Ravera has always been viewed by the growers of Novello as the best part of the municipality for growing nebbiolo.

Main labels

*Barolo Vigneto Terlo Ravera – Marziano ed Enrico Abbona, Dogliani

*Barolo Ravera – Elvio Cogno, Novello

Ravera

Our selection

Population 910
Height 471 metres asl

INFORMATION

Town Hall
Piazza Marconi, 1
Tel. + 39 0173 731147

THE WINERIES

Elvio Cogno
Località Ravera, 2
Tel. + 39 0173 731405
Walter Fissore and his wife Nadia are the enthusiastic owners who run this winery, which was founded by one of Barolo's historic names, Elvio Cogno. Walter supervises winemaking personally with the assistance of consultant, Beppe Caviola. It is thanks to this winery that one of Barolo's historic vineyard selections, Ravera di Novello, has survived

WHERE TO SLEEP

Hotel Barbabuc
Via Giordano, 35
Tel. + 39 0173 731298
Three stars. A small but attractive hotel in a nineteenth-century building, managed by Maria Beccaria amid a profusion of books, paintings and pottery. The rooms are furnished with antique and designer pieces. All are colour coordinated. The generous breakfasts feature jams, cheeses and salami.

Albergo Al Castello da Diego
Castello di Novello
Tel. + 39 0173 744011
Three stars. Located in the nineteenth-century castle, the hotel offers comfortable rooms and suites.

WHAT TO BUY

Bottega Comunale del Vino
Via Roma, 1
Open at weekends, the Bottega Comunale del Vino brings together the production of about 20 local wineries.

THE GREAT VINEYARDS

RAVERA

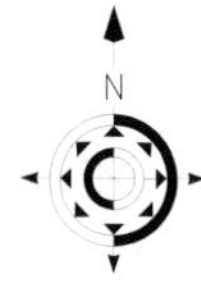

BAROLO DOCG ZONE

GREAT VINEYARDS

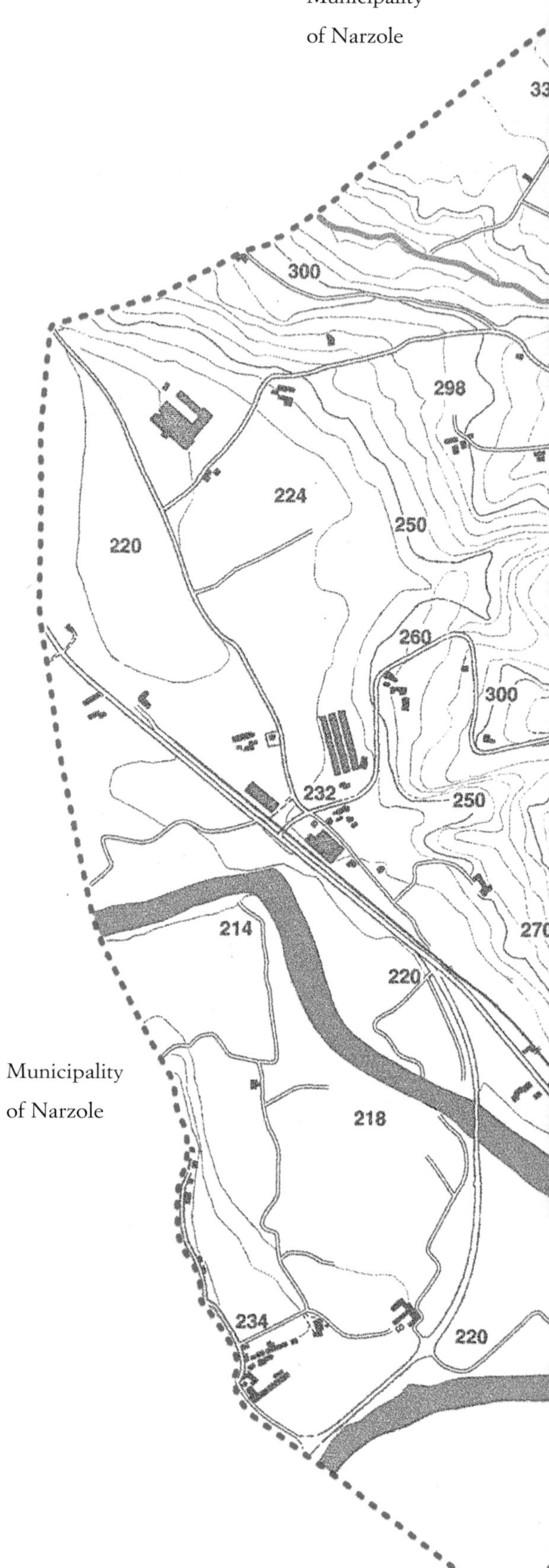

Municipality
of Barolo
Ravera
Municipality
of Monforte d'Alba
Municipality
of Monchiero

Roddi

The name Roddi probably derives from the Celtic word *raud* or *rod*, which means "river", obviously referring to the Tanaro, which flows lower down. In classical times, Roddi was known as *Castrum Rhaudium* and became a strategic link between *Alba Pompeia* and the more important *Pollentia*. Historians know the area for two famous battles that took place here. The first, the battle of the Campi Raudii, saw the Roman general Marius defeat the Cimbrians in 101 BC and the second took place in 403 AD, when Stilicon overcame Alaric's Goths.

After belonging to the bishop of Asti, Roddi was enfeoffed to a number of feudal lords, including the Pico della Mirandola family, until it shared the fate of another 73 Piedmontese municipalities and was annexed by the Savoys under the treaty of Cherasco in 1631.

Standing on a ridge over the flatlands that stretch towards Alba, about seven kilometres away, Roddi is a mediaeval township with a spiral layout. The houses in the historic centre huddle together along the main street that winds its way up to the castle. The castle itself dates back to around the year 1000 AD. Tall, impressive and almost disproportionately bulky, the castle features towers from the twelfth and fifteenth centuries that were not so much added as unceremoniously tacked on to the main body. After passing from one feudal lord to another, Roddi was acquired by king Carlo Alberto from the Marchesi Della Chiesa of Cinzano in 1836, when he extended the nearby Pollenzo estate on the far side of the Tanaro. The old, uncomfortable building was never used as a royal residence and Vittorio Emanuele II lost no time in selling it in 1858, during one of his enforced money-raising campaigns. Other noteworthy buildings are the

imposing thirteenth-century bell tower and the late Baroque parish church of Santa Maria Assunta, whose graceful façade provides an eye-catching backdrop for the dignified Piazzetta del Municipio.

Until a few years ago, Roddi was the home of a singular institution, the *Università del Cane da Tartufo*, or "university for truffle dogs", founded in 1880 by Antonio Monchiero, known as *Baròt*. His son, nicknamed *Baròt II*, carried on where his father had left off and maintained the highest standards until his death in 1960, when the initiative petered out.

Roddi is also noted as a centre of *pallapugno*, or "elastic ball", and it is no coincidence that one of the greatest-ever Italian players, Beppe Corino, national first division champion in 1962, came from the town. The local pallapugno pitch is a broad stretch of Via Sineo, along the side of which runs a rampart supporting the old buildings on Via Carlo Alberto above it. Having introduced Via Sineo, where the Sineo palazzo once stood, we might now mention three famous members of the family. Sebastiano was the military commander who led the siege of Turin in 1706, Francesco Antonio Sineo, with Bonafous and Ranza, founded the Jacobin Republic of Alba in 1796 and took part in the 1821 revolution while Riccardo, a minister on two occasions, was a leading leftwing politician for 30 years, first in the Subalpine Parliament and then in that of the Kingdom of Italy. A determined opponent of Cavour, Riccardo inflicted a memorable defeat on his illustrious adversary in the 1848 elections. Roddi and Cavour's Grinzane were part of the same constituency and while the lawyer, Riccardo Sineo, attracted 193 votes, the future architect of a united Italy won only 12.

The great vineyards

DOC and DOCG	Totale area under vine in hectares	% of area in municipality	% of area in zone
Barbera d'Alba	34.5284	40.24	2.00
Dolcetto d'Alba	25.8925	30.18	1.38
Barolo	**11.6460**	**13.57**	**0.93**
Nebbiolo d'Alba	9.9400	11.58	2.39
Other DOC zones	3.8000	4.43	
TOTAL	85.8069	100.00	
Other DOC zones			
Langhe Freisa	1.7200	2.00	2.87
Langhe Chardonnay	1.2500	1.46	0.49
Langhe Favorita	0.6600	0.77	0.66
Langhe Nebbiolo	0.1700	0.20	0.68

Production

There are 17 wineries in the town, totalling 11.64 hectares with a potential output of 931 quintals of grapes and 652 hectolitres of wine, representing 0.93 per cent of the Barolo DOCG zone.

Our selection

Population 1,294
Height 284 metres asl

INFORMATION

Town Hall
Piazza Umberto I, 3
Tel. + 39 0173 615001

WHERE TO SLEEP

Enomotel Il Convento
Via Cavallotto, 1
Tel. + 39 0173 615286
Three stars. This hotel stands on the road junction at the bottom of the valley between Barolo and Alba. It is an excellent base for excursions into Barolo country.

Agriturismo Cascina Barin
Località Toetto, 21
Tel. + 39 0173 615159
The rooms feature attractive caisson ceilings, wrought-iron beds and some items of antique furniture. In the morning, guests can enjoy a generous breakfast of typical local products.

EATING OUT

La Crota
Piazza Principe Amedeo, 1
Tel. + 39 0173 615187
Danilo Lorusso serves expertly made dishes from the Langhe cuisine, which he enhances with a touch of originality. A few recipes, such as some of his risottos and stews, come from the Savoy tradition. In season, the menu includes game and truffles.

BAROLO

Serralunga d'Alba

The hillslopes are clad with magnificent vineyards that once belonged to the Marchesi Falletti, who obtained fine wines from them for the court of Turin. The town is reached from Alba along the provincial road for Barolo. After Gallo, the turn-off for Serralunga takes you along a panoramic road that runs halfway up the hillside. Your first contact with the town's heritage is the estate and cellars of Fontanafredda, built in 1878 by Emanuele, Conte di Mirafiori. On the estate is the beautifully restored *Casa di Caccia*, or "hunting lodge" of *Bela Rosin*. This was the setting for the celebrated love affair of Vittorio Emanuele II and the good-looking commoner, Rosa, who subsequently became Contessa di Mirafiori and the king's morganatic wife.

Only a few minutes away, on the far side of Baudana, is Serralunga itself. Above the town soar the *tre ciochè*, the name – in the local vernacular – of the distinguishing feature of this, the loveliest castle in the Langhe. The *tre ciochè* are the three bell towers, each one different from the other two, which give the castle its unique vertical thrust. Between the brickwork of the castle and the green expanse of fully 29 Barolo vineyards, the mediaeval town forms an almost intact barrier in a characteristic radial pattern.

Built between 1340 and 1357 by Pietrino and Goffredo Falletti, Serralunga's fortress was designed as a solid, safe base for the warfare of an age that was ignorant of artillery. The castle's vertical lines were useful for keeping a lookout and also for discouraging would-be attackers. Once, a moat surrounded the complex, which was accessible only across a

drawbridge. The radial arrangement of the houses around it also enabled civilian residents to retire into the stronghold quickly to safety. The castle lay in line with the other Falletti strongholds and in its heyday made use of a simple but effective system of optical telegraphy. Communication with other feudal landholders was maintained using torches at night and coloured standards by day.

The plain quadrilateral plan is closed at the corners by the cylindrical tower and the square keep. A third hanging turret, inspired by mediaeval French architecture, emerges from the sharp north-west corner. The residential floor features two-light windows which, with the remains of Ghibelline battlements and rows of hanging arches, are the only decorative elements to adorn this austere building. In 1950, the Italian president of the day, Luigi Einaudi, ordered conservation and restoration work on the castle, which is now public property. Access from the town below is through a gate cut into the walls. Visitors can enjoy a stroll around the mediaeval houses, up and down the steep lanes in the shadow of the Romanesque spire-topped bell tower of the former parish church.

After your stroll, you might stop off for a glass of wine and perhaps toast the health of the Cappellano family, outstanding winemakers at Serralunga in the late nineteenth century. Giovanni, a hotelier from Alba, launched the fashion here for dolcetto grapes as a cure-all for anaemia. His brother Giuseppe, a chemist, made and sold at his pharmacy in Turin the celebrated Barolo Chinato, which he produced with the aid of 13 oriental spices. It was revered as a digestive cordial and panacea for all ailments.

The great vineyards

The number of vineyards – fully 29 – in this municipality, all of which lies in the Barolo DOCG zone, may come as a surprise to readers. It will be less of a surprise, however, to the many growers and viticulturists of the Langhe and the Alba hills, who are well aware of the potential of the territory.

Serralunga's Barolos have two main distinguishing features. The first, sensory, characteristic, is their remarkable tannin structure. In addition, they grapes maintain a very high standard of quality across the entire territory of the municipality.

If you want to get a clear idea of the location of the vineyards, start with the central ridge that the provincial road from Gallo Grinzane runs along on its way first to the township and then Roddino. A number of hills leave this ridge more or less at right angles. Their best slopes enjoy perfect south-facing locations. The vineyards to the left of the road – Cerretta, Pra di Po', Badarina and so on – are mainly south east-facing. Their wines are a shade less tannic and structured because of the cooler,

DOC and DOCG	Total area under vine in hectares	% of area in municipality	% of area in zone
Barolo	**200.9548**	**54.30**	**16.08**
Dolcetto d'Alba	79.2405	21.41	4.24
Moscato d'Asti	38.0500	10.28	0.92
Barbera d'Alba	30.3079	8.19	1.76
Langhe Chardonnay	9.0340	2.44	3.52
Piemonte Pinot Nero	4.8400	1.31	62.17
Other DOC zones	7.6360	2.06	
TOTAL	370.0632	100.00	
Other DOC zones			
Piemonte Brachetto	1.2450	0.34	10.23
Langhe Rosso	1.2250	0.33	1.74
Langhe Nebbiolo	0.6710	0.18	2.68
Langhe Bianco	0.5150	0.14	1.93
Piemonte Grignolino	0.4200	0.11	2.56
Langhe Favorita	0.2400	0.06	0.24
Langhe Freisa	3.3200	0.90	5.53

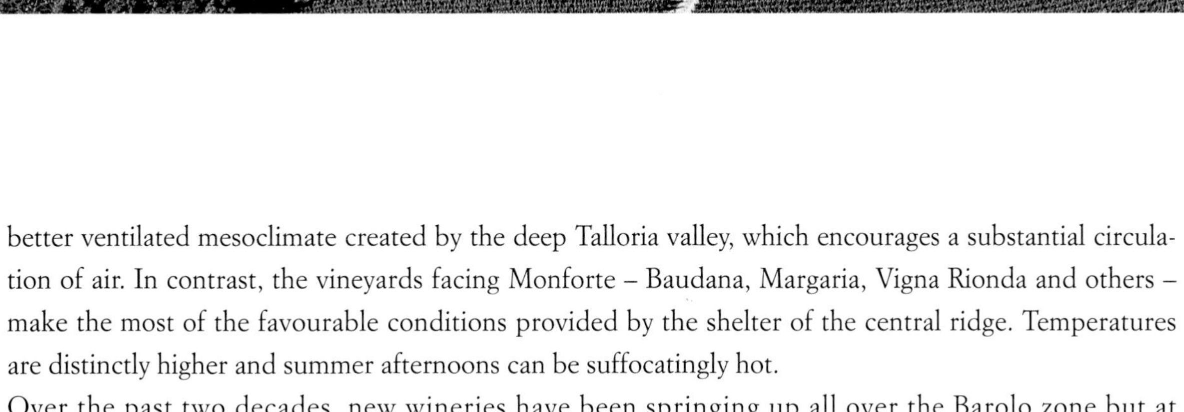

better ventilated mesoclimate created by the deep Talloria valley, which encourages a substantial circulation of air. In contrast, the vineyards facing Monforte – Baudana, Margaria, Vigna Rionda and others – make the most of the favourable conditions provided by the shelter of the central ridge. Temperatures are distinctly higher and summer afternoons can be suffocatingly hot.

Over the past two decades, new wineries have been springing up all over the Barolo zone but at Serralunga, this development has been less marked. One reason is the dominating presence of Fontanafredda, which has traditionally absorbed all the fruit grown locally. Yet, as can be seen from the number of labels cited at the end of each vineyard description, change is in the air at Serralunga and young producers are emerging here, too.

Production

There are 98 wineries, totalling 201 hectares with a potential annual output of 11,178 hectolitres of wine, equivalent to 13 per cent of the entire Barolo DOCG zone.

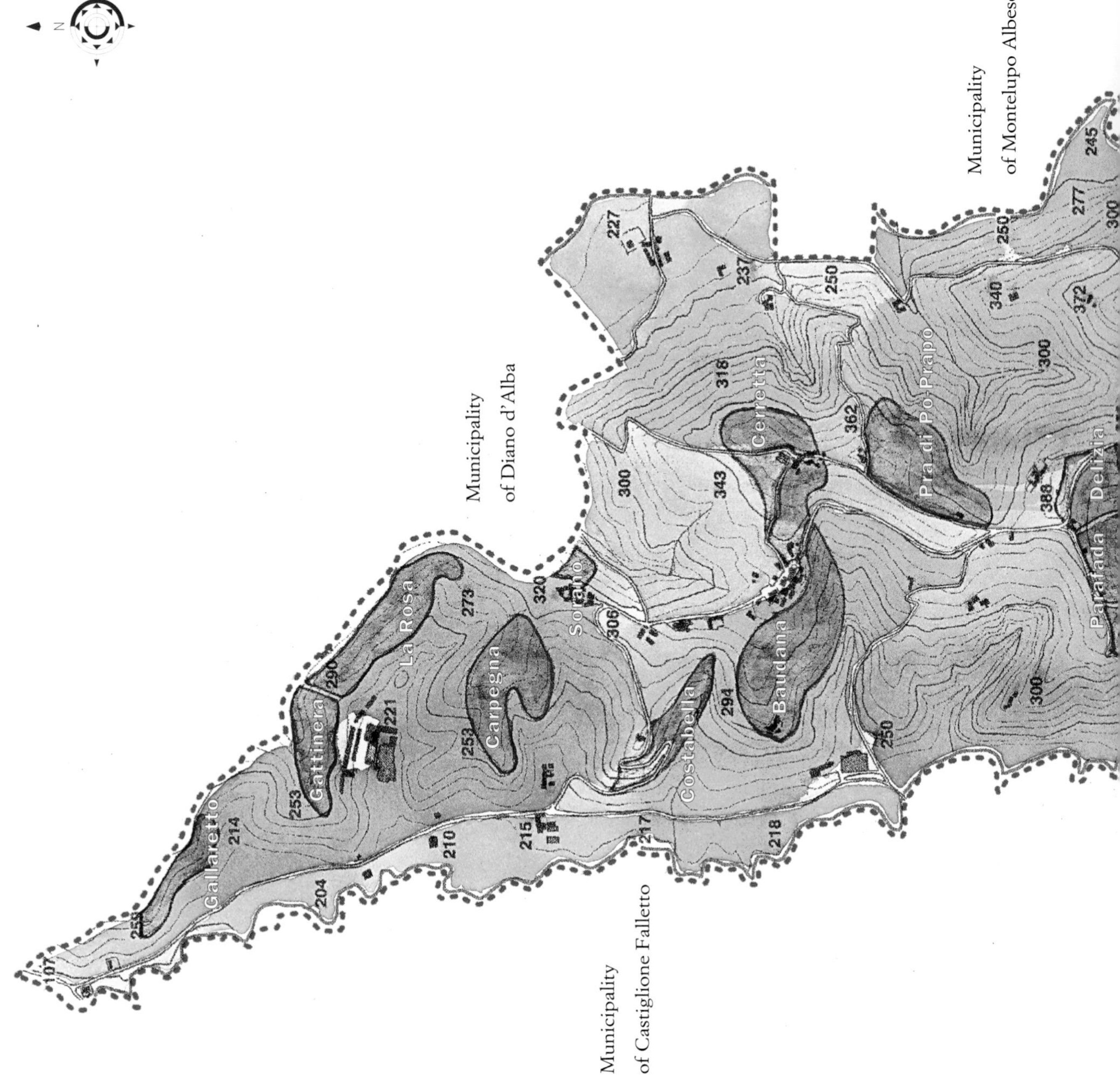

THE GREAT VINEYARDS

ARIONE
BADARINA
BAUDANA
BOSCO ARETO OR BOSCARETO
BRICCOLINA
BROGLIO
CARPEGNA
CERRETTA
COLLARETTO
COLOMBAIO
COSTABELLA OR SAN ROCCO
CUCCO AND POSTEIRONE
FALLETTO
FRANCIA
GABUTTI
GALLARETTO
GATTINERA
LA ROSA
LAZZARITO AND
LAZZARIASCO OR LAZZARIASSO
MARENCA
MARGARIA AND LE TURNE
ORNATO
PARAFADA AND DELIZIA
PRA DI PÒ OR PRAP
RIVETTE
SAN BERNARDO
SANTA CATERINA
SERRA
SORANO
VIGNA RIONDA
VOGHERA AND BRE

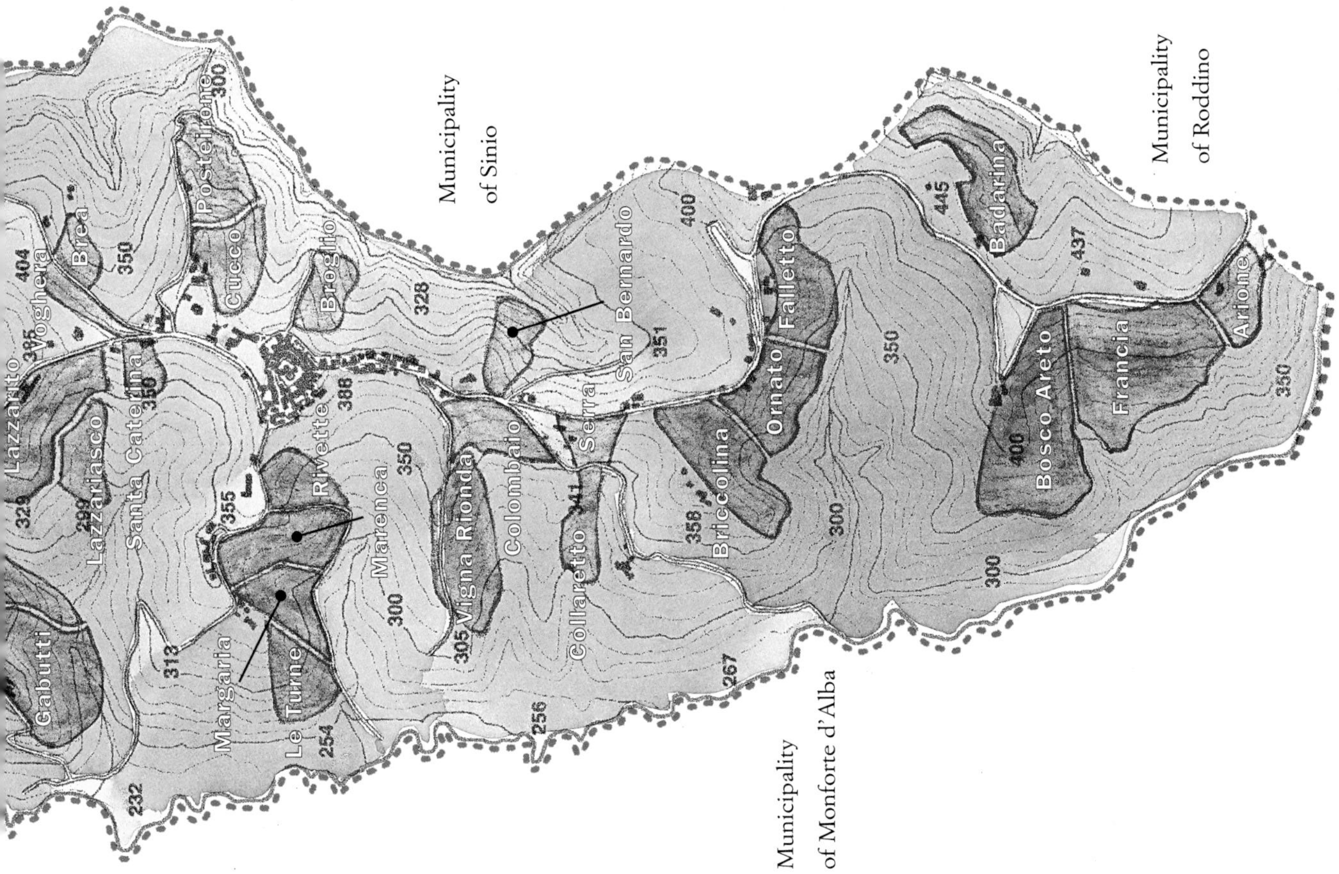

Municipality of Sinio

Municipality of Roddino

Municipality of Monforte d'Alba

Lazzarito, Voghera, Brea, Postelrone, Cucco, Broglio, Lazzariasco, Santa Caterina, Rivette, Marenca, Margaria, Le Turne, Gabutti, Vigna Rionda, Colombaio, Collaretto, Serra, San Bernardo, Briccolina, Ornato, Falletto, Badarina, Bosco Areto, Francia, Arione

BAROLO DOCG ZONE

GREAT VINEYARDS

Arione

On the border of the municipality of Serralunga with Roddino, Arione lies at the edge of the Barolo DOCG zone. The Manera *cascina*, or farmhouse, which dominates this vineyard, is 450 metres above sea level. A little lower down is the attractive *cascina* Arione. The grape-growing area extends over about ten Piedmontese *giornate*, or just under four hectares. It is separated from the Francia vineyard by a large, steep *capezzagna*, or unsurfaced road. Here, the hill faces in another direction and the vines vary in aspect from south west to south as far as *cascina* Arione. Nebbiolo is the variety grown in this part of the vineyard. Beyond the farmhouse to the border with Roddino has always been an area known for its spectacular barbera grapes. On the far side of the river Talloria di Castiglione can be seen the Mosconi, Ginestre and Pilone vineyards, which lie in the municipality of Monforte d'Alba.

MAIN LABELS

*Barolo Arione – Gigi Rosso, Castiglione Falletto

*Barolo Arione Sôrì dell'Ulivo – Gigi Rosso, Castiglione Falletto

Badarina

For a few years now, nebbiolo has been planted at Badarina, in the south of the municipal territory of Serralunga. Once, the variety's uncertain yields and, especially, the vineyard's altitude – we are about 420 metres above sea level – led growers to prefer dolcetto to nebbiolo. Just around the righthand bend at the *cascina* Falletto, to the east of the provincial road for Roddino, we find nebbiolo vines that belong, like those at the adjacent *cascina* Badarina, to the Bersano winery. The area to the north of the farmhouse faces east and south east while to the south of the building, on slope between 420 and 380 metres above sea level, the vines enjoy superb south and south east-facing locations.

MAIN LABELS

*Barolo Badarina – Bersano, Nizza Monferrato

Baudana

A historic vineyard of especial renown, Baudana, fittingly, is mentioned in Ratti's *Carta del Barolo* map but it is also highly regarded by growers. "The *sorì* (slopes) at Baudana are very well aspected and from there up to Briccolina we find the best vine-growing locations in Serralunga". That view, expressed to us by Giuseppe Boasso from Gabutti, is held by almost all the older growers in Serralunga. Geologically speaking, Baudana is on the border between the zones of Sant'Agata Fossili marl known locally as *tov* and the grey-red sandstone alternating with grey marl known as the *Formazione di Lequio*. The soil is compact white clay and sand that is fairly firm in texture. Below the few houses in the vineyard, the vines are steep and the growing area continues, uninterruptedly south-facing, to the west as far as the *cascina* Belvedere, reached along a lane that goes down from the church of San Rocco and skirts the house that once belonged to Virginia Ferrero. From this property, or rather, from the local road that heads towards Meriane, we can admire the whole vineyard, which extends over ten hectares or so at an average height above sea level of 300 metres. There can be no doubt that, since the 1930s, grapes grown in Baudana have helped to make some of the finest Barolos produced. This only confirms the opinion of Baudana voiced by local residents.

Main labels

*Barolo Baudana – Cantina Terre del Barolo, Castiglione Falletto

*Barolo Sorì di Baudana – Attilio Zunino, Serralunga d'Alba

Bosco Areto or Boscareto

Once, *cascina* Areto stood in thick woodland. Indeed, until the 1920s, much of what is now the Langhe wine country was dotted with copses in areas that were less suitable for viticulture, by grazing land at the bottom of the small valleys and by fields set aside for other crops, as was the custom in the mixed agricultural economy of the day.

Year after year, as wine gains in importance and the single-crop cultivation of grapes ecomes more popular, more land is turned over to viticulture. The countryside has changed radically and today, the farmhouse in the woods looks out onto a large expanse of vines. The south-facing part of the slope, where nebbiolo and barbera have long been planted, continues to be an outstanding vineyard and we are happy to note it as such here.

The area concerned is about 32 Piedmontese *giornate*, or 12 hectares, to the south and west of the *cascina*, bordering on the Francia vineyard and the provincial road to Roddino.

Facing Bosco Areto on the Monforte slope is the Ginestre vineyard. In fact, this is an excellent place from which to admire all the finest Monforte vineyards.

Historically, the long strip under vine that now belongs to the Francia vineyard is still part of Boscareto. It is here that Ferdinando Principiano from Monforte harvests his grapes.

Main labels

*Barolo Vigneto Boscareto – Batasiolo, La Morra

*Barolo Boscareto – Ferdinando Principiano, Monforte d'Alba

Briccolina

Briccolina, where it looks onto Bosco Areto forming a small trough in the line of hills, deserves to be regarded as an outstanding cru. Exposure ranges from south west to south, and then south east, while the height above sea level is between 330 and 390 metres. Covering about seven hectares, the vineyard includes a superb plot, known as Corda della Briccolina, all of which is south-facing.

The nebbiolos of Briccolina are excellent. For many years, they were purchased by Dottor Giuseppe Cappellano, who admired their ability to imbue the wine with a remarkable intensity of aroma.

The border with the Ornato vineyard is clearly visible at the edge of the small depression, where the hill turns gently round to face south again.

MAIN LABELS

*Barolo Vigneto Corda della Briccolina – Batasiolo, La Morra

Broglio

From the road around the village of Serralunga, near the attractive Art Nouveau building that was once a nursery school, there is a lane leading down to the Broglio vineyard. Well-aspected to the south at about 360 metres above sea level, this small vineyard is reasonably well sheltered in the valley of a stream, also called Broglio. Many of those we spoke to said that Broglio is a good nebbiolo area and it has always been highly regarded by grape buyers working for the big wine houses around Alba. The best part of the vineyard is just under three hectares in area.

MAIN LABELS

*Barolo Vigna Broglio – Palladino, Serralunga d'Alba

Carpegna

Carpegna links the hamlet of Bruni, situated lower down where the road forks for Castelletto and Serralunga, and Sorano, higher up near Baudana. The slope at Carpegna rolls downhill so that the vineyards are aspected first to the south west, then to the south, and then again to the south west and south. Just beyond Bruni, the hill forms a small, west-facing valley with hazel trees, whose nuts have always provided an alternative crop to grapes in the damper parts of the Langhe.

The finest grapes in Carpegna are grown in an area of about 15 Piedmontese *giornate*, or just under six hectares, at a height above sea level of 250 metres or a little more. Stretching north from the crest of the hill is the Fontanafredda estate, where a small wood runs down to the winery complex. The soil of this lovely vineyard is mainly clay and limestone.

Cerretta

The hamlet of Cerretta is right in the middle of the vineyard of the same name. Local roads lead off in various directions and the plots are variously aspected. The slope that looks towards Baudana has south west-facing vineyards and borders the Alba-Serralunga provincial road. The part overlooking the Talloria valley faces east and south east, with two distinct vineyards. The first, to the north of the cliff, extends almost as far as the *cascina* Teodoro whereas the second, delimited by the local Teodoro road, reaches nearly to the *cascina* Sordo. The small group of houses, in the characteristic pattern of rural settlements with one courtyard backing onto the next, takes you to a height of 380 metres and a small plateau. From here, you can enjoy a view over the Sorano vineyard and the *sorì*, or slopes, of the municipality of Diano d'Alba towards the Talloria valley.

Much of the vine stock belonged in the early twentieth century to *Tota* Virginia Ferrero, who entrusted them to local share-cropping tenant farmers. Even earlier, Cerretta, like much of the municipality of Serralunga, belonged to the Opera Pia Barolo charitable institute, as a detailed register drawn up in 1859 attests. The finest grape-growing area covers about 20 Piedmontese *giornate*, or less than 8 hectares.

MAIN LABELS

*Barolo Cerretta Piani – Luigi e Fiorina Baudana, Serralunga d'Alba
*Barolo Vigna Cerretta – Ca' Romé di Romano Marengo, Barbaresco
*Barolo Cerretta – Ettore Germano, Serralunga d'Alba
*Barolo Collina della Cerretta Vigna Sumot – La Cerretta, Serralunga d'Alba
*Barolo Cerretta – Giovanni Rosso, Serralunga d'Alba

Collaretto

The vines of Collaretto extend downhill at the Serra vineyard from the municipal oad that leads to the village of Collaretto. The low hill lies parallel to the vineyards of Rionda and is oriented slightly more to the west. Most of the vines are uniformly aspected to the south west.

Facing them, on the Monforte side, is the Castelletto vineyard. Collaretto is a good area for nebbiolo but never reaches the heights of quality achieved at nearby Vigna Rionda or Colombaio, the plots being situated too low down to enjoy protracted exposure to sunshine.

Colombaio

The eastern side of Vigna Rionda, separated by a minor road, takes us into Colombaio, its lovely hilltop *cascina*, also named Colombaio, dominating the vineyards of Serralunga. Three roads mark off its boundaries. To the north is the Chiappellere road, to the east, the provincial road from Serralunga to Roddino and to the south the road for Collaretto. Along the provincial road, the vines face west, shifting to south west where they join Vigna Rionda proper. Extending over almost seven *giornate*, or more than two hectares, the vines stand at heights ranging from 340 to 380 metres above sea level. Long known by its own name, the lovely Colombaio vineyard can actually be regarded as part of Vigna Rionda.

Costabella or San Rocco

The vines of Costabella start at the first sharp corners on the road that rises from the bottom of the Talloria valley to Serralunga, extending as far as the church of San Rocco. Once, San Rocco was the realm of *Tota* Virginia Ferrero, a great early twentieth-century wine producer and merchant. From the square in front of the church, there is a fine panoramic view of the vines of Costabella or San Rocco. Below, at the first hairpin bend, the rows of vines face west, then spread out and shift aspect, first to face south west and then south. The soil is white, marly, rich in limestone and fairly compact, lying at between 250 and 300 metres above sea level. San Rocco's finest growing area corresponds to just under ten *giornate*, or three and a half hectares.

Today, the vines on the eastern side of the provincial road, opposite the church, should also be considered part of San Rocco. These few *giornate* may not be well-aspected – in fact, they face east – but the expert hands of Luigi Scavino, from the Azelia winery, coax excellent results from the fruit.

MAIN LABELS

*Barolo San Rocco – Azelia, Castiglione Falletto

*Barolo S. Rocco – Eredi Virginia Ferrero, Serralunga d'Alba

Cucco and Posteirone

Below and alongside the village of Cerrati lie the vineyards of Cucco and Posteirone. The first enjoys an excellent south-facing location and is clearly visible from the centre of Serralunga. Cucco used to belong to Dottor Giuseppe Cappellano, a celebrated figure in the world of Barolo, who was quick to acquire this superb plot when the opportunity arose. It is on the eastern flank of Serralunga and nebbiolo has always been at home on its white, tufaceous soil. The grapes yield a Barolo with outstanding structure, capable of ageing in the cellar for many years. Understandably, wines such as these have generated a certain local pride among the growers of Serralunga. The story goes that during the harvest, Dottor Cappellano would ask, disparagingly, how much the *nebiulin d'La Mura* (the "little nebbiolo" grapes from La Morra) were fetching, so convinced was he of Serralunga's uperiority. Cucco lies from 340 to 390 metres above sea level, covering an area of ten Piedmontese *giornate*, or just under four hectares.

Posteirone is the natural continuation of Cucco and is easily identifiable where the aspect of the slope shifts to the east and moves towards the Talloria valley. The far boundary of Posteirone is formed by the municipal road of the same name that runs down from Cerrati towards the Broglio, at the point where it flows into the torrential Talloria river. As we mentioned above, the aspect of the vines shifts progressively towards the east, at an average height of 360 metres.

For many years, barbera has been grown at Posteirone with excellent results, as may be seen from the archives of the Cappellano family, who once owned the entire vineyard.

MAIN LABELS

*Barolo Cucco – Stroppiana, Serralunga d'Alba

Falletto

Cascina Falletto has a prominent position on its hilltop at a height above sea level of 420 metres. On one side are the vines, almost all facing south and south west on a steep slope, and on the other flank is the road for Roddino, which here forms a long hairpin bend. The vineyard covers 15 or so Piedmontese *giornate*, or less than six hectares. The eastern boundary is formed by the embankment of the provincial road at *cascina* Manocino. In this part of the vineyard, the vines face west but are reasonably well protected from the wind.

On the far side of the road lies the municipality of Sinio, which is outside the Barolo DOCG zone. In fact, the boundaries of the Barolo zone were drawn up only after years of argument. Predictably, local pride blew hot in defence of one growing area or another. Veto countered veto to favour the inclusion of areas with influential friends, as was the case with the small plot in the municipality of Cherasco. In the end, the entire municipality of Serralunga was included in the Barolo DOCG zone, as was absolutely right and proper.

MAIN LABELS

*Barolo Falletto di Serralunga d'Alba – Bruno Giacosa, Neive

Francia

The Ginestra vineyard at Monforte offers a fine view of the extensive, regularly laid out, densely planted Francia vineyards between Arione and Bosco Areto, on the western slope of Serralunga. The height, ranging from 370 to 420 metres, tells you that you are close to the municipality of Roddino, on the edge of the Barolo DOCG zone. Indeed at one time, the main varieties grown here were dolcetto, freisa and barbera. Only recently have growers started planting nebbiolo. The results have been, and continue to be, excellent in our opinion as the composition of the soil and the excellent exposure of the south west-facing vines yield superb raw material. Of course, it is not the stylish, relatively soft-textured Barolo of Barolo, Castiglione Falletto or La Morra. Instead, Francia wines are tannin-rich and reveal their full potential only after seven or eight years in the cellar. In fact, the presence of two vineyards as different as Francia and Gallaretto in the same municipality enables us to appreciate the range of personalities that grapes from Serralunga can express. Francia includes more than ten hectares under vine. It is here that Giacomo Conterno's celebrated wines are made, including Barolo Cascina Francia and Barolo Monfortino.

It should also be noted that recently, new nebbiolo vines were planted in an excellent south east-facing position to the east of the Serralunga-Roddino road, just below the Cascina Francia itself.

Main labels

*Barolo Cascina Francia – Giacomo Conterno, Monforte d'Alba

*Barolo Monfortino – Giacomo Conterno, Monforte d'Alba

Gabutti

We are not exaggerating when we say that Gabutti is the starting point of a long ribbon of vineyards along the side of the most prestigious hill in the municipality of Serralunga, and one of the most outstanding in the entire Barolo DOCG zone. Gabutti and the adjacent vineyards of Parafada and Lazzarito were classified by Ratti as first growths with very high quality profiles. In making this decision, Ratti was certainly supported by the widespread beliefs of growers in the area and by a long-established hierarchy that had taken root in the popular consciousness and was reflected in prices in the market. "When we took the grapes to Fontanafredda, they always paid a couple of lire more than for fruit from other municipalities". We heard statements like this from several growers in the area. It would be interesting to see whether they are borne out by the accounts of the older wineries. Unfortunately, much of the documentation has been lost and it is now extremely difficult to reconstruct the commercial history of Barolo.

Going back to Gabutti, the area planted to vine lies below the houses and can be reached along the local road from Parafada. The road itself marks the boundary for some distance then the hill takes a sharply different direction. To the east, Gabutti borders on Parafada along a long *capezzagna*, or unsurfaced road. The south-facing aspect and the steep slope, as well as shelter from the wind, combine to produce a superb site climate for the cultivation of nebbiolo. Other data about Gabutti: height above sea level – around 320 metres; surface area – about 20 Piedmontese *giornate*, or less than eight hectares.

The hamlet of Gabutti affords a lovely view not just of Serralunga and its splendid castle but also of the noble residence at Castiglione Falletto and the palazzo at Perno.

Main labels

*Barolo Otin Fiorin Collina Gabutti – Cappellano, Serralunga d'Alba

*Barolo Otin Fiorin Collina Gabutti Franco – Cappellano, Serralunga d'Alba

*Barolo Gabutti – Gabutti di Franco Boasso, Serralunga d'Alba

*Barolo Sorì Gabutti – Sordo, Castiglione Falletto

Gallaretto

Situated right at the north end of the long municipality of Serralunga, almost on the border with Alba, Gallaretto is a vineyard that can be admired from the provincial road. The characteristic colours of the lovely farm that dominates it from on high tell you that it is the property of the Tenimenti di Fontanafredda. From up on the ridge, there is a fine view of the gentle vineyards of Grinzane Cavour and, in the middle, the castle that is home to the *Ordine dei Cavalieri del Tartufo e dei Vini Albesi* (Order of the Knights of the Truffle and Alba Wines). Further up is Diano d'Alba and then, on the other slope, the vineyards of La Morra and Castiglione Falletto.
Gallaretto's clay and limestone soil extends over four and a half hectares at an altitude of between 240 and 280 metres. Aspect varies from south west to west. In tastings carried out so far, Gallaretto's wines have stood out for their unforced elegance and intriguing fragrance.
Since 1985, grapes from Gallaretto have no longer been vinified separately. Today, they are blended with the fruit from the Gattinera vineyard to produce Fontanafredda's Barolo Galarey, a wine that flaunts its origins in its dialect name.

Gattinera

Situated next to the ancient cellars and vineyard workers' houses of Tenimenti di Fontanafredda, Gattinera is the pride and joy of the winery created in 1878 by Conte Emanuele Guerrieri, son of Vittorio Emanuele II and his morganatic bride, Contessa Rosa di Mirafiori e Fontanafredda, nicknamed *Bela Rosin*. Gattinera is on the same strip of hillside as La Rosa but has a slightly different orientation so that the entire vineyard is south-facing. Gattinera stretches over almost 15 Piedmontese *giornate*, more than five hectares, at a height that ranges from 250 to 300 metres above sea level. Here, too, it is fascinating to note that the property of the Fontanafredda estate lies in the municipality of Serralunga but enjoys its own special topoclimate. As a result, nebbiolo from Gattinera does not have the robust structure of fruit from Lazzarito and ripens earlier, although it still has all the latter's texture and elegance. Since 1985, grapes from Gattinera have no longer been vinified separately. With the fruit from the Gallaretto vineyard, they today produce Fontanafredda's Barolo Galarey.

La Rosa

There is a fine view down onto the La Rosa vineyard from Sorano. As you go along the side of the hill, the magnificent Tenuta di Fontanafredda unfolds in all its glory. The geometric order of the vines, imposed by the systematic intervention of a single owner, endows these hills with a charm of their own. At the bottom of the hollow, the cellar itself is surrounded by the estate workers' homes.

La Rosa extends over more than nine hectares, at a height that varies from 250 and 300 metres. Almost without exception, the vines face south west. At the top of the hill is the building known as *cascina* La Rosa, decorated in the estate livery. The vineyard is said to take its name from the wild roses that once festooned the walls of the farmhouse. The excellent aspect, soil composition and the steep slope make this area particularly suitable for the cultivation of nebbiolo. The Barolo it yields may not have the tannin-rich fullness of Serralunga's other vineyards but they do stand out for their elegance and harmony.

Main labels

*Barolo Vigna La Rosa – Fontanafredda, Serralunga d'Alba

Lazzarito and Lazzariasco or Lazzariasso

There are no certain indications for the derivation of the vineyard's name, although some claim a lazar house once stood here. However, the name Lazzarito is already used in the land registry of 1610. The imposing *cascina* that dominates the vineyard used to belong to the Opera Pia Barolo, as is clear from the inventory drawn up for the charity in 1859.

Lazzarito is a large vineyard, covering about 20 Piedmontese *giornate*, or just under eight hectares, much of it owned by Fontanafredda, which bought the land in the early 1960s. The altitude of the vines ranges from 350 to 400 metres. The soil is very similar to that on other parts of the hill, although it is perhaps looser packed. Reddish granules of sand can be noted.

Observed from the hamlet of I Vei, Lazzarito is an attractive hollow that forms the natural continuation of the Delizia plot in the Parafada vineyard. The vines range from south through south west to west-facing. It should be noted that the west-facing plot is universally well-regarded as the hollow formed by the hillside provides excellent shelter from the wind.

The chalky nature of the soil keeps yields limited but the quality of the fruit is superb. Lazzarito has always been considered a first class vineyard capable of producing great Barolos with exceptional cellar potential. The lower part of the vineyard is separated by a minor road that starts from the hamlet of I Vei and is known, traditionally, as Lazzariasco. This tiny vineyard of less than two hectares is situated at a height of 300 to 350 metres. Similar in soil type to Lazzarito, it also has excellent potential for quality, thanks in part to its favourable south and south east-facing aspects and in part to an ideal mesoclimate for growing nebbiolo. Sheltered from the wind and protected by the high hillside opposite, Lazzariasco is in the middle of

a valley where the summer heat can be stifling. In short, it has all the requisites of a fine nebbiolo vineyard. It has to be said that all of the older local growers we spoke to assured us that Lazzariasco produces outstanding Barolo and that the tiny plot has always been extremely highly rated.

Main labels

*Barolo Vigna Lazzarito – Fontanafredda, Serralunga d'Alba
*Barolo Vigna Lazzariasco – Guido Porro, Serralunga d'Alba
*Barolo Lazzarito – Vietti, Castiglione Falletto

Marenca

The Marenca vineyard is bounded to the north by the Feja municipal road, to the east and south by the Damiano road, which leads down to the torrential Talloria di Castiglione river, and to the west by the Margaria vineyard. From I Vei, the undulating lines of the hill are clearly visible. In this area, the slope at first has a south-facing aspect, on the border with Rivette, then faces south west, before finally turning to the south again, where an unsurfaced *capezzagna* separates it from Margaria. There is excellent exposure to sunlight, then, at this vineyard, which covers about five hectares at an average altitude of 350 metres.

These vines, always very highly regarded, stand close to the residential part of the town and are probably the longest established in Serralunga. Besides, the town's viticultural heritage is documented in detail by the *Statuti Originali del Comune di Serralunga del Feudo dei Falletti di Barolo*, or the "Original Statutes of the Municipality of Serralunga in the Fief of the Fallettis of Barolo". The statutes date from the first half of the fourteenth century and many of the chapters deal with obligations and duties concerning vineyards, vines, grapes (specifically, those who steal bunches that belong to others) and wine. We would like at this point to draw readers' attention to the statutes of the municipality, notarial deeds and parish archives, in the hope that researchers will investigate them. The results would certainly be of great significance for the entire region.

Main labels

*Barolo Vigneto Marenca – Luigi Pira, Serralunga d'Alba

Margaria and Le Turne

A seriously good vineyard owes its success to a combination of three main factors. First comes soil that is suitable for viticulture; then the varieties grown must have the right charactersitics; and finally the site climate should be congenial. Great wines

Parafada

are, of course, also the result of shrewd vineyard and cellar management techniques. Margaria possesses all the fundamental requisites and can certainly be looked upon as an outstanding vineyard. In this stretch of hills, Margaria is the best-aspected area and its vines look proudly to the south. Naturally, such distinctions are sometimes impalpable but the especially favourable position of the vines at Margaria is worth underlining. Time and the response of the market will, of course, establish just how good the wines are, and where they stand in the hierarchy of merit, but there is no denying that Margaria is a vineyard of rare beauty.

It extends over three and a half hectares at a height above sea level ranging from 280 to 380 metres. To the south, it is bounded by the Damiano road and to the north by the hamlet of Marenca, where you can admire a view of the entire hill.

Where the lovely hillslope turns to the west, making what people from the Langhe call a *sorì d'la seira*, or "evening slope", we find Le Turne. The vines of Le Turne carry on to the large courtyard at the hamlet of Marenca and are marked off by two concentric *capezzagne*, or unsurfaced roads, running along the west side of the hill. Although it may not have the quite the potential of neighbouring vineyards, Le Turne deserves a mention for its admirable wines. The altitude varies from 270 to 340 metres and the vines cover about seven Piedmontese *giornate*, or two and a half hectares.

Main labels

*Barolo Vigneto Margheria – Luigi Pira, Serralunga d'Alba

*Barolo Vigna Margheria – Vigna Riönda di Massolino, Serralunga d'Alba

Ornato

The Ornato family lived on this property until the early 1940s and, as is often the case, the vineyard is named after its former owners.

The Ornato vineyard extends over more than five hectares in the heart of a hillslope area of outstanding viticultural quality. On either side are the Falletto and Briccolina vineyards while the border to the north, at the top of the vineyard, is the Serralunga-Roddino provincial road. The vines face south and the slope of the hillside is relatively steep. Opposite are the rows of Bosco Areto and the broad, vine-clad amphitheatre that looks towards Falletto and Ornato. Here, the aspect turns northwards. Today, the amphitheatre is almost entirely planted to moscato but until the 1920s, it was covered by thick woods.

Barolo Ornato is noted for its intense aromas, which over time acquire a distinct note of tar. Their structure is unmistakably that of a wine from Serralunga, which means they have excellent ageing prospects.

The border with Falletto is marked by a steep unsurfaced *capezzagna* starting from a minor road that turns off the provincial highway for *cascina* Falletto.

Main labels

*Barolo Ornato – Pio Cesare, Alba

Parafada and Delizia

A little higher up the slope than Gabutti is the hamlet of Parafada. Its vineyard is easily visible from the houses at I Vei. From here, there is a clear view of the unsurfaced paths that separate this vineyard from Gabutti to the west. Parafada lies between 280 and 380 metres above sea level. The vines, all facing south, are the pride and joy of local growers, who love to describe in detail the qualities of their fruit. "The agent from a *cascina* that belonged to the Opera Pia Barolo told me one day that the gold medals the Opera Pia has won around the world were always for wines from here" (Giuseppe Boasso, born 1910). In fact, the Opera Pia Barolo owned much of the municipality of Serralunga in the latter half of the nineteenth century. Since the institute was the successor of the Marchesi Falletti, who invented Barolo, it is reasonable to assume that grapes from Serralunga contributed to the very first Barolos. Leaving aside these questions of local pride, which have nonetheless provoked intense argument whenever the demarcation of the Barolo DOCG zone has come under discussion, we may confidently affirm that Parafada, with its 25 Piedmontese *giornate*, or nearly ten hectares, deserves to be listed as one of the great Barolo vineyards.

At Parafada, we also find the Delizia plot, whose main owner is Fontanafredda, as may be deduced from the characteristic farmhouse painted in the livery of the

Tenimenti. The name – it means "delight" – of the *cascina*, which has lovely south-facing vines, is emblematic and at the same time evidence of the quality of this small plot. Delizia borders on Lazzarito and is crossed by the Alba-Serralunga provincial road. Some of the vines stand on the far side of the road at a height of 380 metres. The lower boundary is formed by a minor road that leaves *I Vei* to cross the Lazzarito and Lazzariasco vineyards. In geological terms, the hill marks the start of the so-called *Formazione di Lequio*, the predominant substratum in the municipality of Serralunga. The soil is fairly shallow white clay and limestone marl. In some places, it is quite unstable and as you go further down the slope, it tends to be slightly cooler. The Delizia vineyard covers almost ten Piedmontese *giornate*, or less than four hectares.

Main labels

*Barolo Vigna La Delizia – Fontanafredda, Serralunga d'Alba

*Barolo Parafada – Vigna Riönda di Massolino, Serralunga d'Alba

Pra di Pò or Prapò

The derivation of this odd name is unknown but the quality of its grapes did not escape the notice of Dottor Giuseppe Cappellano, the expert and sophisticated connoisseur of Langhe vineyards. For more than half a century, the Cappellano cellar throve thanks, at least in part, to the grapes he bought at Pra di Pò. The vineyard can be admired from the courtyard in front of the cemetery at Serralunga. It lies on an attractive, fairly steep, hillside with a very sunny summit known as Bricco Cerretta. We have included the Bricco itself in the Cerretta vineyard for historical and geographical reasons. Situated at an altitude of 390 metres, the Bricco has an area of just over one hectare and is perhaps a little too windy. But it does offer a stunning panorama of the entire Langhe. Below this dry, sunny peak, the Pra di Pò vines cover the steep slope at an average altitude of 350 metres above sea level. There are almost seven hectares planted to vine, with aspects ranging from the east-facing *sorì del mattino*, or "morning slope", to the south-east and south-facing *sorì di mezzogiorno*, or "midday slope".

The vineyard is clearly marked off by the road that rises from the provincial highway to the hamlet of Cerretta and by the Cerretta vineyard. The Barolo from this vineyard is tannin-rich, with aromas that acquire classic notes of tar as they age in the cellar.

Main labels

*Barolo Prapò – Bricco Rocche Ceretto, Castiglione Falletto

*Barolo Prapò – Ettore Germano, Serralunga d'Alba

*Barolo Prapò – Mauro Sebaste, Alba

*Barolo Vigneto Prapò – Schiavenza, Serralunga d'Alba

Rivette

In the nineteenth century, Cascina Rivette and the vines round about formed part of the Opera Pia Barolo estate which, in the municipality of Serralunga alone, extended over fully 257 hectares. Subsequent changes of ownership have in no way compromised the prestige of Rivette on the edge of a range of hills halfway between Vigna Rionda and the Gabutti hill. We are right in the heart of Serralunga's great Barolo vineyards.
With Marenca and Margaria, Rivette has always been regarded as an excellent location for growing nebbiolo. Ratti himself considered it a first class area. Rivette stands to the west of Serralunga, just below the village. There is thus an excellent view from Piazza Cappellano. Its boundaries are marked both to the north and to the west by the Damiano municipal road. The rows of vines face south and south west at altitudes of between 330 and 380 metres. The soil is fairly loose-packed marl and limestone, the quality of the grapes beyond dispute. There is an excellent viewpoint from which to observe Rivette, Marenca, Margaria and Le Turne on the local Chiappellere road, at Vigna Rionda. Rivette covers almost nine Piedmontese *giornate*, or just over three hectares.

San Bernardo

This tiny vineyard deserves a mention for its excellent south and south east-facing aspect. The vines are behind the Cascina Colombaio, on the hilltop from which it dominates Vigna Rionda looking towards Sinio, and the vineyard is delimited to the south by the small Lirano municipal road. The Broglio stream runs at the bottom of the valley before it joins the Talloria at Sinio. The San Bernardo vineyard covers only ten Piedmontese *giornate*, or just under four hectares. *Cascina* Colombaio stands at an altitude of 400 metres and the vines lower down are at about 350 metres.

MAIN LABELS

*Barolo Vigna S. Bernardo – Palladino, Serralunga d'Alba

Santa Caterina

Santa Caterina is a small vineyard situated beyond Lazzarito in the direction of the centre of Serralunga. Only part of the vineyard, which takes its name from the *cascina*, is suitable for growing nebbiolo: the section that faces south west. The vines run downhill from the provincial road on fairly cool soil that tends to be richer than the terrain in areas that receive more sunshine. The advantage of vineyards of this kind is that they can provide excellent fruit even in years with very little rain. Santa Caterina covers no more than five Piedmontese *giornate*, or less than two hectares. It lies between 340 and 390 metres above sea level.

MAIN LABELS

*Barolo Vigna Santa Caterina – Guido Porro, Serralunga d'Alba

Serra

Cascina Serra is on the provincial road that leads from Serralunga to Roddino. The main part of this attractive vineyard descends harmoniously to the west of the road, the side that faces the municipality of Monforte. The municipal road of Collaretto marks off the lower part of the vineyard at an altitude of 360 metres. The west and south west-facing positions mean Serra is a classic *sorì d'la seira* that enjoys the last rays of the setting sun. A small part of the vineyard lies below the Serralunga-Roddino provincial road, facing east and south-east. The vineyard covers about three hectares.

Sorano

Most of the Sorano vineyard lies in the municipality of Diano d'Alba. The hamlet stands right on the border with Serralunga and the line of demarcation is the lane that goes from Sorano along the crest of the hill towards the Fontanafredda estate. The plot that belongs to Serralunga is just below the houses and faces south east at an altitude ranging from 270 and 320 metres (see the entry for the municipality of Diano d'Alba).

MAIN LABELS

*Barolo Sorano – Ascheri, Bra

Vigna Rionda

If you ask a resident of Serralunga to name the town's three finest vineyards, one of the trio is sure to be Vigna Rionda.

It is an historic vineyard. The quality of its grapes has been celebrated for hundreds of years and the greatest names in Langhe winemaking have for many years made special efforts to acquire grapes from Vigna Rionda. Great producers have always sought to purchase the finest fruit. As Giovanni Gagna from Monforte pointed out in a report on wine production in the Langhe for the 1879 *Inchiesta Agraria* (agricultural inquiry), "The production of wine is becoming more intensive each year so several producers travel into the countryside to assure supplies of grapes from the best ositions and aspects, or invite the owners to visit them to negotiate their purchase".

Nebbiolo from Vigna Rionda yields fairly tannic Barolos with outstanding structure and excellent ageing potential. "Serralunga Barolo from Vigna Rionda, Parafada, Lazzarito and other vineyards needs time to develop. With patience, you can obtain a wine that is unrivalled" (*Giaculin* Anselma).

The vital statistics of Vigna Rionda are as follows: height above sea level ranges from 300 to 350 metres, mainly south-facing, and the surface area is almost 30 *giornate*, or over ten hectares. Vigna Rionda is known all over the world thanks to the Bruno Giacosa winery at Neive. Giacosa's Barolo Collina Rionda – produced until 1993 – has delighted generations of winelovers.

MAIN LABELS

*Barolo Vigna Rionda – Giacomo Anselma, Serralunga d'Alba
*Barolo Poderi dell'Antica Vigna Riunda – Aldo Canale, Serralunga d'Alba
*Barolo Vigna Rionda – Michele Chiarlo, Calamandrana
*Barolo Vigna Rionda – Fratelli Oddero, La Morra
*Barolo Vigna Rionda – Luigi Pira, Serralunga d'Alba
*Barolo Vigna Riönda – Vigna Riönda di Massolino, Serralunga d'Alba

Vigna Rionda

Voghera and Brea

Voghera and Brea, classified by Ratti as a single vineyard under the name Brea, have their own special characteristics. Lying to the east of Serralunga, the vines start near the provincial road for Alba, not far from where it enters Cerrati. The rows run along both sides of the Tezzo municipal road until they reach, 50 metres lower down, *cascina* Camia at an altitude of 340 metres above sea level. Until the early 1990s, the Brea vineyard, which extends below the Tezzo road and is magnificently located for the cultivation of nebbiolo grapes to make Barolo, was almost entirely grassed over. Today, thankfully, nebbiolo vines have recently been replanted on this slope. Those belonging to the Brovia family from Castiglione Falletto deserve special mention.
Situated above the Tezzo road at just under 400 metres above sea level, the Voghera vines face south east in the plot adjacent to the provincial road, then gradually turn towards the south lower down, above *cascina* Camia. The entire area of the Voghera and Brea vineyards was classified by Ratti as being of especially good quality. Ratti called the area Brea, which is actually the name of the cascina in the middle of this small vineyard.

MAIN LABELS

*Barolo Ca' Mia – Fratelli Brovia, Castiglione Falletto

Our selection

Population 497
Height 414 metres asl

INFORMATION

Town Hall
Via Foglio, 1
Tel. + 39 0173 613101

Castello di Serralunga d'Alba
Via Castello, 5
Tel. + 39 0173 613358

THE WINERIES

Luigi e Fiorina Baudana
Borgata Baudana, 43
Tel. + 39 0173 613354
A small but interesting cellar that we have included because of the fine quality of the first estate wines, the Dolcetto, Barbera and Chardonnay. The first Barolo vintage released was the 1996 and is labelled Cerretta Piani. There are plans to bottle a new selection from Baudana in the next few years.

Gabutti - Franco Boasso
Borgata Gabutti, 3/a
Tel. + 39 0173 613165
Four hectares under vine in Gabutti and Parafada are the trump card of this compact estate. With laudable consistency, the cellar turns out attractive, well-made wines year after year, achieving heights of excellence when fruit from great vintages, such as 1990 and 1998, is available.

Giuseppe Cappellano
Via Alba, 13
Frazione Bruni
Tel. + 39 0173 613103
One of the historic cellars (see the relevant profile in the chapter *The Greats of Barolo*), Cappellano has over the last ten years made some very fine wines with fruit from an outstanding vineyard, Gabutti at Serralunga. Nor should we forget that the winery has promoted the celebrated Barolo Chinato, made with Peruvian bark and other herbs,

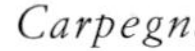

Carpegna

using a recipe that is still a trade secret.

Eredi Virginia Ferrero
Località San Rocco, 71
Tel. + 39 0173 613283
Tota Virginia Ferrero (see the profile in the chapter on *The Greats of Barolo*) was a gruff, enterprising producer whose wine business was not continued after her death by her closest relatives. Today, the cellar is again operating with the twin aims of honouring the heritage left by the formidable *Tota* and of bringing out the potential of a very good vineyard, San Rocco.

Fontanafredda
Via Alba, 15
Tel. + 39 0173 613161
The magnificent estate-owned vineyards and the deep pockets of the owner, the Monte dei Paschi di Siena bank, have enabled this historic winery, which was founded at end of the nineteenth century, to turn out consistently good wines. However, the cellar has never managed to give the name Fontanafredda the status of one of Barolo's front-rank labels. That, however, is the ambitious objective being pursued by the new winery management with Barolo selections that include La Delizia, La Rosa, Lazzarito, Galarey and La Villa, as well as Barolo di Serralunga. Very encouraging results have also recently been achieved with Barbaresco Coste Rubin.

Sergio Germano
Borgata Cerretta, 1
Tel. + 39 0173 613528 - 0173 613112
Production with grapes from estate-owned vines began in 1975 but it is only in the last decade that the cellar has built up a reputation in the market. Since that year, the very capable Sergio himself has been working at the winery full-time. Sergio Germano releases Barolo under two labels, Cerretta and Prapò. Cerretta is more approachable and stylish whereas Prapò is a tannin-rich wine that benefits from ageing in the bottle.

Luigi Pira
Via XX Settembre, 9 bis
Tel. + 39 0173 613106
Giampaolo Pira has only recently taken over this winery but already he has achieved some notable successes. Until now, the cellar has produced two Barolos, about 6,000 bottles of Vigna Margheria and 8,000 or so of Vigna Marenca. The first has a little more tannin and structure while the Vigna Marenca is superbly drinkable only a few years after release.

There is also a Barolo Vigna Rionda 1997 in the pipeline and it promises to be very exciting.

Vigna Rionda - Massolino
Piazza Cappellano, 6
Tel. + 39 0173 613138
Winemaking at this cellar has always been a very traditional affair, as you can see from some of the Barolo Riservas that age in large oak barrels for more than five years. But the arrival of young Franco Massolino has started to make an impact and now, in the attractive underground barrel cellars, built by Franco's father Mario and uncle Giovanni, French barriques stand alongside Slavonian oak. The standard-label Barolo is joined on the list by the proud names of the Margheria, Parafada and Vigna Rionda selections, often also released as Riservas. These are wines with outstanding structure and ageing potential.

WHERE TO SLEEP

Albergo Italia
Piazza Cappellano, 3/a
Tel. + 39 0173 613124
Two stars and eight rooms with bath and telephone. The Italia, a local landmark, stands in the main square of Serralunga and is an excellent base for anyone wanting to explore the Langhe. The hotel offers no-frills accommodation at a moderate price. The owner is Giacomo Anselma, a man of many parts. A grape trader and wine producer, Giacomo is also a restaurateur and above all an outstanding connoisseur of Langhe's vineyards. On the table, you will find home-style Langhe cooking and excellent Anselma Barolos. All at very affordable prices.

EATING OUT

Cascina Schiavenza
Via Mazzini, 4
Tel. + 39 0173 613115
Unswerving loyalty to the local heritage, a simple ambience and a magnificent panoramic view. You will also have an excellent opportunity to sample traditional cuisine accompanied by the house wines from Serralunga's best-known vineyards, Broglio, Cerretta and Prapò. A full meal will cost you about € 30.00.

WHAT TO BUY

Bottega del Vino
Via Foglio, 1
Open on Saturdays and Sundays during summer. Wines from a range of local producers.

L'Infernòt del Castel
Via Roma, 2
A reasonable range of local wines and some gourmet food items.

Cappellano

The history of wine at Alba reveals Dottor Giuseppe Cappellano as one of the most important personalities in the first half of the twentieth century. Few will know that this inspired pharmacist, inventor of Barolo Chinato, only became involved in winemaking after the sudden death of his elder brother Giovanni (1868-1912), who was an equally talented entrepreneur. They were the sons of Filippo Cappellano, a notary who came from a long line of notaries. In 1870, the 48 year old Filippo founded the Cappellano winery, making significant investments to expand the estate to fully 150 *giornate*, or almost 60 hectares of cultivable land. On Filippo's death in 1886, his two daughters were bought out of their inheritance, as was customary at the time, with a dowry of 100,000 lire each, a very large sum of money in those days. Giuseppe, the younger of the two brothers, continued his studies and Giovanni, barely 19 years old, was forced to drop out of university and take care of the family business.

Giovanni did not lack ability or the entrepreneurial spirit. In a few years, he had restructured the cellars at Alba and also opened two hotels, at Alba and Serralunga, with facilities to cater for the Langhe's first tourists. At Serralunga, he launched grape therapy and set up a carriage service to connect his hotel with the railway station at Alba. Meanwhile, wine production did more than merely supply the two Cappellano hotels for it had an appreciative clientele, particularly in Liguria and Piedmont. By 1889, the Cappellano winery had won a bronze medal at the Exposition Universelle held in Paris to celebrate the centenary of the Revolution, and for which, incidentally, the Eiffel Tower was built. After that first award, diplomas, medals and attestations came thick and fast as Giovanni Cappellano's determined spirit begant to make headway in the market.

Giuseppe took an excellent degree in pharmacy and, after working in Turin for a short while, decided to pursue a career as a wine producer and manufacturer of pharmaceutical products. It was in this period that he made the first grape jellies and concentrated medicinal musts as well as inventing the monument to Italian oenology that is Barolo Chinato. This wine-oriented pharmacist created a product that for many years was a legendary elixir and household stand-by, the only real tonic available in the Langhe of poor, or even destitute, agricultural workers.

However, Giuseppe Cappellano's career as an industrialist was brief. In 1912, he was summoned to run the winery left untended after the premature demise of his brother. In that year, Giovanni Cappellano died from a tropical disease contracted in Tunisia, where he had been seeking phylloxera-resistant vines.

At this point, Dottor Giuseppe Cappellano returned to the estate founded by his father and expanded by his brother, Giovanni. When he took over, Giuseppe enhanced the cellar's potential even further thanks to his connections with Turin's upper middle classes and his friendship with Conte Mirafiore. These were years of intense activity for the estate's strategy was not only to make great

Langhe wines and the now celebrated Barolo Chinato but also to acquire new plots in the finest vineyards. However, it was also the period of the family tragedy that so deeply scarred the soul and character of this great winemaker. Giuseppe lost his only daughter to a bout of Spanish influenza. In her memory, he would later donate to the municipality of Serralunga the town's main square, which is still dedicated to Maria Cappellano.

The years that followed are relatively recent history, still recounted by Serralunga's older residents, who remember the gruff gentleman whose word regarding most of the grapes grown in the area was law. The agreement with the Gancia winery at Canelli, who had entrusted Cappellano with the vinification under the Mirafiore label of the *Vini Fini* from Alba, made him the most important purchaser of grapes in the area. Gancia was not the only winery to delegate vinification to Cappellano for other famous Piedmontese labels did so as well. Cappellano bought so much fruit that during the harvest period, it was not unusual to see carts queuing in front of the cellar in an almost endless line. Price was never an issue with Dottor Cappellano. It was already an event if he accepted the grower's grapes. When payment was actually made, the growers compared notes, not always entirely truthfully, to establish the quality classification that Cappellano had drawn up. There could be no appeal. Cappellano was more than familiar with the quality of the fruit, the outstanding vineyards, the growers with ambition when it came to nebbiolo for Barolo and the influence of the various site climates. This authority was universally accepted and even today, many growers regard the fact that they once sold their grapes to Dottor Cappellano as a mark of distinction.

In 1955, Giuseppe Cappellano passed away, leaving his heirs a very substantial estate. After various vicissitudes, and the inevitable carve-up of the estate, the good name of the Dottor Giuseppe Cappellano brand is today held aloft by two great-grandchildren who continue to practise the noble art of making wine.

THE GREATS OF BAROLO

Giuseppe Bressano

1896-1954

The year 1931 was a bad one for the Società Mirafiore Vini Italiani. The phylloxera epidemic, the crisis in the wine trade and various financial problems brought the company to the brink of bankruptcy. The estate at Fontanafredda, and the cellars and olive oil mill at Greve in Chianti, were auctioned off to the Monte dei Paschi di Siena bank. The new owners, who already had several other estates, closed the premises at Greve, and attempted to revive Fontanafredda. First of all, they had to deal with a number of problems that initially almost prompted them to sell off the property without delay.
In the same year, the young wine technician, Giuseppe Bressano, was transferred to Alba from Greve, where he had been working for the Società Mirafiore, to run the estate. At first, Bressano was assisted by Professor Giorgio Garavini, from the faculty of agriculture at the university of Pisa, who was director of the bank's agricultural holdings office. Together, they drew up an agenda for the rational viticultural recovery of the hills at Fontanafredda. In the vineyards, Bressano personally supervised the replanting programme. The fourth child of Giovanni Bressano, the estate manager of the Alba lawyer, Pagliuzzi, Giuseppe loved the land. He had the soil in his blood.
Giuseppe was born on 8 May 1896, 15 years after the family's third child, a daughter. This proved fortunate for his older siblings, financially independent by the time he was studying, were able to contribute to the cost of his education. Giuseppe qualified as a wine technician in 1914. He was then called up and remained in military service until 1918, when the war ended. During the conflict, he was wounded, awarded a bronze medal and given the rank of senior captain. Called up again from 1940 to 1943, Bressano was sent to Albania as a commissioner. This earned for him the rank of lieutenant colonel in the infantry reserve.
In 1919, Bressano was hired by the Società Mirafiore, the new name, acquired that very year, of the Casa E. Mirafiore. It was here that he met his future wife, Vittoria. The couple married just before he left for Greve, where their son Giovanni was born in 1928.
In the early 1930s, awareness of the viticultural potential of the Langhe began to grow. Many producers started to rethink their production strategy and focused on improving quality. The phenomenon led, among other things, to the foundation in 1934 of the Consorzio del Barolo e del Barbaresco, which Cavalier Giuseppe Bressano was to chair from 1949 to 1951. In the meantime, the terrain, climate and locations at Fontanafredda were being assessed. Rigorous studies led to the targeted planting of plots with appropriate varieties. There are still those who can remember Cavalier Bressano, soil auger in hand among the clods of earth, checking that the ground had been broken to a depth of at least one metre. Meanwhile, workers were collecting the trunks and roots of the old, phylloxera-afflicted vines and the cable-driven tractor was dragging its heavy plough.

The new rows were planted in rings around the hill, as if they were in a huge garden. Looking from the bottom of the tracks that led up the slope was almost like gazing along an avenue where, at the end of each row, fruit trees alternated with raspberry and currant bushes. The posts were all made of concrete.

Three families of tenant farmers worked the vineyards, which covered roughly 80 hectares, and other fields were planted to wheat and animal fodder. Sheds for livestock breeding were also built. Fontanafredda was now a full-scale agricultural enterprise.

Next came the restucturing of the cellars, which dated from 1878, the year in which Conte Emanuele di Mirafiore had founded Fontanafredda.

The estate was now well and truly active, with excellent levels of production and wine quality. Marketing and distribution needed to be improved, although the estate had frequent contacts with France, the USA and Switzerland. Wine production could be increased, using bought-in fruit, if new markets could be opened up. This was strategy on which Bressano was working when he was involved in a car accident at Bandito, near Bra, as he was driving to Turin for a meeting with some distributors. It was 28 October 1954. To his wife, Vittoria, who had hurried to his bedside, he said, "You go back to Fontanafredda and take care of the wages. My sister Maddalena will look after me here. The workers have been busy with the vintage in the last few days and we mustn't make them wait just because I have had this accident". At that time, there was no hint that only two days later, Bressano would pass away.

He was an active, much respected man who is remembered with affection. He was also fortunate in having a large bank behind him to back up his policies.

Bressano was a corresponding member of the Accademia della Vite e del Vino (Academy of the Vine and Wine), a member of ONAV, the Italian Winetasters' Association, and a founder member and first president in 1952 of the alumni organisation of the Scuola Enologica (oenological school) at Alba.

THE GREATS OF BAROLO

Tota Virginia Ferrero

1865-1949

Virginia Ferrero was born in Turin on 15 June 1865. Her parents, Giacomo Ferrero and Teresa Gabutti, were both from Serralunga. The Ferreros were reasonably well-off and, although they lived in Turin, they were still able to look after their land and vineyards in their home town. It is not difficult to imagine, then, the significance for Virginia Ferrero of those first harvests and the subsequent winemaking. We have very little documentary evidence of Virginia's life. The story of Barolo itself has yet to be written and no one has so far taken the trouble to collect material from this period. One thing is certain. Among people in the Barolo DOCG zone, old agricultural labourers in Serralunga and Barolo-making families, the memory of Virginia Ferrero, or *Tota* Virginia, as she was called, is very much alive. That memory is pervaded with admiration and respect for a woman who may not have actually worn trousers but was as courageous and determined as any man. Virginia Ferrero was a manager and a model of emancipation in a world – that of wine – which was overwhelmingly dominated by men. Before the end of the nineteenth century, Virginia was already working full-time at Serralunga to follow the winemaking process at first hand. She received no help at all from her brother Francesco, known as *Cichin*, who had an artistic soul and was very much a *bon viveur*, unlike his hardworking, strong-willed sister. When her brother was left a widower, *Tota* Virginia took in her five nephews and nieces, ensuring they were not just fed but also educated and well looked after. Their childhood was certainly much more comfortable than that of most Langhe country-dwellers in the early twentieth century. Prosperity was possible thanks to the drive that Virginia brought to the production and distribution of the wine from the estate, which grew relentlessly, both in terms of assets and of volume.

Year after year, *Tota* Virginia's estate expanded to include several agricultural complexes and over 40 *giornate* of vineyards. At the same time, the cellars bought in fruit from local growers, taking production to almost 6,000 *brente* (kegs) of wine, corresponding to roughly 3,000 hectolitres.

At harvest time, a long line of carts used to stretch in front of the Cantina Ferrero, as the older residents of Serralunga still vividly remember. On the door of the winery in Baudana, opposite the little church of San Rocco, *Tota* Virginia would remark on the grapes from each grower. It was a very thorough examination. Taking your grapes to *Tota* Virginia was like being back in school. The evening before delivery, grapes would be selected bunch by bunch in yards and under porticoes to avoid public humiliation the following day.

The cellar's list was long and varied, encompassing Barolo, Barbera, Dolcetto, Bonarda, Favorita and Brachetto. Even though most wine in those days was sold in demijohns or casks, Ferrero offered a good range of bottled products. The Ferrero winery was in its heyday from the 1920s to the

1940s, and despite her age, *Tota* remained a shrewd businesswoman. The estate must have had a solid financial base if, as people said, the Ferrero winery wanted to purchase Fontanafredda after the latter's bankruptcy. Virginia looked after her customers personally and her horse-drawn carriage frequently crossed the Alps, defying the roads of the day, into Switzerland or France, to visit restaurants in Nice or Montecarlo, as well as Genoa, Turin and Milan. Needless to say, Virginia was at ease with her clients, as she was very communicative and had a cordial, outgoing personality. People in Alba knew her well. On Saturdays, they would watch her arrive in her little gig for the market. She would exchange a few words with the growers in Piazza Savona, visit the bank, where she would deposit the large wad of notes she had tucked down her blouse and then go on to lunch at the Hotel Savona, where she would again converse with other growers.

At Baudana, she supervised cellar operations personally, dealt with correspondence, kept the books and even found time to enquire about local affairs when anyone happened to pass the cellar. She used to say that you had to be inquisitive to be shrewd and she was both. In fact, she was a walking news bulletin on changes of ownership, agricultural and winemaking problems and even the latest gossip from families around the Langhe. She always enjoyed a relationship of mutual respect with Giuseppe Cappellano and the two often exchanged opinions on how to deal with some problem or another.

None of the five nephews and nieces carried on the business when Virginia passed away at the age of 84 on 19 February, 1949, so her estate was broken up. In 1973, her heirs from Milan founded the Eredi Virginia Ferrero winery in the premises that had once belonged to *Tota* Virginia. It is a fitting way to commemorate her name. Virginia, who devoted her entire life to her family and to Barolo, the wine of the Langhe, will not be easily forgotten.

Baudana

EYE-WITNESS REPORTS

The grape agent

Like my father, Felice Anselma, before me, I have always been a grape agent in this area. The best dolcetto grapes were to be had around Serralunga. At Roddi, they had a higher acidity content and greater intensity of colour. During the last few years of Dottor Cappellano's winemaking career, I went to Cerretto Langhe to buy his dolcetto because my father was getting old and in those days you had to walk. Cappellano was the most educated of the great Barolo makers and a good man. He bought a lot of fruit for his own cellar and for Gancia. He would select the grapes before vinification, using the best fruit to produce some great wines. Cappellano knew that even in good vintages, it is not always the same vineyards that give the best results so he would personally check the state of the grapes.

Twenty days before the harvest, my father and Cappellano would go scouting and walk down the rows, checking the quality of this or that grower's grapes. Apart from Serralunga, where he owned many plots, Cappellano's favourite vineyards were in the municipality of La Morra. He bought a lot of fruit from Santa Maria and Serra. Cappellano and Zabaldano, from the chemist's shop at Monforte, have always made good Barolo.

Giacomo Anselma
knonw as *Giacolin*
born 1915
grape agent and
innkeeper
in Serralunga d'Alba

Tota Virginia Ferrero also made good Barolo. Once she asked me to taste a barrel and give her my opinion. She was a *brigadiera*, a "sergeant major" who barked orders like a man, but she knew all about buying and selling wine. You could see she'd had an education, unlike some others. The great Barolos from Serralunga – Vigna Rionda, Parafada and Gabutti – need time to age. At first, they are a little closed but in time they are incomparable. You've got to remind people to be patient and drink them when they are at their best. Many meetings were held at my *osteria* to decide the boundaries of the Barolo DOCG zone. The Cavalieri del Tartufo, or "Knights of the Truffle", initially met in the rooms of my *osteria* because at first the president, Dottor De Giacomi, wanted to make the castle at Serralunga the order's headquarters. (*Summer 1990*)

The wheat between the rows

Aldo Canale
born 1913
grower
in Serralunga

Once, there weren't as many vineyards as there are today. In many of the fields, we used to grow wheat and maize. There weren't very many grapes, not even nebbiolo. The rows stood well apart and we would plant wheat between alternate rows. We used to get three or four stacks of 20 or so sheaves from every row.

I don't want to boast but we have some good grow-

ing spots at Serralunga. In fact, our nebbiolos attract higher prices than fruit from other subzones. *Tota* Virginia Ferrero had a lovely cellar. She grew her own fruit and bought in more. She was a great, big "beast of a woman" who was always glowering. "Are you here for your money already?" she would ask people who had sold her their grapes. But we sold to the Lurgo brothers at Alba.
Once, most wine was sold in demijohns. People bottled very little and left it to age for two years at most before selling it. But it's only a month since I finished racking the Barolo 1986. It was a vintage when not much wine was made. On 28 May that year, there was a terrible hailstorm. We pruned the vines twice. If there is hail before the grapes colour, the surviving shoots produce the bunches. (*Spring 1990*)

Grapes and truffles

Hunting for *trifole* (truffles) is an absorbing passion. I've been a truffle hunter for 78 years. Before I was 10, I had been out once or twice with my late father. I had seen that our bitch was good at finding truffles. Once, I was out with the animal looking for truffles. We were going through a hazelnut grove and she started digging. She found one truffle, and then more. I filled both my pockets. As I was passing the school, the teacher, Miss Servetto, said to me, "Come here a minute. You go truffle hunting instead of studying". I didn't know what to do. My pockets were full of truffles and I didn't dare let her see them. There aren't so many truffles nowadays. Once, I found a truffle weighing 650 grams, and another of half a kilogram, in a single night. I used to give all my truffles to *Giaco Mora* (see the profile of Giacomo Morra in the chapter on *The Greats of Barolo and of Barbaresco*). I was his friend. Truffle hunting since then has changed completely. Then, you would find four or five kilos. Today, you might get a couple of hundred grams. Why do they cost 200,000 lire (€ 100.00) for 100 grams? Because there aren't any left. I have always had good dogs and if the truffle season lasted for three months, then for three months I would leave the house at 11 o'clock every night and come home at six in the morning. Every night. It was hard working in the vineyards all day and then going out again at 11 pm but the truffles helped us make ends meet.

Alberto Germano
born 1902
grower
in Serralunga

It's just as well the truffles were there because there was a lot of poverty in those days. In 1931, I got married and on Sunday 31 August, while I was in Barolo playing *pallone elastico*, a storm blew up, just wind and dust. At the same moment, Cerretta was battered by hail and when I got home at midnight or one in the morning, not a single bunch was left on the vines. A disaster. That year, everyone came to Bricco Cerretta. No one had ever seen anything like it. The following year, there was a drought and we harvested very few grapes. The soil had to be turned over by hand and the workers had to be paid. So I went truffle hunting at night and paid the workers with the money I earned.
Near our house at Cerretta, *Tota* Virginia – there is a profile of Virginia Ferrero in the chapter on *The Greats of Barolo* – had a plot with ten *giornate* (almost 4 hectares) planted to vine and for two years we worked it for her. For several years, I went to work in *Tota* Virginia's cellar in the autumn. Cartloads of demijohns would head for the station at Alba. They all went by rail.
Delivering grapes to Cappellano – discussed at length in the chapter on *The Greats of Barolo* – and *Tota* Virginia was worse than taking an exam. They would make you harvest the fruit in the evening because in the morning it was too

damp. Every bunch had to be cleaned, grape by grape. It's a different story nowadays! *Tota* Virginia bought a lot of fruit and was a bit slow in paying. You had to make a lot of trips to get your money. That woman had a temper, too. Every so often, she would give you the rough edge of her tongue but then she might treat you well. Below her terrace, where we washed the demijohns, Virginia was the boss. She certainly knew how to make her presence felt. She was afraid of no one and did everything herself. She did the accounts, the sales... she was no fool! (*Summer 1990*)

Wine and bread

My father was a baker at Verduno and in 1920, they asked him to go to Fontanafredda, to the village where there was an oven and enough work. The whole family went with him. There were seven of us – I was eight years old – and my two elder brothers, Bastianin and Domenico, got jobs in the winery.
They bottled the wine and washed the bottles. There were no bottling machines then. Everything had to be done by hand. The bottles weren't thrown away. They were put to one side and washed. I remember that outside the winery, there were stacked this high. They were all black and had the crest of the Conti Mirafiore. The wine improved in those bottles.
There were lots of children in the village. My sister Cecilia was born there and her godfather was Cavalier Mollo, one of the bigwigs at Fontanafredda.

Margherita Ravinale
born 1912,
grower
in Serralunga

The Conti Mirafiore were very friendly. Every so often, they would come to the oven and chat with my father. I used to be a ball girl when the Contessa played tennis. The people from villages nearby brought bread to bake in the oven while the ones who worked in the cellar bought it from my father.
A few years later came the Depression and the oven closed. The whole family moved to La Morra and we became tenant farmers, working in the vineyards at Ca' Nere. It's a hard life as a tenant farmer because the owners never divided the crop equally. You always got slightly less than half. There were no guarantees and if the owner sold up you could find yourself out on your ear. At Martinmas, you changed farm. It was a very tough existence. I don't know if I'd want to go back. (*Summer 1990*)

We are not afraid of anyone

Here, we have a wine that ages very well. Take our Dolcetto. You can lay it down for nine of ten years.
A few years ago, a professor from Alessandria came and held a meeting in the parish priest's house. He that that we in Serralunga were lucky because we have a salt in the soil that gives the wine flavour, aroma and ageing potential. Other towns don't have this salt.

Giuseppe Boasso
born 1910
grower
in Serralunga

We're 414 metres above sea level yet if you look at Serralunga from the nearby hills, the village seems to be in a hole. But the soil is good and holds the heat well.
Once, a tenant farmer from one of the estates at Serralunga that belonged to the Opera Pia di Barolo saw me and said, "The gold medals we've won for our Barolo have all been for wines from here".
At Serralunga, we are not afraid of anyone. (*Spring 1990*)

Life behind the counter

I was born in Serralunga and lived in the village. Then when I got married, we moved to Cerretta, where we lived for 30 years. Everyone in the village got on. There was the odd argument, especially in autumn when the hens had to be locked up because otherwise they would eat the grapes in other people's vineyards.
In winter, we used to gather in the biggest barn and play bingo for penny stakes. There were 15 or 20 of us playing bingo and we went to spend the night in the barn. During the week, the women knitted and on Sundays, we all went to play bingo. People helped each other. I remember one family of 12 where the mother was ill. So, the women from three other families would do their laundry and then we all prepared a meal together.
I was very sorry to leave Cerretta but in 1960, we took over the grocery store at Serralunga. It was too good an opportunity to miss. When I came here, there were more people living in Serralunga and all the surrounding villages were populated. They're deserted now. No one lives there. There were 40 of us at Cerretta and 35 or 36 at Collaretto. Now, you see the occasional holidaymaker during the summer.
When I started running the shop, there were still tenant farmers who made me write what they owed in a notebook. One family of tenant farmers asked us, "Can you give us credit?" Money was tight but we said yes. The following year, they paid us and we got on well after that. The family is well-off today. All of them work.

Fiorina Mascarello
born 1913
shopkeeper
in Serralunga

Once, there was a lot of poverty around here but then, with the jobs in the Ferrero factory or at Miroglio, things changed. If one or two people in a family go to work in a factory, then with what you can earn yourself at home and the factory wages, you can live decently. The big problem today is that no one wants to work in the fields any more. I don't know where it will end. (*Summer 1990*)

Verduno

The "flowering hill" of Verduno – the name derives from the Celtic *verdum* – can be reached from Bra via Pollenzo, along the provincial road for La Morra, or from Alba, 12 kilometres away via Roddi, on the provincial road to Barolo. The visitor's first contact with the town is the hill of Monvigliero, Verduno's historic vineyard, which lies just beyond the territory of the municipality of Roddi. Swept by the *marino*, the warm wind from the sea, Monvigliero is one of the area's best-known and most prestigious vineyards. Barolo from Monvigliero made by the legendary Commendator Burlotto went to the Arctic with the Duca degli Abbruzzi's polar expedition in 1900.

Near the historic centre, where the town's most celebrated monuments stand, is the flower-studded meadow of the Belvedere. Although this silent, shady vantage-point is less striking than its namesake at the neighbouring town of La Morra, it offers a fine view over a vast expanse of almost entirely vine-clad Langhe countryside. It is no coincidence that Verduno, the first vine-encircled town on the far side of the Tanaro, is called the "sentinel of the Langhe".

Verduno's artistic heritage is almost entirely to be found in or around Piazza Castello, the civic and religious centre overlooked by the town hall and, side by side, the castle and parish church.

The noble residence that once stood here has disappeared without trace. The present building was erected in the mid-eighteenth century – for Marchese Luigi Caisotti – to plans by Filippo Juvarra. Acquired in the nineteenth century by Carlo Alberto, it became one of the favourite residences of the

Savoy dynasty. It was also the nerve centre of a model wine-producing enterprise, supervised by the oenologist general Staglieno, who was the creator of one of the first Barolos in history. When the Savoys moved to Pollenzo, the castle at Verduno again became a summer residence. It was the home of Oddone, the sickly son of Vittorio Emanuele II, until the young man's death at Genoa in 1861.

The parish church, in the late Baroque idiom, also shows its debt to Juvarra. Evincing the measured solemnity and dark, ominous atmosphere typical of seventeenth-century Catholicism, the church conserves an icon of the Blessed Sebastiano Valfré, born at Verduno in 1629. History blends with myth, and the sacred mingles with the profane, in the story of Valfré yet no one at Verduno doubts a word. Chaplain to the court of Vittorio Amedeo II, Valfré served with distinction during the French siege of Turin in 1706, urging civilians and soldiers to resist the attackers. The people of Verduno, however, ascribe to him the particular merit of having brought the town's signature vine variety to these hills from the area around Saluzzo – Valfré introduced pelaverga. It was not merely for his sanctity that a small sanctuary was erected in 1940 to Valfré, where the house he was born in once stood.

Another illustrious son of Verduno was lieutenant Giovanni Battista Laneri, a leading figure, with the more famous Santorre from Santarosa and Guglielmo Moffa from Lisio, in the Piedmontese revolution of 1821. He was unfortunate enough to be one of the few to hang, along with captain Garelli from Genoa, while the others managed to escape. The rest were sentenced by default and hanged in effigy.

The great vineyards

Verduno, one of the great Barolo municipalities, has a high proportion of growers who are members of the Cantina Terre del Barolo co-operative winery.

The municipal territory embraces two distinct soil types. On one side are the well-aspected slopes that face Roddi and Grinzane Cavour and on the other is the chalky terrain that stretches towards Rivalta at La Morra.

We will describe six vineyards, including the greatest of them all, Monvigliero. Only a small fraction – just over four per cent – of the municipal territory falls within the Barolo DOCG zone but the vineyards fully deserve to be part of the denomination.

Barolo from Verduno may not have the elegance of wines from La Morra, or the full, generous body of the versions from Serralunga, but it ages effortlessly and, in great vintages, its aromas are reminiscent of truffle and autumn leaves.

One of the wine-related singularities of Ver-

DOC and DOCG	Totale area under vine in hectares	% of area in municipality	% of area in zone
Barolo	**54.0911**	**47.53**	**4.33**
Dolcetto d'Alba	31.5411	27.72	1.69
Barbera d'Alba	15.1387	13.30	0.88
Verduno Pelaverga	8.4900	7.46	98.02
Other DOC zones	4.5400	3.99	
TOTAL	113.8009	100.00	
Other DOC zones			
Langhe Chardonnay	2.1400	1.88	0.83
Langhe Rosso	0.6900	0.61	0.98
Langhe Bianco	0.6000	0.53	2.25
Langhe Favorita	0.5000	0.44	0.50
Nebbiolo d'Alba	0.3600	0.32	0.09
Langhe Freisa	0.1500	0,13	0.25
Piemonte Grignolino	0.1000	0.09	0.61

duno is that bottling was common here as early as the nineteenth century, when in the rest of the Langhe, demijohns and casks were the norm. Bottling was certainly encouraged by the town's close relationship with the Savoy court, which held wines from Verduno in high regard.

Verduno's wines owe much of their fame to Giovan Battista Burlotto, to whom we have dedicated a profile in the chapter on *The Greats of Barolo*. Burlotto, in effect, anticipated the modern wine market.

Production

There are 57 wineries in the municipality, with 54 hectares and a potential production of 3,029 hectolitres of wine a year, or 3.99 per cent of the Barolo DOCG zone.

THE GREAT VINEYARDS

BRERI
MASSARA
MONVIGLIERO
PISAPOLLA
RIVA
SAN LORENZO

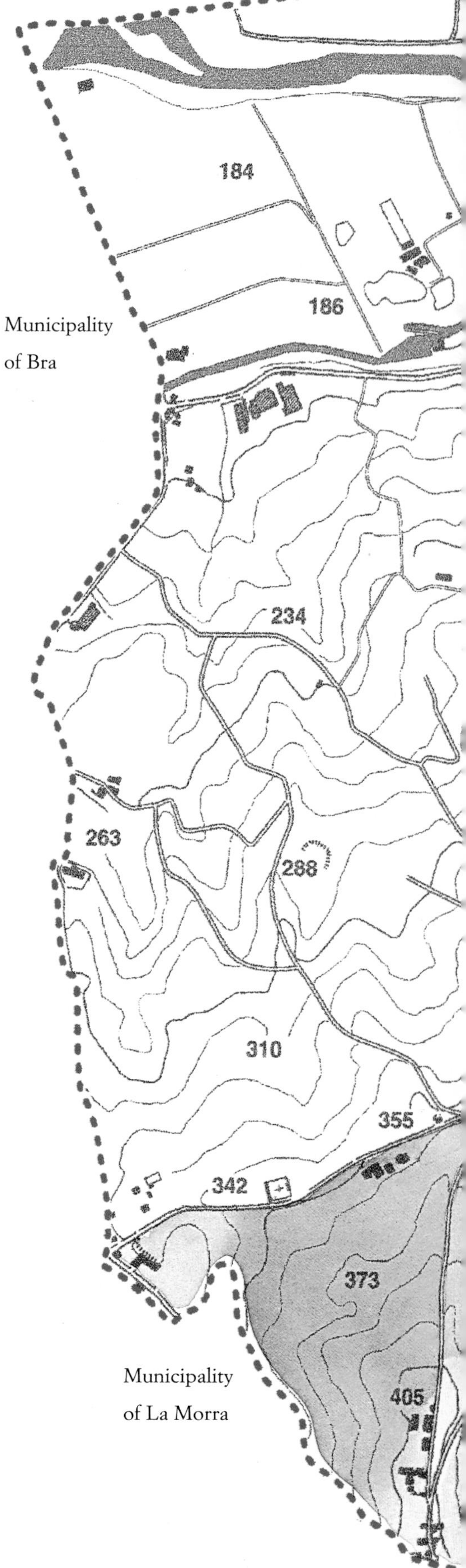

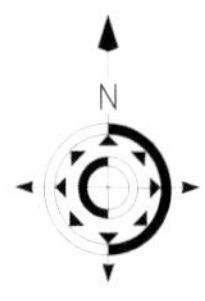

BAROLO DOCG ZONE

GREAT VINEYARDS

Municipality
of Roddi

Monvigliero
Pisapolla
Massara
Breri
San Lorenzo
Riva

180
189
200
238
270
310
287
276
300
226
264
211
342
404
233
230
250
241
352
305
364

Municipality
of La Morra

Massara

Breri

This vineyard lies below the Appiano road, facing Monvigliero, at about 250 metres above sea level and includes the village of Breri. Nebbiolo is cultivated in plots whose positions range from south west to south east-facing. Breri covers about nine *giornate*, or just over three hectares, distributed among several owners.

Once, the main varieties were dolcetto and barbera, sold almost exclusively to private customers and *osterie* on the far bank of the Tanaro. Verduno had an advantage, with respect to other Langhe towns, in this trade as it lies near the flatland towns.

Today, most of the nebbiolo grown here is vinified by the Cantina Terre del Barolo at Castiglione Falletto.

MAIN LABELS

*Barolo Breri – Bel Colle, Verduno

Massara

Massara is perhaps the least fragmented of the vineyards we have selected at Verduno. Its ten *giornate*, or almost four hectares, belong to just two growers, the heirs of Commendator Giovan Battista Burlotto, who purchased the land and castle from the Savoys in 1910.

The vineyard and its *cascina* lie below Pisapolla and have comparable positions and quality characteristics. As well as nebbiolo, the rare pelaverga variety is also cultivated at Massara.

Massara's east-facing location is of the kind known in the Langhe as *sorì d'la matin*, or "morning slope".

MAIN LABELS

*Barolo Vigna Massara – Castello di Verduno, Verduno

*Barolo Cascina Massara – Fratelli Burlotto, Verduno

Monvigliero

Monvigliero lies to the north east of Verduno and includes the farms of Monvigliero, Fava and Marzio.

It is bounded to the north by the crest of the hill, to the south by the Appiano municipal road that links Verduno to Roddi, and to the east by the road from *cascina* Mosca to *cascina* Monvigliero. To the west, it has to be borne in mind, the orientation of the hill changes.

The hill of Monvigliero is entirely south-facing at a height of about 300 metres above sea level. Covering roughly 30 Piedmontese *giornate*, it is divided among 15 or so different owners. Along the top runs a local road with a magnificent panoramic view over the Langhe and Roero.

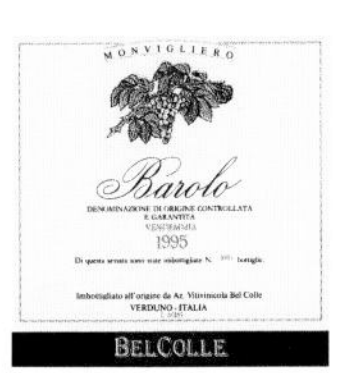

Monvigliero's soil and position have earned it a reputation as an outstanding vineyard for growing nebbiolo for Barolo, as many reports confirm, "Monvigliero's quality is beyond dispute. In the old days, winemakers always considered it the best" (Sabino Grasso). "There has always been rivalry between Barolo and Verduno over the merits of Cannubi and Monvigliero" (Giovanni Laneri).

The soil, which is fairly loose-packed in this area, is a fine white marl. The quality of wine from Monvigliero is confirmed by the fact that a hundred years ago, Commendator Burlotto, the only bottler in the area, bought his nebbiolo for Barolo almost exclusively at Monvigliero, with some from nearby San Lorenzo.

Main labels

*Barolo Vigna Monvigliero – Castello di Verduno, Verduno

*Barolo Vigneto Monvigliero – Commendator G.B. Burlotto, Verduno

*Barolo Monvigliero – Bel Colle, Verduno

*Barolo Monvigliero – Fratelli Alessandria, Verduno

*Barolo Monvigliero – Mauro Sebaste, Alba

*Barolo Monvigliero – Cantina Terre del Barolo, Castiglione Falletto

Pisapolla

Situated near the town of Verduno, Pisapolla lies between the ridge of the hill and the Appiano road. It extends over roughly three hectares and there are ten or so owners.

The vines, almost all nebbiolo, face east at a height of about 300 metres. As elsewhere, barbera was the most important variety at Pisapolla in the past. Today, the vineyard yields good quality nebbiolo.

Previously, consumption of Barolo was very limited. Growers found it easier to sell varieties like barbera and dolcetto, so much to that "in some cases, if you had any nebbiolo, you had to hide it among the barbera to get rid of it" (Mario Valfré).

Main labels

*Barolo Vigna dei Pola – Ascheri, Bra

Riva

Located below the town, Riva stands at the edge of Verduno's wine territory. Further to the south west, the terrain becomes too chalky to cultivate nebbiolo.

Nonetheless, the Riva vineyard is highly regarded by local growers and deserves to be mentioned.

Ownership is very fragmented. There are only ten *giornate*, or less than four hectares, but there are also ten owners. This is perhaps why the area is not entirely planted to vine, despite its excellent south-facing position.

Main labels

*Barolo Riva – Claudio Alario, Diano d'Alba

Monvigliero

San Lorenzo

Another particularly fine vineyard for nebbiolo is San Lorenzo. Standing on the same hillslope as nearby Breri, to the south east of Monvigliero, San Lorenzo is marked off by *cascina* Mosca to the west and the municipal boundary with Roddi to the east.

Almost all of San Lorenzo is south-facing and the vineyard lies at a lower altitude than Monvigliero.

Covering about 20 *giornate*, or just over seven hectares, San Lorenzo is divided up among a ten or so owners.

In years when the weather behaves as it should, Bricat is the best plot at San Lorenzo while quality tends to decline as you go lower down the hillslope.

It appears that, usually, "San Lorenzo fruit has a higher must weight than Monvigliero's" but the resulting wine does not possess the same rich sensory profile, especially on the nose.

Our selection

Population 486
Height 381 metres asl

INFORMATION

Town Hall
Via Roma, 2
Tel. + 39 0172 470121

THE WINERIES

Fratelli Alessandria
Via Beato Valfré, 59
Tel. + 39 0172 470113
Gian Alessandria and his son Vittore run this historic Verduno winery, which specialises in the production of Barolo. Every year, the Alessandrias release 15-20,000 bottles from three vineyard selections, San Lorenzo, Monvigliero and Riva, and a standard-label wine that blends fruit from various estate-owned plots.

Bel Colle
Frazione Castagni, 56
Tel. + 39 0172 470196
Run for the past ten years by oenologist Paolo Torchio, the former technical manager at the Carretta estate in Piobesi, Bel Colle specialises in the production of Verduno's typically austere wines. The Barolo is made with grapes from the estate-owned plot in the Monvigliero vineyard, which was joined last year by the new Barolo Breri label. Bel Colle also releases a limited selection of Barbarescos.

Commendator G.B. Burlotto
Via Vittorio Emanuele, 28
Tel. + 39 0172 470122
An historic winery of Verduno and the entire Barolo area – formerly a supplier of the Savoy royal household – the cellar is managed today by Giuseppe Alessan-

dria, Marina Burlotto and their son Fabio. The range is a combination of innovation and tradition but Barolos are the Burlottos' strong suit. Monvigliero and Cannubi are the estate vineyard selections.

Castello di Verduno
Via Umberto I, 9
Tel. + 39 0172 470284
Castello di Verduno has added to its list, since the marriage some years ago of Franco Bianco and Gabriella Burlotto, one of the Langhe's most important designations of origin, Barbaresco. Monvigliero and Massara for Barolo, and Rabajà and Faset for Barbaresco, are the vineyard selections that have made this cellar's name.

WHERE TO SLEEP

Real Castello di Verduno
Via Umberto I, 9
Tel. + 39 0172 470125
Two stars. Open from March to November.
The hotel occupies one wing of the castle, formerly a residence of Carlo Alberto. The rooms are furnished in a charmingly old-fashioned style. The long-established gardens are beautiful and refreshing, especially in summer.

EATING OUT

Real Castello di Verduno
Via Umberto I, 9
Tel. + 39 0172 470125
Three sisters, Lisetta, Gabriella and Lilli, run the kitchens and the lovely, nineteenth-century dining room. Here, or in the adjacent long room, you can eat warm tongue *in giardino* (with chilli sauce), brain in sauce, *bate 'l gran* (harvest) soup and Piedmontese *giura*, or boiled beef and other cuts. To finish, a thin, dry hazelnut cake made to an old recipe. There is a good list of Alba wines and, of course, all the selections from the house cellar.

John Falstaff
Via Commendatore Schiavino, 1
Tel. + 39 0172 470244
Very exciting, innovative cuisine of dishes from the local territory, selected with care and skill. Visit the lovely, compact cellar under the restaurant, where there are many of Verduno's finest vineyard selections. This restaurant is particularly popular with non-Italian diners as the very competent host has international experience.

Giovan Battista Burlotto

1842-1927

It is more than a century since Cavaliere Ufficiale Giovan Battista Burlotto, also a Commendatore, the title people were wont to call him by, flaunted, with a hint of snobbery, on the bottles he exported all over Europe the extravagant label that bore the prominent legend, *Château*.

In that far-off year of 1881, when he won his first gold medal, Burlotto was a man well on his way to success, the affluent proprietor of an excellent vine-growing estate, a winemaker and a merchant.

How he got there from his humble beginnings in the countryside, no one could quite recall. Born in 1842, Burlotto was a self-made man in an age when Italy was being made around him.

The Commendatore's cellars, in his lovely noble residence, with private chapel, at Verduno, looked out onto the Tanaro valley, and indeed they still do. On a clear day, you could almost see, on the far side of the river, the busy workers at the new factory of Enrico Cinzano, the vermouth maker who in 1867 had purchased from the Savoys the Moscatello estate at Santa Vittoria d'Alba. Commendatore Burlotto was assisted by his brothers, Giuseppe and Francesco, especially the latter, who was to continue the Burlotto line down to the present day, leaving behind him hordes of grandchildren and great-grandchildren.

There is an emblematic anecdote from the early twentieth century. When the king, Vittorio Emanuele III, got out of his carriage, having arrived from Pollenzo, he at once asked Burlotto how "his castle" was, leaving his entourage of members of parliament and other dignitaries dumbfounded. In 1910, Burlotto had finally bought from Carlo Alberto the castle in whose cellars the new Langhe winemaking adventure had began with general Staglieno. In addition, Burlotto was a supplier of the royal household, as he had been of the 1899-1900 Arctic expedition led by the Duca degli Abruzzi, who wrote him on 7 March 1901, "The wine has been conserved in perfect condition".

From the terrace of the house, whose façade still bears traces of many frescoed awards, Burlotto would impart the orders of the day, or the week, when he had to leave on one of his many business trips. The walls of the gallery leading to the cellars were hung with gold medals and diplomas won at exhibitions, including Milan 1881, Turin 1884, Paris 1885 and so on. There were 32 medals all told. The Commendatore was well aware that only a good, well-positioned vineyard could give premium-quality wines. In consequence, he bought plots in the sunniest parts of Bricco Monvigliero at Verduno, near to *cascina* Massara, which he had already acquired with the castle. He even bought a small *cascina* at Cannubi di Barolo, as well as securing the best lots of fruit from vineyards where he owned no plots.

His wines – Barolo, Pelaverga and Barolino – were excellent ambassadors for the Langhe. The Barolino, which had earned him a gold medal as early as 1894, was obtained by passing the just run-off Dolcetto over the still dripping nebbiolo skins. It was a benchmark wine until the Barolo designation was introduced. Burlotto was a great admirer of Pelaverga and it is thanks to his unswerving insistence that the wine is still made today. Giovan Battista Burlotto died in 1927.

When the women travelled with the baggage

Giuseppina Burdese
born 1917
shopkeeper
in Verduno

In January, people would go to the feast of the Blessed Sebastiano Valfré, which was held in church. In the evening, there was a theatre in the town hall but there was no dancing. There were no travelling actors. Young people from the village put on the show. It was ordinary theatre, not religious stuff. This year, they put on a play again because they've repaired the main hall.

On 8 September, there was the feast of the *Madonnina*, the Virgin. The procession went from the parish church to the chapel and a dance stage was set up in the courtyard of Felicin Aimasso's osteria. The other *osteria* was Marengo's. After Aimasso's place closed, the Circolo social club was opened.

Once, there was a bit of rivalry between the two groups in Verduno, but they never came to blows. Then the republic was set up and we had the Garofano (carnation) and the Margherita (daisy). One lot would go to the Circolo and the others used Marengo's *osteria*. Things have changed now but there is still a bit of rivalry. There was also resentment with people from Rivalta. There have always been two shops at Verduno but they didn't carry much stock so people shopped at Rivalta. When we gave up the Rivalta store, the customers told the new manager, "Luciana, don't change anything. Keep everything Ghitina had". That's me. Even a needle is useful because people are ashamed to buy just one.

The coach didn't use to pass through Verduno. It went to Rivalta, where there was a post office. People came here on their way to the post office to catch the coach. They bought things here because they didn't keep thread and lace and such like at Verduno.

My father worked in the fields for three years in America. He came home and bought the shop for 400 lire. When he returned, we thought he was a millionaire. He bought a horse and rode it into Bra every Friday to do the shopping at the market and buy tobacco at the shop. The old coach didn't have glass in the windows, just curtains. In the morning, a team of oxen pulled it out of La Morra. The baggage was put on top and when there wasn't enough room inside, people climbed on top, too. Even women. (*Autumn 1989*)

But the Commendatore slept in the hotel

Andrea Burlotto
born 1911
grower
in Verduno

The cart under the portico has travelled along many roads, particularly the ones for Bra and Turin. We clambered on top of the 14-*brenta* barrels (a *brenta* is about 50 litres) or 60 demijohns, each containing about 54 litres. It was drawn by three lovely horses until the first motor trucks arrived, just before 1939.

On Monday mornings, we left for Turin and, after a stop at

Sommariva Bosco, we reached Moncalieri in the early evening. The horses were unhitched and rested for the night. The stableboy wanted to rub them down but I'd tell him, "No!", and send him off to tend to the other guest's horses. Lots of us spent the night in the stables. I was the youngest, still just a kid, and they used to call me *Burlotin* (little Burlotto).

Early the following morning, my grandfather, Commendator Burlotto, was already at the Moncalieri toll waiting for us. He would take the train from Bra the previous evening and sleep at a hotel in Turin. Grandfather looked after the paperwork and paid the bills. During the day, we took the wine to the cellars of restaurants and private customers, racking it into their barrels or demijohns. We didn't put any bottles on the cart in case they broke. In any case, they had a long way to go so we sent them by rail. Once, though, I had to take them to Racconigi. We'd had a phone call that the king was entertaining at the castle and needed some Barolo and Barolino straight away.

I have seven children. Five are boys and four of them keep the *cascina* going. I opened a bar for the fifth. One looks after the calves, one the vines, and another the cellar. There's plenty of work for everyone. Do you see that ploughed field? We want to plant some favorita (a white variety characteristic of the Roero area). My sons say it should grow well there. (*Spring 1990*)

The birth of ecology

Nebbiolo used to be crushed on the eve of the feast of the Blessed Sebastiano Valfré, in late January. This is what we did. The newly harvested grapes were put into vats and just crushed. Planks were put on top and they were left until January. The juice was run off and the still well-conserved bunches were then trodden. We trod the grapes barefoot all day long. You couldn't eat or smoke. The grapes felt freezing cold underfoot.

It was always the same people who went to Commendator Burlotto's place. I started when I was still a child. The cellar still vinifies part of its nebbiolo that way.

Now there are supervised control experts to tell us when to treat the vines. At first, we didn't believe them when they told us vine moth wasn't a problem and we didn't need to use pesticides. Instead, we treated again and again, all over the vineyards. We got rid of the moths but the vines were invaded by red spider and then by leaf hoppers. There was no end to it. That's when I remembered what they said. So, when the agricultural supplies trader asked me, "Have you given them the stuff for vine moth?", I said, "I'm not going to use it any more. The experts have been round and told me not to use it". "That's just rubbish", he replied. "You're the one that talks rubbish because you make me waste money poisoning my vines. I haven't used pesticide for two years".

The Conte di La Morra used to say that it's the cellar owners who make nebbiolo because they should only buy the best fruit. The growers would then stop leaving too many buds when they prune. They used to leave a lot of buds. Vines ran from post to post on cordons for several metres, one on top of the other. The rows were thick bundles of shoots but the vines produced less fruit. There was no fertilising and crops were sown between the rows – beans, maize, anything. The yield was half what we get today. We used Bordeaux mixture and too much lime, burning the grapes, so there were fewer of them and they had higher must weights. (*Autumn 1989*)

Giovanni Laneri
born 1931
grower
in Verduno

When the grapes were pressed at Christmas

Mario Valfré
born 1920
grower in Verduno

It's the tufa soil that makes good grapes. Fifty years ago, Burlotto bought up the best sites. People from the flatlands and the mountains bought the barbera. It was easier for us here to sell because we're close to the flatland towns. They'd come on horseback from Sommariva Bosco, Carmagnola and Moncalieri, load up the grapes and leave the same day. At Sommariva, some *osterie* bought fruit as a group. They were no fools because they made bottled wine to sell in the *osterie* and a second-choice version for the carters. Maté Ascheri and Manzone came from Bra. Maté supplied the government and made wine for the army.

We didn't press the nebbiolo until Christmas. The wine was thick as liqueur and clear as crystal. We left it to age and in two years it was a first-class Barolo. The stalks gave character to the wine and stayed in the must until Christmas.

When I was still making wine, I had a customer at Villanova Mondovì. I met him at a Christian Democrat party meeting in Cuneo. We ate at the same table. This summer, he paid me a visit with his brother-in-law, who teaches at teacher training school in Cuneo. He had two demijohns to take away some of the Barbera I used to give him. For me, making wine was a pleasure and a source of income. You could make good money with wine and you didn't lose out. If you've got 60 or 100 quintals of grapes to sell and no one wants them, the merchant is only going to take them if the price is right.

In 1958, when they were still building the co-operative winery, we went to see Prunotto, in Alba, and he said, "I don't think you've got any good grapes left to sell. Those are leftovers. We haven't got any more barrels. Bring me them, if they have more than 19 degrees must weight". The following year, he came round. "If you've got any left, bring me them", but I had already signed up at the co-operative. It's more profitable for me to make wine when the grapes are worth 500 lire and the merchant is only offering 300. (*Spring 1990*)

Manure is the best fertiliser

Sabino Grasso
born 1928
grower in Verduno

The grapes were thrown into a vat, given a quick crushing and left to macerate for 15 or 20 days. The wine was racked off, the fruit was pressed thoroughly and the wine was put back again. Barolo made like that tastes the way it used to, when the vines were local plants, not grafted onto American rootstock. Nowadays, the wine has a gamey flavour. It used to be less acidic, less astringent. Don't try to tell me that you shouldn't dig round the vines, or that you don't need to fertilise with manure. I've never used guano because manure is the best fertiliser. Since 1929, there have been two or three years without rain when the vines produced very short shoots, little curly things. And if it continues not to snow, that's what's going to happen this year. Last year, I had to water the sunniest plot because the crop was withering. My vines stand on tufa so they suffer in droughts. If it doesn't rain, the grapes' must weight is low and the co-operative winery is reluctant to buy them. (*Winter 1990*)

Barbaresco

THE BIRTH OF BARBARESCO

As we have seen in the chapter on nebbiolo, several centuries were to pass before the wine called simply "Nebbiolo" became Barbaresco. In the latter half of the nineteenth century, grapes from this area often went into Barolo, as there was not yet a clear distinction between the two wines. The present designation arrived in 1894, when Domizio Cavazza (see the profile in the chapter on *The Greats of Barbaresco*) founded the Cantina Sociale di Barbaresco co-operative winery. That was the year when the first ten tons of grapes were vinified to produce a wine that would at last have the designation Barbaresco printed on its label. There were historical precedents, as visitors to the museum at *cascina* Drago in San Rocco Seno

d'Elvio may note, but these labels are handwritten and we cannot conclude that the name was official or widely used. The more far-sighted of the area's producers arrived at the decision to create a distinct wine, with its own name, because Barolo makers refused to agree to the unification of the hills to the west of Alba with those to the east in a single designated zone.

The production strategy selected by Cavazza and his group was to produce a wine that was more elegant, and less demanding, than Barolo. It should be clearly stated, however, that this does not mean that those pioneering winemakers wanted to create a wine that was particularly different from its rival. In fact, Cavazza himself complained that a number of less than scrupulous bottlers were passing off as Barbaresco wines that had none of the characteristics of "real Barbaresco".

The image of a wine that is "a little more approachable, less austere, more drinkable and less tannic" than Barolo has clung to Barbaresco until recent times. The clearest proof can be found in the regulations for the production of Barbaresco (readers are referred to the full text hereunder), which look like a slightly abridged photocopy of those for Barolo. Certain characteristics are identical, including minimum acidity (five grams per litre) and dry extract (at least 23 grams per litre) but the minimum ageing period is two years, only one of which need be in wood, instead of three, and the minimum alcohol content of the wine must be 12.5 per cent and not 13. The regulations also distinguish the colour of the two wines. Barolo's rich "garnet red" contrasts with the less intense "orangey red" of Barbaresco.

In the first six decades of the twentieth century, many producers accepted this slightly inferior status and, as a result, Barbaresco tended to be referred to as Barolo's "kid brother".

Then came Gaja. He showed that Barbaresco from the finest nebbiolo-growing slopes was in no way inferior in structure or palate to Barolo. Nevertheless, it took years before the right conditions prevailed for the truly great Barbarescos – we should mention here Bruno Giacosa's Santo Stefano and Ceretto's Bricco Asili, at the very least, as ranking alongside Gaja – to become the common heritage of an entire generation of winemakers. In our opinion, this has taken place over the last ten or 15 years.

Despite these developments, the image of Barbaresco as a "lesser Barolo" dies hard. In Piedmont itself, particularly in Turin, you still hear people say that "Barbaresco is a much softer wine than Barolo".

As in Barolo, the most widely planted nebbiolo clone is lampia, although michet is also very popular. The rosé clone has been almost entirely abandoned.

Regulations for the production of Barbaresco

After the creation of the DOC zone by Presidential Decree on 23 April 1966, Registered and Guaranteed Designation of Origin (DOCG) was granted by Presidential Decree on 3 October 1980. It stipulates that:

1. The grapes used must be exclusively the michet, lampia and rosé clones of the nebbiolo variety, grown in the areas listed.
2. The maximum yield of grapes permitted is 80 quintals per hectare and the must-to-fruit ratio cannot exceed 65 per cent at the end of the compulsory period of ageing.
3. Vinification and bottling must be carried out in the grape production area, with some permissible exceptions for wineries in the provinces of Cuneo, Asti and Alessandria.
4. The wine must be aged for at least two years, one of which should be in oak or chestnut barrels, and may be released from 1 January of the third year after the harvest.
5. Back blending with Barbaresco from vintages other than the one mentioned on the label is permitted up to a maximum of 15 per cent.
6. The minimum analytical values are 12.5 per cent alcohol, five grams per litre acidity and 23 grams per litre dry extract.
7. References to geographical areas in the production zone, or to estate brands, are permitted.

Municipalities	Registered wineries	Total area under vine (ha)	Max. yield permitted (q/ha)	Max. yield permitted (hl)	% of DOCG
Barbaresco	105	226.5124	18,120.99	12,684.69	47.16
Neive	167	137.4059	10,992.47	7,694.73	28.61
Treiso	77	93.7778	7,502.22	5,251.56	19.53
San Rocco Seno d'Elvio	14	22.5700	1,805.60	1,263.92	4.70
TOTAL	363	480.2661	38,421.29	26,894.90	100

Year	Production in quintals	Production of wine (65%)	Average yield (%)	Bottles (max 3,329,845)
1994	20,223	13,145	52.63	1,652,667
1995	22,946	14,915	59.72	1,988,667
1996	27,771	18,051	72.28	2,406,800
1997	31,575	20,524	82.18	2,736,533
1998	32,991	21,444	85.87	2,859,200

Production of municipalities included in the Barbaresco DOCG zone (data from 1998)

There were 363 estates registered as growers of nebbiolo for Barbaresco in 1998, accounting for a total area under vine of 480 hectares (an average of 1.32 hectares per estate). In that vintage, the total yield was 32,991 quintals of grapes and 21,444 hectolitres of wine. The production forecast for Barbaresco in 1998 was 2,859,200 bottles, in comparison with 1,752,667 in 1994, 1,988,667 in 1995, 2,406,800 in 1996 and 2,736,533 in 1997.

Year	Registered area under vine in hectares	Actual production in bottles	Hectolitres per hectare
1967	190.21	1,215,067	47.91
1968	190.21	1,184,933	46.72
1969	232.96	1,330,533	42.84
1970	305.11	1,768,533	43.47
1971	326.28	1,506,266	34.62
1972	374.91	0	–
1973	404.03	2,696,733	50.06
1974	441.53	2,92,066	49.72
1975	454.55	2,379,066	39.25
1976	453.85	1,681,733	27.79
1977	468.98	1,671,733	26.73
1978	471.84	1,928,733	30.66
1979	471.78	3,099,866	49.28
1980	471.98	3,142,400	49.93
1981	495.04	2,563,067	38.83
1982	492.53	2,824,800	43.01
1983	520.22	2,986,534	43.06
1984	511.75	1,305,467	19.13
1985	504.56	2,471,867	36.74
1986	508.18	2,475,467	36.53
1987	496.99	2,393,560	36.12
1988	489.76	2,361,467	36.16
1989	488.48	2,173,867	33.38
1990	484.29	2,333,600	36.14
1991	484.23	2,236,533	34.64
1992	482.55	2,008,133	31.21
1993	477.05	2,024,133	31.82
1994	477.78	1,752,667	27.51
1995	479,62	1,988,667	31.10
1996	483.74	2,406,800	37.32
1997	483.48	2,736,533	42.45
1998	480.27	2,859,200	44.65

Total area of Barbaresco DOCG zone

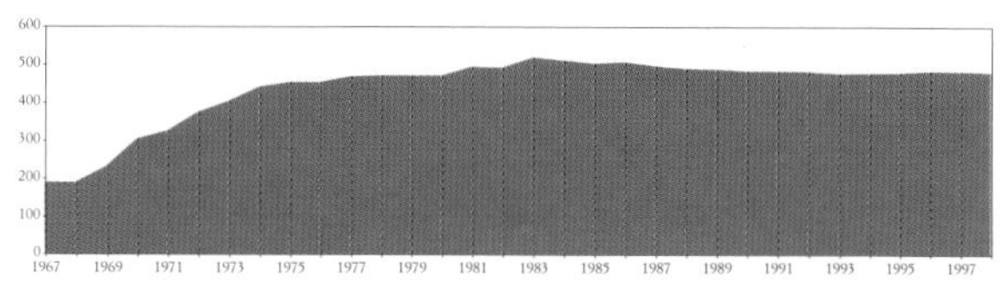

Barbaresco production (number of bottles)

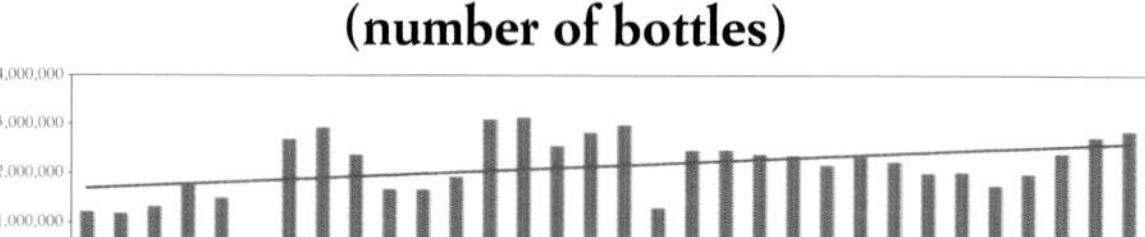

Yields of Barbaresco DOCG zone

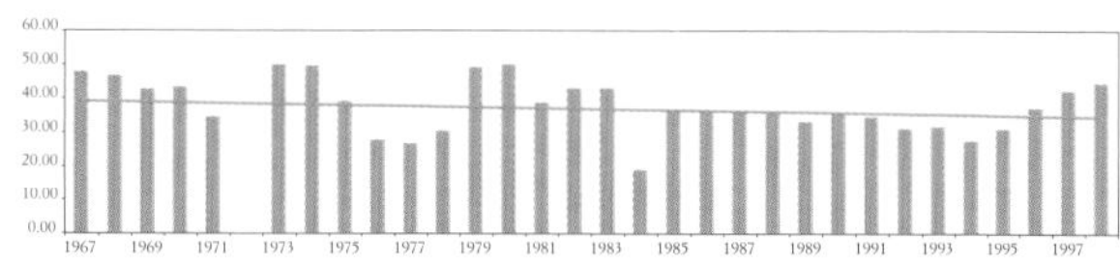

Breakdown of Barbaresco DOCG zone by municipality

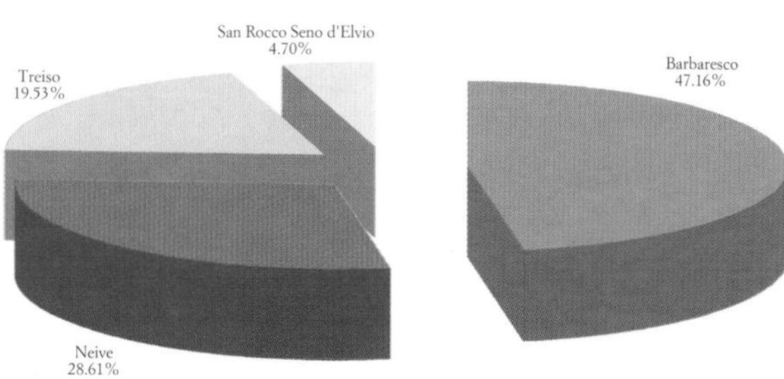

Barbaresco

The hill of Barbaresco can be reached by turning right after Alba, at the Baraccone junction on the Alba-Asti highway. It is visible from a long stretch of the road. The town stands on an almost sheer drop over the river Tanaro in a geologically interesting location, the so-called "Tortonian layer", uncovered by the river's erosive action. The clayey marl, rich in mineral salts, is permeable and therefore continuously damp, creating a highly suitable terrain for viticulture. The wine named after the town has a much smaller DOCG zone than Barolo. Already highly esteemed in classical times, Barbaresco has conserved its fame over the centuries.

History tells us of the Austrian general, Melas, who ordered a *carrà*, or about five hectolitres of wine, to be transported to the square in Bra in celebration of the victory at Genola in 1799.

Colonised by the Ligurian Statielli tribes, Barbaresco may owe its name to the Saracens, or *barbareschi*, who invaded the Langhe in the tenth century. However, there is another possible hypothesis. The wooded area where the Ligurians sought refuge from the advancing Romans was called Barbarica Sylva. The Romans, of course, had the habit of calling other peoples "barbarians".

The Middle Ages were the heyday of the strategic watchtower that, with others scattered around the villages of Roero, formed an important early warning and defence system. Nine metres square and 36 metres high, the tower was impregnable. The most massive such edifice in Piedmont, it was contested for centuries by the towns of Alba and Asti. Once, it was covered by a roof, which was removed in 1821 when the municipality lit a bonfire at the top

of the tower to celebrate the arrival of king Vittorio Emanuele I and queen Maria Teresa at the castle of Govone. The over-enthusiastic welcome for the restored Savoy rulers had the unfortunate effect of decapitating the monument and rendering it more vulnerable to the ravages of wind and rain.
The parish church is dedicated to Saint John the Baptist. It was built between 1719 and 1728 to plans by the Cuneo-born architect, Giovanni Maria Castelli. Inside, there is a carved choir with walnut seats and a sumptuous, coloured marble altar. The houses lie in a semicircle around the church, forming two neat rows that end lower down at the nineteenth-century chapel of San Donato, which today is the home of the Enoteca Regionale del Barbaresco. A little further on, the road leading to the station offers a marvellous view of the trough below from the vineyard of Asili to Rabajà, revealing on one slope *cascina* Martinenga, the former Villa Martis. Here, there was once the forest that the Ligurians had consecrated to Mars, a god they had borrowed from the Etruscans. Nearby is one of the many mineral springs in the area, the same salt springs that housewives used during the last world war, as there was no salt to be found for sale. It also appears that Barbaresco was the birthplace of Publius Helvius Pertinax, emperor of Rome for just 87 days. He has left his name in Monte Elvio, in the torrential stream Seno d'Elvio and the district of Pertinace, which is shared with the municipality of Treiso.
Barbaresco borders to the east with the municipality of Neive, to the south with Treiso, and to the west with Alba, Guarene and Castagnito.

The great vineyards

In the municipality of Barbaresco, almost 60 per cent of the vineyards are planted to nebbiolo, followed by dolcetto, with about 15 per cent, then barbera and chardonnay, both of which account for about six per cent. In all, there are 383 hectares in the register of vineyards. Although Barbaresco has less land planted to vine than Neive or Treiso, it accounts for almost half of the production of the entire DOCG zone. This shows that the entire surface area of the municipality is particularly suited for growing nebbiolo and has strong historic links with the variety.

The 24 vineyards face more towards the south west than the south east. They stand on the main longitudinal ridge (Ovello, Casotto-Loreto, Morassino and Ronchi, largely corresponding to the route of the Alba-Acqui provincial road from the Vicenziana to Rabajà), and on the secondary transverse ridges (Montefico and Montestefano, Secondine, Pagliuzzi, Martinenga, then Roccalini, Roncaglie, Roncagliette and Montaribaldi). Where the ridges meet, they form valleys that are nearly always shaped

DOC and DOCG	Total area under vine in hectares	% of area in municipality	% of area in zone
Barbaresco	**226.5124**	**59.04**	**47.16**
Dolcetto d'Alba	62.9969	16.42	3.37
Barbera d'Alba	26.2242	6.84	1.52
Langhe Chardonnay	23.9366	6.24	9.33
Langhe Rosso	19.1777	5.00	27.27
Langhe Freisa	9.6279	2.51	16.05
Langhe Bianco	6.7653	1.76	25.36
Langhe Nebbiolo	4.0100	1.05	16.04
Other DOC zones	4.3800	1.14	
TOTAL	383.6310	100.00	
Other DOC zones			
Nebbiolo d'Alba	0.9700		0.23
Piemonte	0.8000		4.37
Langhe Favorita	0.1100		0.11
Piemonte Grignolino	1.3600		8.29
Langhe Arneis	1.1400		2.76

Pora

liked amphitheatres, such as Cole, Moccagatta, Pajé and Trifolera. As we move south towards the municipality of Treiso, the valleys become longer and broader, creating distinct site climates, depending on the degree of ventilation they receive from the cool winds.

As well as having lent its name to the DOCG zone, Barbaresco can claim other merits. The town has many of the finest and most celebrated vineyards and is also the home of the Angelo Gaja cellar.

Production

There are 105 wineries in the municipality, with 226 hectares under vine and a potential annual production of 12,684 hectolitres, or 47 per cent of the entire Barbaresco DOCG zone.

THE GREAT VINEYARDS

ASILI
BRICCO OR BRICCO LEMONDO
CASOTTO-LORETO
CAVANNA
COLE
FASET
MARTINENGA
MOCCAGATTA
MONTARIBALDI
MONTEFICO
MONTESTEFANO
MORASSINO
OVELLO
PAGLIUZZI
PAJÉ
PORA
RABAJÀ
RIO SORDO
ROCCALINI
RONCAGLIE
RONCAGLIETTE
RONCHI
SECONDINE
VITALOTTI

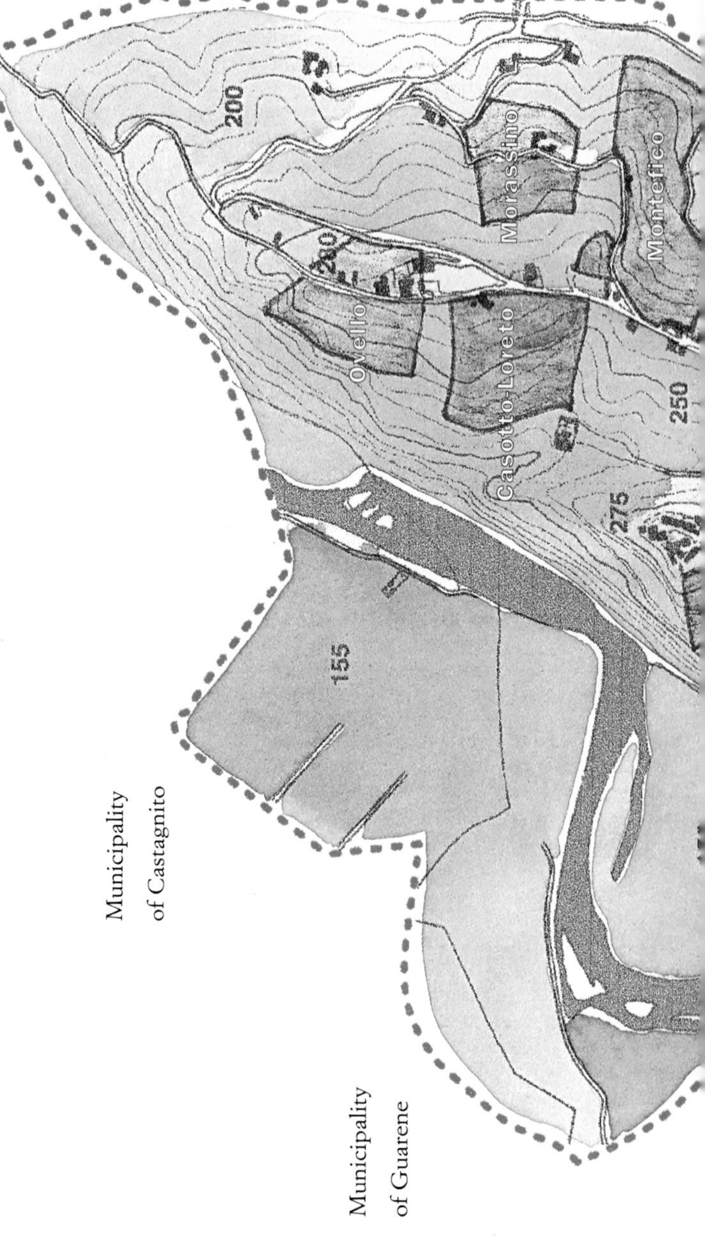

BARBARESCO DOCG ZONE

GREAT VINEYARDS

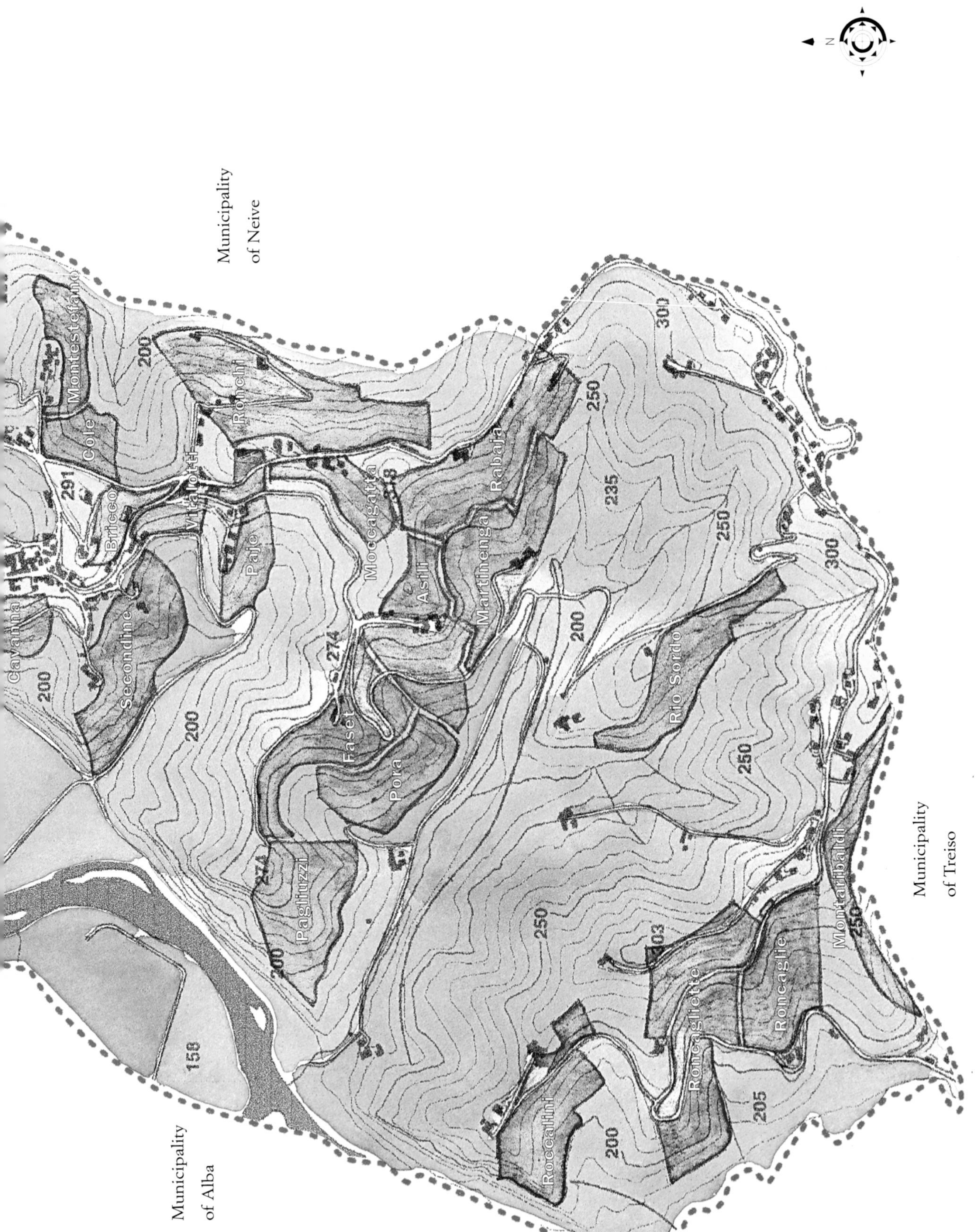

Cavanna
200
291
Montestefano
Cole
Bricco
Secondine
200
Municipality
of Alba
158
200
Vitalotti
Municipality
of Neive
Ronchi
Paje
274
200
Pagliuzzi
274
Faset
Moccagatta
318
Pora
Asili
Martinenga
Rabajà
Roccalini
250
200
200
250
235
Rio Sordo
300
303
Roncagliette
250
205
250
Roncaglie
300
Montaribaldi
250
Municipality
of Treiso

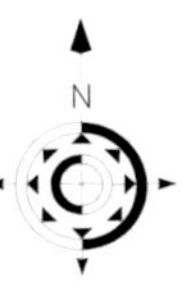

Asili

A vineyard of undeniable fascination, Asili lends Barbaresco a special finesse, elegance and charm. The colour is never as intense as in neighbouring Rabajà but with time, the wine expresses its *terroir* with rare personality. Asili owes its fame historically to the Produttori del Barbaresco, who have been releasing a selection since 1971, and to the Fratelli Ceretto, whose Bricco Asili has made Barbaresco a household name around the world. The vineyard covers an entire hill and takes its name from the village on the western slope.
To the west, Asili borders on the Faset bowl at the top and the Pora hill further down. The eastern edge reaches Rabajà and to the south it extends as far as Martinenga while the northern boundary is the peak of the hill itself. Beyond are other varieties planted in cooler positions. The altitude ranges from 200 to 270 metres. Initially, the vines are west-facing in the Valdrappo section that borders on Faset. They face south west from the village to the Gaiun vineyard at Martinenga and then enjoy a superb south-facing aspect at Rabajà.

MAIN LABELS

*Barbaresco Bricco Asili – Bricco Asili, Barbaresco
*Barbaresco Asili – Ca' del Baio, Treiso
*Barbaresco Asij – Ceretto, Alba
*Barbaresco Asili – Michele Chiarlo, Calamandrana
*Barbaresco Asili di Barbaresco – Bruno Giacosa, Neive
*Barbaresco Asili – Luigi Giordano, Barbaresco
*Barbaresco Vigneti in Asili – Produttori del Barbaresco, Barbaresco

Bricco or Bricco Lemondo

Located near the town, this vineyard is known locally as "Bricco". Nevertheless, we can also accept the name "Bricco Lemondo", deriving from the local Giro del Mondo road that marks its boundary to the east. In the nineteenth century, Bricco was part of the Lemondo district and belonged to Domizio Cavazza. Today, it is owned by the Gaja family.
A stupendously positioned, south-facing vineyard, Bricco has an altitude of between 230 and 290 metres. Almost entirely planted to cabernet sauvignon, it has been the source, since the 1970s, of Gaja's marvellous Darmagi. Once, it was planted to nebbiolo, yielding some of the best fruit in Barbaresco, as some of the older growers were able to tell us. That is why we have included Bricco among the finest vineyards at Barbaresco, even though it is no longer possible to taste a Barbaresco from this vineyard.

Asili

Casotto-Loreto

It is rather difficult to identify the name and extent of this little-known but attractive vineyard, which produces very fine nebbiolo, for a number of historical and territory-related reasons. In the Napoleonic registers, *cascina* Casotto is mentioned as a property that lay on both sides of the hill, separated by the Alba-Acqui provincial road that leads to Barbaresco. Locally, however, the vineyard has always been known as "Loreto", a name that may derive from the Conti di Loreto, who were the *signori* (lords) of Barbaresco about the year 1000 AD. To be precise, Loreto is the lower part of the Casot vineyard, which stands around the *cascina* of the same name on the west and south west-facing slope overlooking the Tanaro. For this reason, we have decided to keep both names, excluding the vines on the other east and north east-facing slope, below the Albano *bricco* where the Distilleria del Barbaresco stands.

The *cascina* is about 280 metres above sea level. It and all its land belonged to the lawyer Carlo Rocca in the nineteenth century and then passed to Professor Domizio Cavazza in the early twentieth century. Currently, the vineyard is owned by several producers.

MAIN LABELS

*Barbaresco Vigna Casot – Carlo Boffa, Barbaresco

*Barbaresco Vigneto Loreto – Albino Rocca, Barbaresco

*Barbaresco Bricco Loreto – Franco e Mario Scrimaglio, Nizzá Monferrato

*Barbaresco Sorì Loreto – Rino Varaldo, Barbaresco

Cavanna

As you go along the Baraccone-Rondò provincial road towards Neive, you will the town of Barbaresco and its castle rising over the Tanaro valley. The Cavanna vineyard can only be clearly seen from here, easily identifiable between the *rocche*, or high cliffs, to the south and the houses of Barbaresco to the north. The vineyard is a very narrow, steep hollow that offers various aspects. One part behind the Secondine vineyard faces north and north west but the other, west-facing area is much more suitable for growing nebbiolo. The elevation ranges from 220 to 280 metres above sea level.

MAIN LABELS

*Barbaresco Cavanna – Luigi Giordano, Barbaresco

Cole

Cole is a steep vineyard that faces east and south east at an altitude of 240-280 metres above sea level. It may be considered the continuation of Montestefano but it is only over the last few decades that the Moccagatta winery, owned by the Minuto brothers, has invested in it. Even though it belongs to the Montestefano district, a Colla vineyard had already been identified in the nineteenth century. In subsequent years, grapes from this vineyard were often sold as coming from the much better known Montestefano. Since 1985, the Minuto brothers have been releasing a Barbaresco Vigna Cole, as did Donato Giacosa, albeit only for that vintage. Barbaresco Cole is an austere, muscular wine with good structure, even in poorer vintages. It has all the ageing potential of Montestefano, which however has superior breadth and complexity on the nose. The western part, known as Collaretto, is the continuation of the eastern sector of Bricco Lemondo.

MAIN LABELS

*Barbaresco Vigneto Cole – Moccagatta, Barbaresco

Faset

In the nineteenth century, Faset belonged to the Conti Cocito of Neive whereas today it is split among a number of small growers. The vineyard is long, looking over the valley of the Rio Sordo. Faset extends over the upper part of the hollow formed by the Pagliuzzi and Pora hills with an additional section, also concave, that borders on Asili, again behind Pora. Since the line of the hillslope is uneven, Faset offers a range of very different aspects. The vines start out facing south east on the border with Pagliuzzi, shifting to south and south west in the central section at Bricco Faset and then west near *cascina* Faset, to go back to south east and south-facing on the border with Asili. The highly irregular configuration of the Faset hillslope, and its considerable extent, make it difficult to draw up a profile for the nebbiolo. What we can say is that the grapes need hot weather to express their innate elegance, even though they never achieve the finesse and complexity of fruit from neighbouring Asili. The altitude is about 250-270 metres.

MAIN LABELS

*Barbaresco Vigna Faset – Marziano e Enrico Abbona, Dogliani
*Barbaresco Fasêt – Bricco Asili, Barbaresco
*Barbaresco Bricco Fasèt – Pietro Berutti, Barbaresco
*Barbaresco Vigna Faset – Castello di Verduno, Verduno

Martinenga

This marvellous amphitheatre of a vineyard is one of the loveliest in Barbaresco. Grey-blue calcareous marl, the largely south west-facing vines and an altitude of between 220 and 280 metres are the factors that make it ideal for nebbiolo, so much so that 30 years ago the price of grapes from Martinenga was a benchmark for the market at Alba.

The name Martinenga is said to derive from the ancient Villa Martis, of Latin origin, the place where the emperor Publius Helvius Pertinax was born. Currently, the entire vineyard belongs to the Cisa Asinaris of Gresy, who acquired it from the Conti Deabbate in the nineteenth century.

The year 1967 was significant for Martinenga because that was when its name appeared for the first time on the label of a selection released by the Cantina dei Produttori.

To the west and north west, the vineyard borders Asili, to the north east and east with Rabajà, and to the south it is marked off by the floor of the Rio Sordo valley, along which the railway line runs. There are two distinct plots in Martinenga that should be noted: the south-facing, almost triangular Gaiun plot on the Asili hill; and the Camp Gros, facing south west in the eastern sector below Rabajà.

MAIN LABELS

*Barbaresco Camp Gros Martinenga – Tenute Cisa Asinari dei Marchesi di Gresy, Barbaresco
*Barbaresco Gaiun Martinenga – Tenute Cisa Asinari dei Marchesi di Gresy, Barbaresco
*Barbaresco Martinenga – Tenute Cisa Asinari dei Marchesi di Gresy, Barbaresco

Moccagatta

The name derives from the Moncagatta family, who once in the nineteenth century owned the vineyard and the land below it that faces west towards Pajé. Today, the *cascina* and some of the vineyards are owned by the Minuto brothers from the Moccagatta cellar. To the north, the vineyard is delimited by Vitalotti, to the east by the Alba-Acqui provincial road, to the south by the Rabajà hill and to the west by the municipal station road. Although it does not enjoy outstanding positions, facing north west under the Rabajà hilltop, nebbiolo from Moccagatta has over recent years achieved a solidly consistent level of quality. There are probably two factors that offset the less than perfect location of the vines. One is the shape of the hill – the same elevation as Rabajà and Martinenga – and the sheltered position under the peak, at the bottom of a fairly narrow, very warm valley. The altitude ranges from 310 metres in the highest part of the vineyard to 270 metres at the lower edge.

MAIN LABELS

*Barbaresco Vigneti in Moccagatta – Produttori del Barbaresco, Barbaresco

Montaribaldi

Montaribaldi is a thin strip of hillside bounded to the north by the north west-facing part of Roncaglie and the Alba-Acqui provincial road, which goes from Alba to Tre Stelle. To the south, the boundary is the old Montaribaldi Roman road, now no longer used, which went to Monte Aribaldo, on the border with Treiso.

The vineyard is marked off to the west by *cascina* Cencio at about 180 metres, then climbs to the east on the ridge that leads to Pajoré at Treiso, passing the *cascina* Quinto, up to the village of Niccolini, at about 300 metres. The altitude varies considerably, causing differences in the ripening rate in the upper and lower parts but the position is very good and the aspect almost uniform, facing south east, south and south west. Grapes from this vineyard have been separately vinified for only a few years but the results have been surprisingly encouraging.

MAIN LABELS

*Barbaresco Sorì Montaribaldi – Montaribaldi, Barbaresco

Montefico

As you go up the Bernino road, the Montefico vineyard begins on your left after you pass *cascina* Morassino, continuing alongside the road until it joins the

Alba-Acqui highway to finish almost at *cascina* Nuova. The hill is roughly in the shape of an open "S" that descends from *cascina* Montefico to the Patricone municipal road. Montefico is one of the finest vineyards in Barbaresco and its central portion enjoys a near-perfect south-facing position that persuaded the lawyer Carlo Rocca and Professor Domizio Cavazza to become its celebrated owners.

Of course, as the slope of the hill changes, so does the position of the vines, which gradually turn to face south east and then east in the first part, the former Canova estate, and to the south west and west in the section that faces Neive. While good nebbiolo can certainly be found in these plots, we are no longer in the historic Montefico vineyard.

It should also be noted that before the junction with the Alba-Acqui highway, to the right of the Bernino local road, there is a small hill that joins another vineyard on the far side (we have not included it in the *Atlas*) between Morassino and Casotto. The plot should be considered an integral part of Montefico for it lies on the same hill. Locally, it is known as *Bric Mentina* and it boasts a splendid south and south east-facing position. Vineyard selections from Bric Mentina have always given excellent results and two local producers do in fact vinify them separately, labelling the wines accordingly.

MAIN LABELS

*Barbaresco Bric Mentina – La Ca' Növa, Barbaresco
*Barbaresco Montefico – La Ca' Növa, Barbaresco
*Barbaresco Montefico – Carlo Giacosa, Barbaresco
*Barbaresco Vigneti in Montefico – Produttori del Barbaresco, Barbaresco
*Barbaresco Bric Mentina – Valfieri, Costigliole d'Asti

Montestefano

The Montestefano vineyard stands on the ridge after, and a few hundred metres south of, Montefico, whose configuration, aspect and altitude it shares. Nevertheless, nebbiolo from Montestefano is remarkably different. Barbaresco Montestefano always has greater structure and length than its fellow from Montefico. It is longer-lived and has a more intense colour. We like to call it "the most Baroloesque of the Barbarescos".

Historically, Montestefano was one of the first vineyard selections to be separately vinified and specified on the label. Beppe Colla of Prunotto released his first Montestefano in 1961 and in 1967, he was followed by the Cantina dei Produttori. In outstanding vintages, like 1971 and 1982, Montestefano still expresses, after 20 or 30 years, an unmistakable *terroir* personality, with deep, austere aromas of leather, tobacco and truffle. In fact, this is one of the finest nebbiolo-based wines in the Langhe.

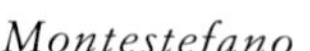

Montestefano

The vineyard has a dizzyingly steep, south-facing central section that begins at the village of Montestefano to descend halfway down the slope over the Ronchi and Cottà valley. To the east, the vines turn to face east and, to the west, it borders on the Cole vineyard, where disputes have raged for years over the exact line of demarcation. We have decided to separate the two vineyards at the point where the hill turns and the orientation changes, ascribing the south eastern portion to Cole and leaving the south-facing vines in Montestefano.

MAIN LABELS

*Barbaresco Vigneti in Montestefano – Produttori del Barbaresco, Barbaresco
*Barbaresco Montestefano – Luigi Giordano, Barbaresco
*Barbaresco Montestefano – La Ca' Növa, Barbaresco
*Barbaresco Montestefano – Serafino Rivella, Barbaresco
*Barbaresco Montestefano di Barbaresco – Accademia Torregiorgi, Neive
*Barbaresco Vigna Montestefano – Mauro Sebaste, Alba
*Barbaresco Montestefano – Prunotto, Alba

Morassino

As you go up towards Barbaresco from the local Bernino road, you will pass *cascina* Vacca and, after a sharp, lefthand bend, you come to the Morassino vineyard. To left and right, you will be able to see nebbiolo vines planted on the far side of *cascina* Morassino – the cellar of Mauro and Roberto Bianco – almost up to the border with Montefico. In the nineteenth century, this hamlet was part of the district of Ovello, a detail that created some uncertainty among local growers over the choice of name for the vineyard. Often, vines obtained from grapes grown here have been released under the label "Barbaresco Ovello". Morassino is a *sorì del mattino*, or "morning slope" that faces mainly to the east. The best vines are the ones below *cascina* Morassino and the ones higher up near the border with Montefico, where the hill turns to face south. These plots produce beautifully rounded, harmonious wines.

MAIN LABELS

*Barbaresco Cascina Morassino – Cascina Morassino, Barbaresco

Ovello

Situated on the border with Casotto-Loreto, Ovello, which takes its name from the *cascina* that used to be called "Aloello", can be reached from the Alba-Acqui provincial road, which forms its eastern border. It stands on the same west and south west-facing slope as Casotto-Loreto and also shares its altitude range of 220-280 metres. Old land registers also consider the eastern slope, which looks towards Neive, as part of Ovello. We have decided to restrict the name to the slope that overlooks the Tanaro, since many of the older growers in Barbaresco claim that this part gives fruit that is much superior. Barbaresco Ovello usually has fresh, fruit-rich aromas and decent tannins that require a good harvest to achieve the fullness and roundness of other vineyard selections.

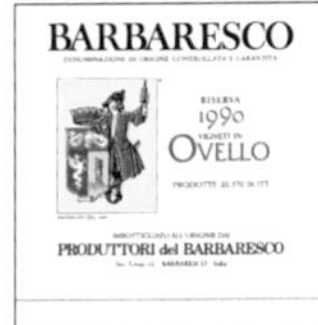

MAIN LABELS

*Barbaresco Vigneto Ovello – Cascina Morassino, Barbaresco
*Barbaresco Vigneto Ovello Ventimesi – Cascina Morassino, Barbaresco
*Barbaresco Vigneti in Ovello – Produttori del Barbaresco, Barbaresco

Pagliuzzi

In 1894, engineer Giovanni Pagliuzzi was one of the founder members of the Cantina Sociale di Barbaresco. At the time, he owned the *cascina* on the far side of the Rio Sordo, the land along the valley floor planted to seed crops and the vines that stood around the circular hill. Even today, the hill is known as Pagliuzzi and some of its plots are exceptionally good. Nonetheless, the name Pagliuzzi has never appeared on a label. The reason is that the fruit is not separately vinified by the owners, going instead to the Cantina dei Produttori del Barbaresco, where traditionally it has been added to the grapes from neighbouring Pora. As a result, Pagliuzzi has never established an identity of its own. For administrative purposes, too, the municipality of Barbaresco designates the entire area bounded by Rio Sordo and the Faset vineyard as "Pora", including the Pagliuzzi hill. We prefer to follow both the ownership history and the usage of the older growers, in the hope that this vineyard will be promoted as it deserves to be in the next few years.

Within Pagliuzzi, where the altitude ranges from 200 to 270 metres above sea level, there is also the Cittadella plot. A magnificent triangular, south-facing position, it is bigger than, but similar in orientation, shape and altitude to, the Gaiun vineyard at Martinenga.

Pajé

This small vineyard stands at the point where the main ridges of Moccagatta and Rabajà meet the secondary ridge of Secondine. Its lovely amphitheatre is almost entirely covered by vines at an altitude that ranges from 220 to 260 metres above sea level, enclosed by the Porto and Asili municipal roads. The slope we have identified faces south and south west below the cascina Paglieri owned by the Roagna family, to whom much of the progress made by this vineyard is due. Nebbiolo from Pajé has hard tannins that lend austerity to its Barbaresco but also a finesse and elegance that are reminiscent of Asili or Rabajà.

Main labels

*Barbaresco Vigneti in Pajé – Produttori del Barbaresco, Barbaresco

*Barbaresco Crichët Pajé – I Paglieri, Barbaresco

Pora

Cascina Pora and the vineyards around it belonged to the lawyer Carlo Rocca, and then to Professor Domizio Cavazza, in the nineteenth century. Today, not many producers own plots in this outstanding Barbaresco vineyard. The first label to bear the name "Pora" dates from 1967 and was released at the initiative of the Cantina dei Produttori, which had already identified Pora for separately vinified selections in the best years.

Located on the sides of the Pora hill and bounded by Pagliuzzi, Faset and Asili, Pora offers excellent nebbiolo-growing positions. Except for the lower section along the floor of the Rio Sordo valley, which is planted to white varieties, and some plots squeezed under Faset, Pora has magnificent exposure to sunlight. The vines are west-facing at first, then turn to face the south in the best positions and finish looking towards the south east on the border with Asili.

Nebbiolo from Pora is aristocratically austere, as is the case in all the finest vineyards, and needs a period of ageing before its full potential emerges and the wine achieves a pinnacle of harmony.

Main labels

*Barbaresco Vigneti in Pora – Produttori del Barbaresco, Barbaresco

*Barbaresco Vigneto Pora – Gigi Bianco, Barbaresco

*Barbaresco Pora – Walter Musso, Barbaresco

Rabajà

Rabajà is a magnificent vineyard that extends more or less uniformly from the highest hill in Barbaresco (311 metres) to a ditch at the end of Camp Gros in Martinenga. This is the historic part of the Rabajà subzone. It then turns slightly to the west and goes down to an area known as "Trifolera". The orientation changes and the positions become less suitable for growing nebbiolo. South west-facing overall, except in the south-facing section, Rabajà borders to the north with Moccagatta and is marked off to the east by the Alba-Acqui provincial road. To the south it reaches Trifolera and to the west Martinenga and Asili.

On old maps, what today is the *cascina* Rabajà, and the home of the Bruno Rocca winery, is indicated as *cascina* Rabagliato, perhaps from the surname of a former owner.

Rabajà is one of the best-known and most celebrated vineyards in Barbaresco, as well as one of the most controversial. For us, the fame of Rabajà is linked to Guido Alciati, the great restaurateur from Costigliole d'Asti who, in the 1970s, introduced the virtues of Rabajà to gourmets and connoisseurs from all over the world by purchasing large quantities from the Cantina dei Produttori and serving the wine in his restaurant. Of course, credit is also due to the producers who in recent years have been able to bring out the full personality of the vineyard in their wines. Rabajà is elegant yet muscular, showing both finesse and breeding. Eminently cellarable, it is equally irresistible when drunk young. This great wine has its principal virtue in its supreme balance.

Recently, there has been much argument among producers, local politicians and journalists over the exact location of Rabajà's boundaries. We have opted for a common-sense solution, as may be seen from the vineyard map, heeding the suggestions of older growers and carrying out on-site inspections while taking

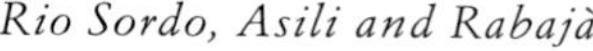

Rio Sordo, Asili and Rabajà

full account of past history and tastings that have taken place over recent years. In short, we were not convinced by the idea of a single large Rabajà vineyard from the foot of Bricco Lemondo to Trifolera. The hill may be the same but aspect and terrain vary considerably. We were also reluctant to relinquish a heritage that has become over recent years so diversified from one plot to the next and from one wine to another by lumping everything together under the single name, Rabajà. This would fly in the face of the very concept of vineyard selection.

Main labels

*Barbaresco Rabajà – Fratelli Barale, Barolo

*Barbaresco Rabajà – Cascina Luisin, Barbaresco

*Barbaresco Vigna Rabajà – Castello di Verduno, Verduno

*Barbaresco Rabajà – Michele Chiarlo, Calamandrana

*Barbaresco Rabajà – Giuseppe Cortese, Barbaresco

*Barbaresco Rabajà – Bruno Giacosa, Neive

*Barbaresco Vigneti in Rabajà – Produttori del Barbaresco, Barbaresco

*Barbaresco Rabajà – Rabajà di Bruno Rocca, Barbaresco

Rio Sordo

In the second valley at Barbaresco, overlooked by Pagliuzzi, Pora and Rabajà, there rises a small, solitary ridge with two slopes. The north eastern slope faces Martinenga and Rabajà but is of little interest for nebbiolo whereas the south west-facing side, opposite the hamlet of Niccolini, has very exciting potential. This is Rio Sordo, a vineyard whose fruit has always been sought after by the agents of the Langhe's best cellars.

The vineyard we have identified starts after the bends in the Rio Sordo road, below Casa Bruciata, and continues at first beside the road and then follows the ridge of the hill almost as far as the houses at *cascina* Rio Sordo. According to the old-timers, the best growing area is the high part of the central section, where yet again the south and south west-facing position, an altitude of 200 to 240 metres and the soil type all come together to create the ideal conditions for making superb quality Barbaresco.

Main labels

*Barbaresco Rio Sordo – Brovia, Castiglione Falletto

*Barbaresco Rio Sordo – Ca' Romé, Barbaresco

*Barbaresco Rio Sordo – Cascina delle Rose, Barbaresco

*Barbaresco Rio Sordo – Giacosa Fratelli, Neive

*Barbaresco Bricco Rio Sordo – Walter Musso, Barbaresco

*Barbaresco Vigneti in Rio Sordo – Produttori del Barbaresco, Barbaresco

Roccalini

Located in the south western part of the municipality of Barbaresco, the Roccalini vineyard is almost unknown except to connoisseurs for a number of reasons. No winery has ever promoted the vineyard, with the exception of Fratelli Giacosa from Neive, who bottled a selection until 1988. After that vintage, the fruit went into a standard-label Barbaresco.

It should also be said that the vineyard is fairly secluded and off the beaten track. For a view of the entire area, you will have to take the Alba-Acqui provincial road for Barbaresco at Pertinace, in Treiso. On the broad bend beyond *cascina* Roncaglie, and before you come to Gaja's *cascina* Roncagliette, a small side road leads off to *cascina* Roccalini and *cascina* Rocca, as well as Villa Como. At the junction, you can see the amphitheatre formed by the vines of Roccalini just below the houses. Located at an altitude of 180 to 250 metres, Roccalini is superbly aspected to the south and south west. In the late nineteenth century, Fantini included it as one of Barbaresco's finest vineyards with the name of Como.

Roncaglie

Roncaglie lies in the southern part of the municipality of Barbaresco, at the start of the ridge that rises up from Barbaresco to Montaribaldi and Pajoré, finally arriving at Treiso. It is located at an altitude that ranges from 190 metres, at *cascina* Roncaglie, to 280 metres in the upper part, which borders on Gaja's Sorì Tildin below the *cascina* Sucré. Apart from this last plot, the entire vineyard is bounded by the two stretches of the Alba-Acqui provincial road that go from Alba to Tre Stelle. The vines face west at first, then turn south to come round to the west again. Despite the high reputation of Roncaglie nebbiolo among the agents of the leading Langhe wineries, the fruit from the vineyard has not been separately vinified. It is only in the last few years that a selection has been released by the Colla winery, which has acquired much of the vine stock.

Main labels

*Barbaresco Tenuta Roncaglia – Poderi Colla, Alba

*Barbaresco Roncaglie – Bel Colle, Verduno

Roncagliette

Situated between Roncaglie to the south and the northern part of the Roccalini vineyard, Roncagliette, named after the *cascina* of the same name, has gone down in history thanks to Angelo Gaja. He called the two most exciting vineyards in the entire area Sorì Tildìn and Costa Russi, taking Barbaresco into the empyrean of world winemaking.

Roncagliette as we have defined it can be divided into four distinct plots. The first lies below the curve where the road leads to Roccalini at an average altitude of 200 metres. The vines face uniformly south and south west, forming Costa Russi. The central part, in the elbow formed by the two stretches of the Alba-Acqui road, is also owned by Gaja and is planted *a ritocchino*, with the vines arranged vertically to follow the steepest slopes. Bordering the Roncaglie vineyard, it has an altitude of 240 metres and faces south west and west. Then there is the part between the top of the hill and the road, at an average altitude of 270 metres. This is the legendary Sorì Tildin.

The vineyard, owned by the Gaja family since 1967, has been separately vinified since 1970. The configuration is less regular than the other plots. It follows the ridge of the hill and concave, amphitheatre-shaped sections alternate with convex humpbacked portions.

The last section of Roncagliette is the triangular-shaped area below *cascina* Berchialla and above Sorì Tildin, which is also south west-facing near the summit.

Ronchi

This is one of the most extensive vineyards in the DOCG zone. Located on the eastern slope of the main ridge that cuts across the municipality of Barbaresco, opposite the villages of Tetti and Cottà at Neive. Its position is almost entirely east-facing with slight deviations to south east. The soil, too, is uniform. Nevertheless, the finest nebbiolo-growing area is the upper band of vines below the Alba-Acqui road. Lower down towards the valley floor, other varieties are more popular.

Recently, a number of very interesting Barbarescos have been made from selections at Ronchi. Their complexity on the nose and excellent structure put them on a par with the finest Barbaresco selections.

The altitude ranges from the 200 metres of *cascina* Ronchi to the 300 metres of Bricco Vitalotti.

Main labels

*Barbaresco Ronchi – Alfonso Rocca, Barbaresco

*Barbaresco Vigneto Brich Ronchi – Albino Rocca, Barbaresco

Secondine

The name may derive from a past owner called Secondo, whose *cascina* and the land round about came over the years to be known as "Secondine".

We are right next to the town of Barbaresco, looking onto the short valley that goes from the Tanaro to Moccagatta, by way of the Pajé hollow.

The Gaja family bought the central part of the vineyard, also known as Masué, as long ago as 1964, when there were very few vines here and most of the land was under wheat. The first vintage of Barbaresco Sorì San Lorenzo, as the vineyard was called, was the 1967.

The Secondine vineyard may be divided easily into three distinct zones. The first of these, also known as "Sorì Secondine", lies behind the cliffs and faces south and south west. Separated by a lane that was once the Montà municipal road, we find the second plot, which embraces Sorì San Lorenzo, after which the hillside turns away to face west.

The third and final plot lies below *cascina* Ghiga, opposite Vitalotti and the northern part of Pajé. This south east-facing vineyard was already included among the finest nebbiolo-growing areas for Barbaresco by both Fantini and Renato Ratti.

The altitude ranges from 200 to 270 metres.

Vitalotti

Vitalotti takes its name from the *cascina* owned by the Bianco family of Castello di Verduno in the nineteenth century. To the north, it borders on Bricco Lemondo, to the east on Ronchi, to the south with Moccagatta and to the west with Pajé. Part of Vitalotti is claimed by some producers as belonging to Rabajà because, in the past, the hamlet of Rabajà included both Rabajà and Moccagatta, which at the time reached the central section of Vitalotti. We believe it is more correct to identify the vineyard with the name of the *cascina*. The area can be split up into three very similar plots with comparable south west and west-facing positions and an altitude that ranges from 220 to 300 metres. The first section goes down from Bricco Lemondo to the valley floor until it reaches the old Porto municipal road, where it continues to form the slope behind Pajé, which we have described elsewhere. The second, central part lies between the junction of the Asili municipal road and the Alba-Acqui highway, and the Moccagatta vineyards, held to be the historic core of the vineyard. Finally, the third portion lies beyond the provincial road near Bricco Vitalotti at about 300 metres, behind Ronchi.

MAIN LABELS

*Barbaresco Vigna Vitalotti – Carlo Boffa, Barbaresco

Pajè

Ronchi

Our selection

Population 645
Height 274 metres asl

INFORMATION

Town Hall
Via Torino, 5
Tel. + 39 0173 635234

Enoteca regionale del Barbaresco
Via Torino, 8/a
Tel. + 39 0173 635251

THE WINERIES

Bricco Asili
Località Asili
Tel. + 39 0173 282582
This winery is one of the jewels in the Ceretto crown and the cellar where the estate's most prestigious Barbarescos are made. Since 1974, Barbaresco Bricco Asili has been separately vinified so that the natural elegance and sophistication of the vineyard's grapes is fully expressed. The '78, '85, '89 and '96 vintages were memorable. The Faset is a notch or two lower, a worthy stablemate that never quite reaches the heights of Bricco Asili. The 1997 vintage saw a new vineyard with a famous past come onstream: Bernardot at Treiso.

Ca' Romé Romano Marengo
Via Rabajà, 36
Tel. + 39 0173 635126
The cellar's total output of Barbaresco and Barolo is about 20,000 bottles a year. The vineyard in front of the cellar, at the southern edge of Rabajà, yields the grapes for Barbaresco Maria di Brun. The standard-label Barbaresco has always been obtained largely from vines at Rio Sordo and the vineyard's name will be on the labels from the 1998 vintage. Ca' Romé also releases two Barolos from estate-owned plots at Serralunga d'Alba, Cerretta and Rapet.

Cascina Luisin
Via Rabajà, 23
Tel. + 39 0173 635154
Since young Roberto Minuto arrived, this cellar has made enormous progress and is now able to offer wines that are as good as any in the Langhe. The cellar's Barbarescos include a Sorì Paolin, from the Basarin vineyard, a wine that is elegant and captivating when still young, and a second wine, which is labelled Rabajà for historic reasons but actually comes from Vitalotti and has excellent structure and ageability.

Tenute Cisa Asinari dei Marchesi di Gresy
Via Rabajà, 43
Tel. + 39 0173 635222
The Tenute Cisa Asinari has belonged to the Marchesi di Gresy for more than 200 years and is located in one of the most attractive sites in the entire DOCG zone. Although the grapes from Martinenga have long been considered some of the best in Barbaresco, the family only started to make wine in 1973. Their just over 12 hectares planted to nebbiolo yield about 50,000 bottles of Barbaresco, released under three labels. Martinenga is the estate's standard label, taking up a position halfway between the aroma-rich and pleasing, if less full, Gaiun, from the lower part of the Asili vineyard, and the austere, muscular, long-lived Camp Gros, located at the other end of the amphitheatre, right below the celebrated Rabajà cru.

Giuseppe Cortese
Via Rabajà, 35
Tel. + 39 0173 635131
From roughly three hectares planted to nebbiolo, at the southern edge of Rabajà, the Cortese family produces about 16,000 bottles of Barbaresco that reflect the vineyard's impressive tannin structure and austerity. This is definitely a wine that needs a few years to mellow out.

Gaja
Via Torino, 36/a
Tel. + 39 0173 635158
When you talk about Barbaresco you are talking about Angelo Gaja. The estate's more than 50 hectares under nebbiolo produce wines that have shaped Italy's oenological destiny in the world, Barbaresco, Barbaresco Costa Russi, Barbaresco Sorì San Lorenzo, Barbaresco Sorì Tildin and Barolo Sperss. The cellar's roughly 110,000 bottles of Barbaresco each year come from 14

Ronchi

different vineyards, including the celebrated Pajoré cru, which brings its contribution of structure and fullness of body. Costa Russi, from the Roncagliette vineyard, was first released in 1978 and is the softest and most aroma-rich of the stable. Sorì Tildin has been made since 1970 and also comes from Roncagliette but offers more vigour and fullness. The origins of the Sorì San Lorenzo, separately vinified for the first time in 1967, lie in the Secondine vineyard, which lends the wine more tannic potency and makes it rather austere when young. In 1988, Gaja bought just under 30 hectares at Serralunga d'Alba, in the Marenca and Rivette vineyards, much of it planted to nebbiolo. The vines gave birth to the powerful, richly flavoured Barolo Sperss.

In 2000, Angelo Gaja decided to use the Langhe Nebbiolo designation for his Barolos and Barbarescos.

I Paglieri
Alfredo Roagna
Via Rabajà, 8
Tel. + 39 0173 635109
The Alfredo Roagna cellar is the place to go if you are looking for owerful, long-lived Barbarescos and Barolos whose tannins will mellow over the years to achieve an astonishing velvet smoothness. Barriques may have been introduced here more than 20 years ago but these wines, like their maker, offer no easy concessions to modern tastes.

In addition to a blended Barbaresco, the cellar produces the Crichët Pajé. Released for almost 20 years as a vino da tavolo, with the 1996 vintage it became once again a Barbaresco DOCG.

For several years, Roagna has been vinifying a Barolo La Rocca e La Pira that has all the austere sensory characteristics of the Barolos from Castiglione Falletto.

Moccagatta
Via Rabajà, 24
Tel. + 39 0173 635152 - 0173 635228
The estate of brothers Franco and Sergio Minuto embraces about 11 hectares under vine, of which roughly 40 per cent is nebbiolo for Barbaresco. Today, the cellar releases three vineyard selections. Basarin, made since 1982, is the leanest of the trio, thanks to its soil type, whereas Cole, also produced since 1982, is big and rougher, a characteristic that barrique-ageing

has at least partly reined in over the last few years. Bric Balin, from Moccagatta, is the jewel in the cellar's crown. Fermented entirely in part-new barriques, Bric Balin is the densest and most velvety of the three wines.

Cascina Morassino
Via Ovello, 32
Tel. + 39 0173 635149
Roberto Bianco keeps a firm hand on the tiller at this small winery, which has a total of five hectares in the vast, heterogeneous subzone of Ovello. The 10,500 or so bottles of Barbaresco are split as follows: 6,000 bottles of the rugged Barbaresco Morassino, the vines for which stand just below the cascina; and 4,500 bottles of Barbaresco Ovello, harvested in the Ovello subzone or, to be more precise, in the Albano-Morassino vineyard overlooking the cellar.

Walter Musso
Via D. Cavazza, 5
Tel. + 39 0173 635129
Walter Musso is lucky enough to have nearly five hectares planted to nebbiolo in two of the most envied vineyards in the municipality of Barbaresco, Pora and Rio Sordo. The resulting wines have good complexity and structure, with a little extra length and density in the case of the Pora.

Produttori del Barbaresco
Via Torino, 52
Tel. + 39 0173 635139
This co-operative winery, run by Celestino and Duccio Vacca, is a worthy successor to the one founded more than a century ago by Professor Domizio Cavazza. The 60 members tend almost 110 hectares of nebbiolo for Barbaresco, representing more than 22 per cent of the total for the DOCG zone. The Produttori turn out more than 300,000 bottles of Barbaresco. There is a 60-40 split between standard labels and Riservas, the fruit coming from some of the municipality's most famous vineyards (Asili, Rabajà, Rio Sordo, Ovello, Montestefano, Pajé, Moccagatta, Montefico and Pora). The winery offers drinkers a rare opportunity to explore the different characteristics of Barbaresco's finest vineyards.

Albino Rocca
Via Rabajà, 15
Tel. + 39 0173 635145
Although the estate does not include any out-standing nebbiolo-growing positions, Angelo Rocca still releases great wines every year, thanks to careful control of cropping levels and scrupulous work in the cellar. His almost five hectares of nebbiolo produce two vineyard selections, the Brich Ronchi, whose south east-facing vines stand below the *cascina*, and Loreto, which faces south west and the Tanaro valley. Brich Ronchi is aged in part-new barriques and explodes onto the palate with a velvety tannic fullness that sets it apart from the crowd. In contrast, Loreto is part aged in large barrels and generally has less potency but greater aromatic complexity, which makes it a much more approachable bottle.

Moccagatta

Bruno Rocca
Via Rabajà, 29
Tel. + 39 0173 635112
Bruno Rocca may be fairly young but his is a name that must be mentioned when you are talking about the Barbaresco renaissance. Bruno was not content to conserve the heritage left by his father in 1978. Instead, he concentrated on improving it still further with painstaking work in vineyard and cellar. Of course, we cannot ignore the contribution of his superb plot in the heart of Rabajà but today, Bruno's Rabajà selection fears no rivals, combining structure and softness thanks to very low yields and the skilful use of new barriques for ageing. It should be noted that from the 1995 vintage, the winery has been releasing another Barbaresco, a blend of fruit from Fausoni and Pajoré, under the Coparossa label. Bruno is confident that as the vine stock gets older, Coparossa will prove to be a first-rank vineyard.

Rino Varaldo
Via Secondine, 2
Tel. + 39 0173 635160
Rino and Michele Varaldo's cellar is not yet one of Barbaresco's best known but the two Barbaresco selections, of which 10,500 bottles are released, leave no room for doubt about their quality policy. The Sorì Loreto di Barbaresco, aged in barrels of Slavonian oak, is distinctly austere and the Bricco Libero di Neive, a blend of grapes from Gallina and Albesani aged in barriques, is a softer wine. The Varaldos also release a few bottles of Barolo Vigna di Aldo.

Cantina del Pino
Via Ovello, 15
Tel. + 39 0173 635147
The Vacca family's winery was founded only recently and in fact the first Barbaresco released came from the 1997 vintage. By assembling grapes from their various plots in Ovello – Loreto and Albano – and by carefully exploiting their three hectares, which yield a total of roughly 15,000 bottles of barrique-aged Barbaresco Ovello, the Vaccas have already achieved excellent results.

Carlo Giacosa
Via Ovello, 8
Tel. + 39 0173 635116
The Carlo Giacosa cellar released two types of Barbaresco, both of good quality. Since 1993, the cellar has turned out 9,000 bottles of Montefico, aged in large barrels that enhance the complexity of the wine on the

nose, and a further 9,000 bottles of Narin, from Asili, Cole and Canova. Named after grandfather Donato, the barrique-aged Narin has a softer, gentler palate. It should also be noted that until the early 1990s, a Sorì Secondine was produced, before it made way for the Montefico.

La Ca' Növa
Via Ovello, 1
Tel. + 39 0173 635123
The Rocca brothers, Pietro, Giulio and Franco, are not men to compromise. Their Barbaresco is aged in large barrels of Slavonian oak to conserve the typicity of its nose. They release four versions, a blended Barbaresco, a Montefico, a Bric Mentina and a Montestefano, all of which have attractive aromatic complexity and remarkably powerful tannins. For many years, the grapes from Montestefano were sold to Prunotto but they started to be vinified at the cellar again in 1995.

Montaribaldi
Via Rio Sordo, 30
Frazione Tre Stelle
Tel. + 39 0173 638220
From the splendid if little known vineyard of Montaribaldi, young brothers Luciano and Roberto Taliano make about 6,000 bottles of an excellent Barbaresco that owes its rich fruit and full palate in part to careful ageing in part-new barriques. This interesting young winery is definitely a rising star. Watch out for Monteribaldi in the next few years.

Ronchi
Via Rabajà, 14
Tel. + 39 0173 635156
Giancarlo Rocca, cousin of the more famous Angelo, looks after three hectares of nebbiolo that the family owns in the Ronchi vineyard. As he is just starting out, only part of his wine goes into the bottle (about 5,000 units) and the rest is sold wholesale. Giancarlo's Barbaresco is part-aged in barriques. It concentrates on power on the palate more than elegance on the nose.

WHERE TO SLEEP

Vecchio Tre Stelle
Frazione Tre Stelle
Via Rio Sordo, 13
Tel. + 39 0173 638192
Three stars. Eight double rooms provide an unfussy, welcoming ambience that offers a good base for exploring the hills of Barbaresco. The restaurant has a territory-dedicated menu that keeps in step with the season. Prices are very affordable.

Rio Sordo

Cascina delle Rose
Località Tre Stelle
Via Rio Sordo, 17
Tel. + 39 0173 638292 - 0173 638322
An *agriturismo*, or farm holiday centre, with a few comfortable rooms in a delightful setting. There are lovely views over the hills of Barbaresco and Roero. The farm's excellent fruit, vegetables and Barbaresco, from the Rio Sordo vineyard, are all available for guests to enjoy. There are no catering facilities but guests can prepare their own breakfast in a large living area with kitchenette.

EATING OUT

Antica Torre
Via Torino, 8
Tel. + 39 0173 635170
The Antica Torre, run by the Albarello family, serves well-prepared Piedmontese cuisine, with all the classic dishes and, occasionally, harder to find delights such as pig's head in sweet and sour sauce. The wine list is long and carefully chosen, featuring almost the entire range of Barbarescos. Expect to spend around € 30.00 without wine.

Antiné
Via Torino, 34 a
Tel. + 39 0173 635294
The ambience, furnishings and cuisine at Antiné are in the modern idiom, and the accent is on light dishes. The menu includes the classic *ravioli del plin* and *tajarin* pastas as well as rabbit in Barberesco. The very decent wine list foregrounds Barbarescos. A full meal will cost around € 35.00, excluding wine.

Rabajà
Via Rabajà, 9
Tel. + 39 0173 635223
A restaurant in a rustic but delightfully neat setting in the midst of the vines, just below Rabajà and a stone's throw from Pajé. The traditional cuisine follows the progress of the seasons. Lovers of good wine will admire the list of more than 300 labels, mainly from the Langhe and Roero.

WHAT TO BUY

Distilleria del Barbaresco
Via Bricco Albano, 3
Tel. + 39 0173 635251
The distillery produces first-quality grappa for grower members from all over the Barbaresco area.

Domizio Cavazza

1856-1913

The coat of arms of the Cavazza family has a vine leaning on two large elm branches, a training technique that was once widespread in Emilia. The symbol was a surprising foretaste of Domizio Cavazza's future career.

Domizio was born at Concordia sul Secchia, a town near Modena, in 1856. His mother, Anna, was a noblewoman, who came from the baronial Zanoli family. His father, Luigi, was the municipal notary and came from a historically important family, as may be seen from a deed dated 1699, but the Cavazzas were not on the official roll of noble families. Domizio's grandfather had a degree in pharmacy, his uncle was a graduate in medicine and his father had a law degree. The Cavazzas were a solid, civic-minded family with a level of education that was distinctly higher than the average for the times. Domizio took his degree *con molto plauso* ("magna cum laude") in agronomy and land surveying at the university of Milan, going on to complete further studies, first at Versailles and then at Montpellier. Two of his teachers, the celebrated scholars Viala and Foëx, recognised the young graduate's potential and recommended him to the Italian minister for agriculture, with whom they were in contact. Domizio was able to observe at first hand the devastation caused by phylloxera, which in France had already reduced vast tracts of wine country to deserts, and of downy mildew, discovered in those years by Professor Planchon of Montpellier on Jaquez vines. When the ministry invited him to found the "Scuola Pratica di Viticoltura ed Enologia", or Practical School of Viticulture and Oenology, at Alba in 1881, Domizio had built up outstanding contacts and experience in the sector.

Cavazza became the school's first principal, a post he filled with efficiency and generous commitment. Readers will find an account of his work in the profile of the school. In those years, Cavazza's interest and indeed love for the Langhe grew. His wife, Amalia Vitali, "a wise, cultured and exceptionally devout woman", was from Piedmont.

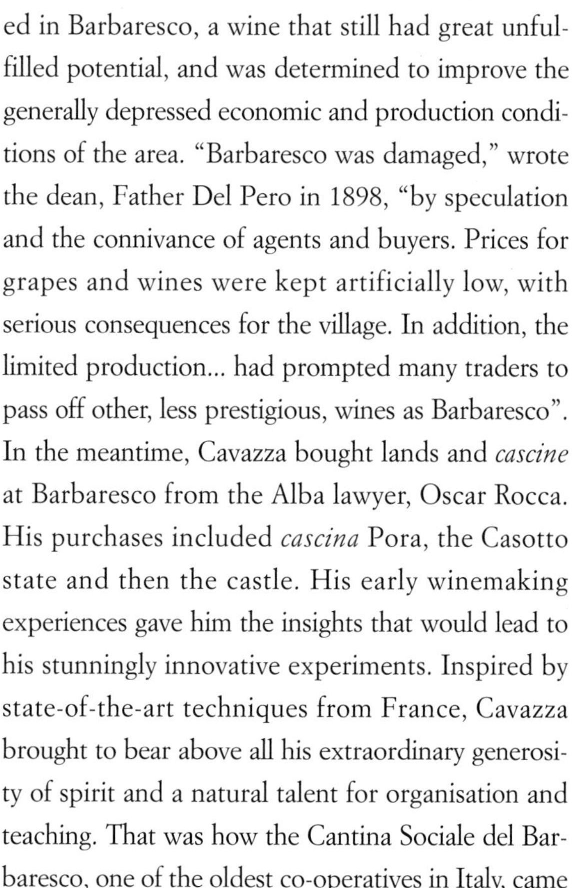

Domizio became particularly interested in Barbaresco, a wine that still had great unfulfilled potential, and was determined to improve the generally depressed economic and production conditions of the area. "Barbaresco was damaged," wrote the dean, Father Del Pero in 1898, "by speculation and the connivance of agents and buyers. Prices for grapes and wines were kept artificially low, with serious consequences for the village. In addition, the limited production... had prompted many traders to pass off other, less prestigious, wines as Barbaresco".

In the meantime, Cavazza bought lands and *cascine* at Barbaresco from the Alba lawyer, Oscar Rocca. His purchases included *cascina* Pora, the Casotto state and then the castle. His early winemaking experiences gave him the insights that would lead to his stunningly innovative experiments. Inspired by state-of-the-art techniques from France, Cavazza brought to bear above all his extraordinary generosity of spirit and a natural talent for organisation and teaching. That was how the Cantina Sociale del Barbaresco, one of the oldest co-operatives in Italy, came

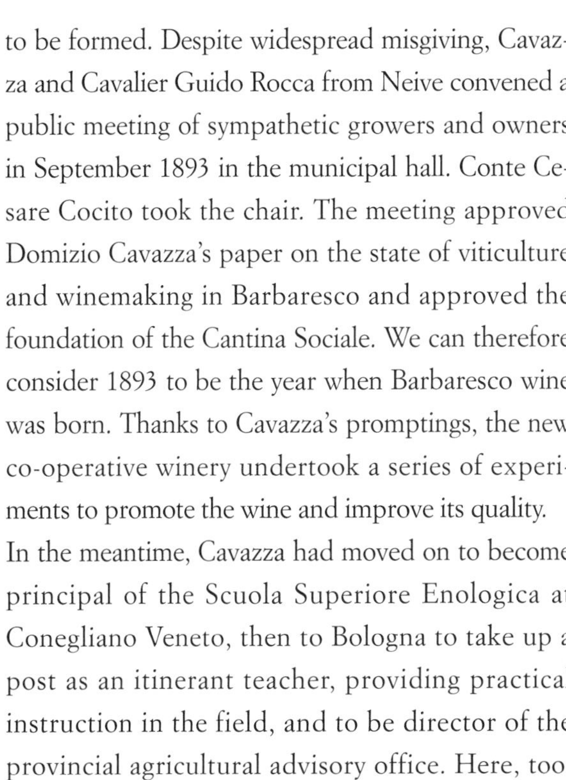

to be formed. Despite widespread misgiving, Cavazza and Cavalier Guido Rocca from Neive convened a public meeting of sympathetic growers and owners in September 1893 in the municipal hall. Conte Cesare Cocito took the chair. The meeting approved Domizio Cavazza's paper on the state of viticulture and winemaking in Barbaresco and approved the foundation of the Cantina Sociale. We can therefore consider 1893 to be the year when Barbaresco wine was born. Thanks to Cavazza's promptings, the new co-operative winery undertook a series of experiments to promote the wine and improve its quality.

In the meantime, Cavazza had moved on to become principal of the Scuola Superiore Enologica at Conegliano Veneto, then to Bologna to take up a post as an itinerant teacher, providing practical instruction in the field, and to be director of the provincial agricultural advisory office. Here, too, Cavazza was outstanding for his enterprise and skill. He produced remarkable research work on poplars, the selection of wheat and on the regeneration of the peach tree. But Cavazza's heart and mind were with the vineyards of Barbaresco. He returned every autumn and remained in charge of the Cantina Sociale, which was housed at his castle. In 1911, he suffered a severe stroke at Bologna. Medical treatment enabled him to survive for a further 29 months, although his health was never stable. Cavazza did manage to move back to his castle at Barbaresco, where he died on 9 August 1913.

The final days of his life were saddened by violent hailstorms that ravaged the Langhe. Only a few hours before he died, Cavazza confided to his friend Teobaldo Calissano that he was worried about the hail damage. Cavazza's final thoughts were for Barbaresco and its vines.

Gaja

In the book, *Immagini per Una Storia di Barbaresco* (Images for a History of Barbaresco), published by the municipality, there are two photographs that sum up the Gaja family better than any biography. The first is from 1902 and portrays Angelo's grandfather, also called Angelo, resplendent in moustache and hat beside his mule. The other picture dates from 1958 and shows Giovanni, a surveyor, making his first fficial speech after being elected mayor. The two snapshots illustrate two different ages. Indeed, they seem to come from different planets. Grandfather Angelo is a good-looking young man with a bright, jaunty air. But he is wearing boots and work pants. He gives the impression of not being comfortable in his jacket. In contrast, it is easy to pick out Giovanni among his fellow citizens. His elegant, well-cut coat, immaculate shirt, Borsalino hat, gaunt features and authoritative, sweeping gestures belong to a born politician.

It was with Giovanni Gaja that the winery began the irresistible rise that has taken it in recent years to the front ranks of Italian winemaking. Gaja's roots go back to 1859. Great-grandfather Giovanni owned a flourishing transport company (he was a *cartoné*, or "carter") and was able, thanks to his hard work and that of his five boys and two girls, to leave a *cascina* to each of his children. Three of the boys, in the time-honoured Langhe tradition, squandered their inheritance at the gambling table. *Barba Cit* (or "Little Uncle", as the youngest, a two metre-tall giant of a man, was nicknamed) even managed to gamble away the two *cascine* that his extremely wealthy wife had brought as a dowry. The second youngest boy Angelo, the man with the mule, was a very different character. "He went around holding a rosary", people said of him. Angelo was to marry Clotilde Rey, a severe woman who had studied to be a primary school teacher at Chambéry. Everyone in Barbaresco called her *Madama*, the local equivalent of *Signora*. Only her closest relatives were allowed to use the familiar diminutive, *Tildin*. Inflexible but intelligent, Clotilde had very clear ideas on what constituted quality and a job well done. She immediately took over the running of the family *osteria*, the "Osteria del Vapore", working shoulder to shoulder with four daughters-in-law and totally re-organising activities. She was equally incisive in the cellar.

The children were sent to Alba to study. Giovanni, born in 1908, qualified as a surveyor before joining the family business. He was an enterprising man, with an extraordinary nose for business, and was active in the construction industry as well as brokerage. In those days, the village surveyor was an economic advisor, an arbitrator in the inevitable angry disputes that broke out among heirs or neighbours, and a broker for property sales. Naturally, since the surveyor had all the relevant information, he was generally the one who got the best deal. A man like that also had to be on the side of the political powers that be. Under Fascism, Giovanni was the *podestà*, or governor, of Lequio Beria and the political secretary of Barbaresco, later becoming the town's mayor from 1958 to 1983. He was well-liked by local residents. The partisans never harmed him and his fellow

citizens were happy to keep re-electing him. Having studied at Alba, Giovanni went into business with a Turin-based company during the boom years, supervising building work all over Piedmont. Although he had little time to spend at the winery, he invested all his earnings in the land.

It was grandmother *Tildin*, widowed in 1944, who ran the cellar. At the time, the Gajas sold wine only to private customers but they were famous families, such as the Somainis from Milan, the Zegnas and the Nasis. All were households that had their own cooks and a cellar full of French *grands crus*. They bought their Barbaresco in demijohns, bottled it themselves and served it as "table wine". The Gajas therefore had a good market for their wine, which they sold without difficulty. It could stay in the vats for ten years waiting for a customer to come along. Grandmother *Tildin*, however, insisted on quality and rigour, even in those early days. When Angelo Gaja joined the winery in 1961, he found an enviably solid financial situation, a name that was already well-known in Italy and 33 hectares of superbly positioned vineyards at Barbaresco. In 1965 and 1966, when he decided to enter the restaurant market, he already had an excellent range of wines. Then came the vineyard selections. The first, San Lorenzo, was vinified in 1967. However, Giovanni had always bought his fruit from the plot in the Secondine vineyard that he thought was one of the finest in Barbaresco. The Gajas acquired it in 1964. In 1970, the wine technician, Ezio Rivella, joined the estate. In the same year, Sorì Tildin was created, followed in 1978 by Costa Russi. This, however, is recent history, a chronicle that Angelo Gaja is still writing with his wines and which Edward Steinberg's book *Sorì San Lorenzo*, published by Slow Food in 1996, tells in greater detail.

The professors were looking for phylloxera

Luigi Bianco
born 1910
grower
in Barbaresco

When Cavazza founded his co-operative winery, up at the castle, there weren't very many of us making wine here at Barbaresco. I still have the newspaper article reporting the event and our name is right there. Some people told me it was advertising. It wasn't anything of the sort. We didn't know about advertising back then. The fact is that everyone here sold all the grapes. Calissano, Gancia and Pio used to come. They had all the addresses and took all the fruit. One year, there was an epic hailstorm. It was 1922 and I remember coming back from the May Festival in Alba to find hail lying half a metre deep on the road. I'm not exaggerating; it looked like snow. But over at Neive, there hadn't been any hail at all. We didn't have a single bunch so we bought fruit, too. We paid 33 lire for the grapes. An incredible amount! The following year, the price dropped back to nine lire and we had ridiculously expensive wine in the cellar that we couldn't sell. Luckily, Commendator Calissano sold it off for us in America. He had us rack it into new ten-litre demijohns and send it away. We did exactly what he told us and breathed a huge sigh of relief.

Those were difficult years and phylloxera was devastating the vineyards. I was very young but Professor Ferraris from the Scuola Enologica at Alba made me go to school twice a week to learn how to graft. I would walk across the vineyards then follow the electricity lines downhill, and always arrived at school on time. Sometimes, I would go with him into the vineyards. There were three of them, all professors, and they were looking for phylloxera. Some growers were hard to convince. They said it was impossible and that the vineyard was healthy. The next year, everything would be shrivelled and dried up.

Here at Barbaresco, there has always been nebbiolo. It's not like Treiso, where they've planted and ripped it out two or three times! Truth to tell, they planted nebbiolo where nothing else would grow, in *sorì*, or slopes, where you could only plant maize or beans because the slope was too exposed and dry. That's where the old-timers used to plant nebbiolo. Now, they're the most famous vineyards, the crus. But don't think that they were big zones. Now, they want to call everywhere Strada Rabajà goes "Rabajà" but that's not right. Rabajà is a small area, just the zone around the *cascina* Rabajà. All the vineyards here in Barbaresco take their names from the villages or more important *cascine*. (*November 1995*)

A lousy life

We used to sell the grapes to Calissano, Fontanafredda and Gancia. We never took them to Alba because the agents came here. Terranino from Neive, for example, and Musso, the father of the Musso who makes wine now. We joined the co-operative winery straight away, in 1958, the first year. After then, things got better. We never made much money before that.

The good areas were already the ones that are famous today. Paglieri, Pagliuzzi and Martinenga are wonderful positions. No one ever talks about Paglieri because the *cascina* is low down and north-facing but the vines have a lovely location and get lots of sunshine. *Cascina* Pora is at the end of Cittadella. Pora belongs almost entirely to the Manzone family, who are very hard-working, except for the Musso plot. The Gaja holding has always been called Bricco and nebbiolo has always been grown there. Now, there's cabernet.
One year, we harvested all the grapes and couldn't sell them. Luckily, the tenants from further up couldn't sell theirs because they were poor quality so they came to buy ours, at nine lire.

Luigi Giordano
born 1915
grower
in Barbaresco

But it was a poor kind of life, *da pioi* (lousy). The Cantina Social got us out of a real hole. Today, they buy on must weight. It's still must weight that sets the price.
Once, when there was a bit of space between the rows, we would plant chickpeas, which is a vegetable you can pick after 100 days. After phylloxera, we began to rip up the soil. We'd dig down for a metre or a metre and a half.
Vines that lie perpendicular to the slope are easy to work with a tractor but terrible if you have to work manually. You've always got one leg bent. Do you know who plants like that? People who don't work the vines but get someone else to do it! (*November 1995*)

But it was worse during the war

When I was young, life was hard but it was worse during the war. I was called up in 1940 and I did two years in Russia. Even though I was a gunner and looked after the animals – mules and horses – I did the whole retreat on foot. Because by the time we began to move back, we had eaten all the animals. We and the prisoners, because the commanding officer wanted everyone to eat the same food. One of my friends was luckier. He got – let's be frank, he stole – a marvellous topcoat with a fur collar. So one day, he reported to the lieutenant, who said to him, "If you give me the coat, I'll send you home". That's how he got a comfortable ride home on a lorry while I had to walk for 2,000 kilometres. It took me four months. The worst moment was when we were crossing the frozen river Nieper (Dnepr) – 1,200 metres of ice. As soon as we were across, the bombardment started. The shells broke the ice and I saw sheets as big as a *giornata* of land thrown into the air. It was an awesome spectacle. Thinking about it, it was beautiful but at the time... I was terrified!
Luckily, after I got home in 1945, things slowly began to get better. If I think that my grandfather used to take wine to Turin with an ox-cart, a rabel. It took him two days. He left when it was still dark and stopped to sleep halfway to Turin. But he took the hay for the animals and his own food with him because he had no money. He had one bag of walnuts and one of bread. And wine, of course. That was his food for a journey that lasted two days and two nights. (*November 1995*)

Mario Minuto
born 1910,
grower
in Barbaresco

An artist remembers

I finished the fourth year of primary school here in Barbaresco. Then a teacher came from Alessandria and said I should do the fifth year, too. I did it at night school. I was already carving wood when I was eight or nine. The teacher had made a museum. The girls brought embroidery and borders, the boys made sledges and chairs, and I brought a yoke, my very first piece. No one in my family ever sculpted. My uncle did the odd job on the tools, like spade handles or knives. My wife is Francesca Pellissero, from *cascina* Crosa, the sister of Pasquale who makes wine at Neive. When I was 12, the family split up. There were 18 of us. Three brothers, that is my father and two uncles, my father's five children, five more of one uncle and the other was a bachelor. The first went to Neive in 1921. In 1925, we bought Casotto for 100,000 lire, with nine *giornate*. The vineyard is Ovello and like all subzones, there are good plots and bad ones. We're at Bernino. And we go as far as Montefico. When we split up, they had me putting on sulphur with the machine. I've seen people using bags but I was already using the machine. My great-grandfather was born here but I think his family came from Mango. My grandfather was one of the founder members of the Cooperativa di Cavazza. I'm a founder member of the Produttori di Barbaresco co-operative.

Francesco Vacca
born 1913
sculptor
in Barbaresco

Once, there was an *opio*, that is a maple, a special one that looked like a box tree. It was a wild maple, hard as marble, with no veining. It stayed smooth and didn't hurt the necks of the animals whereas walnut wood chafes. It was magnificent, a one-off. And I worked at night, always at night, before I went off to join up. I made this lovely piece in 1950. I did reptiles, snails, frogs. Then birds. Then vegetables, fruit, water-pepper, wheat and corn. Then the bridge, the train, the house, the cars. It's unique. At Castiglione, I made eight yokes from *opio* wood. To make them took me two or three years, working at night. I must have made hundreds of yokes. Some were decorated with a dog's head, or birds.

One day, a man from Castelrotto stopped me and said he'd bring me his yoke, which had Barbaresco on it, to tidy it up. I was to wax and oil it, not put on *flatin* (flatting paste), which leaves an encrustation. I went to pick it up and he said, "I've sold it, to some people from Sanremo". It was 50 years old and worn with use. They paid 3,000,000 lire for it.

I made some yokes at Carmagnola. There's one at Mussotto, at Agliano. Seven or eight well used ones are still in circulation. It was like for cars today, the more ambitious types wanted them painted and decorated the way they do with luxury cars.

The first bust I did was my grandfather, Giuseppe. They gave me some plastiline in Turin and I tried it out. I couldn't do much with it. I did my first real bust for Vacca from the station. Before he died, he said to his children, "I want a bust by *Cichin*". It must be 20 years ago now. We did a swap for this sofa.

First, I did those 20 centimetre-high statues that are in the civic museum in Turin today. They weren't signed. They put an iron plaque on them. My grandson saw them on a school trip and told us about them – I've never seen them in the museum. I went once but it was closed – he said to us, "It's a pity the Pietà was cracked".

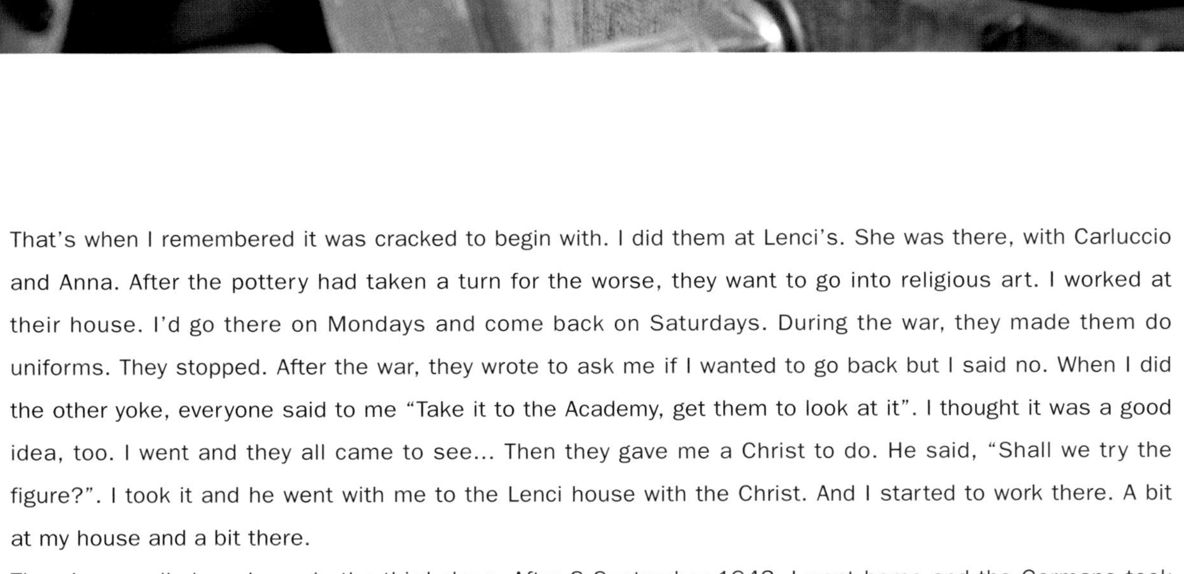

That's when I remembered it was cracked to begin with. I did them at Lenci's. She was there, with Carluccio and Anna. After the pottery had taken a turn for the worse, they want to go into religious art. I worked at their house. I'd go there on Mondays and come back on Saturdays. During the war, they made them do uniforms. They stopped. After the war, they wrote to ask me if I wanted to go back but I said no. When I did the other yoke, everyone said to me "Take it to the Academy, get them to look at it". I thought it was a good idea, too. I went and they all came to see... Then they gave me a Christ to do. He said, "Shall we try the figure?". I took it and he went with me to the Lenci house with the Christ. And I started to work there. A bit at my house and a bit there.

Then I was called up. I was in the third class. After 8 September 1943, I went home and the Germans took me hostage. I was in the first ten. If any Germans had died, they would have shot me. They took me all over, to Turin and the Torino Cavalleria, in Corso Unione Sovietica. Then a black-shirt captain from Barbaresco turned up. I knew him well. I used to graft the apple trees at his place. He sent me home.

I had three grafting diplomas from Professor Ferraris.

Oh, how many vines I grafted after the war! They planted the American vine, then in spring or August I would go round grafting from Asti to Serravalle. At Carretta, for instance, I did everything. I grafted 5,000 vines so I know the whole area. We give the nebbiolo to the Cantina Sociale. Once, we couldn't give the co-operative everything because we produced too much. In recent years, what we do produce hasn't been enough. (*November 1995*)

B A R B A R E S C O

Neive

The best way to arrive in Neive is to skirt the magnificent rows of nebbiolo lining the road that leaves Alba and passes through Tre Stelle, then Barbaresco. Towards the end of summer, there is a stupendous array of dolcetto, barbera and nebbiolo in a riot of colour that varies with the slope and its exposure to the warm Langhe sunshine.

The name Neive derives from Nevius, of the *Gens Nevia*, who may have been the second century AD poet and composer of a history in verse as well as numerous plays. The site of the town itself belonged to the Camillia tribe. In the Middle Ages, Neive was ravaged by barbarian invasions and then contested by Alba and Asti, passing under the control of Manfredi I of Busca and of Galeazzo Visconti and his daughter Valentina, the bride of Louis d'Orléans. Subsequently, a number of families became the *signori*, or lords, of Neive, which passed to the Savoys after Napoleon, who occupied the town during his first Italian campaign, lost it when he was banished to the island of Elba.

Neive has, as it were, two souls. Borgonuovo is the commercial town, the place where carts heading for Alba once stopped at the restaurants for refreshment and the stables to change horses. The lower town, having expanded in the architectural anarchy of the 1960s, now surrounds the historic centre on the hilltop. Beyond time, the upper town of Neive Alta has preserved its seventeenth and eighteenth-century palazzos from the over-enthusiastic restructuring of the past or, worse, demolition.

Old Neive has come down to us unchanged, huddled on its hilltop around a bell tower built by the citizens of Asti in to complete the ancient *ricetto*, or shelter. About the year 1000 AD, the Signori of Neive built the

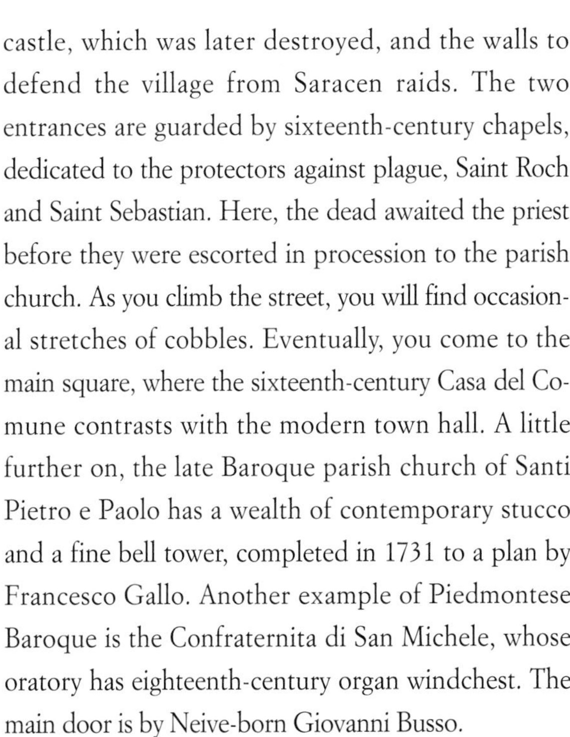

castle, which was later destroyed, and the walls to defend the village from Saracen raids. The two entrances are guarded by sixteenth-century chapels, dedicated to the protectors against plague, Saint Roch and Saint Sebastian. Here, the dead awaited the priest before they were escorted in procession to the parish church. As you climb the street, you will find occasional stretches of cobbles. Eventually, you come to the main square, where the sixteenth-century Casa del Comune contrasts with the modern town hall. A little further on, the late Baroque parish church of Santi Pietro e Paolo has a wealth of contemporary stucco and a fine bell tower, completed in 1731 to a plan by Francesco Gallo. Another example of Piedmontese Baroque is the Confraternita di San Michele, whose oratory has eighteenth-century organ windchest. The main door is by Neive-born Giovanni Busso.

The entire historic centre of Neive is therefore worth visiting carefully, with its noble palazzos (Palazzo Cotto, Palazzo Borgese, Palazzo Bongioanni, Palazzo Cocito and the Casaforte Cotto), its fine stone houses, its well-restored wooden doors and the road that curves past scrupulously tended gardens, offering delightful views of the surrounding countryside.

At Borgonuovo, on the road to Mango, you will find the ancient sacristy of the twelfth-century abbey of Santa Maria del Piano, or rather what is left of it for only one side wall and the Romanesque bell tower survive. Its walls were clearly made with material dating from Roman times.

To the north and east, Neive is bounded by the municipality of Castagnole Lanze, to the south east by Mango and to the south by Neviglie and Treiso. The entire western section is contiguous with Barbaresco.

The great vineyards

The municipality of Neive is the most extensive in the Barbaresco DOCG zone. Only about 20 per cent of the area under vine is planted to nebbiolo. Currently, the most widely planted variety is moscato, followed by nebbiolo, barbera and dolcetto.

The 18 vineyards lie on the slopes of seven hills arranged in a circle around Neive Alta. Beginning in the north, we find Serracapelli, then Starderi, Bordini and Balluri. Next comes the Albesani hill, then Gallina and so on to Basarin and San Cristoforo to the south.

There is also another area that is equally suitable for growing nebbiolo in the eastern part of the municipality. This lies beyond the railway line and is called Bricco di Neive. Here, we find Serraboella, Bricco and Canova. These three hills lie almost parallel to each other and their soil becomes progressively sandier the further one proceeds towards Castagnole Lanze. Nebbiolo is planted mainly on the slopes that face south, from west to east. On the north-facing hillsides, we find moscato or

DOC and DOCG	Total area under vine in hectares	% of area in municipality	% of area in zone
Moscato d'Asti	208.0378	32.90	5.02
Barbaresco	**137.4059**	**21.73**	**28.61**
Barbera d'Alba	133.2189	21.07	7.73
Dolcetto d'Alba	105.0868	16.62	5.62
Langhe Chardonnay	20.2816	3.21	7.90
Langhe Arneis	9.7680	1.54	23.69
Other DOC zones	18.5244	2.93	
TOTAL	632.3234	100.00	
Other DOC zones			
Langhe Freisa	3.3205	0.53	5.53
Piemonte Grignolino	2.7050	0.43	16.49
Langhe Favorita	2.5658	0.41	2.57
Piemonte Brachetto	2.5300	0.40	20.78
Piemonte	2.1200	0.34	11.58
Langhe Nebbiolo	2.0543	0.32	8.22
Piemonte Cortese	1.3188	0.21	10.24
Langhe Rosso	0.9600	0.15	1.36
Langhe Bianco	0.3500	0.06	1.31
Piemonte Chardonnay	0.3400	0.05	10.62
Piemonte Moscato	0.2600	0.04	1.78

dolcetto, as well as on the parts that are nearly flat and the areas where the land is reddish because of the presence of clay or richer soil types.

Although Neive was left out by Fantini when he wrote his monograph on viticulture in the province of Cuneo, there are several vineyards that show excellent potential, beginning with the Santo Stefano that is so magisterially vinified by Bruno Giacosa.

Production

There are 167 wineries in the municipality, con 137 hectares and a potential annual production of 7,695 hectolitres, or 28.6 per cent of the entire Barbaresco DOCG zone.

THE GREAT VINEYARDS

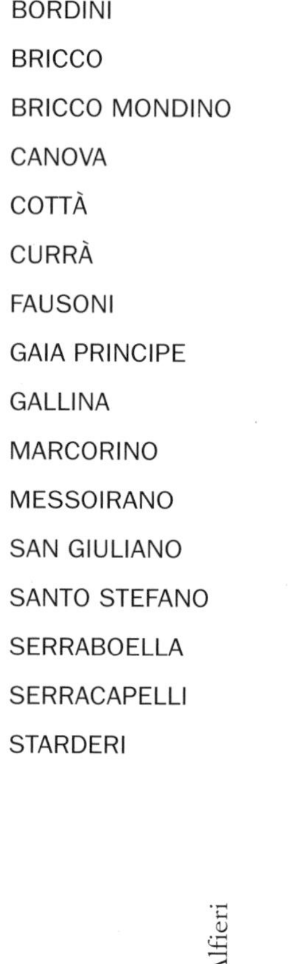

ALBESANI
BASARIN
BORDINI
BRICCO
BRICCO MONDINO
CANOVA
COTTÀ
CURRÀ
FAUSONI
GAIA PRINCIPE
GALLINA
MARCORINO
MESSOIRANO
SAN GIULIANO
SANTO STEFANO
SERRABOELLA
SERRACAPELLI
STARDERI

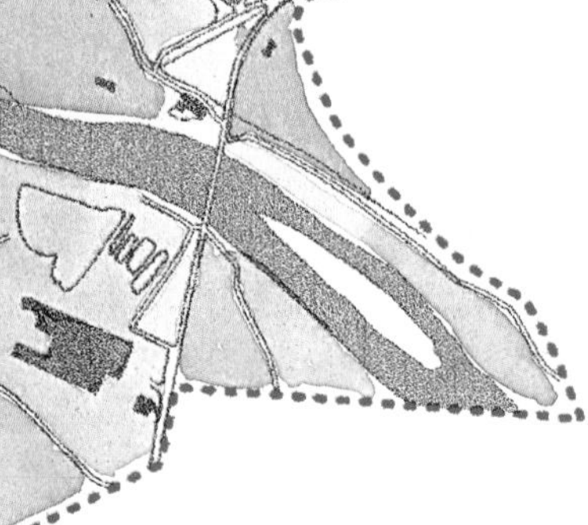

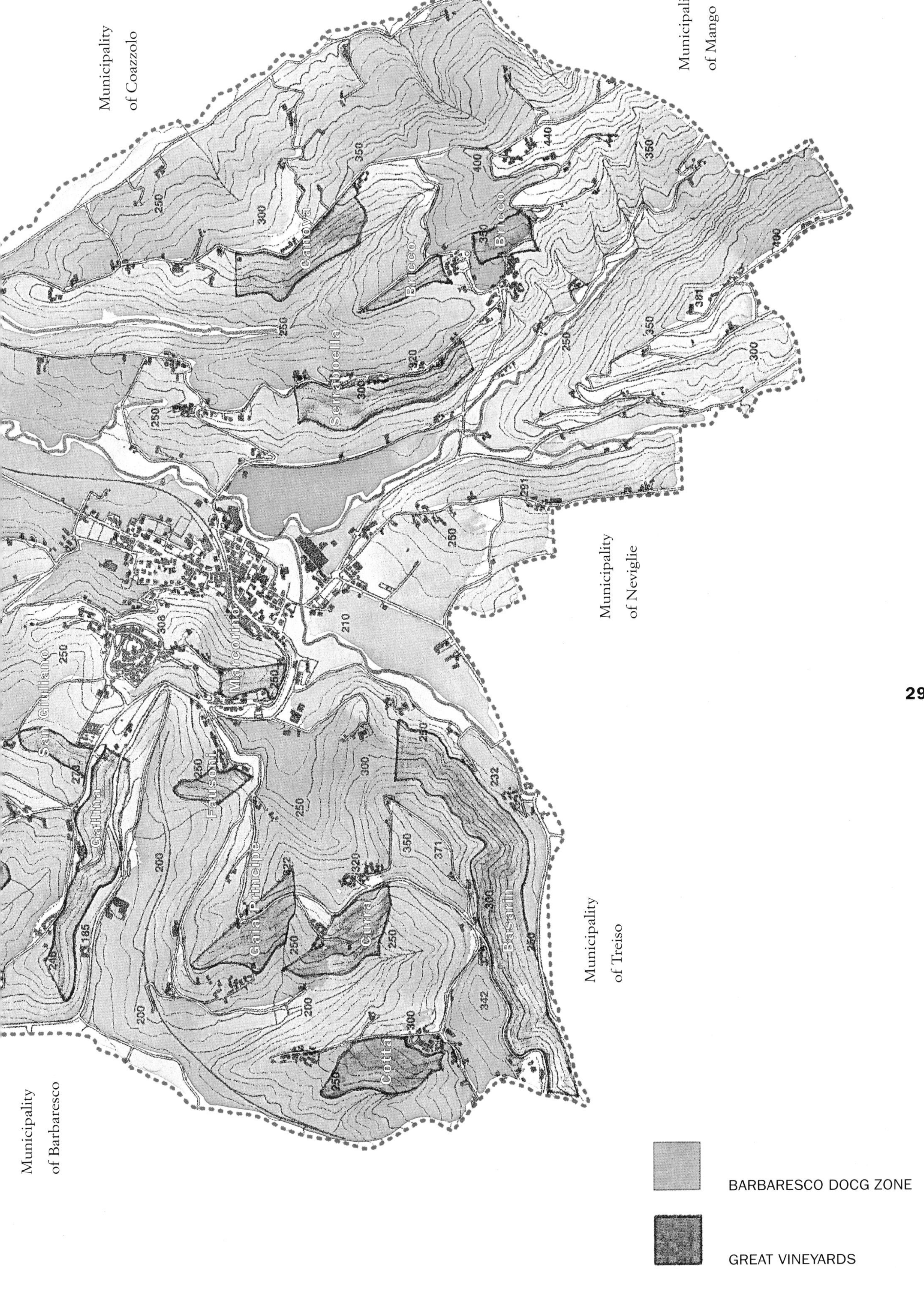
Municipality of Coazzolo
Municipality of Mango
Canova
Bricco
Bricco
Serraboella
Municipality of Neviglie
Marcorino
San Giuliano
Gallina
Fausoni
Gaia Principe
Currà
Basarin
Cotta
Municipality of Treiso
Municipality of Barbaresco
BARBARESCO DOCG ZONE
GREAT VINEYARDS

Albesani

The hill of Albesani lies between Balluri to the north and Gallina to the south. The road of the same name, which goes up to the cemetery, passes over the ridge that marks off the slope overlooking Balluri, which is of little interest since it is north-facing, and the slope that faces Gallina, a much better aspected hillside facing west and south west. The Albesani vineyard we are considering here has as its upper boundary the Albesani road that goes from the *cascina* Ronchi, where the Bernardino Gastaldi cellar stands, to *cascina* Bricchetto. To the south, the border is the Rondò-Baraccone provincial road as far as cascina Santo Stefano and from there a hypothetical line that joins *cascina* Santo Stefano to *cascina* Bricchetto. The Santo Stefano vineyard, which we have examined separately, is excluded from this area. The vineyard from Santo Stefano to *cascina* Bricchetto is known as Borgese. A Barbaresco selection from Borgese has been produced with great success for some years by Piero Busso.

MAIN LABELS

*Barbaresco Vigna Borgese – Piero Busso, Neive

*Barbaresco Vigna Ronco – Cantina del Brichetto, Neive

Basarin

Although Basarin is a superb vineyard both in extent and in orientation – many plots are entirely south-facing – it has never given nebbiolos to rival the great crus. Instead, its most impressive wines are obtained from dolcetto or barbera. The old-timers claim that this is a consequence of the subzone's soil type (they say there is too much sand for nebbiolo), the high altitude at Bricco San Cristoforo and in general of the winds from the north east and the Tinella river valley. To the west, Basarin is delimited by the boundary between Neive and Barbaresco, near Giorgio Pelissero's Vanotu vineyard. To the north, the boundary is the ridge that separates Basarin from Cottà, continuing along the local San Cristoforo road. The border then goes down to the *cascina* Zocco, at first following the course of the Tinella and then the Tre Stelle-Valgrande-Borgonuovo provincial road.

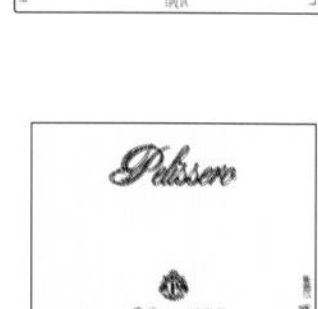

MAIN LABELS

*Barbaresco Vigneto Basarin – Moccagatta, Barbaresco

*Barbaresco Vanotu – Giorgio Pelissero, Treiso

Bordini

The hill of Bordini, which takes its name from *cascina* Bordini, cuts across the lower parts of Balluri and Starderi, with two slopes. One faces south east and the other, less interesting slope looks north, except for Bricco Mondino, which stands at the junction with Balluri and which we have examined separately. Bordini is a superb vineyard as well as being, unusually for Neive, a south west-facing *sorì del mattino* that looks towards the Borgo Antico. The hamlet of Bordini stands at an altitude of 280 metres and the lower limit of the vineyard is 220 metres. At certain points near the houses, the slopes face directly south. The soil is light in colour and the slopes are steep, both characteristics that are crucial to the production of elegant, well-structured wines.

MAIN LABELS

*Barbaresco Sorì di Burdin – Fontanabianca, Neive

Bricco

Bricco stands on the south west slope of the hill of the same name between Serraboella and Canova but at the higher altitude of 300 to 350 metres above sea level, almost at the upper limit for growing nebbiolo. As has been the case with many other vineyards in the municipality of Neive, history decreed in the past that other varieties unable to exploit the subzone's potential should be planted. But for the past few years, the nebbiolo harvested at Bricco has been giving good results and a wine that is longer on elegance than on structure, perhaps because of the sandy nature of the soil. The vineyard faces the northern slope of Serraboella, extending from the first curves in the road that leads to Bricco Spessa, just above the hamlet of Bricco di Neive, and keeping slightly below the ridge itself. Bricco then carries on to the hamlet of Moniprandi, where the hill peters out into poor positions that face north west, and then north east.

MAIN LABELS

*Barbaresco Bricco di Neuveis – Dante Rivetti, Neive

*Barbaresco Bricco – Cigliuti, Neive

Bricco Mondino

Bricco Mondino is a small vineyard on a hilltop. Crossed by the Balluri road, it is bordered to the south by the Bordini road and to the north by *cascina* Mondino. The highest point in the vineyard is about 280 metres above sea level and it then descends towards a low point in the west of 240 metres in the direction of Valle Possa. Since the hilltop faces slightly to the west, the vines almost always enjoy sunshine until late in the evening. Nebbiolo from *cascina* Mondino was always much prized by grape merchants in the past.

MAIN LABELS

*Barbaresco Bricco Mondino – Piero Busso, Neive

Canova

The lovely hill that closes off the Canova vineyard on its south west slope lies parallel to nearby Serraboella and is the most easterly elevation in the municipality of Neive, bordering on the municipal territory of Castagnole Lanze in the province of Asti. This is not a traditional area for the cultivation of nebbiolo for Barbaresco but the excellent positions of some stretches and the altitude, which is not excessive for this part of Neive (280-350 metres above sea level), make it a potentially exciting vineyard for Barbaresco. Canova covers a large area below the road that follows the ridge on top of the hill to reach Bricco Spessa. More precisely, it includes the part that leaves cascina Nova, after which the road is named, and turns near *cascina* Merone to arrive at *cascina* Caloglio, with a magnificent south west-facing location.

MAIN LABELS

*Barbaresco Canova – Cascina Vano, Neive

Cottà

Located in the most westerly part of Neive, almost on the border with the municipality of Barbaresco, this vineyard takes its name from the hamlet of Cottà, which looks onto the slope of Moccagatta and Ronchi as far as Montestefano. Observed from *cascina* Ronchi at Barbaresco, the vineyard's boundaries are easy to pick out. They are formed by the houses of Cottà itself to the south, the road on the ridge leading to the Tetti vineyard to the east, and the lane going down from the Sottimanos' *cascina* Maté to the hamlet of Tetti to the west. The hill has a highest point of 300 metres and slopes gently down to the 240 metres of the valley floor, enjoying sunshine until the late afternoon.

MAIN LABELS

*Barbaresco Cottà Vigna Brichet – Sottimano, Neive

*Barbaresco Masseria – Vietti, Castiglione Falletto

*Barbaresco Tettineive – Scarpa, Nizza Monferrato

Currà

The name probably derives from a holding that belonged to some *curato*, or parish priest, in the past. A small vineyard, Currà is bounded to the west by Cottà, by Bricco San Cristoforo to the east and by Gaia Principe to the north. As you travel along the Tre Stelle-Rondò provincial road towards Neive, you will see Currà on your left below the road, near the group of houses at *cascina* Pastura. It extends up to the righthand bend,

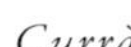

Currà

where the hill turns away offering positions that are less suitable for nebbiolo. Between these two landmarks, the vines run gently downhill on the south west-facing slope to reach *cascina* Rio, below the hamlet of Currà, on one side and the woods at the bottom of the *capezzagna*, or unsurfaced lane, that starts from the houses at *cascina* Pastura, on the other. The elevation ranges from 220 to 300 metres above sea level.

Main labels

*Barbaresco Currà Vigna Masué – Sottimano, Neive

*Barbaresco Vigneto Curà – Cantina del Glicine, Neive

Fausoni

Fausoni is a very small vineyard lying between the Borgo Antico of Neive and the aia-Principe hill, beneath the group of houses on the peak known as Fausoni Cadetto from the name of the two *cascine*. If you stand at the junction of the Tre Stelle-Rondò provincial highway and the local Gaia road, you will see the whole of Fausoni rising

gently up to the houses. The vineyard is very similar in position to Gaia Principe – it faces south west – and in elevation (270-230 metres). It has recently been developed by the Sottimano winery, which owns the Vigna del Salto at Fausoni.

MAIN LABELS

*Barbaresco Fausoni Vigna del Salto – Sottimano, Neive

Gaia Principe

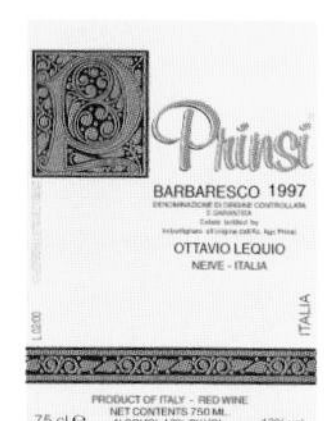

The hill of the Gaia Principe vineyard is divided over two slopes at *cascina* Slizza. The first faces north east towards Gallina while the other, south west-facing, overlooks the hamlet of Tetti.

The latter slope has an elevation of between 230 and 280 metres above sea level and is suitable for nebbiolo, particularly the area enclosed by the Tre Stelle-Rondò provincial road to the east, the lane bordering the Currà hill to the south and the local Gaia road to the west up to *cascina* Principe to the north.

MAIN LABELS

*Barbaresco Prinsi – Prinsi, Neive

*Barbaresco Gaia Principe – Mainerdo Fratelli, Neive

Gallina

As you arrive in Neive from the Baraccone-Rondò provincial road, you will see on your left the long Gallina hill, which ends near the Borgo Antico. The slope you can see has a better position than the side that looks towards Albesani, which is entirely north-facing. Gallina is undoubtedly the best known vineyard in the entire Neive area since it was one of the first to be mentioned on the labels of celebrated wineries, such as Parroco di Neive and Bruno Giacosa. There are two main reasons for this. One is the superior quality of the grapes, which lends depth and elegance to the wine, and the second is that it has always been possible to select the finest lots of fruit from a very large area planted to vine.

The best area is a broad strip below the road that cuts through the hamlet of Gallina. The swathe goes from the bend near *cascina* Rigo to the houses by the cemetery, descending almost to the provincial road. The position of the vines varies continuously from south west to south because of the irregular hillslope and the small hillocks that line the main ridge. In contrast, the elevation is fairly uniform, ranging from 250 metres at the hamlet of Gallina to the 200 metres of *cascina* Rigo. In addition to nebbiolo, rows of barbera have always been planted at Gallina, yielding some of the Langhe's most complex, richly textured wines.

Main labels

*Barbaresco Gallina di Neive – Bruno Giacosa, Neive

*Barbaresco Vigneto Gallina Vürsù – La Spinetta, Castagnole Lanze

*Barbaresco Gallina – Ugo Lequio, Neive

*Barbaresco Gallina – Giuseppe Negro, Neive

*Barbaresco Gallina – Prinsi, Neive

*Barbaresco Vigneto Gallina – San Michele, Neive

*Barbaresco Gallina di Neive – Mainerdo, Neive

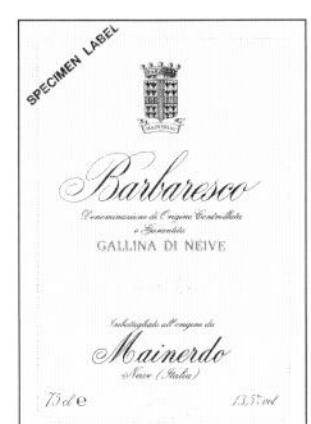

Marcorino

Marcorino is a small vineyard that rises up from the Rondò-Baraccone provincial highway, at the Bruno Giacosa cellar, situated 250 metres above sea level, to the peak at about 300 metres, in the direction of Neive Alta. For many years, the nebbiolos from the south west-facing upper part of the vineyard have been vinified by the Cantina del Glicine whereas lower down, and on the other south east-facing slope, which looks towards Borgonuovo, we find other varieties, such as arneis and dolcetto.

Main labels

*Barbaresco Marcorino – Cantina del Glicine, Neive

Messoirano

The hill where the hamlet of Serracapelli is located continues beyond *cascina* Monteoberto to the south until it joins the Valledoglio municipal road. Here, the hill rises to a lovely peak that is almost perfectly round. As you look at the vineyard from *cascina* Valdoglio, you realise that the position varies from south east to south west, with a substantial stretch to the left of the *cascina* Montebertotto facing directly south. The altitude ranges from the 300 metres of the upper part, near *cascina* Messoirano (so called because it was once the home of *contadini messori*, the workers who harvested the wheat), to the 220 metres of the lower area near the road.

Main labels

*Barbaresco Vigneto Messoirano – Cantine del Castello, Neive

San Giuliano

San Giuliano is a small but very beautiful vineyard. It borders to the south with the last part of Gallina, climbing the hill to the left of the cemetery and extending almost as far as *cascina* Crosa on the other side. The altitude ranges from 240 to 280 metres. The location gets plenty of sunlight and faces south east in the first part, near the cemetery, then east near the hilltop. Further on, the vines face north east and there is no nebbiolo in the area behind. Nebbiolo from San Giuliano has always been bought by local wineries and blended with grapes from other vineyards, sacrificing the identity of the cru.

MAIN LABELS

*Barbaresco Cascina Crosa – Pasquale Pelissero, Neive

Santo Stefano

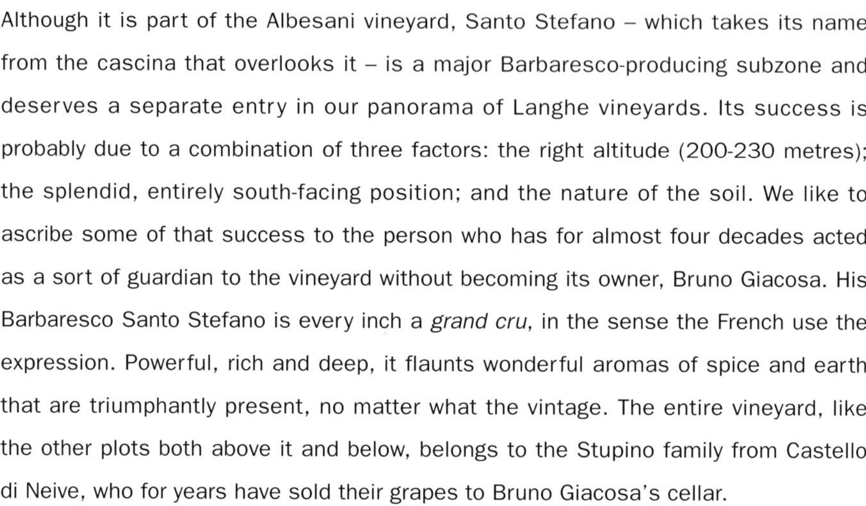

Although it is part of the Albesani vineyard, Santo Stefano – which takes its name from the cascina that overlooks it – is a major Barbaresco-producing subzone and deserves a separate entry in our panorama of Langhe vineyards. Its success is probably due to a combination of three factors: the right altitude (200-230 metres); the splendid, entirely south-facing position; and the nature of the soil. We like to ascribe some of that success to the person who has for almost four decades acted as a sort of guardian to the vineyard without becoming its owner, Bruno Giacosa. His Barbaresco Santo Stefano is every inch a *grand cru*, in the sense the French use the expression. Powerful, rich and deep, it flaunts wonderful aromas of spice and earth that are triumphantly present, no matter what the vintage. The entire vineyard, like the other plots both above it and below, belongs to the Stupino family from Castello di Neive, who for years have sold their grapes to Bruno Giacosa's cellar.

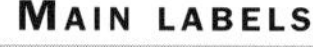

MAIN LABELS

*Barbaresco Santo Stefano di Neive – Bruno Giacosa, Neive
*Barbaresco Santo Stefano – Cantine del Castello, Neive
*Barbaresco La Rocca di Santo Stefano – Cantine del Castello, Neive

Serraboella

Serraboella is the most famous and important vineyard in the eastern part of the municipality of Neive, known as Bricco di Neive, thanks to the progress made at the initiative of Renato Cigliuti. For decades, Renato's name has been synonymous with Barbaresco Serraboella. Nebbiolo is a relatively recent variety in this part of the area. For many years, the market demanded, and paid higher prices for, other grapes, like dolcetto and moscato. In fact, there arose a belief that the plots at Bricco were unsuitable for the cultivation of nebbiolo. Over time, however, the Barbarescos from Bricco have expressed personality that is well above average. They possess fine structure, firm tannins and excellent cellarability. The vines stand on the slope facing the village of Neive, below the Serraboella road that goes over the ridge of the hill from the Cigliuti cellar to the north, until just past the Paitin cellar of Pasquero-Elia to the south. The rows mainly face west, although some are south west-facing. The altitude ranges from 250 to 320 metres.

Main labels

*Barbaresco Serraboella – Fratelli Cigliuti, Neive

*Barbaresco Sorì Paitin – Paitin, Neive

Serracapelli

Here, we are at the northern limit of the Barbaresco DOCG zone. Further on, we find only the moscato and barbera of the municipality of Castagnole Lanze. The vineyard takes its name from the hamlet of Serracapelli, which stands on the ridge of the hill at a height of 310 metres. It begins below the road running through the hamlet at the point between *cascina* Monteoberto and the last of the houses. The vines then run downhill towards the valley floor at about 240 metres, where the first hazelnut groves are to be found. Despite its south west-facing position and the good soil quality, Serracapelli has yet to be fully exploited. The reason may be that no winery has so far been able to bring out the character of the grapes grown here and the name Serracapelli has, in fact, yet to appear on a wine label as a vineyard selection.

Starderi

The hamlet of Starderi is a group of holiday homes where city-dwellers come to spend their weekends in peace and quiet. It stands on the ridge of the Starderi hill between Balluri to the east, Serracapelli to the west and Bordini to the south. To the north, the slope goes gently down to the river Tanaro. The best area for growing Barbaresco nebbiolo extends from the first group of houses at Starderi, dropping steeply down to the valley floor very near the hamlet of Pellisseri. The vines face south west and the altitude ranges from 200 to 270 metres. One producer who has long believed in this vineyard is the La Spinetta winery, owned by the Rivetti brothers, who have been vinifying a selection since 1996 with outstanding success.

Main labels

*Barbaresco Vigneto Starderi Vürsù – La Spinetta, Castagnole Lanze

*Barbaresco Starderi – Giuseppe Traversa, Neive

Our selection

Population 2,937
Height 308 metres asl

INFORMATION

Town Hall
Piazza Italia
Tel. + 39 0173 67004 - 0173 67110

Bottega dei Vini di Neive
Piazza Italia
Tel. + 39 0173 67004

THE WINERIES

Piero Busso
Borgata Albesani, 8
Tel. + 39 0173 67156
The philosophy of this small producer is to make modern, approachable wines by getting the best out of every vintage while respecting tradition in terms of style and taste. There are two Barbarescos (the Vigna Borgese and the Bricco Mondino), a Dolcetto and a Barbera, as well as a decently structured white from chardonnay and sauvignon, released under the label Bianco di Busso.

Cantina del Glicine
Via Giulio Cesare, 1
Tel. + 39 0173 67215
The cellar has been making wine for decades under the tireless supervision of Adriana Marzi, in the heart of Neive's historic centre. Its wines include a Roero Arneis, the well-typed Dolcetto d'Alba, an unusual Barbera d'Alba "Nebbiolata", and then the Marcorino and Vigneto Curà Barbarescos.

Cascina Crosa
Borgata Crosa, 56
Tel. + 39 0173 67376
Pasquale Pelissero is one of the stalwarts of Neive winemaking. His bottles are fine examples of territory-dedicated typicity. The range is limited to the very attractive Dolcetto d'Alba and an austere Barbaresco Cascina Crosa, made with grapes from the San Giuliano vineyard near the cemetery.

Santo Stefano

Cascina Vano
Via Rivetti, 9
Tel. + 39 0173 677705
Bruno Rivetti, assisted by his father, Beppe, has exactly what it takes to uphold the reputation of wines from beyond the Tinella, at Bricco di Neive. At the time of writing, Cascina Vano only markets a standard-label Barbaresco but will soon be releasing a Barbaresco Canova from the 1998 vintage.

Castello di Neive
Via Castelborgo, 1
Tel. + 39 0173 67171
This splendid castle, which once belonged to the Conti Riccardi, is today the property of the Stupino family. The roughly 25 hectares under vine produce Barbaresco Santo Stefano, and in some years Rocca di Santo Stefano and Messoirano selections as well.

Fratelli Cigliuti
Località Serra Boella, 17
Tel. + 39 0173 677185
Renato Cigliuti is a benchmark producer for the younger growers at Neive, as well as an older brother from whom they can always pick up useful tips. Renato's Serraboella vineyard yields Dolcetto, Barbera and Barbaresco. The Bricco plot yields fruit for much of the Briccosera, a blend of nebbiolo and barbera, and a Barbaresco, beginning with the 1997 vintage.

Fontanabianca
Frazione Bordini, 15
Tel. + 39 0173 67195
The new winery run by Aldo Pola and Bruno Ferro has got off to a good start. The wines are modern, stylish and elegant. The pair's ten hectares yield a total of 50,000 bottles, including the Barbaresco Surì Burdin and a standard-label version, a Dolcetto and a Chardonnay.

Gastaldi
Via Albesani, 20
Tel. + 39 0173 677400
Bernardino Gastaldi is a very demanding and sophisticated producer. In some vintages, his wines are among the finest to be found in the Langhe. For the time being, Bernardino's Barbaresco is a blend of two vineyards, Serraboella and Starderi. His Rosso Gastaldi is also very successful. It is a powerful, mature wine obtained mainly from nebbiolo. We should also note that Bernardino has recently acquired a small plot in the Barolo DOCG zone, in the Le Coste vineyard at Monforte d'Alba.

Bruno Giacosa
Via XX Settembre, 52
Tel. + 39 0173 67027
Bruno Giacosa is one of the fathers of Langhe winemaking. His Barbarescos and Barolos are considered by many to be the finest expressions ever of

the nebbiolo variety. Frequently, tasters can only gasp in amazement when they uncork a properly aged bottle of these wines. At present, Giacosa releases a standard-label Barbaresco and the Santo Stefano, Gallina and Asili vineyard selections. From the 1996 vintage on, the cellar is vinifying estate-owned grapes from the legendary Rabajà vineyard. Finally, Villero and Falletto come from the Barolo DOCG zone. It should also be noted that Bruno Giacosa was one of the most enthusiastic supporters of Serralunga Barolos and his Collina Rionda, produced until 1993, is the finest example of the quality that can be coaxed from the soil of that municipality.

Fratelli Giacosa
Via XX Settembre, 64
Tel. + 39 0173 67013
Paolo and Maurizio Giacosa represent the fourth generation of this winery, founded at Neive more than a century ago. Currently, the cellar releases over 300,000 bottles. The best bottles in the range are the Barbaresco Rio Sordo and the Bussia and Vigna Mandorlo Barolos.

Ugo Lequio
Via del Molino, 10
Tel. + 39 0173 677224
Ugo Lequio's cellar is small but very attractive and, over the last few years, it has astonished many a tasting panel. There are no estate-owned plots so the winery purchases the finest grapes available to vinify them expertly in the cellar. The Barbaresco Gallina is often outstanding.

Paitin - Pasquero Elia
Via Serra Boella, 20
Tel. + 39 0173 67343
Valerio and Giovanni, with their father Secondo, obtain about 50,000 bottles from their ten hectares in the Serraboella vineyard. Top of the range is the Barbaresco Sorì Paitin and the Langhe Rosso Paitìn, a blend of nebbiolo, barbera, cabernet sauvignon and syrah.

Sottimano
Località Cottà, 21
Tel. + 39 0173 635186
The progress made over the last few years by this small winery is simply astonishing. Located on the border of Neive and Barbaresco, it is run by the hard-working Sottimano family. Rino has found a highly competent assistant in his son, Andrea, who, in addition to working in vineyard and cellar, has his own ideas for creating new wines. The Cottà, Currà, Fausoni and Pajoré Barbarescos from recent vintages have all been excellent.

WHERE TO SLEEP

Locanda La Contea
Piazza Cocito, 8
Tel. + 39 0173 67126
Next to the well-known restaurant, which is under the same management, you will find a few quiet, comfortable rooms in an ancient noble palazzo that looks onto Piazza Cocito.

EATING OUT

La Cantina del Rondò
Frazione Rondò
Località Fausoni, 7
Tel. + 39 0173 679808
The Cantina del Rondò is the latest venture of Francarlo Negro, whose enthusiasm has created a pleasantly relaxing atmosphere that makes no secret of its roots in the *osteria* tradition. The cuisine, which uses only ingredients of outstanding quality, also receives lavish attention. As well as a

full menu, diners can also enjoy *merende sinoire*, generous portions of cold meats, cheeses and anchovies that fall somewhere between a snack and a full dinner. Wine is available in bottles but some fine local vintages are available on tap. Reckon on spending about € 35.00 without wine.

La Contea
Piazza Cocito, 8
Tel. + 39 0173 67126
La Contea is a lovely restaurant, set in a series of small nineteenth-century rooms with antique furniture and frescoed ceilings. It is run by Claudia and Tonino Verro, who offer ravioli, *tajarin* pasta, shin of beef, roast lamb, rabbit *al brusco* (in vinegar) and mushrooms or truffles in season. There is a fine selection of cheeses and an impressive wine list, with a wide range of Barolos and Barbarescos. The bill will come to between € 40.00 and € 50.00, not including wine.

La Luna nel Pozzo
Piazza Italia, 23
Tel. + 39 0173 67098
A friendly restaurant where classic Piedmontese cuisine is reinterpreted with exquisite taste. The raw meat, veal with tuna sauce, *ravioli del plin*, *tajarin* and beef stewed in Barolo are all good. The wine list offers the best bottles from the area. Expect to spend around € 35.00 without wine.

WHAT TO BUY

Romano Levi
Via Borgo Stazione
Romano Levi is a character. His hand-labelled grappas – each label is drawn by Romano himself with a surreal touch – have helped to make Neive and the Langhe better known around the world. Visitors are always welcome but it won't be easy to get your hands on one of the bottles. Romano is very loath to part with his creations.

Al Nido della Cinciallegra
Piazza Cocito
This is another venture by Tonino Verro from La Contea. The *enoteca* can offer a fine selection of wines, particularly Barbaresco, grappas, robiola d'Alba cheeses, nougat, chocolate and, in season, truffles. The shop also stocks its own range of salamis, wines and grappas.

L'Aromatario
Piazza Negro, 4
Rita Pastura proposes a selection of local wines, hazelnut cakes, nougat, cornflour cakes, jams and spices. On the upper floor, there are two double rooms with bathrooms, available at around € 25.00 per person.

The parish benefice

Don Giuseppe Cogno
born 1928
parish priest in Neive

I came to the parish in 1961 and things were already beginning to move on the wine front at Neive. The first signs of change were already perceptible. Some, like the Conte of Neive, Guido Riccardi Candiani di Castelborgo, had failed to note which way the wind was blowing. In fact, it was then that he sold all his holdings, about ten *cascine* and the castle, to the "pork butcher from Porta Palazzo", as he was called by the Contesse Cocito. We've always had plenty of nobility here at Neive and they were distinctly snobby. The "pork butcher" in question was the uncle of Marcarino, the present owner of the Punsèt winery. He got the lot for 80,000,000 lire. He kept two *cascine* and sold the rest, including the castle.

There were lots of meadows in those days. The slope of Barbaresco that faces Neive (Bernino) was all meadowland. Then bit by bit, a little here and a little more there, they began to plant vines. But the land of the parish benefice was exactly what it is today. You've only got to read the land register for 1755, which we have here in the parish, and you can get a full picture of the vineyards at the time. (*November 1995*)

S. Rocco Seno d'Elvio

The last district of Alba to the north of the town, and the southern tip of the small triangle that marks off Barbaresco territory, San Rocco Seno d'Elvio is little more than a square, a few low houses, an *osteria* and up in the air on the wire netting that closes off the street, a wooden board for the game of *pantalera*, a local version of *pallone elastico*.

The surrounding countryside does not yet present a favourable topography for viticulture and the slopes are dotted with old hazelnut trees, poplars, reeds and cluster pines clinging to the tufa ledges.

If you book ahead, you can visit the Museo del Drago, at *cascina* Drago, with its collection of rural memorabilia conserved by Dottor De Giacomi, the local chemist. The exhibits include two seventeenth-century winepresses, copper stills from the eighteenth century and early twentieth-century equipment for making sparkling wine. Your journey through this area might begin with the first three bottles of Barbaresco ever made, from 1870 (with handwritten labels), and continue to nearby Alba, a somewhat anomalous main town as it is on the flatlands yet serves as a capital for the Langhe hills, which form a natural amphitheatre in front.

Alba sits between the folds of the Roero and the Langhe hills, like a ship becalmed in the gently rolling landscape, while its actual waters, the lazy river Tanaro, flow sluggishly on to Asti.

An international town, Alba is world-famous for its confectionery (Ferrero), fabrics (Miroglio), graphics (San Paolo) and rubber (Mondo Rubber) industries. Above all, however, it is known for its great wines, white truffles and superb cuisine.

The historic centre is one of the most intriguing in the south of Piedmont. The surviving towers in this "city of a hundred towers" frame the Piazza del Duomo, the heart of the town and a Roman forum in the days of *Alba Pompeia*.

On the left of the piazza is the town hall, also built on previous Roman remains. Inside, visitors can admire a number of important mediaeval and renaissance paintings. One splendid work is the *Concerto* by Mattia Preti and equally interesting are the frescoes on the walls of the main staircase, which come from the Gothic church of San Domenico, recently restored and converted into an exhibition space and concert hall.

The impressive brick-faced façade of the cathedral, dedicated to Saint Lawrence, overlooks the piazza, or main square. Building began in 1486 to a design by, and under the direction of, bishop Novelli. Work was completed in 1517, although the present-day edifice has undergone alterations over the intervening centuries.

From Piazza del Duomo, we will take Via Vittorio Emanuele II, here called Via Maestra, which crosses the entire historic centre. This is where residents enjoy their afternoon stroll among a medly of architectural styles that range from mediaeval to Art Nouveau. Finally, both the Maddalena church in Via Maestra and the church of San Giovanni Battista in Piazza Elvio Pertinace are worth a visit. There are numerous works of art, including the fourteenth-century panel by Barnaba da Modena and an altarpiece from the workshop of Macrino depicting a *Virgin and Child with Saint Augustine and Saint Lucy*.

The great vineyards

When people are talking about Barbaresco, they tend to forget that part of the district of Alba known as San Rocco Seno d'Elvio, because it was the birthplace of the Roman emperor Publius Helvius Pertinax, actually belongs to the Barbaresco DOCG zone. It has to be said, however, that Alba, with its 22 hectares of Barbaresco DOCG, accounts for less than five per cent of the zone. San Rocco Seno d'Elvio is in fact the south western boundary of Barbaresco territory. As you go from Altavilla towards the town of Barbaresco, before you reach the hamlet of Pertinace you will find on your right a lane that takes you to San Rocco Seno d'Elvio. After you go through San Rocco, continue along the road that runs parallel to the valley of the Seno d'Elvio torrential stream, which ends a few kilometres further south at the *cascina* Castellengo. All the vines on your left, to the east, are in the Barbaresco DOCG while those on your right fall outside it. However, even in the Barbaresco zone, little nebbiolo is planted because of the fairly cool site climate of the Seno d'Elvio valley and the very steep slopes of the

DOC and DOCG	Total area under vine in hectares	% of area in municipality	% of area in zone
Dolcetto d'Alba	230.4025	30.89	12.33
Moscato d'Asti	210.3816	28.20	5.07
Barbera d'Alba	187.5514	25.14	10.88
Nebbiolo d'Alba	34.7370	4.66	8.36
Langhe Chardonnay	24.3600	3.27	9.49
Barbaresco	**22.5700**	**3.03**	**4.70**
Other DOC zones	35.9650	4.82	
TOTAL	745.9675	100.00	
Other DOC zones			
Langhe Arneis	8.8100	1.18	21.37
Langhe Freisa	8.6000	1.15	14.34
Langhe Favorita	5.6350	0.76	14.34
Langhe Rosso	3.8500	0.52	5.47
Piemonte	2.9800	0.40	16.27
Piemonte Cortese	1.9300	0.26	14.99
Langhe Bianco	1.4400	0.19	5.40
Piemonte Brachetto	1.1700	0.16	9.61
Piemonte Moscato	0.8600	0.12	5.88
Piemonte Barbera	0.3800	0.05	0.71
Piemonte Grignolino	0.3100	0.04	1.89

Rizzi

hills. Older growers prefer moscato or dolcetto. The best growing areas of San Rocco Seno d'Elvio are the final sections of the hills that descend from Treiso towards the valley. It may justly be claimed that the vineyards of San Rocco Seno d'Elvio are shared with those of the western part of Treiso, whose names they also bear (Rizzi, Basso, Montersino, Meruzzano and so on). For this reason, we have described the best vineyards of San Rocco Seno d'Elvio in the chapter on the municipality of Treiso.

Production

There are 14 wineries in the municipality, with 22.5 hectares under vine and a potential annual production of 1,263 hectolitres, or 4.7 per cent of the entire Barbaresco DOCG zone.

Our selection

Population 29,700
Height 172 metres asl

INFORMATION

Ente Turismo Alba, Bra, Langhe e Roero
Piazza Medford, 3
Tel. + 39 0173 35833

Ufficio Turismo
Via Vittorio Emanuele, 19
Tel. + 39 0173 362807

Turismo in Langa
Via Cavour, 16
Tel. + 39 0173 364030

WINERIES IN ALBA

Silvano e Elena Boroli
Frazione Como, 34
Tel. + 39 0173 35865
After acquiring the Bompé winery in Alba, the Borolis purchased Brunella at Castiglione Falletto and, above all, a major holding in the magnificent Villero vineyard. Their Dolcetto and Moscato are excellent. The first Barolo to be released was also astonishingly good. Keep an eye on this producer.

Ceretto
Località
San Cassiano, 34
Tel. + 39 0173 282582
The splendid Bernardina estate has for several years been the nerve centre of the Ceretto brothers' wineries, at least as far as their more innovative wines are concerned (Arneis Blangé, Spumante Brut and international wines). But it is also here that they vinify Barolo Zonchera and Barbaresco Asij, their standard-label versions of the two DOCGs.

Lano
Strada Basso, 38
Tel. + 39 0173 286958
Since he took over the family winery in 1992, Gianluigi Lano has been managing his six hectares under vine without recourse to chemical products. His Barbaresco, a wine that needs several years to mellow out its robust tannins, is a blend of nebbiolo grapes from Treiso and San Rocco Seno d'Elvio.

Montersino

Pio Cesare
Via Cesare Balbo, 6
Tel. + 39 0173 440386
This historic Langhe winery is inextricably associated with traditional-style Barolo and Barbaresco in which fruit from different vineyards in blended together. Today, things are changing and Pio Boffa now has two superb estates whose separately fermented grapes are the cellar's pride and joy: one is Ornato at Serralunga d'Alba and the other is Bricco at Treiso. Again at Serralunga, Pio Cesare owns the Colombaio vineyard. Although it is a fine location for Barolo, the estate has planted it to barbera and chardonnay. Recently, new purchases have been made, in the municipality of La Morra at Roncagliette di Santa Maria, in Grinzane, right under the castle itself, and at Treiso.

Poderi Colla
Frazione San Rocco
Seno d'Elvio, 82
Tel. + 39 0173 290148
The Poderi Colla cellars are just outside the Barbaresco DOCG zone in the former cascina Drago. After a long spell at Prunotto, Tino Colla continues, with his brother Beppe and niece Federica, to bring out the best in nebbiolo grapes from the Langhe's great vineyards. Here, the accent is on the finesse and complexity of the varietal aroma, although muscular tannins are also in evidence, as is amply demonstrated by the Barbaresco from the Roncaglia di Barbaresco estate and the Barolo Bussia Dardi Le Rose from Monforte d'Alba.

Prunotto
Località San Cassiano, 4/g
Tel. + 39 0173 280017
In the 1920s, Alfredo Prunotto built up one of Piedmont's most prestigious wineries. The cellar then passed to the very competent Colla brothers, gaining fame and recognition internationally for its Barolo and Barbaresco. In 1961, these began to be released as vineyard selections.
The wines that deservedly made the cellar's reputation, and continue to win plaudits for the new owners, Antinori, are the Cannubi and Bussia Barolos. The magnificent Barbaresco Montestefano is no longer produced but with the 1996 vintage, a new Barbaresco has come onstream. It is the Bric Turot, which now flanks the standard-label version. Another of the estate's flagship wines, again from nebbiolo but grown in the Roero area, is the Nebbiolo d'Alba Occhetti.

Francesco Rinaldi e Figli
Via Sacco, 4
Tel. + 39 0173 440484
Luciano Rinaldi is heir to a family winemaking tradition that dates back to 1870.
He has always made premium-quality Barolo from the ten hectares of estate-owned vines in excellent sites, such as Cannubi, from which he obtains his Barolo Cannubbio, and Brunate, where the enviably positioned vines stand adjacent to those of Giuseppe Rinaldi.

WHERE TO SLEEP

I Castelli
Corso Torino, 14
Tel. + 39 0173 361978
Four stars, three suites and 84 rooms. This recently built hotel, very close to the centre of town, offers all the comforts of a four-star establishment. Breakfast is a treat to look forward to and there are rooms suitable for disabled guests.

Motel Alba
Corso Asti, 5
Località Rondò
Tel. + 39 0173 363251
Three stars, 94 rooms. Standing on the main road to Asti at the entrance to the town, the Motel Alba is particularly convenient for those who wish to tour the nearby Barbaresco hills. Friendly and comfortable.

Savona
Via Roma, 1
Tel. + 39 0173 440440
Three stars, 99 rooms. Right in the centre of town, the Savona is Alba's historic hotel. The rooms are comfortable and access is easy.

EATING OUT

Il Vicoletto
Via Bertero, 6
Tel. + 39 0173 363196
One of the most sophisticated eateries in Italy's truffle capital, Il Vicoletto is elegant and comfortable. The cuisine offers a modern interpretation of the local tradition, using only first-quality ingredients. The selection of cheeses is extensive and the desserts are mouthwatering. Your bill will come to about € 50.00.

Osteria dell'Arco
Piazza Savona, 5
Tel. + 39 0173 363974
You will find a friendly, impeccably courteous welcome, and superbly prepared food at very reasonable prices, even if you select one of the more challenging bottles from a carefully chosen wine list with all the Langhe's finest products, starting with Barolo and Barbaresco. Budget for a bill of around € 25.00, excluding wine.

Osteria Italia
Frazione San Rocco Seno d'Elvio, 8
Tel. + 39 0173 441547
This is an *osteria*, as the sign proclaims, and it stands in the square at San Rocco Seno d'Elvio, at the start of the Barbaresco DOCG zone. You can either pop in for a snack of cold meat and cheese or sit down to enjoy a full meal of tempting traditional dishes from the local kitchen. There is a small selection of good local wines. A meal costs from € 20.00 to € 30.00.

Osteria Lalibera
Via Pertinace, 24/a
Tel. + 39 0173 293155

Excellent service and superb quality ingredients are the keys to the success of this small restaurant in the heart of Alba's historic centre. The wines are good and prices are very reasonable.

WINE SHOP

Burdese
Via Vittorio
Emanuele, 13

Drogheria Carosso
Via Vittorio
Emanuele, 23

Enolibreria
I Sapori del Gusto
Via Vittorio
Emanuele, 23

Enoteca del Centro
Via Roma, 8

Enoteca Fracchia
Via Vernazza, 9

Enoteca I Castelli
Corso Torino, 14/c

Enoteca Terra Gentile
Via Cavour, 5/a

Grandi Vini
Via Vittorio
Emanuele, 1/a

Peccati di Gola
Via Cavour, 11

As well as being the main town of the Langhe, Alba is also the hub around which food and wine tourism in southern Piedmont revolves. In recent years, a considerable trade in food and wine products has grown up and many new outlets have opened.
The people of Alba are born traders and have not let this opportunity slip past them. Many enoteche, or wine shops, have sprung up in a short period of time.
Although each shop has its own specialisations, we have grouped them together into one category, confident that each can offer a first-class service focusing on the territory's wines and food products.

Luciano de Giacomi

1921-1995

Luciano de Giacomi was a man who went straight to the heart of things. He was a little like Godfrey of Bouillon, the knight who led the First Crusade against the unbelievers. Godfrey and his men left for the Holy Land and conquered Jerusalem, driving out the Muslims. Luciano, too, was a man of action, who had no time for coming to terms with those who stood in his way. Like the eleventh-century crusader, he considered his adversaries to be heretics and enemies of the truth, to be annihilated or driven from the field of battle. Contradicting de Giacomi, or simply expressing an opinion he did not share, was not just risky: it was received as an unpardonable affront. Such a betrayal could end forever a long-established friendship, despite years of shared experience and understanding. There was no appeal. Luciano demanded absolute, supreme power, without reserve and without debate.

He was, in short, a difficult man. It was no coincidence that he founded a mediaeval-style confraternity, the "Cavalieri del Tartufo e dei Vini d'Alba" (Knights of the Truffle and Wines of Alba), of which he was Grand Master. Access to the order was only by acclaim and took place at a ceremony, with cloak and sword, accompanied by a fanfare sounded by trumpeters in colourful costumes. The ceremony was a sort of initiation rite, at which neophytes pledged themselves under oath to serve the cause. There were also official uniforms. Emerald green tunics, purple cloaks and plumed Byzantine turbans were all part of a multifarious and somewhat garish, but very striking, wardrobe.

After the investiture, the Knights had only one mission: to defend the wines and the traditions of the Langhe kitchen. The Langhe is a vast spider's web of vineyards and tangled shoots that resembles a stormy sea, with wave-like hills rising, falling, sweeping across the valleys and thrusting skyward. The breathtakingly beautiful landscape embraces woods and groves where the area's other much prized products – truffles – grow.

It is these hills that bring forth Barolo, Barbaresco, Nebbiolo, Barbera, Dolcetto, Freisa, Moscato and other less well known wines that make up a significant part of Italy's oenological heritage and of the rural tradition that has brought them to perfection.

Each wine is tied to a geographical area of origin and subject to production regulations, called *disciplinari*, but Luciano de Giacomi, who had little time for rules that he could not control, decided to personally select not just his Knights but also the Langhe wines to put on show in his *enoteca*. The dream came true, after many years of tenacious hard work, when the *enoteca* opened at the castle of Grinzane Cavour, not far from Alba. This restored noble residence was where the young Cavour, not yet a minister of the Savoy crown, began his oenological and viticultural experiments. It was also the seat of the Order, where a team of tasters decided what wines would be admitted to the *enoteca*. Selection was rigorous and the only criterion was the quality of the wine itself. There were no compromises and no favouritisms. Even today, the *enoteca* at

Grinzane is a benchmark for quality, providing a guarantee for the consumer, that ever-anxious, and often indecisive, winelover looking for a little certainty and bottles that can be trusted.

At the castle of Grinzane, de Giacomi also opened a restaurant that hosts the gastronomic chapters of the Order and has, since its creation, been a favourite haunt of gourmets. It specialises in simple, and on occasion rudimentary, dishes from the tradition of the poor country kitchen of tenant farmers and agricultural workers. Dishes such as *bagna caoda* and *lasagne al sangue* have been adapted for modern palates and restored to dignity by the imagination of expert cooks.

Luciano was a lover of conversation, even when he was cooking. He abhorred fast food and modern trends, spending many hours poring over old recipe books and the grease-stained notebooks of housewives of his own and earlier generations who had noted menus and instructions for dinners and other meals. He wanted to recapture the table of the past, down to the tiniest, least important detail, such as boiling *tagliatelle* in water drawn from a well rather than tapwater. It was not an easy rule to follow but Luciano insisted.

De Giacomi and his Knights were also active abroad. Armed with bottles and baskets of comestibles, they arrived one day in Paris. In a fashionable restaurant on the Champs Elysées, a group of France's most refined palates was waiting. There were food academicians, food writers and food journalists, actors and artists, all rather diffident, even haughty, guests. But when the bottles were uncorked and the first flakes of white Alba truffle floated down like butterflies onto the *fonduta*, the Piedmontese fondue, the triumph was assured and the guests broke into applause. When they returned to Italy, the Knights organised another expedition, this time to London. Luciano hired a DC 9 and filled it with bottles, *agnolotti col plin*, garlic, demijohns of Ligurian olive oil, thistles, peppers, haunches of Piedmontese beef, homemade tomato preserve, hazelnut cakes, bunches of rosemary and the other ingredients necessary to prepare a memorable old-fashioned Piedmontese *cascina* dinner. On this occasion, too, the Knights found themselves up against a coolish reception but the very first course, an unexpected anchovy-based *acciughe al verde*, elicited unrestrained approval. Godfrey of Bouillon had managed to cross the Thames.

De Giacomi's life was a *chanson de geste* to wine and good food but it was not lived in the manner of Rabelais' gluttonous Gargantua. Not for Luciano the greed-driven eating and drinking of diners who are only interested in filling their bellies. Despite himself being an extremely healthy eater, Luciano had a palate as sensitive as Bach's well-tempered clavier. And of course he loved only the food and wine of his own land, a heritage that was in danger of extinction. "There may have been grapes and truffles here," he once said, "when the dinosaurs walked the earth. It's a heritage we must conserve". De Giacomi's indomitable faith would surely have prompted him to arm his Knights and depart on other crusades but one day in 1995, he collapsed. At the time, he was in Alba behind the counter of his chemist's shop. The indomitable, indefatigable Luciano passed away at the age of 74.

Treiso

This small village in the lower Langhe lies at the point where five hills meet, between the Tinella and Seno d'Elvio torrential rivers. The approach from Alba is along the main highway 231. Take the turn-off at the Barbaresco-Neive junction. From the top of the village, the panorama opens up stunning views against the backdrop of the Barolo and Roero Langhe, shading away into the watery colours of the encircling Alps.

The history of Treiso began 5,000 years ago, as is shown by the polished stones from the Neolithic era found at Pertinace. In ancient documents, Treiso is frequently mentioned with the names "Trayso", "Trasio", "Tresio" or "Traizo", from the Latin for "three" – *tres* – as the village was located at the third milestone on the Roman road from Alba. Treiso was a post where Roman armies arriving from Savona could change their horses. Contested by Alba and Asti in mediaeval times, it was the scene of many bloody battles. In 1617, it passed to the Savoys and its history merged with that of Barbaresco until 1958, when it became an independent municipality.

The square, built for the rural existence of days long gone, is dominated by the bulk of the parish church. Classical in style, with Baroque decoration, its red brick façade is adorned with the statues of three saints completed in 1773 by Unia from Racconigi. About the same time, ox-teams went to Turin to bring the main bell for the tower built in 1767 by Traversa. Perhaps the building's most interesting feature, the bell tower leans slightly to one side and was fixed to the

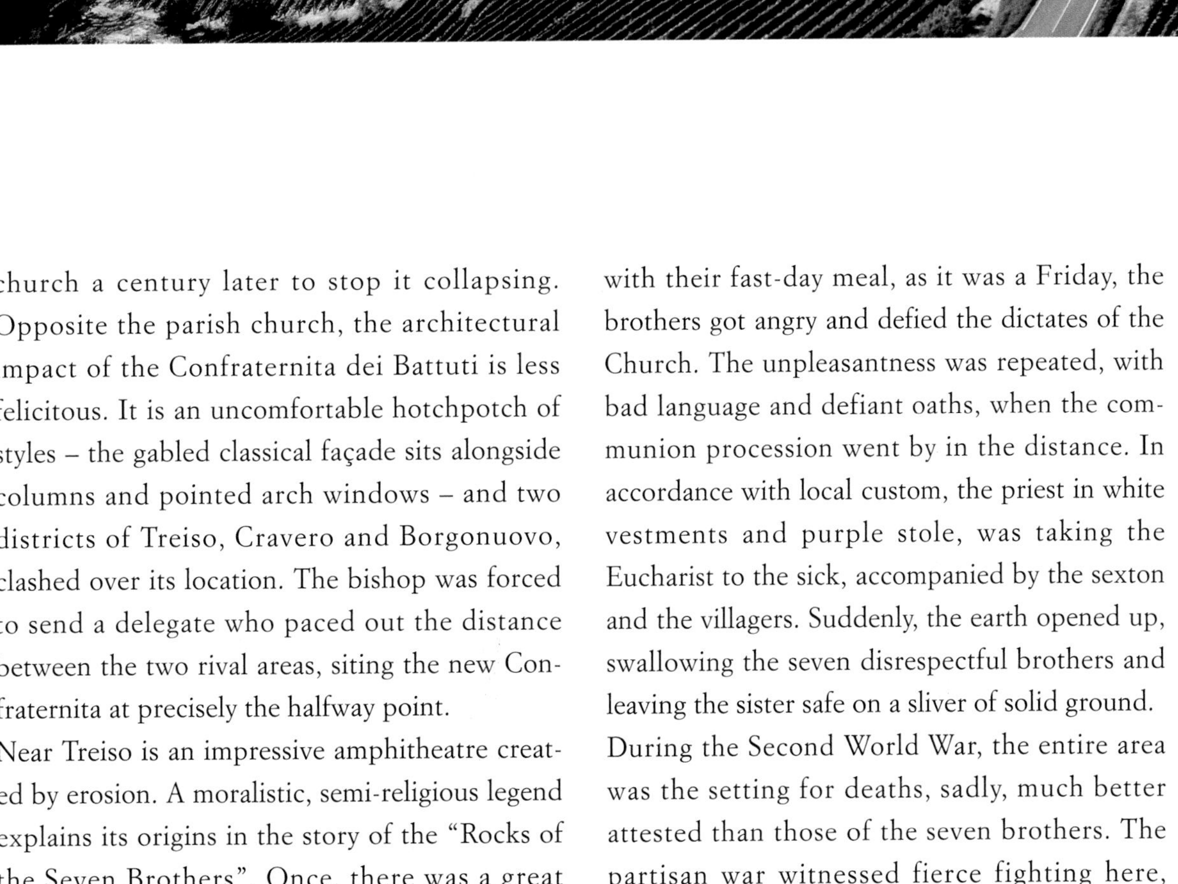

church a century later to stop it collapsing. Opposite the parish church, the architectural impact of the Confraternita dei Battuti is less felicitous. It is an uncomfortable hotchpotch of styles – the gabled classical façade sits alongside columns and pointed arch windows – and two districts of Treiso, Cravero and Borgonuovo, clashed over its location. The bishop was forced to send a delegate who paced out the distance between the two rival areas, siting the new Confraternita at precisely the halfway point.

Near Treiso is an impressive amphitheatre created by erosion. A moralistic, semi-religious legend explains its origins in the story of the "Rocks of the Seven Brothers". Once, there was a great meadow here and seven brothers came to make hay. When their sister arrived towards noon with their fast-day meal, as it was a Friday, the brothers got angry and defied the dictates of the Church. The unpleasantness was repeated, with bad language and defiant oaths, when the communion procession went by in the distance. In accordance with local custom, the priest in white vestments and purple stole, was taking the Eucharist to the sick, accompanied by the sexton and the villagers. Suddenly, the earth opened up, swallowing the seven disrespectful brothers and leaving the sister safe on a sliver of solid ground.

During the Second World War, the entire area was the setting for deaths, sadly, much better attested than those of the seven brothers. The partisan war witnessed fierce fighting here, which claimed the lives of many young people who had embraced the ideals of the Resistance.

The great vineyards

When people talk about Barbaresco, the municipalities mentioned are almost inevitably Barbaresco and Neive. The former has an exceptional number of excellent vineyards and also gave its name to the entire DOCG zone. Neive, too, can boast a number of outstanding winemakers who have brought out the best in its vineyards. Often, Treiso is simply forgotten, despite the fact that it is an older winemaking subzone than Neive. Its activity dates back to the last quarter of the nineteenth century, when Fantini in his *Monografia sulla Viticultura ed Enologia nella Provincia di Cuneo* (Monograph on Viticulture and Oenology in the Province of Cuneo) listed several Treiso vineyards among the finest in the area. It is likely that the poor opinion of Treiso derives from the fact that much of the municipal territory lies at more than 400 metres above sea level, an altitude considered to high for nebbiolo to ripen fully. This, and poor sales of Barbaresco during the 1950s, prompted many growers to turn to more popular varieties, such as moscato and dolcetto, for which, paradoxically, Treiso can today boast a long-established tradition.

Luckily, improved demand for Barbaresco in

DOC and DOCG	Total area under vine in hectares	% of area in municipality	% of area in zone
Moscato d'Asti	158.8419	37.28	3.83
Dolcetto d'Alba	112.9630	26.51	6.04
Barbaresco	**93.7778**	**22.01**	**19.53**
Barbera d'Alba	27.2409	6.39	1.58
Langhe Chardonnay	22.2430	5.22	8.37
Other DOC zones	10.9900	2.58	
TOTAL	426.0566	100.00	
Other DOC zones			
Langhe Favorita	2.69	0.63	2.70
Langhe Rosso	1.91	0.45	2.72
Langhe Nebbiolo	1.80	0.42	7.20
Langhe Freisa	1.08	0.25	1.80
Piemonte	0.90	0.21	4.92
Piemonte Pinot Nero	0.79	0.19	10.15
Piemonte Cortese	0.71	0.17	5.51
Langhe Bianco	0.55	0.13	2.06
Piemonte Grignolino	0.36	0.08	2.19
Piemonte Barbera	0.2000	0.05	0.38

Rocche dei Sette Fratelli

recent years has seen the return of nebbiolo to the best positions and the roughly 94 hectares planted to the variety represent almost 20 per cent of the entire DOCG zone.

A series of vine-covered ridges fan out from the centre of the town, which lies at an altitude of about 420 metres above sea level. The best growing areas are on the slopes that run down towards the Tanaro, passing through Tre Stelle and Pertinace, the Pajoré, Valeriano and Rizzi hills. The sunny slopes of these hills, in the northern part of the municipal territory, are ideal for nebbiolo, thanks to their lower altitude. The east and south of the territory, where it borders with Neviglie and Trezzo Tinella, are higher and the valleys are longer. Air circulates more freely, producing a cooler site climate where nebbiolo ripens only with difficulty. These slopes are more suitable for moscato and dolcetto.

Production

There are 88 wineries, with 94 hectares altogether and a potential production of 5,191 hectolitres, representing 19 per cent of the total for the Barbaresco DOC zone.

THE GREAT VINEYARDS

BERNARDOT OR BERNARDOTTI
BORDINO
BRICCO
CASOT
CASTELLIZZANO
MANZOLA
MARCARINI
MONTERSINO
NERVO
PAJORÉ
RIZZI
ROMBONE
VALEIRANO

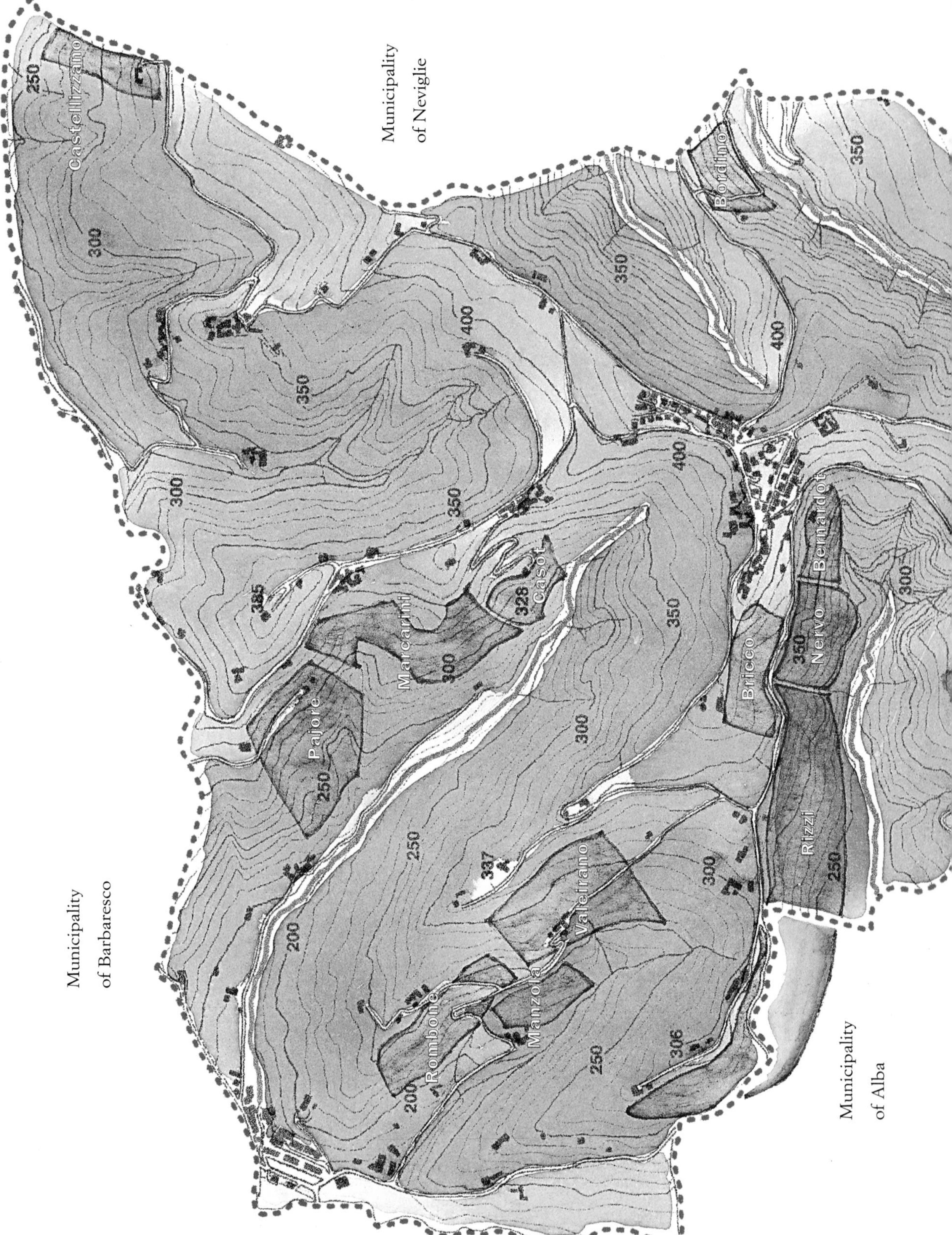

BARBARESCO DOCG ZONE

GREAT VINEYARDS

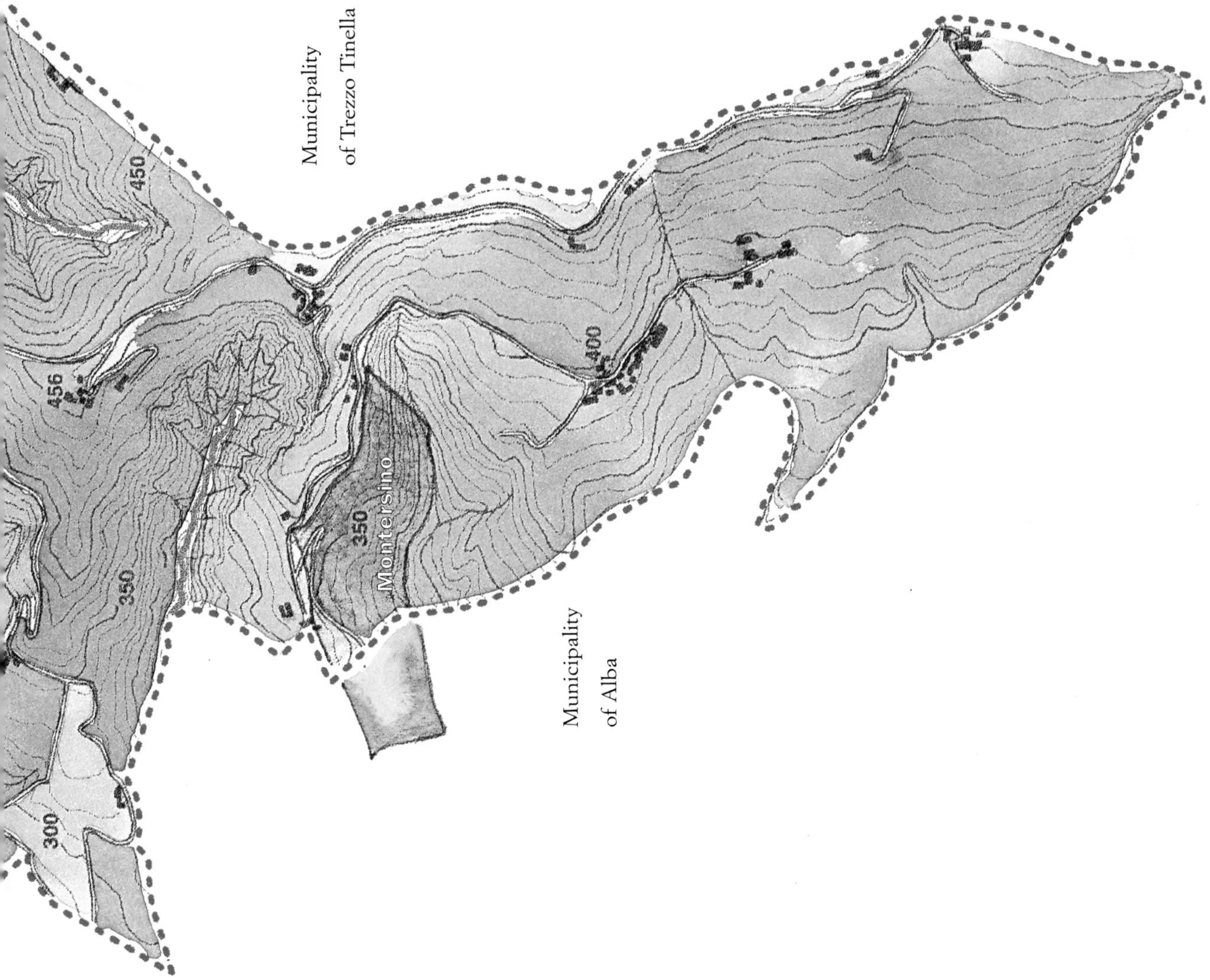

Municipality
of Trezzo Tinella

450

456

400

350

Montersino

350

300

Municipality
of Alba

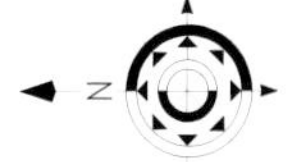

Bernardot or Bernardotti

If you turn left at the first righthand hairpin bend as you come down from the centre of Treiso towards Pertinace, then go a few metres along the Basso road, you will be in the perfect spot to admire Bernardot. This fairly small vineyard has been considered one of the finest in Treiso for more than a century. Today, however, it is familiar only to a few specialists.

It lies below the *cascina* Bernardot, in a fairly narrow natural bowl. The sheltered location offsets its altitude, which ranges from 350 to 400 metres above sea level. Bernardot is the natural continuation of the Nervo vineyard and the first part, to the west of the *cascina*, shares the aspect and soil type of its neighbour. To the east, the vineyard follows the hill gradually round to the south west. Bernardot concludes the series of great vineyards on the Rizzi and Nervo hills.

Main labels

*Barbaresco Bernardot – Bricco Asili, Barbaresco

Bordino

Lying further south than Ferrere and Castellizzano, this part of Treiso holds further pleasant surprises for lovers of Barbaresco. Part of the area known as *Bongioan*, the Bordino vineyard owes its name to the *cascina*, no longer standing, that overlooked the rows until a few years ago. Compared with Castellizzano, Bordino has whiter, lighter soil and good, south east-facing slopes. Thanks partly to their altitude, which ranges from 300 to 360 metres, the grapes yield wines that are elegant, rather than muscular. As in other vineyards on the south eastern edge of the DOCG zone, many of the slopes at Bordino are extremely steep.

MAIN LABELS

*Barbaresco Cascina Bordino – Tenuta Carretta, Piobesi d'Alba

Bricco

From the Rizzi provincial road, the majestic Bricco di Treiso hill rises on your left before you reach the town. The *cascina* itself, the highest point in the northern part of the municipality, is perched on top at an altitude of 410 metres above sea level. Since it is a hilltop, it receives sunshine on all sides but, naturally, the nebbiolo-growing slopes that concern us are the south-facing ones. This particular section is not extensive. The good, south-facing position, with no hills to create shade, offsets the considerable altitude, ranging from 340 to 410 metres above sea level, and an unprotected approach that exposes the vines at Bricco to strong winds.

The interesting Cravero vineyard – *Cravè* to locals – lies to the east, between Bricco and the centre of Treiso. We have included it in Bricco as its characteristics are very similar.

MAIN LABELS

*Barbaresco Il Bricco – Pio Cesare, Alba

Casot

Casot has a relatively small surface area but its quality and, above all, history make it a very important vineyard for the municipality of Treiso. Pierin Meinardi, one of the first to vinify Barbaresco at Treiso, recalls that when the municipality grew mainly dolcetto and moscato, merchants from Alba would

come to buy fruit at Casot and Marcarini, where they also found good quantities of nebbiolo.
The small vineyard is entirely south west-facing and descends from the border with Giacosa, extending beneath and beyond the hamlet of Casot. The altitude ranges from 290 to 330 metres above sea level and the sheltered location is virtually ideal. In contrast, the vines of Giacosa, which are also well-aspected, are a little too high up to ensure that the nebbiolo will ripen perfectly every year.

Main labels

*Barbaresco Poderi Casotto – Giuseppe Nada, Treiso

Castellizzano

It is clear that the areas to the east of Treiso, on the border with Neviglie and, further south, Trezzo Tinello, cannot lay claim to the same traditions as the western part of the municipal territory. Nonetheless, methodical investigation soon reveals one or two noteworthy vineyards. Of these, Castellizzano is one that merits most respect. Despite its deep reddish soil and positions that are not always ideal, ranging from east to south east at altitudes of 260 to 350 metres above sea level, Castellizzano yields muscular wines with good cellar potential. In dry years, they are often superior to Treiso's other vineyards.
The biggest disappointment is that the best-placed sites, comprising very steep plots over the Tinella valley, are in the municipal territory of Neviglie, and therefore lie outside the Barbaresco DOCG zone.

Main labels

*Barbaresco Vigneto Castellizzano – Cantina Vignaioli Elvio Pertinace, Treiso

Manzola

This is the smallest vineyard in the municipality of Treiso but its special position, bounded to the north by Rombone, by Valeriano to the east and by the Manzola river to the west, ensures it a place in the front rank. In the late nineteenth century, Fantini had already noted its qualities, above all an unbroken south west-facing orientation and a moderate elevation, ranging from 210 to 250 metres above sea level. These give the vineyard a relatively warm mesoclimate and protect it from excessive ventilation. The only small blemishes in this profile are the very gentle slope and the proximity of the Rizzi hill, which can reduce the duration and intensity of the sunlight.

Marcarini

Marcarini is the natural continuation to the south of the Pajoré vineyard. Although it lies on the same slope, its characteristics are slightly different. Above all, the hill rises towards the village of Treiso and the vineyards are at a higher altitude of 290 to 360 metres. The vines, south west-facing at first, also gradually turn towards the west. However, this stretch of hillslope, and the neighbouring vineyards of Casot and Giacosa, is particularly prone to landslips. At certain points, heavy rain can lead to accumulations of water that tend to make the soil unstable, as has happened in the past. It is thus easy to understand why the slope is not uniform.

The above description deliberately leaves out the vines that stand above the road from Tre Stelle to Treiso. This part, on Monte Aribaldo below the Marchesi di Gresy estate, lies at a higher altitude that makes dolcetto the variety of choice.

*Barbaresco Vigneto Marcarini – Cantina Vignaioli Elvio Pertinace, Treiso

Montersino

Like many other vineyards in the south of the municipality, Montersino has a relatively high altitude that, in cooler years, can prevent nebbiolo from ripening fully. The problem has been solved by the local growers, who plant nebbiolo only in choice, south-facing locations. Just below *cascina* Montersino, at an altitude of about 400 metres above sea level, lies an excellent vineyard where nebbiolo gives outstanding results over a range of elevations spanning almost 120 metres.

It should also be noted that, as in the case of Rizzi and Meruzzano, Barbaresco vines at Montersino are split between the municipalities of Treiso and Alba. It can safely be stated that the part of Montersino in San Rocco Seno d'Elvio is also superbly aspected.

MAIN LABELS

*Barbaresco Vigna Montersino – Orlando Abrigo, Treiso

Nervo

As you go back up to the village of Treiso, at *cascina* Fornace, to the right of the Rizzi provincial road, the vineyards of Nervò are laid out before your eyes. Everything conspires to make this one of the finest vineyards in the entire Barbaresco area. First of all, the vines enjoy a perfect south-facing location, with heights above sea level that range from 230 to 350 metres, similar to those in almost all the most renowned Langhe vineyards. In addition, the very steep slope makes work in the vineyard difficult and even dangerous but it also improves drainage and, above all, ensures greater exposure to sunlight. Finally, this idyllic picture is completed by the soil composition, which is a very unfertile white marl that manages to imbue the grapes with elegance and power in equal measure.

MAIN LABELS

*Barbaresco Vigneto Nervo – Cantina Vignaioli Elvio Pertinace, Treiso

Pajoré

Bordering the vines of Roncaglie and Montaribaldi, in the municipality of Barbaresco, Pajoré is incontestably one of the most famous vineyards in the Langhe. The story goes that after assessing the quality of the wine made by Enrico Giovannini Moresco from his Pajoré plot in 1971, Angelo Gaja decided to purchase the vineyard, as in fact he did a few years later.

If you follow the lane that takes you from the village to the *cascina* of the Molino family and look northwards, you will have a superb panorama of the Giacosa hill. At the lefthand bend on the road that leads from Tre Stelle to Treiso, the steep vineyard of Pajoré covers the hillslope.

The heart of Pajoré enjoys a near-perfect elevation from the 300 metres of the *cascina* Pairolero to the roughly 230 metres of the last nebbiolo-worthy rows, before going further downhill to *cascina* Chirella. The finest plots, however, have superb south or south west-facing aspects and very lean marly soil.

MAIN LABELS

*Barbaresco Pajoré Vigna Lunetta – Sottimano, Neive

Rizzi

Rizzi

If you approach Pertinace from Alba via Altavilla, taking the righthand turn for Treiso, you will be travelling across the middle of one of Treiso's most impressive vine-clad hills. It starts from Garassino and embraces some of the most famous Barbaresco vineyards, such as Boito, Rizzi, Fratin, Nervo and Bernardot. The Rizzi vineyard is extensive so it is no surprise that within it, there are substantial variations in aspect and altitude. The first part begins just north of *cascina* Boito and is outstanding in the section that climbs up from the Rizzi provincial road Rizzi, at about 220 metres above sea level, to the *cascina* itself, at 295 metres. This part is west to south west-facing. Just before the *cascina* Rizzi, the slope turns to face southwards, dropping steeply from 300 metres down almost as far as the *cascina* Fratino, at about 200 metres above sea level. Here, we are in the heart of Rizzi, although the rows along the provincial road belong to San Rocco Seno d'Elvio, in the municipality of Alba.

Main labels

*Barbaresco Rizzi – Rizzi di Ernesto Dellapiana, Treiso

Rombone

For the time being, the name of this vineyard is little used on labels but its best plots deserve to be numbered among the great vineyards of Treiso, although they cannot lay claim to the long, prestigious history of other sites. Nebbiolo at Rombone area dates back to the 1940s, when the Nada family came to live here. *Cascina* Rombone stands on the last stretch of the hill that extends to Pertinace in the north west and it is entirely surrounded by vineyards, only some planted to nebbiolo. From the *cascina* at 260 metres, Rombone's superb vines run down the hill to about 200 metres above sea level, facing the least suitable part of the Rizzi hill for vine growing. Like lmost all the vineyards in Treiso, Rombone enjoys an unbroken south west-facing aspect that enables it to soak up the last rays of the setting sun.

Main labels

*Barbaresco Rombone – Fiorenzo Nada, Treiso

Valeirano

Valeirano has a profile that makes it one of the finest vineyards in the municipality of Treiso, as Lorenzo Fantini noted over a century ago in his *Monografia sulla Viticultura ed Enologia nella Provincia di Cuneo* (Monograph on Viticulture and Oenology in the Province of Cuneo). The terrain has a relatively uniform slope and elevation of 250 to 300 metres above sea level. It includes the little village of Valeirano and is laid out in a long strip along the hillside. The south west-facing position is typical of the northern part of Treiso and the marly soil is only moderately fertile. The best-known of the owners are the Rivetti family from Castagnole Lanze, who have obtained gratifying results here.

We should also include here the small part of the Ausario vineyard that escends from the *cascina* Magallo to Valeirano as, except for the greater altitude of 300 to 340 metres, its characteristics are very similar.

Main labels

*Barbaresco Valeirano – Ada Nada, Treiso

*Barbaresco Vigneto Valeirano Vürsù – La Spinetta, Castagnole Lanze

Rombone

Our selection

Population 756
Height 410 metres asl

INFORMATION

Town Hall
Piazza Italia
Tel. + 39 0173 67004

THE WINERIES

Orlando Abrigo
Frazione Cappelletto, 5
Tel. + 39 0173 630232
The Abrigo winery, today run by Gianni Abrigo, is not one of the subzone's most famous, partly because of its out-of-the-way location on Barbaresco's southern border. The cellar releases about 20,000 bottles of Barbaresco, soon to become 25,000, split between Montersino and Rongallo, parallel hillslopes that enjoy the same aspect and elevation. They show off to good effect the elegance achievable in these vineyards.

Ca' del Baio
Via Ferrere, 33
Tel. + 39 0173 638219
The Grasso family estate is in the municipality di Treiso but for now, the Barbarescos come from the celebrated Asili vineyard at Barbaresco. Two versions of the selection are released: one is a more complex wine aged in large barrels; the other is softer and barrique-aged. The 1998 vintage saw the release of a new selection from the estate's nebbiolo vines at Valgrande in Treiso.

Ada Nada
Località Rombone
Tel. + 39 0173 638127
Although Giancarlo Nada cannot lay claim to the experience of his cousin Bruno, he does seem to have acquired considerable skill at vinifying his

two Barbarescos, which account for a total of about 16,000 bottles a year. The 12,000 bottles of Valeirano are aged in small oak casks, a mixture of new and pre-used barriques and tonneaux. In contrast, the 4,000 bottles of Cichin are made with fruit from Rombone and the wine is aged in larger barrels.

Fiorenzo Nada
Località Rombone
Tel. + 39 0173 638254
Despite his youth, Bruno Nada may be regarded as one of the elder statesmen of Barbaresco at Treiso. For the time being, all the winery's nebbiolo vines are near the *cascina* on the hill at Rombone but it was only recently that the cellar started releasing just over 4,000 bottles of Barbaresco as a vineyard selection. Since the 1997 harvest, a Barbaresco Rombone made with selected fruit from the Rombone vineyard has flanked the cellar's blended Barbaresco. Aged in small new oak casks, the Rombone is the more alluring wine. The basic version is aged in larger barrels and needs cellar time to mellow out its rough edges. With the 2001 harvest, a new plot of about one hectare in the Manzola vineyard will come onstream. In the future, it may provide a third estate Barbaresco, if the results come up to expectations.

Pelissero
Via Ferrere, 19
Tel. + 39 0173 638136 - 0173 638430
Giorgio Pelissero has gone down a different road from most other Langhe growers. Separate vinification of the most prestigious vineyard selections fails to reflect the Piedmontese tradition of blending but Pelissero's cellar has always released a single-vineyard Barbaresco. Bordering the Basarin vineyard at the meeting point of the municipalities of Treiso, Neive and Barbaresco, the plot yields a wine called Vanotu – a Piedmontese diminutive of "Giovanni" – in tribute to Gianni's grandfather. The soil here is fairly sandy and limestone-rich and it produces a softly tannic wine that is well able to take ageing in new barriques. Since the 1994 vintage, Vanotu has been joined by a Barbaresco from the more clayey soil of Ferrere and San Stunet, which is only part-aged in new oak. Recently, Giorgio and Luigi have planted more nebbiolo at Casot.

Vignaioli Elvio Pertinace
Località Pertinace, 2
Tel. + 39 0173 442238
Managed with flair by young Cesare Barbero, this co-operative winery is a benchmark for many growers around Treiso and for large numbers of Piedmontese winelovers. In addition to an attractively priced standard-label Barbaresco, Vignaioli Elvio Pertinace releases three selections, Castellizzano, Nervo and Marcarini. For some years, the cellar has not released its Barbaresco Casot.

WHERE TO SLEEP

Il Ciliegio
Via Meruzzano, 21
Tel. + 39 0173 630126 - 0173 638267
Three four-bed rooms

Montersino

with bathroom and four four-bed apartments with bathroom and kitchenette-dinette. Prices: double room € 47.00; triple € 62.00; quadruple € 73.00; apartment € 362.00 per week for two guests, € 414.00 for four.
An ideal *agriturismo* for a holiday in the country and a convenient base for cycling and walking excursions, or for exploring the hills. Wine, fruit, vegetables, chickens and rabbits can all be purchased on the estate.

Ada Nada
Via Ausario, 12
Località Rombone
Tel. + 39 0173 638127
A lovely restructured eighteenth-century *cascina* in the heart of the vineyards, Ada Nada offers five comfortable rooms with views over the hills of Barbaresco. The generous meals feature artisan produce, such as bread, jam, cakes, cold meats, cheese and vegetable crudités.

Villa Ile
Strada Rizzi, 18
Tel. + 39 0173 362333
The three comfortable rooms are looked after by Ileana Cordini, who is first and foremost a winemaker. Her Barbaresco and Garassino are worth investigating. The estate also offers fruit and vegetables for sale. Some apartments are also planned for the near future.

EATING OUT

La Ciau del Tornavento
Piazza Baracco, 7
Tel. + 39 0173 638333
After his success at La Ciau, near Pinerolo, Maurilio Garola had little difficulty in earning a fine reputation in the Langhe. The territory-based menu includes potato and leek-filled *agnolotti* pasta cooked in water and hay, Barolo risotto with quail and other traditional dishes. There is also a slightly more daring alternative menu. The selection of cheeses and the wine list are extensive, offering the best the area has to offer. A meal will cost from € 40.00 to € 50.00 without wine.

Osteria dell'Unione
Via Alba, 1
Tel. + 39 0173 638303
A historic Langhe *osteria* and one of the first Slow Food eateries, Pina Bongiovanni and Beppe Marcarino's Unione offers ever-reliable and beautifully prepared traditional cuisine in a temptingly vigorous style. The cellar has a fine range of Langhe wines. Expect to spend around € 25.00 without wine.

Felice Bonardi

(1861-1946)

The group of winemakers who dominated the Langhe grape and wine market in the late nineteenth century is so distinctive and, in some respects, so intriguing, that it deserves closer study. First of all, these individuals called themselves, and were referred to by others, as "wine merchants" – *negozianti da vino* – like the French *négociants*. Only later did the term *commerciante*, or "trader", come into vogue. But in those days, the merchant was in many ways the motor that drove a poor, backward agricultural economy. The main characteristic of figures like Pio, Bonardi and Serafino was their consummate skill as traders. As they used to say in the Langhe, "they would deal in anything". They bought cascine that they sold on to individuals they trusted. They started up restaurants or hotels with stables to place their wines. They traded in silkworm cocoons during the summer when the cellars were empty and they bought wine from the south for their routine trade. In short, they were utterly at home in their economic environment.

Felice Bonardi was a fine example of the type. He was born at Bra, the town where the first cellars that made and distributed Barolo were located. The Bonardis, a family of *cartoné* (carters or hauliers), transported goods to and from neighbouring Liguria, which was a major outlet for trade at the time. Long convoys of horse-drawn carts crossed the Colle di Nava pass, travelling for two days and two nights. They took agricultural produce and wine from Piedmont, bringing back Ligurian fish and olive oil.

As early as 1890, Felice Bonardi was trading in wine and vinifying small lots of grapes at Fossano, where he had moved. He sourced his fruit near Saluzzo in a zone not renowned for quality but which was once a productive area. For example, moscato was grown at Costigliole Saluzzo.

In 1911, Bonardi took the decision that was to change his life. He opened a winery at Alba. Having purchased 20,000 square metres of land, Bonardi erected Alba's first concrete building, investing in production facilities and fermentation vessels. Thus began an adventure that was to have surprising developments over the next half century. The Alba cellar was followed by those at Bra, Tonco and Correggio, then in 1928 he purchased the Melini winery in Chianti. In 1932, Bonardi sold Melini but at the same time consolidated his facilities at Alba, where he became one of the leading figures in local society, as well as business circles. He was honoured, becoming a *Cavaliere Ufficiale*, and nominated vice president of the Scuola Enologica, a position of which he was extremely proud.

As a long-standing supporter of the liberal statesman Giolitti, Bonardi never joined the Fascist party and remained aloof from politics. He looked after customer relations personally, announcing each visit in advance and planning every detail of his business trips. At first the train, then the motor car driven by his faithful chauffeur, took Bonardi regularly to Turin, Genoa and Milan. At Genoa, Bonardi's wine could be found in the most sophisticated patisseries as well as in the rather less elegant watering holes frequented by the dockers.

Bonardi was a patriarchal family man, gruff but with a

heart of gold. He married twice. His first wife bore him four children and when he was left a widower at the end of the nineteenth century, he married Caterina Fissolo from Levaldigi, who gave him another seven, three boys and four girls. Bonardi's winery enjoyed its heyday from the 1930s to the 1950s. It would not be an exaggeration to say that few people in Piedmont at that time could compete with Bonardi.

On 25 July 1946, Felice Bonardi passed away at the venerable age of 85. With him went yet another of the Piedmont wine scene's old guard. Like Pio Cesare, Burlotto and many others, Bonardi took with him a unique knowledge of the region's finest vineyards – the sites that had made his, and his peers', wines great. Today, those vineyards continue to make the great wines of the Langhe.

Moccagatta at Barbaresco

Luigi Calissano

(1830-1913)

Even today, it is still a mystery how a forty-something blacksmith managed to become a leading, industrial-scale winemaker in only a few years. Yet that is exactly what Luigi Calissano achieved.

Born in Alba in 1830, he abandoned his smithy one day and turned instead, with the help of his three sons, Giovanni, Vincenzo and Pietro, to buying and selling Alba wines. The Luigi Calissano company was founded in 1872, although some people put the date as 1878, the year Calissano went into partnership with Domenico Vassallo. Iron was replaced by wine at the Calissano workshop in Via Macrino. In 1879, the first batch of wine left for France and Calissano took his seat on the town council, where he would remain until his death.

In that period, he opened three sales outlets: one in Turin headed by his son, Giovanni; one at Milan with Pietro; and a third at Genoa under Vincenzo. It was in 1883 that Luigi decided to make his big move. He bought 2,600 square metres of land on the Savona road with the intention of building new premises, which were inaugurated in 1897. In 1891, he split with his former partner and set up entirely on his own. This was the beginning of "Luigi Calissano e Figli" and customers were informed of the change in a handwritten letter dated 10 August.

In 1895, Vincenzo left the company. His holding was acquired by Giovanni, who was proving to be no less able and insightful than his father.

In the early twentieth century, entire trainloads of Calissano Barbera and Dolcetto were leaving the port of Genoa for America. In 1901, 15 goods wagons headed for Argentina. The Calissanos were no strangers in New York, where they had bottling plant that operated round the clock. In short, business was booming. There were about 80 workers at the plant in Alba, as well as a dozen office staff. The accounts for 1908 reveal that turnover was about 200,000 lire a month, an impressive figure if we remember that a bottle cost an average of 0.30-0.40 lire.

At this point, Luigi joined the company. Vincenzo's son and a trained chemist, Luigi went to France to learn how to make sparkling wine by the *méthode champenoise*. Shortly afterwards, the house released Duca d'Alba, a dry spumante advertised in 1919 by an Art Nouveau poster featuring a just uncorked bottle from which emerge a tail-coated dandy and patriotic red, white and green ribbons. Some date the Duca d'Alba, or rather the first experiments for the product, as far back as 1879. It was at that time that Luigi Calissano is said to have first been informed about French sparkling and still wines by Domenico Rossano, land agent of the Conti di Neive and a pupil of Cavour's oenologist, Oudart. What is known is that in January 1879, Calissano sent to a certain M. Terrier in France more than 100 hectolitres of wine.

It would be very interesting to find out whether, and to what extent, the rapid rise of Luigi's

company was due to support from his cousin, Teobaldo Calissano, the minister of posts and telegraphy in Giolitti's government. Born in 1857 and a lawyer of liberal convictions, Teobaldo was elected to parliament in 1897 in the Cherasco constituency, helped in part by the votes of catholics who ignored the papal instruction to abstain. We shall never know the relationship of the two cousins, both of whom passed away in 1913.
On the founder's death, the Calissano company was taken over by Giovanni. It was still expanding strongly and there was no indication of the storms that would hit it at the end of the 1920s. After years of boom, the United States fell victim to the great crash of 1929 and prohibition outlawed the importation or sale of alcoholic beverages. For the Alba-based company, this spelled disaster. An entire shipload of wine was thrown into the sea off the coast of America. New partners were sought and for a short time the Vetreria glassworks at Savona showed interest, only to withdraw. Attempts were made to sell grape juice in north America but came to nothing because the must fermented and so fell foul of prohibitionist legislation.
The star of the Luigi Calissano e Figli company was on the wane. The success that had lasted for half a century was founded on the United States trade that also brought it to an end.
The company was swiftly sold to a wine firm based in Reggio Emilia. In the early 1970s, Calissano was acquired by the Winefood multinational, which kept it open for a decade. Finally, it was closed down.

Pio Cesare

(1861-1919)

Pio Cesare was born into a humble family of farm workers on 30 September 1861 at Prassotere, in the small municipality of Mango. He was orphaned at the age of nine, when both his parents died in a smallpox epidemic. The childhood of this man, destined to become one of the most famous wine personalities in Alba, was not an easy one. Besides, living conditions generally in the countryside in the province of Cuneo and the Langhe hills at the time could only be described as desperately poor. Young Pio therefore had little alternative but to roll up his sleeves, leave the *cascina* to his elder brother Battista, and seek employment in nearby Alba, and subsequently in Bra.

It was at Bra that the not yet 20 year old Pio met Maria Rinaldi, who became his wife and helped him to set up in 1881 as a winemaker in Alba. In 1881, a combination of savings and borrowings enabled Pio Cesare to purchase premises on the main street of Alba near Porta Cherasca. Here, he set up his capacious cellars.

Pio Cesare began making Alba wines, which he sold mainly in casks and demijohns. A thrifty farming lad, Pio saved his first earnings and started a family that was to include three daughters, Luigina, Antonietta and Domenica, and a son, Giuseppe, born in 1891.

A stylishly elegant price list from the early twentieth century presents the range in three broad categories: 1. premium wines for bottling sold in casks and demijohns (the cellar gave complimentary labels and basic bottling instructions); 2. superior table wines (the inevitable "Barolino" and a curious Dolcetto d'Alba "Barberato"; 3. bottled wines in cases of 12 (Extravecchio Classico Barolo and Barbaresco and Asti Gran Spumante).

This complete and well-promoted range enabled Pio Cesare to take on challenging markets like Switzerland and Belgium while barrels of Moscato headed for France.

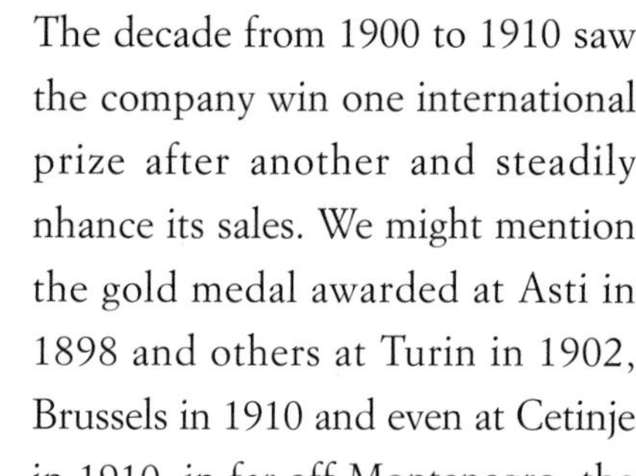

The decade from 1900 to 1910 saw the company win one international prize after another and steadily nhance its sales. We might mention the gold medal awarded at Asti in 1898 and others at Turin in 1902, Brussels in 1910 and even at Cetinje in 1910, in far-off Montenegro, the homeland of Italy's queen Elena. The son of poor farming folk from Mango now travelled all over Europe, investing in new hotels and restaurants where his wine was sold exclusively. Station buffets were excellent outlets, allowing Cesare to buy one of the largest hotels with stables in Alba, "I Buoi Rossi". It was perhaps this strong commercial orientation that ensured Pio Cesare's success. The investments he made in the company were substantial and in 1910 he opened a distillery. Wealth and fortune meant that Pio's son Giuseppe was able to attend a private school at Rolle, in French-speaking Switzerland. The decision was partly inspired by a desire to make up for Pio's own impoverished childhood and partly by a far-sighted, internationally-oriented commercial strategy.

When the First World War arrived, the company

was expanding as fast as it could. Pio, whose health was failing, was left to run the business because Giuseppe had been called up. Sheer willpower and tenacity nonetheless enabled Pio to find time to sit on the town council at Alba and in 1915, he purchased the castle in his home town of Mango for 26,000 lire.

This prestigious new residence was a kind of Pio Cesare *château* but the enterprising winemaker was unable to enjoy it to the full. He died in July 1919 at the Ospedale Mauriziano in Turin from heart failure.

At the time, *La Bandiera*, the Alba newspaper unsympathetic to Pio Cesare's politics, wrote, "We who honourably and openly opposed the public and political career of Pio Cesare, today, with the sincere condolences of friendship, salute an indefatigable worker and a man who owed everything to himself alone. It was to his own effort, his own genius and his own courage as a producer that Pio Cesare owed the fine reputation and worldly success he achieved in the winemaking industry". Pio Cesare's work would be continued by his son, who went on to consolidate the image of the cellar, the quality of its wines and its solid position in the market. Now in its fourth generation, the Pio Cesare company can boast a label that is a household name all over the world.

Sorano at Diano d'Alba

Giacomo Morra

(1889-1963)

In 1889, the *cascina* Manescotto, owned by the Conti Falletti from Castiglione in the municipality of La Morra, was farmed by a poor family of tenants. That year saw the birth at the *cascina* of Giacomo Morra, a man who was destined for fame and would influence the entire economy of Alba. Strictly speaking, Giacomo was not a "great" of either Barolo of Barbaresco but his wide-ranging activities as a hotelier, restaurateur and promoter of tourism ensured that his influence on the destiny of Langhe wines was substantial.

Morra worked on the *cascina* until he was 19, then moved to Alba with his brothers, Andrea, Giovanni and Matteo, who also intended to open *osterie*.

In 1923, Giacomo moved to Turin, where he opened a trattoria serving Langhe wines in Corso Nizza, opposite the faculty of veterinary science. But the enterprising young man from La Morra felt ill at ease in the big city and dreamed of returning to his friends in Alba. The opportunity arrived in the mid 1920s, when he was offered the chance of acquiring the rundown and near bankrupt Hotel Savona. The Savona was a luxury hotel that was perhaps too ambitious for Alba in the early twentieth century. Giacomo Morra understood the problem and set about transforming the excessively opulent structure into a hotel where everyone could feel at home. To that end, he immediately opened a café, later adding a billiard hall and an unpretentious dining room. In only a few years, the Savona became one of the focal points of business life at Alba, not just for the activities of the Morra family but also for the wine trade: the grape market was held in the piazza in front of the hotel. Winemakers would lunch at the Savona on market days and meet merchants in the café while all Alba's important dinners were held at the hotel.

Organising this commercial enterprise demanded skill in the procurement raw materials. To fulfil that need, Giacomo set up the *cascina* Gorreto at nearby Vaccheria to breed calves and pigs. The winemaking cellar was also expanded in this period.

At the same time, Morra also saw how important truffles were for Alba's culinary heritage and, thanks to his contacts in the world of journalism, created an aura of legend around them that year after year attracted tens of thousands of people to the town from all over the world.

The Fiera del Tartufo, or "truffle fair", launched in 1930, gained increasing prestige. Special trains were laid on for participants and the Savona served as many as 3,000 meals in a single day, employing more than 100 waiters and chefs. Most of the staff were farm workers, who were thus able to earn extra cash for their meagre family budget.

The price of Alba truffles skyrocketed. Morra began to look at ways of conserving truffles and got people to call him the "truffle king", purchasing as much as 300 kilograms from his trusted truffle hunters in a single day.

From the 1930s to the 1950s, the image of Alba as one of Italy's food and wine capitals became firmly established and Giacomo Morra was the first to create an efficient catering machine. Morra's fragile figure concealed an iron will and an exceptional ability to communicate. He was generous by nature, but not inclined to waste. On his death in 1963, he left a veritable empire, not just a collection of assets. The "Tartufi Morra" brand is still today a benchmark for many buyers.

Grinzane Cavour

Alfredo Prunotto

(1881-1960)

Alfredo Prunotto was already 40 years old when he began to make wine for himself. The Great War had only recently ended and the wine economy at Alba was swiftly getting back on its feet.

Prunotto's experience in the field was by no means superficial for he had been involved in the wine trade since his youth. After graduating from technical school in Alba, he went to work in the cellars of Commendator Burlotto at Verduno, immediately coming into contact with the winemaking élite of the Langhe. From Verduno, Prunotto went on to Fontanafredda, then known as Cantina Mirafiore, and stayed there for several years. His final experience as an employee was with Pio Cesare at Alba. It was at this winery that Prunotto met Luigina, daughter of the great Pio Cesare himself. The couple were subsequently to marry.

In the 1920s, Prunotto acquired the premises of the bankrupt former "Ai Vini delle Langhe" co-operative winery and began to make wine. As a result, Alfredo's relations with his in-laws took a distinct turn for the worse. As usually happens in such circumstances, established customers were drifting away and at that time, the customers constituted a considerable business asset. At the turn of the twentieth century, restaurateurs and hoteliers did not generally have a range of sources but used a single supplier. Purchase quantities thus tended to be very large indeed and the distribution pattern also highlights the fact that consumer demand was not particularly discriminating. Wine merely had to be cheap and free of major defects so cellars responded by releasing their entire output in barrels and demijohns before the end of spring. It is now easy to see why most cellars turned in summer to secondary activities such as selling silkworm cocoons. As early as the 1930s, the Prunotto cellar had established itself as a serious winemaker. It exported to South America, particularly Argentina where there were many emigrants from Piedmont, then from 1936 to 1940 it also found a market in Italy's African colonies. From what we can see from the price lists and labels, the wine production at the time deserves close study, not just from a documentary point of view but also to reconstruct the evolution of tastes and the changes that were taking place in cellar techniques. Wines like Barolino, Barberato, Nebbiolo Dolce, Barolo Extravecchio Classico and others should be classified and studied, if only because for many years they sustained a flourishing economy.

The third phase of Alba wine exports, which found a market in the United States, again saw Prunotto active, in the select company of Fontanafredda, the Opera Pia and Pio Cesare. These producers formed a wine aristocracy that was beginning to make a name for itself all over the world.

Prunotto, Borgogno, Bonardi, Serafino, Calissano, Cappellano and a few others could be found in Alba on market days at the Hotel Savona. Their relations, as one might expect of good Piedmontese, were cordial and distinguished by their respectful formality. Their shared rural background made them thrifty, disinclined to generosity and averse to flaunting their wealth. This thumbnail sketch of Alba's winemakers in the 1920s, 30s and 40s hints at what a restricted, fairly close-knit circle they formed.

The Second World War brought with it for the Prunotto cellar a process of slow decline. The obvious difficulties of distribution entailed by the hostilities, the absence of key family figures – for example, Alfredo's three daughters decided not to follow him into the firm – and serious health problems all conspired to induce Prunotto to give up the struggle in the early 1950s. Those were black years for Alba wines in general. Italy's economic boom was taking off and mass emigration from the countryside led to the collapse of the wine sector. After two or three attempts to sell his business, Prunotto decided to close the winery, and in 1955, he had not even made any wine.

It was sheer chance that a young wine technician from Santo Stefano Belbo, Beppe Colla, contacted the elderly Prunottos. Alfredo and Luigina offered Colla attractive conditions of purchase and on 16 September 1956, the handover took place. The Prunotto cellar would live on.

In the final years before his death in the spring of 1960, Alfredo passed on to Beppe Colla the knowledge and prestige he had accumulated, and which growers universally acknowledged, in his many years of activity. It may well be for that reason that the cellar continues to bear his name and honour his memory.

Neive

Glossary

Agriturismo
Plural *agriturismi*. A farm holiday centre offering accommodation, often with catering, cooking and other facilities on-site.

Albo dei vigneti
The *albo dei vigneti*, or register of vineyards, for each province is held at the local chamber of commerce. It records all areas planted to vine for the production of DOC and DOCG wines.

Ampelography
The branch of botany that deals with the classification and description of the various species and varieties of vine.

Anthocyans
Phenolic pigments, found mainly in the skin of the grape, which are responsible for the red colour of wine.

Bordeaux mixture
A mixture of copper sulphate and lime dissolved in water once widely used as an effective treatment against downy mildew, or peronospera.

Bouquet
A French term indicating the overall impression of olfactory sensations, usually referring to mature wines.

Brenta
Plural *brente*. A keg used for transporting or racking wine. As a unit of measurement, one *brenta* is equivalent to a volume of 50 litres.

Bricco
Plural *bricchi*. Piedmontese term for a hilltop or hillslope vineyard.

Cabreo
Piedmontese term for land register or map.

Capezzagna
Plural *capezzagne*. An unsurfaced access road leading to the vineyards, sometimes used as a boundary to delimit a property.

Cascina
Plural *cascine*. A farm building or, by extension, a small farm. The present-day, grape-growing *cascine* of the Langhe were in the past multiple-crop farms, often rented to tenant farmers.

Cap
The solid parts of the grape, mainly skins and seeds, that tend to rise to the surface during the tumultuous alcoholic fermentation of nebbiolo and red wines in general.

Clonal selection
Laboratory reproduction by vegetative propagation of vines belonging to a given variety, selected for specific desirable characteristics.

Clone
A plant generated by vegetative, or agamic, propagation from a mother vine, often by grafting.

Cru
French term for a vineyard where the site climate, position and other factors, both natural and artificial, give the wine special characteristics that distinguish it from wines produced on other, neighbouring plots.

Cultivar
A variety of a cultivated plant or clone from the same vine.

DOC (DOCG)
The abbreviation for *denominazione di origine controllata (e garantita)*, or "registered (and guaranteed) designation of origin". Individual DOC regulations are laid down by presidential or ministerial decree and published in the *Gazzetta Ufficiale*, the Official Journal of the Republic of Italy.

Downy mildew
See **peronospera**.

DPR
The abbreviation for *decreto del presidente della repubblica*, or presidential decree.

Enoteca
Plural *enoteche*. A wine shop, either privately owned or run by a regional authority or other public body, which may or may not also sell food and offer tasting facilities.

Fruit cane
A one year old shoot bearing the fruitful buds from which the bunches will grow.

Fruit set
The transformation of the vine flowers into grape berries. Each fertilised flower grows into a berry.

Giornata
Plural *giornate*. Originally, the area of land that could be tilled in one day (*giorno*). Later, it became a local unit of measurement equal to 3,810 square metres. One hectare corresponds to 2.624 *giornate*.

Girapoggio
Planting pattern in which all the vines in each row are on the same level and the rows lie parallel to the top of the hill.

Goudron
French tasting term. *Goudron* is used to indicate the elegant gustatory and olfactory sensation of tar perceptible in mature red wines, including Barolo and Barbaresco.

Grafting
An operation comprising the transfer and connection of a portion of bud-bearing vine onto rootstock or a shoot from another plant.

Maceration
Contact of the must with the solid parts of the grape (skins, seeds and, very occasionally, stalks).

Maderized (Italian ***maderizzato*** or ***marsalato***)
An adjective that indicates the perceptible alteration of the wine by slow oxidation so that the flavour is reminiscent of Madera or Marsala fortified wine. This defect is sometimes apparent in Barolos or Barbarescos more than 30 years old.

Marl
Grey-blue calcareous clay that inhibits the ripening of the grape and enhances its acidity.

Mass selection
Reproduction by vegetative propagation of vines belonging to a variety with specific characteristics, operating on the entire mass of a vineyard.

Masué (or **masoé**)
Piedmontese term. Tenant farmer.

Mesoclimate
An intermediate term referring to an area smaller than a macroclimate, or regional climate, and larger than a microclimate, which is measurable in a few metres. Mesoclimate is a near synonym of "site climate" and "topoclimate".

Must
Grape juice in which alcoholic fermentation has not yet started.

Must weight
Measurement of sugars in grape juice or must to assess ripeness. Various systems of measurement have been developed.

Neirano
A red grape variety that was fairly widely planted in Monferrato and the Langhe until a few decades ago. Today, it has almost entirely disappeared.

Osteria
Plural *osterie*. A tavern or public house that sells wine and food.

Oxidation
A natural process caused by oxygen that dissolves in the wine to produce undesirable alterations to the colour, nose and palate. Oxidation may be observed in Barolo or Barbaresco with defective corks, or which has been stored in unsuitable conditions, or has aged for too long.

Peronospera
Also known as "downy mildew", peronospera is a vine disease caused by a fungus that attacks the leaves and buds. Downy mildew arrived in the Barolo and Barbaresco area in the early twentieth century, causing severe damage to vineyards. It is often controlled by applying Bordeaux mixture (*bouillie bordelaise*), a mixture of copper sulphate and lime dissolved in water.

Phenolics
Chemical compounds, mainly anthocyans and tannins, that oxidise and tend to be deposited as the wine ages.

Phylloxera
A parasite that attacks the roots of *vitis vinifera*. Phylloxera was controlled by grafting the European vine, whose leaves are not attacked, onto American rootstock, which is resistant to the pest.

Racking
Removing clear wine from the sediment that has collected in the bottom of a container.

Rootstock (or **stock vine)**
Plant with a root system onto which a scion is grafted.

Reduction
Unpleasant olfactory sensation due to the reduction of available oxygen in the wine. Sometimes, the phenomenon disappears with aeration.

Ripping
Breaking up the soil to enable water to penetrate and roots to grow deeper. "Ripping out" is the process of clearing a vineyard, for example, in order to plant new varieties.

Ritocchino
Planting pattern in which the rows are arranged vertically, running down from the top of the hill to the bottom.

Sand
Small particles of rock and minerals that have been broken up over time. Sand has poor water retention and gives rise to a warm soil type. Wines from sandy terrain are richer in aromas than in structure.

Scion
Piece of a fruiting *Vitis vinifera* vine, with one or more buds, which is grafted onto another vine.

Site climate
The climate of a specific vineyard or plot.

Soldo
Plural *soldi*. One twentieth of a lira.

Sorì (or **sorito**)
Piedmontese term. A sunny plot, usually on a hillslope.

Spur
Fruit cane with two or three buds.

Tannin
A particularly astringent phenolic contained in the stalks, seeds and skins of grapes.

Terroir
A French term for a unique set of biological, geographical, climatic and geological factors.

Topoclimate
The local climate of a hillside or an area of similar size. A near synonym of "site climate" and the slightly less specific term, "mesoclimate".

Tov (or **tuv**)
Piedmontese term. Whitish siliceous marl or tufa.

Training
Since vines are not self-supporting, they must be established in the required shape. Usually, the vine is trained to a supporting structure.

Veraison
The change in colour, from green to dark red, of berries during the first stage of ripening. The corresponding Italian term is *invaiatura*.

Vino da tavola
Table wine. In the European Union, the term is used to indicate any wine that is not classified as a superior quality wine.

VQPRD
Abbreviation of *vino di qualità prodotto in regione determinata*, or quality wine produced in a specific region. This is the acronym used by the European Union to indicate DOC and DOCG wines.